Turning Points in Baptist History

MERCER
UNIVERSITY PRESS

Endowed by
TOM WATSON BROWN
and
THE WATSON-BROWN FOUNDATION, INC.

Turning Points in Baptist History

A Festschrift in Honor of Harry Leon McBeth

Edited by

Michael E. Williams, Sr. and Walter B. Shurden

MERCER UNIVERSITY PRESS
MACON, GEORGIA

THE JAMES N. GRIFFITH SERIES IN BAPTIST STUDIES

This series on Baptist life and thought explores and investigates Baptist history, offers analyses of Baptist theologies, provides studies in hymnody, and examines the role of Baptists in societies and cultures around the world. The series also includes classics of Baptist literature, letters, diaries, and other writings.
Walter B. Shurden
Series Editor

MUP/P430

© 2008 Mercer University Press
1400 Coleman Avenue
Macon, Georgia 31207
All rights reserved
Paperback edition 2011.

Mercer University Press is a member of Green Press Initiative (greenpressinitiative.org), a nonprofit organization working to help publishers and printers increase their use of recycled paper and decrease their use of fiber derived from endangered forests. This book is printed on recycled paper.

Books published by Mercer University Press are printed on acid free paper that meets the requirements of American National Standard for Information Sciences—Permanence of Paper for Printed Library Materials.

Library of Congress Cataloging-in-Publication Data

Turning points in Baptist history : a festschrift in honor of Harry Leon McBeth / edited by Michael E. Williams, Sr., and Walter B. Shurden. -- 1st ed.
p. cm.
Includes bibliographical references and index.
ISBN-13: 978-0-88146-244-9 (paperback : alk. paper)
1. Baptists--History. I. McBeth, Leon.
II. Williams, Michael E. (Michael Edward), 1960- III. Shurden, Walter B.
BX6231.T87 2008
286.09--dc22
2008014052

In honor of Harry Leon McBeth

Professor, Scholar, Colleague, and Friend

Contents

Introduction

Michael E. Williams Sr.

In recent years historians in many different theological disciplines have begun to consider vital or decisive moments in Christian history. In 1989 Donald McKim, for example, published *Theological Turning Points: Major Issues in Christian Thought*. Mark A. Noll followed in 2000 with *Turning Points: Decisive Moments in the History of Christianity*. The "turning points" motif has not been limited, however, to the writing of theology or church history. Indeed, entire series of books have been published, such as Oxford University Press's Pivotal Moments in American History, which includes volumes on "Moments" such as George Washington's crossing of the Delaware, James Madison's struggle for the Bill of Rights, and the landmark *Brown vs. Board of Education* decision. We thought a similar volume focusing exclusively upon Baptist history would be a worthy project. Such a volume is especially germane since Baptists are approaching the quadricentennial celebration of the founding of the first Baptist Church in 1609 in Amsterdam, Holland.

This volume is not intended to serve as a history of Baptists in the world, as it generally focuses upon English-speaking Baptists. It is not intended to be a comprehensive treatment of Baptist history. Rather, it is intended to highlight the pivotal moments in Baptist history. We have intentionally tried to write with students and laity in mind, suppressing academic jargon and utilizing limited endnotes where possible. We wanted to compile a book that would introduce college and seminary students, as well as laypersons, to the richness of Baptist history and the Baptist vision of the Christian faith. We wanted to do this with historical accuracy, viable interpretations, and in simple language. Candidly, we wanted to avoid the appearance of the often tedious work of technical academic scholarship, long footnotes, dense language, and extensive quotations from primary sources. For that reason, the "Suggested Reading" at the conclusion of each chapter is vitally important for this work. We wanted to point the readers to other significant sources without burdening them with that material within the various chapters. One will not but help notice the heavy emphasis on Baptists in the United States and the English-speaking world. Also, while we attempted to provide something of a chronological approach, we were content to live with some inevitable overlapping.

Turning Points in Baptist History is dedicated to Harry Leon McBeth, one of the foremost Baptist historians in the world. Among many other contributions, his landmark study, *The Baptist Heritage: Four Centuries of Baptist Witness,* and its companion, *A Sourcebook for Baptist Heritage,* have set the standard for Baptist history for two decades and have served as a major reference point for anyone studying Baptist history. For more than forty years, McBeth taught thousands of students in Baptist history and other topics in church history at Southwestern Baptist Theological Seminary. He directed many doctoral students and influenced the preservation of Baptist history through his work with the Southern Baptist Convention's Historical Commission. Additionally, he taught many laypersons Baptist history, not only through his writing, but also through his preaching and teaching ministry in Baptist churches.

The contributors to this volume are McBeth's former students, colleagues, and contemporaries, or they are recognized experts in the subject of the chapter they have written. The topics were assigned to them by the editors. The volume includes a timeline of McBeth's life that highlights key points in his life and ministry and also a selected bibliography of his books, articles, and addresses. Each contributor joins with the editors in expressing our appreciation and respect for McBeth's scholarship, his encouragement to his students, and his deep love for his family and God and his church. It is our hope that *Turning Points in Baptist History* will prove to be a fitting tribute to Dr. McBeth and will serve to educate a new generation of students of Baptist history.

CHAPTER 1

The Context of Baptist Beginnings: 1517–1609

Michael E Williams Sr.

Contrary to the attitudes of some, God did not say on the eighth day, "Let there be Baptists." Likewise, contrary to the beliefs of some, Baptists did not begin with John the Baptist, Jesus, and the Jordan River. Jesus' disciples did not organize the First Baptist Church of Jerusalem, nor were Paul's epistles addressed to the first Baptist churches of Ephesus, Corinth, and Philippi.

On the other hand, the first identifiable Baptist churches to emerge in the seventeenth century did not suddenly and miraculously appear. People like John Smyth, Thomas Helwys, John Murton, Anne Broadmead, William Broadmead, Richard Blunt, William Kiffin, and John Spilsbury did not read the New Testament and decide overnight that the Bible commanded all Christians to commit to believer's baptism and that the continental Anabaptists were correct in many of their theological and biblical presumptions. The context out of which the first Baptists developed was a culmination of many significant cultural events, pioneering theologians, and courageous leaders.

The Cultural Context

At the beginning of the sixteenth century, Europeans found their world in an incredible state of flux. Tremendous change shattered the worldview held by most Europeans for centuries, forcing people to reconsider the very foundations of their society and its belief systems. A number of factors contributed to the context out of which the first Baptist and other Protestant churches arose.

For centuries after the fall of the Roman Empire, the Roman Catholic Church served as the dominant institution in Western Europe. Government, economics, education, military, social, and cultural life all revolved around the Church. With this type of monolithic body in place, often controlling almost every aspect of life, corruption and abuse frequently occurred. Furthermore, groups and individuals who challenged the authority of the Church in any way often found themselves crushed. Even with these problems, many devout believers sought to live out their faith in the best ways that they knew how. The power of the Roman Catholic Church reached its zenith in the High Middle Ages about AD 1215. From that date forward, the Church's power and influence steadily declined. As the period known as the Renaissance developed and the modern era dawned, the status quo that had held society together since ancient times was challenged from a number of directions.

One development came in the area of business and technology. The Crusades beginning in 1095 introduced Europe to new goods produced in Asia that Europeans encountered while fighting in the Holy Land. As returning Crusaders brought these silks, perfumes, medications, dyes, and spices to other Europeans, the demand for these goods and the desire for the profit these goods generated created an exciting climate that budding commercial centers in Italian city-states like Genoa and Venice sought to exploit. These city-states then invested significant effort and capital in developing trade routes that combined overland and water passages to acquire goods from China, India, and the so-called Spice Islands (modern-day Malaysia and Indonesia). The commercial revolution that followed, especially in northern Italy but also in other parts of Europe, led to the emergence of banking houses, including the Medicis of Florence, Italy, and the Fuggers of Augsburg, Germany. This commercial revolution also led to the emergence of a wealthy class of businessmen and the increasing urbanization of Europe.[1]

During the late Middle Ages, Italian traders dominated the only known water routes that provided access to the land routes to the Far East. A lack of reliable sea-going technology forced these commercial ventures to use only known routes. However, new technology developed during the Renaissance—the astrolabe, the caravel sailing vessel, and the compass—allowed other nations such as Portugal to begin venturing into unknown parts of the seas such as the south Atlantic. Thus began a rush to find an all-water route to the Far East.

This competition in exploration drove an enterprising Italian sailor named Christopher Columbus to make his daring proposal to reach the East by sailing

---

[1] See Eugene F. Rice, Jr. and Anthony Grafton, *Foundations of Early Modern Europe, 1460–1559*, 2nd ed. (New York and London: W. W. Norton & Company, 1994) 45–60 and John Merriman, *A History of Modern Europe: From the Renaissance to the Age of Napoleon*, 2nd ed., 2 vols. (New York and London: W. W. Norton & Company, 2004) 1:22–26.

west into the unexplored Atlantic Ocean. Ultimately, the Spanish monarchs Ferdinand and Isabella reluctantly agreed to finance Columbus's gamble. Of course, Columbus was correct in his assumption about navigation but wrong in his understanding of the globe's vast dimensions. His mistake led to the European discovery of the Americas and contributed to a radical era of change that took place in the sixteenth century. His discovery also led to Spanish domination of the New World and the emergence of significant Spanish power and influence in European geopolitics throughout the sixteenth century. With Spanish backing, the Roman Catholic Church also gained significant influence in directing the religious development of the New World, especially of the Caribbean and Central and South America.

Not only did sea-going technology contribute to the extreme changes shaking Europe in the sixteenth and early seventeenth century, other forms of technology also contributed to these revolutionary alterations in European life. The introduction of gunpowder and firearms transformed warfare in Europe. Gunpowder equalized fighting on the battlefield as armor-piercing weapons threatened and then destroyed the dominance of wealthy and heavily armored lords on the battlefield. Gunpowder also neutralized the effectiveness of stone castles held by feudal lords and eventually democratized European warfare. Yet while gunpowder served to democratize warfare, it also gave advantages to monarchs who utilized new technology to liberate themselves from their reliance upon local knights and nobles for their power. This development allowed some monarchs to expand their territories but also increased the emerging monarchs' dependence upon banking houses to provide the capital needed to equip their armies with the new technology. While these modifications in the ways that Europeans fought wars were not completed in this era, the transformation had begun.[2]

The invention of the movable type printing press by Europeans such as Johannes Gutenberg further contributed to the dramatic revolution taking place in Europe. Whereas once the Roman Catholic Church and the wealthy controlled education and reading, the development of the printing press made education, literature, and especially the dissemination of information much more available to the general public. As more people learned to read, an insatiable desire for literature and information spread throughout much of Western Europe, a situation not entirely pleasing to the Church.[3]

---

[2] Merriman, *A History of Modern Europe*, 1:34–35.
[3] Ibid., 1:36–37.

These aforementioned technological innovations contributed significantly to the rise of the modern nation-state. As monarchs utilized technology and financial capital to consolidate their control over their subjects, they also challenged the traditional power structures of Europe, especially those of the Roman Catholic Church. An inherent sense of nationalism began to develop in England, France, Spain, the Austrian Hapsburg realms, and the smaller Germanic states. These challenges came against the backdrop of a decline in the authority of the Church in a number of realms.[4]

Even as new developments in business, government, geography, and technology occurred, so too did new developments in science. Scientists such as Nicholas Copernicus, and eventually Johannes Kepler and Galileo Galilei, quietly confronted previously unchallenged ideas on astronomy and the universe. The penultimate Renaissance man, Leonardo da Vinci, issued his own scientific experiments that further opposed traditional Renaissance viewpoints.

The Theological Context

Further challenges to the medieval worldview originated in theological and philosophical studies. Frustrated with the corruption and ignorance they found inherent in the medieval Church, individuals such as John Wycliffe and John Huss launched abortive attempts to reform the Church from within. Textual studies in ancient Greek texts motivated many brilliant young scholars such as Johannes Reuchlin, John Colet, and Desiderus Erasmus to question the dominant Catholic scholasticism of their day. Prior to the sixteenth century such attempts failed to overthrow the Church's great authority.

In the early sixteenth century, however, the situation was ripe for reform. Today's observer looking through the 20/20 lenses of history can see that it was not so much a question of whether reform of the church and society would occur but when and where. Where it occurred might have been a surprise to the people of that day and certainly the "who" of reform would have shocked them. The movement ultimately known as the Protestant Reformation began in an obscure German city, Wittenberg, in the electorate of Saxony, and was led by an equally obscure German monk, Martin Luther. While Luther did not initially intend to overthrow the Roman Catholic Church, the sources of dissension into which he tapped ultimately brought about not only a

---

[4] William R. Estep, *Renaissance & Reformation* (Grand Rapids: William B. Eerdmans Publishing Company, 1986) 97–101.

reformation but a true revolution. Originally, Luther sought only to address the problems he perceived to be the greatest abuses within the Church, especially concerning the sale of indulgences. In the end, however, he created a climate out of which a new paradigm for the Christian church would emerge.

Luther and other reformers like his contemporary Ulrich Zwingli and, later, John Calvin, stressed the importance of scripture for understanding the relationship of the individual to God. This principle of *sola scriptura*, or scripture alone, replaced the doctrine that the ultimate authority resided in the Roman Catholic Church. Luther and others argued that the Bible, not the Church, was the final word on God. The reformers coupled this emphasis upon scripture with an intense desire to put the Bible in the hands of all people in their own language rather than in the inaccessible Latin of the Roman Catholic Church. The reformers were not the first to have this desire. Wycliffe and his Lollard followers more than two centuries earlier had made a concentrated effort in England to make the Bible accessible to common people. No sooner had Luther taken his stand before the Holy Roman Emperor at the Diet of Worms, than he began a concentrated effort to translate the Bible into the German of the common people. His *September Bible*, as it was called, became the finished product of his efforts. Later reformers continued with this focus upon *sola scriptura* and the effort to put the Bible in the people's language. Some, like Luther, also sought to create music in the language of the people as well in order to enhance the corporate worship experience.[5]

The reformers also focused on the concept of *sola gratia*, or grace alone, and *sola fides*, or faith alone, for salvation. Rejecting the concept that the Church was the vehicle of salvation and that outside the Church there was no salvation, Luther and others argued that scripture taught that men and women are justified by faith alone and that this justification is an expression of God's grace toward human beings. The reformers also carried this understanding of justification a step further by teaching that each believer is a priest before God and does not require a priestly intermediary. This principle, usually called "the priesthood of believers," became a key principle of many of the reformers as well and was linked with the idea of the authority of scripture to magnify the idea that each believer was free to read and interpret scripture for himself or herself.

With their emphasis upon God's written word, the reformers shifted the focus of the church's worship experience and ministry away from the Roman

---

[5] Ibid., 153–55.

Catholic Mass to the preaching event. For the reformers, preaching became the occasion for the proclamation of the gospel of God's grace and for the emphasis on the importance of each believer's personal faith. Preaching tied together the three *solas* in the minds of the reformers.[6]

Just as preaching allowed the reformers to present their theology to the Church's people, so too did the availability of the printing press. A tremendous hunger for information and reading material increased as literacy increased, and the availability of affordable books, pamphlets, and papers gave the reformers a remarkable opportunity to spread their ideas to the common people as never before. Rising currents of nationalism also encouraged the masses to join in the reformers' protest against distant Rome.

Once Luther opened Pandora's box of revolt, the Roman Catholic Church could not put reform back inside. In addition to the more mainstream or "magisterial" reformers like Luther, Zwingli, and John Calvin—so called because they had the support of their governments—were those who came to be known as the "radicals." A myriad of people, ideas, and backgrounds formed this radical wing of the Reformation. Generally speaking, the radicals fell outside the scope of the magisterial reformers. In fact, the radicals usually found themselves at odds with both the magisterial reformers and the Roman Catholic Church. While a variety of groups fell within the category of radical, those best known and ultimately most influential were ridiculed as the "Anabaptists."

Emerging initially in Geneva under the influence of the Swiss Reformer Zwingli, these radicals took the principle of *sola scriptura* to its logical conclusion. Their study of scripture convinced them that the Roman Catholic Church created infant baptism and that the Bible taught believer's baptism alone—hence the name Anabaptists or "again baptizers." This assertion brought them into direct conflict with Zwingli and his supporters. The years that followed were bloody ones for Anabaptists as they found themselves persecuted by both the Protestants and the Roman Catholic Church. Anabaptists also found themselves discredited by those radicals who used the Anabaptist name but carried their conclusions too far. The most notorious was the infamous Munster episode in 1534. Beginning in Switzerland, many Anabaptists suffered martyrdom. Others went underground or adopted strict codes of conduct to distinguish themselves from the radicals who abused their ideas. Some of those people became known as Mennonites because they based their beliefs on the teachings of Menno Simons, a second generation Anabaptist. While historians

---

[6] Ibid., 155–58.

have typically been unable to identify a direct link between these European Anabaptists and the English Baptists who arose in the early seventeenth century, the Anabaptists certainly created a climate of dissent on the continent that later Baptists adopted. Many European Baptists have claimed these Anabaptists to be their theological ancestors.[7]

The Context in England

Meanwhile, in England, the flames of reform were much slower to stir. In the Middle Ages, England experienced the waxing and waning of papal influence and fought an ongoing conflict with France. England also encountered its own internal power struggles. Eventually, English nationalism stirred strongly in the late Middle Ages. Wycliffe tapped into this nationalism with his emphasis on producing an English translation of the scripture. Despite persecution, Wycliffe's Lollard heirs persevered in carrying his ideas and the English Bible to the common people while the Renaissance stirred the minds and souls of English intellectuals and upper classes.[8] Simultaneously, as the various lords of the realm struggled for control of England, a tremendous desire for unity eclipsed the interests of local lords. Some of the aforementioned changes taking place in European culture added to this growth of nationalism. In 1485 Henry Tudor, who came to be known as Henry VII, ended the Wars of the Roses and unified England.

During his reign from 1485 until his death in 1509, Henry VII sought to solidify his control over England by forging alliances with other European nations and within England through marriages. The marriage of his eldest daughter, Margaret, to James IV, king of Scotland, secured England's northern border. The marriage of his eldest son, Arthur, to Catherine of Aragon, daughter of the powerful Spanish monarchs Ferdinand and Isabella, appeared to create a partnership with the nation emerging as the great world power. Unfortunately, Arthur died of consumption in 1502 after being married only a few months.

Undeterred, Henry and Ferdinand sought a papal dispensation that would allow Henry's younger son, also named Henry, to marry Catherine. They based this request on the argument that Arthur and Catherine had never

---

[7] Ibid., 195–220. See also W. R. Estep, *The Anabaptist Story*, 3rd ed. (Grand Rapids: William B. Eerdmans Publishing Company, 1996).

[8] A. G. Dickens, *The English Reformation*, 2nd ed. (University Park: Penn State University Press, 1989) 46–56.

consummated their marriage. More a pragmatic politician than a spiritual leader, Pope Julius II granted the dispensation. In 1509, the same year that he ascended the throne of England, Henry VIII married Catherine.

Unfortunately for the Machiavellian schemes of monarchs and popes, Catherine bore eight children, but only one, a female named Mary, survived to adulthood. Henry's overwhelming desire to produce a male heir and solidify his control over England led him to petition for a papal annulment of his marriage. Caught between Henry's petition and Spain's tremendous power, Pope Clement VII denied his request. In response, Henry drew upon English nationalism and led the English church to separate from the Roman Catholic Church. He established himself as the temporal head of the Church of England and appointed the Archbishop of Canterbury as its spiritual head. He then requested his divorce from the Archbishop. When the first Archbishop of Canterbury refused, Henry replaced him with Thomas Cranmer, who promptly granted Henry's divorce. Henry then married Anne Boleyn, by whom he had a daughter, Elizabeth. Later, Henry executed Anne and remarried again, this time to Lady Jane Seymour, who finally produced a male heir, the sickly young Edward, before she died. Henry married a total of six times and upon his death, his son Edward, though still in his minority, assumed the throne. During Edward's reign, Protestants further consolidated control of England.[9]

Regrettably for English Protestants, death abbreviated Edward's reign. Henry's eldest daughter, the loyal Roman Catholic Mary, assumed the throne and instituted a five-year period of persecution of Protestant church leaders. Some of those not executed fled to the continent where they were further exposed to the ideas of the Reformation, especially those espoused by the Genevan reformer John Calvin. The exposure to Calvin's theology became critical in later years.

Mary only ruled for five years before she succumbed to what was most likely a cancerous tumor. Henry's only surviving heir, Elizabeth, the daughter of Anne Boleyn, succeeded Mary, thus ushering in a reign of forty-five years during which she stabilized the monarchy and led England to become truly a world power. England began to expand its colonies abroad and used its growing naval power to challenge the New World dominance of Spain. Among the decisions Queen Elizabeth I made, many related to the religious future of England. Rather than choose a continuation of Roman Catholicism as her half

---

[9] Estep, *Renaissance & Reformation*, 254–56 and H. Leon McBeth, *The Baptist Heritage: Four Centuries of Baptist Witness* (Nashville: Broadman Press, 1987) 22–23.

sister had done or fully embrace the Reformation as some of her advisors hoped, Elizabeth chose the *via media*, or middle way between.

Protestantism and Roman Catholicism. The English church anglicized the liturgy of the Church, but in many external appearances it retained the Catholic theology and liturgy with an English twist. The *via media* disappointed English citizens who had enjoyed significant change during Edward's reign, including those who had experienced the continental reformation during the Marian exile, or those who sought a more "English" experience. Increasingly, these English men and women pursued other avenues of worship, Bible study, and reflection. In the latter part of Elizabeth's reign, these reformers within the English church came to be known as "Puritans" because they sought to "purify" the English church of the last vestiges of Roman Catholicism. During the 1630s, almost thirty years after Elizabeth's death, these Puritans would challenge royal supremacy and the domination of the Church of England.[10]

Not all English reformers remained content to be simply Puritans. Others insisted that Catholicism had so corrupted the English church that reform could not fully purify it. They believed that true believers should separate entirely from the Church of England. The Church of England severely persecuted these English dissenters led by individuals like Robert Browne and Francis Johnson, both of whom had attended Cambridge University. By the time that a young Anglican minister named John Smyth arrived in 1586, Cambridge had become a hotbed of Separatism. Eventually rejecting both Anglicanism and Puritanism, Smyth led a Separatist congregation in Gainesborough. Out of this congregation surfaced two groups. One group led by John Robinson, William Brewster, and William Bradford migrated for a time to Holland as did many other persecuted Separatists. They eventually became known as the "Pilgrims" of Massachusetts after they traveled on the *Mayflower* and settled in the New World. The other group, led by John Smyth and a wealthy layman named Thomas Helwys, also migrated to Holland for a time. There they formed what Leon McBeth identifies as "the first identifiable Baptist church of modern times."[11] Later, this Baptist branch became known as the General Baptists.

---

[10] McBeth, *The Baptist Heritage*, 23–24. For more information on the origins of Puritanism, see William Haller, *The Rise of Puritanism*, 2nd ed. (Philadelphia: University of Pennsylvania, 1984).

[11] McBeth, *The Baptist Heritage*, 27–32.

Another branch of Separatists founded a congregation in London under the leadership of Henry Jacob. While Jacob and his immediate successors never became Baptists, they planted seeds that others would harvest. Out of this church, usually known as the "JLJ church" after the initials of its first three pastors, the roots of another branch of English Baptist life grew. These Baptists, eventually known as Particular Baptists to distinguish them from the General Baptists on the basis of their different viewpoints on atonement, adopted believer's baptism by immersion under the separate influences of Richard Blunt, William Kiffin, and John Spilsbury.[12]

While these latter developments will be discussed in greater detail in the following chapters, it is important to note that both the first General and Particular Baptists who emerged out of English Separatism resulted from a variety of cultural circumstances. A changing world both produced and shaped them in a social, political, and religious context consistent with the revolutionary world of which they were a part. Events set the stage upon which Baptists soon appeared.[13]

Suggested Reading

Estep, William R. *Renaissance & Reformation*. Grand Rapids: William B Eerdmans Publishing Co, 1986.

Haller, William. *The Rise of Puritanism*. 2nd edition. Philadelphia: University of Pennsylvania, 1984.

McBeth, H. Leon. *The Baptist Heritage: Four Centuries of Baptist Witness*. Nashville: Broadman Press, 1987.

Rice, Eugene F. Jr., and Anthony Grafton. *Foundations of Early Modern Europe, 1460–1559*. New York and London: W. W. Norton & Company, 1994.

---

[12] Ibid., 39–47. See chapter 2.

[13] The author gratefully acknowledges the insights of another of Dr. McBeth's former M.Div. student, Dr. Deirdre Lanoue, in the preparation of this chapter.

CHAPTER 2

Baptist Beginnings and the Turn toward a Believers' Church: 1609/1612/1633/1639

Charles W. Deweese

Punctuated with persecution, Baptist origins took several decades to complete, assumed an international character, stayed close to biblical authority, and reflected Baptist participation in the Believers' Church. Anabaptists, those radical reformers who claimed that the Mainline Protestant Reformation had stopped short of reestablishing some critically important biblical principles, preceded Baptists in asserting the imperative need for the Believers' Church and may have contributed to Baptist participation in it. However, independent reading of scripture most likely convinced Baptists to sign on with the Believers' Church. Believer's baptism and discipleship lay at the heart of the Believers' Church.

Believers' Church: A Key to Understanding Baptist Origins

The concept of a Believers' Church penetrated every phase of Baptist beginnings; in fact, its integrating quality served as a defining element of the totality of Baptist origins. The Believers' Church injected a congregational ingredient into the launching of the Baptist pilgrimage. The Believers' Church became a distinctive calling card of Baptists for future advancement.

Congregational in character from day one, Baptists nailed down the point that only those persons previously regenerated by the Holy Spirit could be legitimate church members; that excluded infants and non-believing youth and adults. Consequently, the earliest Baptists insisted that every church should be comprised of faithful people who separated from the world and covenanted with God and one another through baptism upon a voluntary confession of faith and sins, produced by the preaching of the gospel. These believers were to worship together, administer the ordinances, minister to one another, exercise church discipline, and adopt biblical ethics for daily living.

The Believers' Church, represented by early Baptists, equalized all church members and churches. Even if a church had no officers or if the officers were in prison, sick, or otherwise hindered, the congregation was obligated to meet, pray, prophesy, and administer the ordinances. Further, in 1609–1612 deacons were to be men and women, all experiencing fasting, prayer, and the laying on of hands. Each church, under the Lordship of Christ, possessed congregational freedom to make its own decisions about ministers, ministries, relationships, and money.[1]

Baptist participation in the Believers' Church meant that they practiced responsible church membership. Responsibility resulted because individuals made personal decisions to join churches, and churches made congregational decisions to admit members meeting biblical qualifications. Early Baptists paid careful attention to the credentials of candidates for church membership, adopted congregationally approved admission procedures, expected voluntary covenantal commitments from members, and held one another to biblical standards for membership.

Baptists believed that the New Testament insisted on rigorous standards for church membership. Although driven by voluntarism and individual decisions, Baptists, in the context of the Believers' Church, injected accountability into membership practices. Gradually, they expressed their views about the Believers' Church in written letters, confessions of faith, church covenants, statements of disciplines, and church manuals.

Baptist Origins in Holland, England, and America

Baptist churches originated in separate but integrated ways in Holland in 1609, in England in 1612 and in another branch independently in England in 1633, and in America in 1639. The concept of a Believers' Church guided the process on every occasion. The General Baptists (favoring a general atonement) created the first Baptist church in history in Amsterdam in 1609 when a small group of English Separatists, who had gone there to find religious freedom, adopted believer's baptism. John Smyth and Thomas Helwys, a layman, were their leaders.

---

[1] William L. Lumpkin, *Baptist Confessions of Faith*, rev. ed. (Valley Forge: Judson Press, 1969) 119–22.

Soon after arriving in Amsterdam, these English exiles came into contact with the Dutch Mennonites, Anabaptists who practiced religious liberty and believer's baptism. The degree of influence the Mennonites may have had upon early Baptist entrance into the Believers' Church is difficult to ascertain. The Smyth-Helwys group continued to study the Bible, resulting in their decision to become Baptists through personal confession of faith in Christ followed by believer's baptism. Smyth baptized himself and the other believers, either by pouring or sprinkling.

Few documents characterize the nature of a congregation committed to the Believers' Church better than a 1609 letter written by Hughe and Anne Bromheade, two members of Smyth's church, to a relative back in London. This was the first (and now the oldest) written description of a Baptist worship service. These early believing Baptists worshiped together, including prayers, readings from the Bible, comments and conversation about the readings, prophesyings (preaching), a contribution for the poor, and the conducting of church business.[2]

The Bromheades also shared why they and others had separated from the state church of England and participated in the formation of a Baptist church in Amsterdam. Among reasons given were their desires to find "peace and protection," so they could worship freely; to create a church with a true constitution, true covenant, true baptism, true ministry, true worship, and true government; and to form a church with a biblical basis, one matching the expectations of Christ.[3] Essentially, the Bromheades sought a Believers' Church.

What was going on here? Baptized believers, in exile but in freedom, were exercising the opportunities and responsibilities of church membership. For them, worship of God had to happen at whatever cost. Unknowingly, they were establishing a Believers' Church legacy for all future Baptists throughout the world. Soon, they would take this model straight back to England where the state church of that country, which demanded conformity in patterns of faith and practice, would go to many lengths to disrupt their nonconforming, dissenting way of doing Believers' Church.

Smyth soon concluded that he had erred in baptizing himself and applied to become a Mennonite. Although he died in 1612 before his acceptance, his

---

[2] H. Leon McBeth, *A Sourcebook for Baptist Heritage* (Nashville: Broadman Press, 1990) 22.

[3] Ibid., 21.

followers did successfully join the Mennonites in 1615. Meanwhile, Thomas Helwys led the remaining group of early Baptists back to Spitalfield, England, where they formed the first Baptist church on English soil in 1612. A 1611 confession of faith of this group, apparently written by Helwys, made clear their view that a church should consist only of baptized believers who followed the biblical model; further, churches constituted in any other way did not have a New Testament basis.[4]

Helwys was a pastor willing to die for the cause of Baptist participation in the Believers' Church, and he did. A bold defender of religious liberty in a country that stifled it, he wrote a book titled *A Short Declaration of the Mistery of Iniquity* (1612), often described as the first major defense of religious liberty in the English language. Unable to present a personal copy to King James I, he autographed a copy on the flyleaf and sent it to the king. The king apparently did not like Helwys's explicit appeal for religious freedom. Helwys soon found himself in Newgate Prison, where he apparently died in 1616. What a pastor. Through his life and death, Helwys helped to establish an essential principle for his congregation and for the entire Believers' Church: The church that Jesus Christ established and for which he died requires thoroughgoing commitment, even unto death. Infringements on the faith patterns of others, self-centered individualism, and mediocre patterns of involvement were unacceptable options.

John Murton succeeded Helwys as pastor of the first General Baptist church in England. General Baptists soon began to expand the number of their churches. Baptists did not tend to wander around England as detached individuals; rather, they typically created congregations of believers.

In the 1630s Particular Baptists appeared in England. They taught a particular atonement, meaning that Christ died only for a particular group, the elect. The teachings of John Calvin, a mainline Protestant leader, influenced their views about the atonement. Some Independent churches in England preferred autonomous congregations without a radical break from the state church. By 1616 Henry Jacob led an Independent church, and John Lathrop and Henry Jessey succeeded him as pastor. This church is sometimes known as the JLJ church, based on the initials of the first three leaders. In 1633 some members withdrew from this church and formed a separate congregation. Some were likely baptized as believers. This congregation, later joined by others also adopting believer's baptism, served as the basis for the first Baptist church in the

---

[4] Lumpkin, *Baptist Confessions of Faith*, 120.

Particular Baptist tradition. In 1633 it clearly set in motion a new version of Baptist participation in the Believers' Church.

Like the first General Baptists in 1609, these Baptists of the 1630s practiced baptism by sprinkling or pouring. The first Baptist confession of faith to prescribe baptism by immersion was the London Confession of Faith (1644). For the earliest Baptists, the Believers' Church did not depend on the mode of baptism. Rather, it hinged solely on whether the person being baptized was a believer.

When the Particular Baptists adopted their first major confession of faith in 1644, they made certain that the concept of Believers' Church received primary attention. Article 33 required that all church members "be called & separated from the world by the word and Spirit of God" on the basis of a "visible profession of the faith of the Gospel, being baptized into that faith."[5] Quite simply, covenantal relationships within the life of early Baptist churches automatically assumed that every person entering such relationships had made a voluntary profession of faith in Christ prior to baptism.

The rise of the first Baptist church in America, in Providence, Rhode Island, in 1639, involved dynamics similar to those affecting the rise of Baptist churches in England. Roger Williams (c.1603–1684), the founder of the Providence church, was born, raised, and educated in England. Like Smyth and Helwys, he grew up in the Church of England. Like them, he eventually viewed that church as a false church and became a Separatist. Like those who fled to Holland to escape persecution because of their Separatist views, he fled to America, arriving there in 1631. He practiced his Separatist views in Salem and Plymouth, Massachusetts, from 1631 until early 1636 when state church authorities decided to force him to return to England. He escaped by fleeing to what he named Providence Plantations, founded upon land he purchased from the Native Americans. There, in early 1639, he and others formed the first Baptist church in the new world.

Under the date of 16 March 1639, Governor John Winthrop of Massachusetts recorded in his journal that Anne Hutchinson had convinced Williams "to make open profession" of his faith, that Ezekiel Holliman baptized him, that Williams in turn baptized Holliman and ten others, and that all the

---

[5] Ibid., 165.

new members of this church "denied the baptizing of infants."[6] These developments constituted a brand new manifestation of the Believers' Church.

Although independent of the rise of Baptist churches in 1609, 1612, and 1633, the formation of this Baptist congregation in Providence also shared some common denominators with those earlier developments. Mounting disagreements with the conforming requirements of state churches resulted in patterns of religious dissent that refused to continue buying into top-down patterns of coerced faith. Smyth, Helwys, Murton, former members of the Jacob/Lathrop/Jessey church, and Williams all decided that church really made no sense when involuntary infant baptism prevailed, when the secularized state church based its authority on non-biblical traditions, when the ministry had sold its soul to the state, and when that state church persecuted individuals who opted for voluntary approaches to belief and practice.

The concept of a Believers' Church permeated the development of Baptist life in colonial America. One illustration relates to the formation of the First Baptist Church in Boston, Massachusetts, in 1665. That year, the church prepared the first Baptist confession of faith adopted in America. The confession asserted that the only persons eligible to be members of the church were those who "received the word & are baptized." A church consisted of a competent number of such persons joined in a covenant and the fellowship of the gospel. Further, this church had the power to receive into its fellowship other "visible believers." Duties of the church included choosing officers, administering the ordinances, executing church discipline, meeting for worship, and affirming religious freedom.[7]

Important evidence of the interaction between English and American Baptists relating to the Believers' Church lay in the fact that the Philadelphia Baptist Association in 1742 would adopt the Second London Confession of English Particular Baptists dating from 1677. These confessions shared a common emphasis on the fact that church members were those who had previously professed faith in Christ and then had been baptized. As a conviction that could not be compromised, the Believers' Church tied together Baptists in England and America from 1639 forward.

---

[6] H. Leon McBeth, *The Baptist Heritage: Four Centuries of Baptist Witness* (Nashville: Broadman Press, 1987) 131.

[7] McBeth, *A Sourcebook*, 95–96.

The Meaning and Implications of the Believers' Church

In a sense, a Baptist way of thinking emerged in the second generation of the Protestant movement. Preceded by Anabaptism, this Baptist mindset made the Believers' Church the center of its strategy. The Believers' Church centered around the idea of a regenerate church membership. From the early 1600s, the concept of a regenerate church membership would always be a distinguishing mark of Baptists and would permeate their teachings and writings on the nature of the church. Although the idea of a regenerate membership existed in Protestantism before the arrival of Baptists, they would lead the way in contributing the doctrine to Protestant development.

What was regeneration to the earliest Baptists? It was an act of the Holy Spirit that changed individuals' outlook on life; they became people seeking, finding, and following God in Christ. The regenerate included those persons who had received new birth from the Holy Spirit. As a 1611 Baptist confession put it, they were people for whom baptism was "the outward manifestation of dying unto sin, and walking in newness of life" and therefore did not apply to infants.[8] Only the regenerate could legitimately be members of the church; thus, the Believers' Church took root in Baptist life. The implications were obvious: The regenerate could fulfill their response to God only within the context of the church, and the church could achieve its mission for God only if comprised of the regenerate.

It was no accident that from day one Baptists emphasized religious liberty. The Believers' Church could not possibly consist by political and/or ecclesiastical mandate of all people born in a particular geographical region; that would make church membership equivalent to national citizenship. Such a church of non-believers would not be comprised of gathered believers, but rather of involuntary participants who might or might not be regenerated by the Holy Spirit. That kind of climate would simply force all citizens, baptized as infants, regenerate and non-regenerate alike, into a common church with questionable biblical credentials.

For Baptists a regenerate church membership could be a reality only when religious liberty and separation of church and state would allow both the voluntary aspect of church membership and the requirement that every member be a baptized believer to function apart from outside intervention. Thus, religious liberty and regenerate church membership went hand in hand.

---

[8] Lumpkin, *Baptist Confessions of Faith*, 120.

The earliest Baptists used the following logic in implementing their views of regenerate church membership and therefore of the Believers' Church. Believer's baptism played a central role in safeguarding the rise of a regenerate membership. To safeguard the preservation of a regenerate membership, churches regularly celebrated the Lord's Supper and engaged in other forms of worship, used church covenants as pledges that regenerate members made to God and one another, practiced church discipline, and engaged in discipleship.

Participation by Baptists in the Believers' Church in the early 1600s always risked persecution. Many Baptists in England and America were persecuted on account of their faith. Thomas Hardcastle demonstrated through his personal life that Baptists were willing to go to jail in behalf of the Believers' Church. As pastor of the Broadmead Baptist Church in Bristol, England, in the 1670s, Hardcastle, according to the church's actual records, was imprisoned seven times in 1675–1676 by the state church of England. During those imprisonments, he wrote twenty-two letters of encouragement to his congregation, drilling into his church members the need both to defend against all odds their right to be free and to use their liberty responsibly.

Hardcastle took his faith seriously. The Lordship of Christ meant something to him. The authority of the Bible affected his sense of mission. Believer's baptism connected him to his church in an unbreakable bond. Liberty of conscience drove him to defend the right of the Believers' Church to be free and responsible. Prison was not a source of bondage; rather, it was another pulpit from which to preach. For Hardcastle, being a Baptist Christian in the Believer's Church was worth dying for.[9]

For early Baptists, the stakes were high. They signed on with the Believers' Church at considerable risk, but they knew that to do less would shatter the Baptist witness and neutralize their witness. So the legacy they left for future generations of Baptists read something like this: Read the New Testament carefully to see what it says about radical faith and the church. Baptize believers only. Initiate and regularly renew covenantal vows with God and fellow church members. Develop disciplined patterns of conduct, discipleship, and ministry. Highlight freedom, cooperation, and accountability in church membership practices.

---

[9] Edward Bean Underhill, ed., *The Records of a Church of Christ, Meeting in Broadmead, Bristol, 1640–1687* (London: J. Haddon for the Hanserd Knollys Society, 1847) scattered pages.

Suggested Reading

Brackney, William H. *Doing Baptism Baptist Style: Believer's Baptism*. Brentwood TN: Baptist History and Heritage Society, 2001.

Briggs, John. "Baptist Origins." Baptist History & Heritage Society. http://www.baptisthistory.org/contissues/briggs.htm.

Durso, Pamela R., and Keith E. Durso. *The Story of Baptists in the United States*. Brentwood TN: Baptist History and Heritage Society, 2006.

Goodwin, Everett C. *Down by the Riverside: A Brief History of Baptist Faith*. Valley Forge: Judson Press, 2002. See especially chapter 11: The Church.

Holcomb, Carol C. *Doing Church Baptist Style: Congregationalism*. Brentwood TN: Baptist History and Heritage Society, 2001.

Leonard, Bill J. *Baptist Ways: A History*. Valley Forge: Judson Press, 2003.

———. *An Introduction to Baptist Principles*. Brentwood TN: Baptist History and Heritage Society, 2005.

Lumpkin, William L. *Baptist Confessions of Faith*. Revised edition. Valley Forge: Judson Press, 1969.

McBeth, H. Leon. "Baptist Beginnings." Baptist History & Heritage Society. http://www.baptisthistory.org/baptistbeginnings.htm.

———. *The Baptist Heritage: Four Centuries of Baptist Witness*. Nashville: Broadman Press, 1987.

———. *A Sourcebook for Baptist Heritage*. Nashville: Broadman Press, 1990.

Pinson, William M. Jr. *Issues Testing Baptist Polity*. Brentwood TN: Baptist History and Heritage Society, 2003.

Shurden, Walter B. *Turning Points in Baptist History*. Brentwood TN: Baptist History and Heritage Society, 2001.

CHAPTER 3

Baptist Freedom and the Turn toward a Free Conscience: 1612/1652

Walter B. Shurden

Introduction

In the interest of historical accuracy, this chapter title needs a bit of tweaking. Baptists did not *turn* toward the idea of "a free conscience." They *began* in the seventeenth century screaming and agitating for liberty of conscience. The Baptist people did not accidentally stumble upon the idea of religious liberty after years of opposing the idea; they were born crying for freedom of expression. Historically, the Baptists have spoken harmoniously and unambiguously for absolute religious liberty for all people throughout most of their 400 year history. They stubbed their toes at times, but when at their best Baptists have advocated absolute religious liberty for all based upon principle, not expediency.

Why have Baptists been such zealous advocates of absolute freedom of conscience and religious liberty? There is no doubt that Baptists have been stalwart defenders of religious freedom. Even their fiercest historical opponents affirm this. How did Baptists arrive at this intoxicating idea of freedom of conscience for absolutely everybody?

The Baptists' embrace of the idea of a free conscience is rooted in two major factors: Baptist history and Baptist theology. First, Baptists turned toward the idea of a free conscience because of the antagonistic political/ religious context in which they emerged. Second, Baptists turned toward the ideas of freedom because of their unique spiritual convictions that encouraged religious diversity. So the Baptist plea for religious liberty has something to do with their original historical context and their initial spiritual convictions, with their birthing and their believing.

The Baptist *turn* toward a free conscience can be illustrated with two early and critically important Baptist books. Thomas Helwys, one of Baptists' spiritual fathers, wrote and published the first Baptist book in England in 1612. While he addressed a number of themes, the underlying theme was that of freedom of conscience. He wrote because of the oppressive religious conditions in England. Helwys took the strange title for his book, *A Short Declaration of the Mystery of Iniquity*,[1] from 2 Thessalonians 2:7 where the biblical writer spoke of "the mystery of lawlessness (iniquity)." Helwys interpreted the "mystery of iniquity" as "a working power of Satan." Given the historical context of Thomas Helwys, he saw this evil especially in the pomp, power, and polity of the Roman Catholic and Anglican Churches who conspired with governments to deny freedom of conscience to dissenters. More generally, however, Helwys identified the "mystery of iniquity" as the satanic spirit of domination and oppression.

John Clarke, the most important Baptist in seventeenth-century America, wrote the second book considered here. He published it in 1652 and titled it *Ill Newes from New England*.[2] Clarke described, as the title suggested, the religious tyranny that ran wild in New England, not old England. While Clarke described the New England situation, he actually published the book in London, England, in 1652. He probably would never have found a publisher for it in New England! *The Mystery of Iniquity* and *Ill Newes* appeared only forty years apart, and they appeared when the Baptist movement was a tiny speck on the religious landscapes of England and America.

It is important to underscore that Baptists published these two highly controversial books at the beginning of the denomination's history. *The Mystery* was probably the earliest document calling for freedom of conscience in England, and it was also the first document published by Baptists in England. *Ill Newes*, while not the first document in America calling for a free conscience, was one of the first Baptist documents addressing the subject. Together these books clearly signaled the adoption by Baptists of what came to be one of their most celebrated distinctives, the idea of freedom of conscience and religious liberty. Indeed, much of what Baptists would say for the next 400 years on religious freedom may be found either explicitly or implicitly in these two

---

[1] Thomas Helwys, *A Short Declaration of the Mystery of Iniquity* (1612), ed. Richard Groves (Macon GA: Mercer University Press, 1998).

[2] John Clarke, *Ill Newes from New-England* (1652), in *Colonial Baptists, Massachusetts and Rhode Island*, Baptist Tradition Series (New York: Arno Press, 1980).

seventeenth-century documents. They are seminal for probing the Baptist identity as that identity unfolded in the seventeenth century. They are indispensable for understanding what Baptists would call "soul freedom."

Baptists' Turn toward Freedom of Conscience: Historical Context

These two books first appeared in a period of harsh history for the Baptist people. Baptists emerged from their seventeenth-century religious womb like all infants, struggling, bloody, and crying for their independent existence. Unlike most babies, however, Baptists were unwanted. They landed immediately in hostile territory, both in old England and in New England. It was a strange era. People assumed that political stability required religious uniformity, that social cohesion was impossible without religious cohesion. Baptists thought otherwise. For Baptist Christians, political stability required religious freedom, not religious uniformity. Most of the politicians and religious leaders of that period also assumed that religion needed the support of the state. Baptists loudly and often cried "No!" So Baptists emerged as a minority religious denomination in the midst of crippling religious restrictions in both old England and New England. So *how* and *where* and *why* did our two documents originate? In other words, what is the context in which Baptists began their protests for freedom?

Baptists are children of the seventeenth-century English Reformation. Born in the midst of tumultuous religious conflict, Baptists are great-grandchildren of Anglicanism, grandchildren of Puritanism, and children of English Separatism. Thomas Helwys founded the first Baptist church in England in 1611 in a place outside London with the quaint sounding name of Spitalfield. The year 1611 is remembered as an important date in Christian history not because of the founding of this little Baptist church but because it is the year of the publication of the King James translation of the Bible. Baptists and other nonconformists, however, remember King James himself less for his authorized Bible translation than for his strong arm of oppression.

Dissenters thought they saw a friend coming to the throne in 1603 with the crowning of James I. After all, James had been king over Protestant Scotland. Surely, thought the Baptists, James would relax the rigidity of the Anglican religious establishment. James reacted, however, with horror to the idea of liberty of conscience. He affirmed the divine right of kings and the divine right of bishops as one and the same. It was a scrambled-eggs society. The Anglican Church and the English state came on the same plate and all mixed together. Baptists wanted to unscramble the political-ecclesiastical eggs, maintaining, among other things, that the state has no say over the soul of a person.

Like so many of his age, King James simply could not conceive of a society built on the freedom to choose one's faith or to choose no faith at all. James made his position clear when he said of the troubling nonconformists, "I shall make them conform themselves, or I will harry them out of the land, or else do worse."[3]

Not surprisingly, during the reign of James I a little group of Separatist Christians at Gainsborough, led by John Smyth and Thomas Helwys, pioneers of the Baptist movement, left their homeland in England in 1608 to find religious refuge in Holland. In Amsterdam in 1609 they formed what most historians consider to be the first Baptist church. For a number of reasons Helwys returned to England with a remnant of the Baptist group in 1611. Almost immediately upon landing in his native land, he published his book. Possessed with far more courage than wisdom, Helwys sent an autographed copy to King James. James promptly rewarded Helwys with a prison sentence, but not before this pioneer Baptist freely defended not merely the Baptists but the Roman Catholics of England to James. These early Baptists wanted freedom of religion not only for themselves but for all people. One should not be surprised to learn that Thomas Helwys probably died in Newgate Prison.[4]

Freedom of religion fared no better in New England, only the Establishment changed from Anglicanism to Puritanism. Roger Williams, a dissenter so radical that one critic said that he had "windmills in his head," stubbornly advocated religious freedom and earned himself exile from his home. He had to flee for his life from the Puritan Commonwealth of Massachusetts in early winter 1636. In 1638 he organized the First Baptist Church of Providence, Rhode Island, the first Baptist church founded in America. Rhode Island subsequently became a haven for Baptists and all others who dissented from supporting the Puritan churches. Williams is often called the father of Baptists in America. In one sense, that designation is altogether

---

[3] Quoted in Edward P. Cheyney, ed., *Readings in English History Drawn from the Original Sources* (New York: Ginn and Company, 1922) 431.

[4] For further discussion on religious liberty in England, see H. Leon McBeth, *English Baptist Literature on Religious Liberty to 1689* (New York: Arno Press, 1980). This book, a reprint of McBeth's 1961 doctoral dissertation at Southwestern Baptist Theological Seminary in Fort Worth, Texas, is a marvelous resource for the subject at issue.

appropriate. However, he stuck with Baptists only a few months and then became a Seeker. Williams said that he could not find the true church among the churches of his time. However, he wrote some powerful and influential works on freedom of conscience, and he exercised a formative influence on Baptists on both sides of the Atlantic. No Baptists would want to minimize the importance of Roger Williams for the Baptist family. More significant, however, than Roger Williams for Baptist life in seventeenth-century New England was Dr. John Clarke.

A physician, Clarke worked on more than sick bodies. He worked on a sick society, one that denied freedom of religion. Clarke founded the second Baptist church in America, the First Baptist Church in Newport (1644), Rhode Island. One of the most ardent advocates of liberty of conscience in America's history, John Clarke stands out as one of the mountain peaks of Baptist history in America. No spiritual isolationist who kept his distance from messy politics, Clarke secured from King Charles II of England in 1652 a new charter for Rhode Island Colony. The charter guaranteed full religious liberty for the little colony

Deserved to be remembered for many roles—pastor, theologian, physician, politician, diplomat, and biblical scholar—Clarke is primarily remembered for *Ill Newes from New England.* This fiery Baptist tract exposed religious persecution in seventeenth-century New England. Written during a period when dissenters in England had discovered some "good news" regarding religious freedom, he wanted to describe the "bad news" from New England where magistrates sadly wielded the "sword of steel" to repress conscience.

The myth stubbornly persists in American history that the founders of this country came here to establish religious liberty for *all* people. Not so! It is true that many of the earliest settlers came here to escape religious persecution. Many came to America, however, to establish religious liberty for themselves, not for all citizens. In fact, few people anywhere in the seventeenth century believed in religious liberty as a principle for all people. Universal religious liberty evolved as a hard-earned freedom in America. Anti-establishment forces dismantled the last state church in this country only in 1833. This was more than two centuries after the founding of the earliest colonies. Baptists helped lead the parade for universal liberty of conscience. Dr. John Clarke was the Baptist drum major for freedom in seventeenth century America. Due to the benign neglect of their own heritage, most Baptists have never heard of this wise and courageous man.

In 1651 John Clarke and two of his church members, John Crandall and Obadiah Holmes, courageously traveled from Newport, Rhode Island, to Lynn, Massachusetts, to conduct a worship service in the home of William Witter, a blind and aging Baptist. That trip became one of the most famous events in colonial American Baptist history. It also became the occasion for John Clarke's *Ill Newes from New England.*

Civil authorities brusquely interrupted the Baptist worship service in old man Witter's house that day. Then they arrested Clarke, Crandall, and Holmes, eventually taking them to Boston to be tried for breaking the laws of Massachusetts for not worshiping according to the pattern of the established Congregational churches. Friends paid fines for Clarke and Crandall, and they were released. But Obadiah Holmes, a stubborn cuss if ever there was one, refused to permit his fine to be paid by anyone. As a result he was lashed thirty times with a "three-corded whip" on Market Street in downtown Boston. At the end of the humiliating whipping, Holmes looked to the civil magistrates and said, "You have struck me as with Roses."[5]

While in the Boston prison in 1651, Clarke had requested an opportunity to debate the Puritans on the questions surrounding freedom of worship. The Puritans refused. But the next year, 1652, while living in England and seeking a new charter for Rhode Island, Clarke wrote *Ill Newes from New-England.* He intentionally sent a copy to the Parliament of England. He fervently hoped that the document would become political leverage for the magistrates of England to rid New England of its intolerance. In *Ill Newes* Clarke called for New England Puritans to repent of their religious discrimination. He wanted the Puritans delivered from their false zeal for God which led to what he called "soul murdering." He said that it is unbiblical, unchristlike, unnatural, and unspiritual to coerce conscience.[6]

So born in the midst of great pain with freedom denied, Baptists, a minority people, grounded their plea for religious freedom to some degree in their own historical experience of deprivation. Few things are quite as strong as the testimony of the oppressed, unless it is the testimony of the oppressed that have gone public so that all can see and hear. Martin Luther King Jr., a twentieth-century Baptist prophet, suffered enormous criticism because, as some said, "He was simply trying to attract the media." King pled guilty to that charge, saying that public attention was precisely his goal. He aimed to attract a

---

[5] Clarke, *Ill Newes*, 51.

[6] Ibid., 6, 10, 97–109.

crowd in order to expose to the nation and the world the horrors of segregation and the denial of basic human rights. Thomas Helwys and John Clarke penned their blistering words for precisely the same reason. Just as the civil rights movement of the 1960s was born from freedoms denied, the religious rights movement of the seventeenth and eighteenth centuries emerged because of the religious freedom denied. The earliest Baptists got red in the face on issues of religious liberty because they were deprived of basic human rights.

Baptists' Turn toward Liberty of Conscience: Spiritual Convictions

Baptists' commitment to soul freedom did not come solely from historical circumstances and the fact that they were a minority people. Baptists turned toward freedom of conscience primarily because their peculiar interpretations of the Christian faith drove them there. Given their suffering, Baptists surely had some self-interest in pleading for freedom. However, if Baptists had never felt the sting of religious and civil oppression, their distinctive spirituality, if logically followed, would have still turned them to liberty of conscience for all people. Baptists, it is important to repeat, did not stumble upon the principle of religious liberty; it was not an accident of history. Rather, their fundamental principles made them the unyielding advocates of religious liberty and religious diversity.

To say that Baptists' convictions encouraged diversity does not suggest in the least that Baptists had no firm certainties regarding cardinal Christian truths. Nor is it to say that their opinions were flabby with an "anything goes" approach to the Bible and theology. They were as certain and dogmatic about their views as the most fervent bishops in the Church of England and the most rigid Puritans of New England. The difference, however, was that the bishops' and the Puritans' theological dogmatism led to uniformity while the theological convictions of Baptists' led to diversity. A huge difference.

Before enumerating some of those principles, one should enter a denominational *mea culpa*. Baptists are as riddled by sin as any religious group that ever lived. Baptists are as liable to conscript the Bible and theology in the service of self-interest as anybody. It is easy to cry "Freedom" when some theological dictator has his foot on your neck. It is a more principled position, however, to cry for freedom when you are in the majority but still lift up your voice on behalf of new minorities. When one reads the historical record of Baptists whole, one sees that Baptists committed themselves to spiritual principles that compelled them to plead for religious liberty on the basis of principle, not self-interest alone.

What were some of those ideas? First, Baptists believed that while the state has legitimate civil authority, Almighty God alone is Lord of conscience. This is a dominant and recurring theme in both *The Mystery of Iniquity* and *Ill Newes from New England*. In a copy of his book that he autographed for King James I, Thomas Helwys boldly declared, "The king is a mortal man, not God, therefore has no power over the immortal souls of his subjects."[7] Likewise, John Clarke candidly stated that "it is not the will of the Lord that any one should have dominion over another man's conscience." Declaring the satanic nature of spiritual tyranny, Clarke, using much the same biblical text as Helwys, said that for anyone other than Christ to rule conscience is "the very highest design of the spirit of Antichrist."[8] Conscience, said the physician from Rhode Island, "is such a sparkling beam from the Father of lights and spirits that it cannot be lorded over, commanded, or forced, either by men, devils, or angels."[9]

Baptists stubbornly refused to subjugate their spiritual lives to civil authorities. Their critics, therefore, often portrayed Baptists as anarchists, a people opposed to orderly government. In an effort to underscore this charge their enemies often utilized a fear tactic and equated Baptists with the Anabaptists of Europe. While the Anabaptists were not nearly as anarchistic as their opponents charged, the Anabaptists' refusal to let their people serve as civil servants and the tragic and violent events at Munster in 1534 fueled the fear of Anabaptism.

Helwys and Clarke repeatedly, almost to the point of monotony, affirmed the loyalty of Baptists to the temporal authority of the state. While Baptists must, as Helwys said, "keep their conscience to God," they had not the slightest inclination toward sedition.[10] He described Baptists to King James as "poor subjects who ought and will obey you in all things with body, life, and goods, or else let their lives be taken from the earth."[11] The king had an altogether justifiable earthly kingdom and to that kingdom belonged "all earthly obedience, service and duty."[12] John Clarke had no hesitancy in speaking

---

[7] Helwys, *A Short Declaration*, vi.
[8] Clarke, *Ill Newes*, 103.
[9] Ibid., 6.
[10] Helwys, *A Short Declaration*, 62.
[11] Ibid., vi.
[12] Ibid., 59.

affirmatively of the "sword of steel" with which civil officers implemented justice and order in society.[13] He also deferentially addressed the English House of Parliament as "the Right Honorable" and even the Massachusetts authorities as "the Honored Magistracy." But for all their respect toward duly established governments, Baptists such as Helwys and Clarke considered the soul the sanctuary of a sovereign God.

Second, just as God was Lord of Conscience, these early Baptists spoke of Christ as Lord of the Church. Like all people, Baptists went to the Bible with lenses that refracted the truth of God to them in a certain way. Seventeenth-century Anglicans and Puritans tended to read church-state issues in light of the Old Testament. They liked, for example, the king motif in the history of Israel. It was not unusual for religious people of all stripes in this era to speak of the godly magistrate and the magistrate's authority to punish religious error, basing this on the power of Old Testament kings. Baptists, on the other hand, spent much of their time interpreting church/state issues in light of the New Testament.

Baptists, for example, went to the New Testament to persuade others of the separation of the civil and spiritual kingdoms. Baptists saw two spheres in the Bible. Romans 13 was for the civil, but James 4:12—"There is one lawgiver and judge"—was for the church.[14] The state was under the authority of civil rulers, but the church was under the Lordship of Jesus Christ. Commanding and ordering the household of faith was the clear prerogative of Christ. For Baptists that meant that neither an established government nor an established church could tell them what to believe, how to worship, or who could be their spiritual leaders.

Third, Baptists pled for freedom of conscience because of their understanding of faith and the nature of the spiritual life. "To be authentic," Baptists yelled, "faith must be free." Religion that is genuine, they insisted, must be a voluntary obedience to God. Baptists said it in many ways, but it lay at the heart of their spirituality. They said, "If faith is to be valid, it must be voluntary." "To cram a creed down a person's throat is rape of the soul." "Where there is no autonomy, there is no authenticity." "The only conversion that counts is conversion by conviction." Helwys and Clarke each spoke of the importance of "spiritual obedience" and "spiritual worship," by which they

---

[13] Clarke, *Ill Newes*, 5.

[14] Helwys, *A Short Declaration*, 46; Clarke, *Ill Newes*, 81.

meant the unrestrained freedom to follow Christ and to worship God. Later Baptist theologians would call this the "the voluntary principle in religion."

The voluntary principle is the core value of the Baptist people. The opposite of voluntary faith is coerced faith of any kind. Early Baptists deplored the latter and lauded the former. The voluntary principle had numerous implications for Baptists. They rejected infant baptism because it represented an imposed rather than a chosen faith. They spurned the biblical interpretations of the established clerics because it meant that they lacked the freedom to interpret scripture for themselves. They insisted that Christians should be free voluntarily to support the church of their choosing. They denounced state-enforced religion because it made hypocrites of people, causing them to say that they believed what they did not in fact believe. Clarke spoke for all Baptists of his own and of later times when he said that at the center of Christianity is a discipleship that "obeys from the heart, readily, willingly, and cheerfully."[15]

Fourth, Baptists argued that faith must be freely chosen and practiced because the individual alone must one day stand before a judging God. "Is it not most fair that men should choose their religion themselves," asked Helwys, "seeing they only must stand themselves before the judgment seat of God to answer for themselves, when it shall be no excuse for them to say we were commanded or compelled to be of this religion by the king or by them that had authority from him?"[16] Clarke echoed the precise same sentiment from New England: "Every man...shall appear before the judgment seat of Christ, and must give an account of himself to God, and therefore ought to be fully persuaded in his own mind for what he undertakes."[17]

These four arguments are only a few of the ways Helwys, Clarke, and the early Baptists made their case for a free conscience. No passage in early Baptist writings summarizes the Baptist case better than the statement of Helwys to King James I in which Helwys exonerated Baptists of plotting against the Roman Catholics:

> We still pray our lord the king that we may be free from suspect, from having any thought of provoking evil against them of the Romish religion, in regard of their profession, if they are true and faithful subjects of the king. For we do freely profess that our lord the

---

[15] Clarke, *Ill Newes*, 81.

[16] Helwys, *A Short Declaration*, 37.

[17] Clarke, *Ill Newes*, 37

king has no more power over their consciences than over ours, and that is none at all. For our lord the king is but an earthly king, and he has no authority as a king but in earthly causes. And if the king's people be obedient and true subjects, obeying all human laws made by the king, our lord the king can require no more. For men's religion to God is between God and themselves. The king shall not answer for it. Neither may the king be judge between God and man. Let them be heretic, Turks, Jews, or whatsoever, it appertains not to the earthly power to punish them in the least measure. This is made evident to our lord the king by the scriptures.[18]

In this quotation, one of the most widely quoted from early Baptist writings, Helwys said that the king had no authority over conscience. He implied that Baptists were "obedient and true subjects." He said that religion is voluntary, between human beings and God. He stated that the king could not answer before God for an individual's faith. He said that coercion in matters religious is not the domain of the state. And he affirmed that all of this was biblical.

The issues of religious liberty and separation of church and state have become far more complex and knotty since the time of Helwys and Clarke. The religious landscape in America has become increasingly, staggeringly pluralistic. This pluralism frightens many Americans, including some Baptist people. The temptation is to mute the plea for freedom of religion. The Baptist call for freedom of conscience, however, is needed now in America more than at any time since the Baptist call first went out in the seventeenth century. Helwys and Clarke, and a host of other Baptists in the seventeenth and eighteenth centuries learned the hard way the truth expressed in Pascal's dictum that "men never do evil so completely and cheerfully as when they do it from religious conviction."

Suggested Reading

Clarke, John. *Ill Newes from New-England*, in *Colonial Baptists: Massachusetts and Rhode Island*, in *The Baptist Tradition*. Edited by Edwin S. Gaustad (New York: Arno Press, A New York Times Company, 1980).

Gaustad, Edwin S. editor, *Baptist Piety: The Last Will and Testimony of Obadiah Holmes* (Tuscaloosa: University of Alabama Press, 2005).

---

[18] Helwys, *A Short Declaration*, 53.

Helwys, Thomas. *A Short Declaration of the Mystery of Iniquity* (1612). Edited and introduced by Richard Groves (Macon GA: Mercer University Press, 1998).

James, Sydney V. *John Clarke and His Legacies: Religion and Law in Colonial Rhode Island 1638–1750*. Edited by Theodore Dwight Bozeman (University Park: The Pennsylvania State University Press, 1999).

McBeth, H. Leon. *English Baptist Literature on Religious Liberty to 1689* (New York: Arno Press, 1980).

Shurden, Walter B. "John Clarke, Ill News from New England." Center for Baptist Studies. www.centerforbaptiststudies.org/resources/illnewes.htm.

Wikipedia. "John Clarke, (1609–76)." Wikipedia. http://en.wikipedia.org/wiki/John_Clarke (1609–1676).

CHAPTER 4

Baptist Baptism and the Turn toward Believer's Baptism by Immersion: 1642

Wm. Loyd Allen

Baptists added immersion to believer's baptism about 1642. Historically and theologically, believer's baptism has priority over immersion in Baptist origins and identity. In other words, Baptists were concerned about the *subject* of baptism before being concerned about the *mode* of baptism. The two in combination—the subject and mode of baptism—became Baptists' clearest identifying marker.

Christian Immersion before Baptists

Immersion baptism did not enter Christian tradition through Baptists. Baptists were, however, the first major Christian tradition to make believer's baptism by immersion the ordinary means to constitute a true church.

Immersion baptism of infants was widely practiced long before 1642 by Roman Catholics and Protestants, especially those in England. The *Didache*, a sort of church manual written before AD 300, recommends immersion. The Eastern Orthodox churches have always immersed infants. In the West immersion remained the most common mode until at least the fourteenth century. Supreme Medieval Catholic theologian Thomas Aquinas in his thirteenth-century *Summa Theologica*, expressed a preference for immersion because it was more commonly used and more clearly represented Christ's burial.

Baptism by immersion was well known in sixteenth-century Anglican churches, though falling out of fashion. The trend toward sprinkling probably began in northern France and came late to England, according to Wes

Harrison.[1] The first edition of the *Book of Common Prayer* in 1549 prescribes infant immersion unless the recipient is "weak."[2] Sixteenth-century Puritan Charles Chauncey, before becoming second president of Harvard, lost his pulpit at Plymouth by insisting on immersing the infants he baptized (and he lost more than one opportunity to baptize after immersing his own child in water so cold it fainted away).[3]

At the beginning of the seventeenth century, only Anabaptists argued against infant baptism. Very few of them, however, linked believer's baptism to immersion baptism. Foes condemned the first Baptists as Anabaptists, but this was because of believer's baptism, not immersion. Immersion, which Anglicans had long practiced, was not at first identified as an Anabaptist marker. Baptists did more to create this common misperception than inherit it.

Swiss and German Anabaptists knew of the practice of immersion, considered it in biblical perspective, saw the burial and rising imagery in it, and proceeded with few exceptions to retain the common practices of sprinkling and pouring.[4]

Other than possible individual or very short lived exceptions, believer's baptism by immersion first became a vital matter and common practice among a sect of re-baptizers in Poland and Lithuania, after Anabaptism filtered into that territory in the second half of the 1500s.[5] The 1574 Polish Anabaptist catechism taught believer's baptism by immersion.

---

[1] I am indebted to Wes Harrison, "The Renewal of the Practice of Adult Baptism by Immersion during the Reformation Era, 1525–1700," *The Restoration Quarterly* 43/2 (1998), http://www.restorationquarterly.org/Volume_043/rq04302harrison.htm (accessed 31 July 2006) for his summary of the history of immersion baptism before and during the Reformation.

[2] "On Baptisme, bothe publique and private," *The Book of Common Prayer* (1549), http://justus.anglican.org/resources/bcp/1549/Baptism_1549.htm (accessed 31 July 2006).

[3] George Winthrop's *Journal* 1/95, 120, quoted in Isaac Backus, ed., with notes by David Weston (editor of 1871 ed.), *A History of New England with Particular Reference to the Denomination of Christians Called Baptists* (1777) (Newton MA: The Backus Historical Society, 1871; repr., New York: Arno Press, 1969) 95.

[4] Harold Bender, "Immersion," *Global Anabaptist Mennonite Encyclopedia Online*, http://www.gameo.org/encyclopedia/contents/o850.html (accessed 31 July 2006).

[5] George H. Williams, *Protestants in the Ukrainian Lands of the Polish-Lithuanian Commonwealth* (Cambridge MA: Ukranian Research Institute, Harvard University, n.d.).

Polish Anabaptists, such as Christoph Ostordt, brought believer's baptism by immersion into German and Dutch Anabaptist territory.[6] An unsuccessful evangelist among the Dutch Waterlander Mennonites and the Swiss Brethren, Ostordt had few converts before he died in 1611. He did succeed, however, in making the doctrine of believer's baptism by immersion familiar, if not popular, in Amsterdam.

As early as 1896 William H. Whitsitt knew immersion among Anabaptists was rare.[7] Yet the conviction of Anabaptist believer's baptism by immersion persists to this day in surprising places. For example, Justo González ~~on page fifty-five of~~ in his widely used college and seminary textbook, *The Story of Christianity, Volume 2,* teaches that Swiss Anabaptists began to practice immersion soon after their Zurich debut.[8] This lasting misunderstanding is likely due to its widespread dissemination by early Baptist historians.

The Baptist tradition began about 1609 with the acceptance and practice of believer's baptism by John Smyth, Thomas Helwys, and their Separatist Puritan congregation, who are called General Baptists because of their belief in a general atonement.

Smyth and Helwys's contacts with Waterlander Mennonites undoubtedly contributed to Baptist origins. Baptism was surely one topic of intense dialogue between the English, who were reassessing their baptismal heritage, and the Waterlanders, who valued baptism so highly they preferred to be called *Doopsgezinden* (baptism minded) rather than Mennonites.[9] Waterlander Mennonite influence on General Baptists is an argument *against* immersion as the mode of Smyth's se-baptism (self-baptism). Any investigator of Baptists' immersion history needs to keep in mind Anabaptist historian Harold Bender's conclusion: "General Anabaptist recognition of immersion or practice of it on an optional basis has not been demonstrated.... The general historic practice of Mennonites up to 1860, with few exceptions, was pouring or sprinkling."[10]

---

[6] Robert Friedman, "Ostorodt, Christoph (d. 1611)" *Global Anabaptist Mennonite Encyclopedia Online,* http://www.gamco.org/encyclopedia/contents10850.html 31 July 2006.

[7] William H. Whitsitt, *A Question in Baptist History: Whether the Anabaptists in England Practiced Immersion Before the Year 1641?* (Louisville: Chas. T. Dearing, 1896) 47.

[8] Justo Gonzalez, *The Story of Christianity,* 2 vols. (San Francisco: Harper, 1985) 2:55.

[9] Nanne van der Zijpp, "Waterlanders," *Global Mennonie Encyclopedia Online.*

[10] Bender, "Immersion."

John Smyth rejected his Anglican infant baptism. He administered believer's baptism to himself. He died petitioning for a third baptism at the hands of the Waterlander Mennonites. Immersion did not figure in any of the three.

General Baptists' acceptance of immersion came during or after its widespread acceptance by Particular Baptists in the 1640s. The first confessional statement by General Baptists requiring immersion is found in the Standard Confession of 1660.

English Particular Baptists and Believer's Baptism by Immersion

Particular Baptists brought immersion of believers into the Baptist mainstream. Called Particular for their Calvinist doctrine of a limited atonement, they provide the first clear evidence of a Baptist church constituted by believer's immersion.

Sorting out the genesis of Particular Baptists is like trying to untangle a snarled fishing line in the dark. The "Kiffin Manuscript," supplemented by the "Jessey Memoranda" (or Jessey Records), is the only document to describe the first gathering of the Baptist church credited with introducing Baptists to believer's baptism by immersion.[11] The earliest surviving forms of the "Jessey Memoranda" (no 1) and the "Kiffin Manuscript" (no 2) are copies transcribed into a notebook by Benjamin Stinton about 1711 along with other documents.[12] The first gives a brief history up to 1641 of Henry Jacob's church, often called the JLJ church after its first three pastors, Jacob, Lathrop, and Jessey. The second, the anonymous "Kiffin Manuscript," is the gold standard for information concerning the origins of Particular Baptists and immersion among Baptists. The following account of immersion baptism in Particular Baptist origins is necessarily based on these documents.

Particular Baptists developed from a semi-separatist congregation Henry Jacob founded in 1616. Semi-separatist means separated from the Anglican parishes, but not declaring the established church false, or at least not rejecting

---

[11] This summary of the beginnings of the Particular Baptists from the JLJ church is based mainly on two primary sources, "The Kiffin Manuscript" and the "Jessey Memorandum," as reprinted and analyzed in Barrie R. White, "Baptist Beginnings and the 'Kiffin Manuscript,'" *Baptist History and Heritage* 2/1 (January 1967): 27–37; H. Leon McBeth, *A Sourcebook for Baptist Heritage* (Nashville: Broadman, 1990) 22–27, contains edited portions of these documents as well.

[12] The two in focus here are customarily cited as "no. 1" and "no. 2," respectively, reflecting the order of their appearance in the notebook.

its infant baptism. A strict Separatist offshoot of the JLJ church organized as a congregation in September 1633.

Several names on its early membership lists are later associated with believer's baptism by immersion. One of these is William Kiffin, to whom the work is attributed by Thomas Crosby a century later. Kiffin says he joined the group in 1638.[13] Another is Samuel Eaton. He, along with "some others," received a "further baptism" (no. 2). Whether this signified only a rejection of Anglican baptism or a turn to believer's baptism is obscure. The manner of this "further baptism" is also unknown.

In June 1638, six members of the JLJ mother church rejected infant baptism in favor of believer's baptism and joined a like-minded congregation led by John Spilsbury. Spilsbury's connections to Eaton, whom Spilsbury baptized according to a 1641 source by John Taylor, or to the 1633 daughter church of the JLJ, if any, are unclear. The pieces of this historical jigsaw puzzle, some of which are missing, reveal a Particular Baptist church of baptized believers possibly by 1633 and certainly by 1638. Immersion was added to their tradition in January 1642.

About 1640 Henry Jessey, by then pastor of one-half of the JLJ mother church, and Richard Blunt of the 1633 JLJ daughter congregation, now a Baptist church, conferred together about the nature of true baptism. Jessey, Blunt, portions of their congregations, and others affiliated with the JLJ tradition came to mutual agreement: baptism "ought to be by dipping the Body into the water, resembling Burial and rising again. 2 Col: 2. 12. Rom: 6. 4" (no. 2). At this time, Jessey began practicing infant immersion.[14] He was immersed in 1645 but continued to accept members into his congregation without regard for the age of the subject or the mode, a stance called "open membership."

About 1640 some in Blunt's and Jessey's congregations became convinced the New Testament model necessitated believer's baptism by immersion. They felt compelled to join this practice to believer's baptism in order to restore the true church, but the potential congregation found itself stymied. Some Baptists in the early seventeenth century, called successionists, believed the authority to baptize must come from a true church. They had rejected their own Anglican

---

[13] Stephen Wright, "Baptist Alignments and the Restoration of Immersion, 1638–44, Part II," *Baptist Quarterly* 40/6 (April 2004): 265.

[14] Stephen Wright, "Baptist Alignments and the Restoration of Immersion, 1638–44, Part I," *Baptist Quarterly* 40/5 (January 2004): 264, citing another of document attributed to Jessey in Stinton's copybook.

baptisms on this basis. Now they needed a true church with the authority to baptize them, thus creating their own restored church. They searched on their island in vain, "none having then so practiced in England to professed Believers" (no. 2). Having heard "that some in the Nether Lands had so practiced" (no. 2), they sent Richard Blunt, who spoke Dutch, to seek out immersionists on the Continent.

He found them. The "Kiffin Manuscript" says Blunt "returned with Letters from them Jo: Batte a Teacher there, & from that Church to such as sent him." Longstanding opinion holds Blunt's advisors were Collegiants somewhere in Holland. Collegiants is the name taken by a loosely organized movement begun in response to the 1619 Synod of Dort and the ensuing religious persecution. Centered in Rijnsburg, they shared many similarities to the Mennonite churches, including believer's baptism. In addition, the Collegiants required immersion, perhaps through contact with Polish Socinian Mennonites, whose theology held numerous parallels to their own. The Collegiants, or Rijnsburgers, were widely known for semi-annual public ceremonies of believer's baptism by immersion.[15]

Believer's baptism, immersion and Baptists fused in January 1642. Blunt returned with his findings. Those who sent him agreed to "proceed alike together" (no. 2). They decided to dispense with a covenant, which was "scrupled by some of them" (no. 2) and to organize by immersion baptism. Not all wished to receive immersion. Those who did set Blunt apart to baptize the rest. He first baptized a Mr. Blacklock, a "Teacher amongst them," and then, "Mr. Blunt being Baptized," he and Blacklock "baptized the rest of their friends that were so minded." Forty-one names are listed in the "Kiffin Manuscript" as baptized in this great immersion. Two other lists, one of four names and the other of twelve, who were apparently added soon after, complete the tally of immersed membership available in the manuscript.

The fifty-three believers immersed by Blunt and Blacklock in January 1642 increased and joined with others of like mind to become seven congregations of Particular Baptists by 1644. These joined together that year to publish *The London Confession* to distinguish themselves from General Baptists and Anabaptists.[16] It is the first Baptist statement of faith to prescribe believer's baptism by immersion.

---

[15] Bender, "Immersion."

[16] Printed in McBeth, *Sourcebook*, 45–53.

Article 39 of the *London Confession* declares baptism an ordinance "to be dispensed only upon persons professing faith," and article 40 says, "The way and manner of the dispensing of this Ordinance the Scripture holds to be dipping or plunging the whole body under water: it being a sign must answer the thing signified."[17] It goes on to say the things signified are the soul washed in the blood of Christ; the believers' participation in the death, burial, and resurrection of Christ; and confirmation that the bodies of believers will be raised to reign with Christ. These articles express an enduring Baptist position based on biblical and theological arguments: Believer's baptism by immersion is the sole complete symbol of public profession of Christ and initiation into Christ's body, the church.

Believer's Baptism by Immersion in America

The most influential Baptist institution in colonial America, the Philadelphia Baptist Association, adopted a slightly modified version of the *London Confession* in 1742. Believer's baptism by immersion first appeared in America about a century earlier with a link to the British Particular Baptist story.

William McLoughlin says the first Baptist church in America, founded by Roger Williams, was "the first [in America] to adopt baptism (for them re-baptism) of adult believers by immersion as the only proper basis for church membership,"[18] but the immersion part is almost certainly false. Believer's baptism by immersion most likely entered into America by way of a later British connection, not through Roger Williams. The story of Baptist origins in America invariably begins with Roger Williams; the story of believer's baptism by immersion in America begins by refuting his part in it.

Roger Williams and some who joined him in exile at Providence Plantation began a Baptist church in spring 1639. It was the first Baptist church on the continent. An entry in the journal of Massachusetts Governor John Winthrop is the only surviving description of its founding. Winthrop reports Katherine Marberry Scott,[19] sister to famous radical Anne Hutchinson,

---

[17] *London Confession* in McBeth, *Sourcebook*, 50.

[18] William G. McLoughlin, *New England Dissent 1630–1833: The Baptists and the Separation of Church and State* (Cambridge MA: Harvard University Press, 1971) 10.

[19] George Partridge, *History of Bellingham* (1919), quoted in Bruce W. Lord, "The Signers," chap. 3 of *History of the Town of Bellingham, 1660–1780*, sec. 17http://www.bellinghamma.org/Historical/Chapter3.htm (accessed 31 July 2006).

"emboldened" Williams to profess her "Anabaptistry" and be "rebaptized" at the hand of one "Holyman" (Ezekiel Holliman) from Salem. Then Williams rebaptized Holliman and "some ten more." The church explicitly rejected infant baptism and "wanted no magistrate."[20]

McLoughlin's conclusion that Williams was immersed may be based on a hostile letter written almost four decades after the fact that is printed in Isaac Backus's *History of the Baptists*.[21] Katherine Scott held believer's baptism before Williams, according to Winthrop. McBeth tentatively suggests she might have brought those views from England.[22] Katherine, who became a Quaker, is not explicitly named as one of those baptized by Williams. Even if Katherine brought Baptist tradition to Williams from England, the likelihood that Williams practiced or received immersion is very small indeed. Williams's rebaptism occurred before immersion became common among English Baptists.

Williams was not a Baptist long enough to have a part in introducing immersion later. He founded the first Baptist church in America by March 1639, was a Seeker by 1640, and remained so the rest of his life.[23] Katherine's husband, Richard Scott, writing years later, says Williams remained with the Baptists only three or four months. Then he left, having decided as Smyth had before him in Amsterdam, "'Their baptism could not be right because it was not administered by an apostle.'"[24] The same fate for the same reason, according to Wright, befell Blunt's congregation, which "'broke into pieces, and some went one way, some another, divers fell off to no church at all.'"[25] Believer's baptism by immersion is not part of Roger Williams's legacy in America.

Dr. John Clarke's church is the probable source of believer's baptism by immersion in America. Clarke was an English minister, lawyer, and physician. In 1637, at twenty-eight, he immigrated to Boston. Immediately caught up in the controversy surrounding Anne Hutchinson, he joined her group of

[20] Excerpt on Roger Williams from John Winthrop's *Journal*, in McBeth, *Sourcebook*, 83.
[21] See W. H. Whitsitt's "Appendix: Baptism of Roger Williams," 161 and Whitsitt, *A Question in Baptist History*, 147–64.
[22] H. Leon McBeth, *The Baptist Heritage: Four Centuries of Baptist Witness* (Nashville: Broadman, 1987) 131.
[23] See McBeth, *Baptist Heritage*, 124–36 for a summary of Williams's life, views, and contributions to Baptist life.
[24] Printed in Backus, *A History of New England*, 89.
[25] Stephen Wright, "Baptist Alignments, Part II," 357.

dissidents. Clarke followed her into exile, first in New Hampshire and then at the founding of Portsmouth in 1639.

The date John Clarke accepted Baptist principles is unclear. The nature of the worshiping community at Portsmouth, which Clarke apparently led, was a fluid mix of radicals: separatists, Antinomians, perhaps some Baptists, and certainly some future Baptists. By 1641 Clarke led a split with Anne Hutchinson's supporters, who had shifted toward the Quakers. Clarke's congregation moved south to Newport. By then Clarke had found ample opportunity to consider why Williams and his little band had become Baptists in 1639. From 1637 Clarke associated with Anne Hutchinson, whose sister Katherine held Baptist views before the church at Providence began, and he met with Williams in 1638 to discuss a place of refuge, settling on Portsmouth.

Within three years after the move to Newport, Clarke's congregation was most likely a Baptist one; it was certainly such by 1648.[26] Mark Lucar (or Luker) immigrated to New England and joined the church at Newport soon after receiving immersion from Blunt or Blacklock in January 1642. If Lucar accompanied Roger Williams on his return to America from England in 1644, as William Whitsitt proposes, Lucar's arrival and the tradition of a 1644 beginning at Newport fit neatly together.[27] Immersion of believers perhaps arrived in America along with him.

Lucar's name is one of fifteen Newport Baptist's members enrolled in 1648, according to Comer. Lucar and John Clarke are at the center of the first sure report of believer's baptism by immersion in America. The reporter is Roger Williams. In a letter of 10 November 1649, Williams wrote to Governor John Winthrop:[28]

> At Secunck a great many have lately Concurred with Mr Jo: [John] Clarke and our Providence men about the point of a New Baptism, and the manner by Dipping; and Mr. Jo. Clarke hath been there lately (and Mr Lucar) and hath dipped them. I believe their practice comes nearer the first practices of our great Founder Christ <Jesus> than

---

[26] Backus, *A History of New England*, 125.

[27] Whitsitt, *A Question*, 159.

[28] Glenn W. LaFantasie, ed., *The Correspondence of Roger Williams, Volume 2: 1654–1682*, Glenn H. Horton assisted by Robert S. Cocroft and Pamela A. Kennedy, and revised from an unpublished manuscript edited by Bradford F. Swan (Hanover: Brown University Press/University Press of New England, 1988) 302.

other practices of Religion do and yet I have not satisfaction neither in the Authority by which it is done nor in the manner.

This letter is the earliest document clearly describing believer's baptism by immersion on American soil. It shows immersion already popular in Newport and Providence and spreading into Sekunk (Rehoboth), Plymouth Colony's jurisdiction. In 1649 Roger Williams considered it new. He approves of its form in comparison to others, but Seeker Williams cannot quite accept its source of authority or its form.

Soon after, Clarke and one of the Sekunk immersed believers, Obadiah Holmes, took the "New Baptisme" into Massachusetts itself, where they were imprisoned. Baptists' believer's baptism by immersion so alarmed the Massachusetts authority that they had Holmes brutally and publicly whipped.

McLoughlin is correct in saying Baptists "waged their fight for reform upon the most controversial and unsettled ground in the whole Puritan system": believer's baptism by immersion.[29] If believers could decide for themselves what constituted a true church and the civil magistrate had no power to interfere, the religious, political, and social foundations of Puritan New England rested on shifting sand. American believer's baptism by immersion embodied public resistance to a double shackle of state and established church, the last remnant of which did not fall away until 1833.

Some Loose Ends

When Baptists joined believer's baptism and immersion, they created a potent symbol of a community of faith consisting of voluntary believers whose public profession at baptism is a clear expression of dying to an old life to be raised to a new one of Christian discipleship. The outlines of this turning point in Baptist life are generally accepted. Further historical work remains, both in suppressing repetition of former errors and in exploring unanswered questions.

With whom did Richard Blunt meet in the Netherlands? Did Richard Blunt consult with Collegiants in Holland? Almost everyone thinks so. A meeting between Blunt and the Collegiants rests on three assumptions. First, in 1740 earliest Baptist historian Thomas Crosby interpreted "Jo: Batte" in the "Kiffin Manuscript" as a teacher of the unnamed Netherland immersing congregation. Second, subsequent historians identified "Jo: Batte" as a misspelling of Jan

---

[29] McLoughlin, *New England Dissent*, 7.

Batten [of Leyden], a Collegiant leader about 1620 found in the writings of eighteenth-century Anabaptist historian G. Brandt.[30] Third, there is corroborating evidence from Mennonite historians. For instance, Barrie White judiciously states, "This matter needs more investigation," and then points the reader to a Mennonite encyclopedia article as a further resource.[31]

Stephen Wright's recent research raises new questions about "Jo: Batte." Taken in reverse order, he says no contemporary "Dutch archival documents" corroborate a meeting between Richard Blunt and Jan Batten. In fact, he found the Anabaptist historians dependent upon Baptist secondary sources. In his words, "All roads lead back to Crosby."[32] Second, reading "Jo: Batte" as Jan Batten assumes an N is omitted in the Stinton copybook. What if, Wright argues, "Batte" is really the name intended? He proposes the "teacher" to be Timothy Batte, an English Baptist living in Holland about 1640, who soon appeared in England immersing believers alongside Thomas Lamb. The abbreviations in eighteenth-century script for John (Ino) and Timothy (Tmo) are quite similar. If Stinton copied "Batte" correctly, but mistook the abbreviation of Timothy for that of John, then Blunt may have had a General Baptist exile advising him concerning immersion. Finally, the sentence does not require Crosby's designation of "Jo: Batte" as the teacher of the aforementioned church. The article is "a" not "the," opening the possibility it may be read: "[Blunt] Returned with Letters from them[:] Jo: Batte a Teacher there[,] & from that church to such as sent him" (no. 2). This reading can be understood to separate consultation with the teacher from consultation with the church. White was right; this matter calls for more investigation.

When Was Blunt Immersed? Was Blunt immersed while in Holland or after his return to England? The crucial text here is the ambiguous line in the "Kiffin Manuscript": "Mr. Blunt Baptized Mr. Blacklock that was a teacher amongst them, & Mr. Blunt being Baptized, he & Mr. Blacklock Baptized the rest." Does this mean that Blacklock baptized Blunt in turn and then Blunt and Blacklock baptized the rest or that Blunt had already been baptized in the Netherlands? Various eminent Baptist historians, following Crosby, choose the latter, including among others Joseph Ivimey, W. H. Whitsitt, and E. A. Payne. Leon McBeth in *The Baptist Heritage* agrees these authorities are "probably

---

[30] See Champlain Burrage, "The Collegiants or Rynsburgers of Holland," *The Review and Expositor* 7/4 (October 1910): 526–74, and Wright, "Baptist Alignments Part I," 270.

[31] White, "Baptist Beginnings," 36n54.

[32] Wright, "Baptist Alignments, Part I," 271.

correct."[33] Bill Leonard in *Baptist Ways* offers the opinion that "the sources do not offer enough evidence to support any of these conclusions completely."[34] Robert Torbet, Barrie White, and Stephen Wright disagree. They and others find Champlain Burrage's 1912 arguments against Blunt's immersion outside England decisive, as do I.[35]

Burrage's evidence is too dependent upon its cumulative power to lend itself easily to summarization. The gist of his strategy is to marshal comments by Blunt's contemporaries, most of whom criticize Blunt's audacity in committing se-baptism after going to Holland in search of baptismal succession. One of these comes from Blunt's close associate, Henry Jessey, who wrote in his 1650 book, *A Storehouse of Provision*, "If none but *baptized* ones are *owned* to be *disciples*; then the *first* restorers of baptism [immersion] were *not owned* to be *disciples* [evidently, because their first administrator (Blunt) of immersion had not himself been immersed when he began to administer that ordinance]."[36] These remarks are made in the context of two contrasting Particular Baptist views toward restoring believer's baptism by immersion. One group, represented by Blunt, sought a baptismal succession; the other, expressed here by Jessey, renewed immersion of believers solely on the basis of scriptural warrant for the practice.[37]

What Year Did Blunt and Blacklock Begin Immersing? When did Blunt and Blacklock perform the fifty-three immersions? Some historians opt for January 1641, including Whitsitt, Lofton, McBeth, and Leonard. Others date it January 1642, including Whitely, Burrage, White, and Wright, with whom I agree. The choice hinges on year dates written by an anonymous hand in the margins of Stinton copy of the "Kiffin Manuscript." Since the document is considered reliable, the dates are generally consistent with other writings of the time and no better alternative presents itself, the manuscript's margins hold the decisive references.

The last year entered before the first list of immersed believers is 1641, placed beside the words introducing the immersion ceremony, "They proceeded on.... " Fourteen lines later, over the columns of the first list of

---

[33] McBeth, *Baptist Heritage*, 46.

[34] Bill J. Leonard, *Baptist Ways: A History* (Valley Forge: Judson Press, 2003) 30.

[35] Champlin Burrage, "The Restoration of Immersion by the English Anabaptists and Baptists (1640–1700)," *The American Journal of Theology* 16/1 (July 1912): 70–89.

[36] Quoted in Burrage, "The Restoration of Immersion," 76. Brackets by Burrage.

[37] McBeth, *Baptist Heritage*, 47.

baptized is written "11. Mo.Ianu: begin." The second list of immersed members is headed "1641 11 January 9 added." As Whitely first pointed out, if the year preceding the first January entry is accepted, as seems natural, the second date can best be read as 9 January, the eleventh month of 1641, which is January 1642 by our way of calculating the passage of time.[38]

In seventeenth-century Europe, two calendars were in use.[39] One observed the beginning of the year on 1 January; the other on 25 March. English society used both, one for civil purposes and the other for traditional holidays and the like. To convey a date accurately, in this case the date of the immersions, the writer had to give the year (1641), the month (January), the day of the month (9 for the second list; none for the first), and a number related to the month (11 in both cases) to designate which calendar the year signified (in this case the year beginning in March since January is its eleventh month, not its first). The immersions, therefore, took place in January 1641 on calendars beginning in March and January 1642 on calendars beginning with January, such as those used today. Contemporary practice often signifies the date of the immersions as January 1641\1642. This does not mean either 1641 or 1642, but January of 1641 "old style" calendar and January 1642 "new style" calendar, which are the same month.

The "Kiffin Manuscript" is our only peephole through an opaque fence of lost or fragmentary evidence. This has sometimes created a rather neat impression: Baptists did not immerse; then Blunt brought immersion back from Holland; and soon everyone was doing it, even the General Baptists.

The earlier date, 1641, makes Blunt's ministry as almost exclusive gateway easier to maintain than does the later date. The 1642 date resets the context for Baptist immersion evidence typically considered less central. Defense of believer's baptism by immersion in 1641 by General Baptist Edward Barber is universally acknowledged, for example.[40] McBeth's *The Baptist Heritage* mentions that Leonard Busher advocated immersion in 1614 and Marke Luker (Lucar) in the mid–1630s, all as prelude to the main feature.[41] Wright suggests General Baptist Thomas Lambe performed rebaptisms in the Severn River near

---

[38] White, "Baptist Beginnings," 32, n. 29.

[39] See Mike Spathaky, "Old Style and New Style Dates and the Change to the Gregorian Calendar," *GENUKI: UK & Ireland Geneology*, http://www.genfair.com/dates.htm (accessed 8 August 2006).

[40] A portion of Edward Barber's *A Small Treatise on Baptisme, or Dipping*, 1641, is printed in McBeth, *Sourcebook*, 41–42.

[41] McBeth, *The Baptist Heritage*, 44–45.

Gloucester, England, some time before 11 February 1642.[42]

In view of these possibilities, precise dates take on new importance. Two current standard surveys of general Baptist history are McBeth's and Leonard's.[43] McBeth gives two block quotes from the "Kiffin Manuscript."[44] The first includes the Stinton transcript's 1640 date for Blunt's return next to the description of Blunt returning from England, but the second omits a crucial 1641 date in the section detailing the immersions, though the dates stand in the same relation to their respective texts. The source McBeth cites for the block quotations, Champlain Burrage's *Early English Dissenters*, contains the missing date.[45] Larger portions of the "Kiffin Manuscript" are printed in McBeth's *Sourcebook*.[46] There the 1641 date missing in *The Baptist Heritage* is omitted again without notation. (All the member lists and accompanying month notations are edited out with a three point ellipsis.)

In *Baptist Ways*, Leonard says, "Blunt returned in January 1641 and instituted a ceremony of 'dipping.'"[47] In the next paragraph, he states, "Underwood concluded that Blunt did receive baptism from the Collegiants, sometime in 1641." This could be construed to suggest Underwood, against all others, thought Blunt returned to Holland after the great immersion, but this is surely not what Leonard means to convey. The point is to show Underwood's position on the geography of Blunt's immersion, not its time. The inclusion of the date is irrelevant and slightly confusing, standing as it does apart from any recognition of uncertainty regarding it.

Neither McBeth nor Leonard intentionally misrepresent or intend to mislead. Their purposes do not include establishing the date of the events, which they evidently assume to be more or less settled and relatively unimportant. The imprecision does mark the need to revisit the question.

What Manner Immersion? A question of interest for historians of worship is what manner of immersion did Baptists practice around 1642? A remarkable variety of Baptist immersion methods arose during the first half of the 1700s. Baptists dipped, plunged, thrice immersed, and washed by rubbing hands over

---

[42] Wright, "Baptist Alignments Part II," 348–49.

[43] McBeth, *The Baptist Heritage*; Leonard, *Baptist Ways*.

[44] Ibid., 45.

[45] Champlin Burrage, *The Early English Dissenters in the Light of Recent Research (1550–1641)*, 2 vols., 1912, repr. in The Dissent and Nonconformity series (Paris AK: The Baptist Standard Bearer, Inc., Cambridge University Press, n.d.) 302–303.

[46] McBeth, *Sourcebook*, 26–27.

[47] Leonard, *Baptist Ways*, 29.

the baptizee's body and then immersed. They immersed forward and backward, clothed and unclothed. Open communion [semi?]-Baptist churches accepted believer's baptism by immersion, believer's baptism by sprinkling, or either mode applied to infants. Other Baptist congregations continued to sprinkle believers long after 1642; some accepted various modes of believer's baptism; and some, "closed membership" Baptists, required immersion for admittance, the norm for many Baptist churches today.[48] The frontispiece to Daniel Featley's 1645 book, *The Dippers Dipt*, shows various modes of immersion baptism from the 1640s. What such glyphics say about Baptist theology and liturgy awaits someone to translate their significance.

Who Brought Immersion to America and When? If John Clarke's church was the first to practice believer's baptism by immersion in America, who brought the mode to his attention? Mark Lucar is the prime suspect, but too little is known about his whereabouts between the time Blunt or Blacklock immersed him and the time he shows up on the rolls at Newport in 1648. Whitsitt's view that Lucar came over from England on the ship with the returning Williams in 1644 is plausible and appealing, but conjectural.

Suggested Reading

Burrage, Champlin. *The Early English Dissenters in the Light of Recent Research (1550–1641)*. 2 volumes. 1912. The Dissent and Nonconformity series. Paris AK: The Baptist Standard Bearer, Inc., Cambridge University Press, n.d.

White, Barrie R. "Who Really Wrote the 'Kiffin Manuscript?'" *Baptist History and Heritage* 1/3 (October 1966): 3–10, 14.

———. "Baptist Beginnings and the 'Kiffin Manuscript.'" *Baptist History and Heritage* 2/1 (January 1967): 27–37.

Whitsitt, William H. *A Question in Baptist History: Whether the Anabaptists in England Practiced Immersion before the Year 1641?* Louisville: Chas. T. Dearing, 1896.

Wright, Stephen. "Baptist Alignments and the Restoration of Immersion, 1638–44, Part I." *Baptist Quarterly* 40/5 (January 2004): 261–82.

———. "Baptist Alignments and the Restoration of Immersion, 1638–44, Part II." *Baptist Quarterly* 40/6 (April 2004): 346–68.

———. *Early English Baptists, 1603–1649*. Rochester NY: Boydell Press, 2006.

---

[48] See Burrage, "The Restoration of Immersion," 70–89.

CHAPTER 5

Baptist Confessions of Faith and the Turn toward Public Theology: 1644

Fisher Humphreys

*Baptists often used confessions not to proclaim "Baptist distinctives"
but instead to show how similar Baptists were to other orthodox
Christians.[1]*

Introduction

It is an honor and a pleasure to contribute to a book honoring Dr. Leon McBeth, to whose work in Baptist history I have been indebted for many years. The quotation above is from a passage in which Dr. McBeth provides a helpful analysis of diverse uses for which Baptists have created confessions of faith. One of those uses, as Dr. McBeth says, is to display Baptists' similarities to other Christians; these Baptist confessions are for constructing bridges rather than walls.

That is one of the uses of the confession that was first published on 16 October 1644 and revised and/or reprinted in 1646, 1651, 1652, and 1653.[2] It was written to show that the Baptist understanding of the Christian faith had much in common with other Christians' understanding and that, where it differed from theirs, it differed in order to be faithful to Christ and to the Bible.

Clearly, a major aim of their confession is to point to a clear relationship with other Christians. There is, in their view, no such thing as a "Baptist"

---

[1] H. Leon McBeth, *The Baptist Heritage: Four Centuries of Baptist Witness* (Nashville: Broadman Press, 1987) 68.

[2] B. R. White, "The Doctrine of the Church in the Particular Baptist Confession of 1644," *Journal of Theological Studies*, New Series 19/2 (October 1968): 570, n. 3.

belief. Rather, there is a Christian belief, to which Baptists were calling all to be faithful.[3]

The First London Confession, as it is usually called, is an original in several ways. It was the first confession by the Calvinistic Particular Baptists. It was the first Baptist confession in which immersion is said to be the proper method of baptism. It was the first Baptist confession issued by a group of churches rather than by an individual or a single congregation; it was signed by fifteen men representing seven congregations in London.

To begin our review of how this confession served as a bridge to other Christian churches and thereby launched Baptists onto the enterprise of public and ecumenical theology, we will consider briefly the historical context in which it was issued.

The Historical Context

The historical context was one of political, social, and religious conflict. King Charles I, who reigned 1625–1649, believed in the divine right of kings to rule, which put him in a continual struggle against Parliament, which was committed to a more participatory form of government. From 1629 to1640 Charles refused to call a Parliament and ruled England in an "Eleven Years' Tyranny." In 1640 he was forced to call a Parliament; known as "the long Parliament," it sat for about thirteen years (1640–1653). The details of the struggle between king and Parliament may seem technical now, but the outcome was that king and Parliament created separate armies and entered into a Civil War (1642–1648). The army of Parliament was victorious, and in 1649 King Charles was beheaded. Initially, Parliament ruled England as a Commonwealth (1649–1653), but as society lurched toward anarchy, the leader of the army, Oliver Cromwell, became Lord Protector (1653–1658). The Protectorate was no more successful than the Commonwealth, and in 1660 Charles II, son of Charles I, returned from exile in France, and the monarchy was restored.

The years between 1642, when the armed conflict began, and 1660, were golden years for the Baptists. Free for a time from persecution, they managed during this period to grow dramatically in numbers, to plant new churches

---

[3] Charles R. Andrews, "The Maine Wheele That Sets Us Aworke," *Foundations* 1/3 (July 1958): 31.

throughout much of Great Britain, to form associations of churches,[4] and, in the case of the Particular Baptists, to transform much of society's image of them from being a strange, contemptible sect (think Moonies) to being a branch on the great tree of Protestantism.

The conflict between the king and Parliament was a political one. The kingdom was also engaged in a social conflict that was principally a contest between the royalty and aristocracy on one hand and the gentry on the other, though it also included more radical individuals and movements who called for the full equality of all persons, a concept that seems natural to people today but that suggested anarchy to class-conscious England in the seventeenth century.

And then there were the religious conflicts. On a grand scale there was the Thirty Years War (1618–1648) in which Catholic nations and Protestant nations struggled for dominance on the continent of Europe; this war formed a background against which Protestants in England, including Baptists, worked out their own issues, for the threat of Catholic domination was quite real; among other things, King Charles's wife Henrietta Maria was a Catholic, and Ireland, one of the three kingdoms over which Charles ruled, was staunchly Catholic.

On a national scale there was conflict between the Church of England, which was the established church, and all other expressions of the Christian faith. The Church of England had the king as its head, and he had appointed a rigorist Archbishop of Canterbury, William Laud, to carry forward his anti-Puritan program for the church. As Owen Chadwick writes, Laud's influence was such that "Charles I began his reign by asking for a list of clergy to promote; and William Laud marked the list with the letters P (for Puritan) and O (for Orthodox)."[5] When the conflict between king and Parliament heated up, not surprisingly the largely Puritan Parliament imprisoned Laud; he was imprisoned in the Tower in London when Baptists published their confession in 1644, and early the next year he was beheaded.

The two largest groups who opposed Laud and his program were the Presbyterians and the Independents, as Congregationalists were then called. These groups shared a common Calvinistic theology, but they differed concerning church government. The Independents wanted congregations to be self-governing; the Presbyterians favored an established church, such as Calvin

---

[4] B. R. White, "The Organisation of the Particular Baptists, 1644–1660," *Journal of Ecclesiastical History* 17/2 (October 1966): 209–26.

[5] Owen Chadwick, *The Reformation* (Baltimore: Penguin Books, 1968) 222.

had in Geneva and the Presbyterians had in Scotland, and a connectional form of church government. Initially, the Presbyterians were the stronger of the two groups, but beginning in 1647 with the increasing prominence of Oliver Cromwell, who was an Independent, the Independents became the stronger group. It was to these two groups that the Baptists were building a bridge with the confession of 1644.

First Some Walls, Then the Bridge

In order to display how much they had in common with the Presbyterians and the Independents, the Calvinistic Baptists needed to distinguish themselves carefully from a number of other religious groups. Baptists were not Roman Catholics and they were not Anglicans. They held a different theology, a different form of church government, and a different attitude toward religious liberty than these two churches. The Catholic Church's sacramental system was entirely alien to the Baptists. So was governance by bishops appointed by the Pope (Roman Catholic) or the king (Church of England).

Baptists needed to distinguish themselves from other Christian groups also. For example, the Particular Baptists had to show that, unlike the General Baptists, they were not Arminian in their theology, but they enthusiastically embraced the principles of Calvinism. They did this at length in the confession of 1644.

They also needed to distinguish themselves from the Anabaptists, the radical wing of the Reformation. In 1644 Baptists were not yet called "Baptists," and as often as not they were called "Anabaptists"; in fact, the title of the 1644 confession is "The Confession of Faith of Those Churches Which Are Commonly (Though Falsly) Called Anabaptists." In the mind of many English people in 1644, Baptists were associated with a violent uprising of Anabaptists in the city of Münster in northern Germany just over a century earlier. Though Anabaptists had since shown themselves to be peaceable, and many of them were actually pacifists, many English people still regarded them as anarchists who were not to be trusted. In addition, Anabaptists were opposed to Christians serving as magistrates and to taking oaths. Baptists needed to make it clear that they were supportive of magistracy and oaths and that their political and social views excluded anarchy and violence. They did this in the confession of 1644.

Baptists also needed to show that, except for one issue to be discussed below, they were not social extremists. During the Interregnum, the number of groups of social extremists increased dramatically and included, among others,

Diggers, Levellers, Muggletonians, Ranters, Quakers, Seekers, and Fifth Monarchy Men. Unlike the Diggers, Baptists were not communists. Unlike the Levellers, Baptists respected the supreme magistracy of the king and of Parliament as representative of the people of Britain. Unlike the Muggletonians, the Ranters, and the Quakers, Baptists looked to the Bible, rather than to visions given to individuals, as their authority in religion. Unlike the Seekers, Baptists believed that there is a true church of the Lord Jesus in the world and that Christians should affiliate with that church while awaiting the return of the Lord. Unlike the Fifth Monarchy Men, most Baptists, including those who did think of the new republican order in Britain as the coming of the Fifth Monarchy (succeeding the four monarchies mentioned in Daniel 2), did not understand their millenarian views to entail a call to oppose all human government or to revolt against established governments.[6] Though the First London Confession does not mention these groups by name, it does address many of their issues, most indirectly but some such as Arminianism and magistracy directly.

The one issue on which the position of the Baptists may be described as radical was their total commitment to full religious liberty. In his comprehensive review of the early English Baptist literature on religious freedom, Leon McBeth has demonstrated that Baptists were fully committed to complete liberty and that at the time when Baptists began to address the question, they were a distinct minority. He wrote of the confession of 1644, "No doubt the articles on religious liberty were as formative as the doctrinal articles."[7]

Religious liberty was on people's minds in 1643. Just three months before the First London Confession was issued, a book was published in London that was representative of the Baptist commitment to freedom. Written by the founder of the first Baptist church in America, Roger Williams, it was titled *The Bloudy Tenent of Persecution*, and it was a plea for full religious liberty for all persons. Williams had come to London in order to get from Parliament a charter for Providence Plantations (Rhode Island), the colony that he had founded in America. In March he received the charter; in July *The Bloody Tenent* was published; and in August, by order of Parliament, it was burned by the

---

[6] B. R. White, "John Pendarves, the Calvinistic Baptists and the Fifth Monarchy," *The Baptist Quarterly* 25/6 (April 1974): 251–71.

[7] H. Leon McBeth, *English Baptist Literature on Religious Liberty to 1689* (New York: Arno Press, 1980) 85–86.

public hangman in London. But Parliament was unable to arrest Williams, as he has just sailed for America.[8]

A public theology is one in which, among other things, issues are addressed that are of interest and concern not only to one's own church but to the larger society. In distinguishing themselves from these other groups, and in speaking to the public question of religious liberty, Baptists were engaging in the practice of public theology.

Sources for the First London Confession

Historians have devoted careful attention to the question of sources for the First London Confession.[9] The consensus is that the principal source is the True Confession of 1596, an early confession of Separates.

B. R. White has proposed that the confession of 1644 incorporated the five themes that were promoted in the Canons of the Synod of Dort (1618–1619).[10] These five themes concern salvation, and they have become perhaps the most popular account of Calvinism in the English-speaking world in part because they can be presented with the acronym TULIP: total depravity, unconditional election, limited atonement, irresistible grace, and the perseverance of the saints.

Leon McBeth has hinted that the Westminster Confession itself may have been a source for the First London Confession.[11] The Westminster Confession was the product of the Westminster Assembly, a group appointed by Parliament that began meeting in London in summer 1643. In the assembly the two principal groups were Presbyterians and Independents; the confession affirms a presbyterian rather than a congregational form of church government. The assembly did not complete the confession until late in 1646, so their finished document was not available to the Baptists in 1644. However, the assembly began its work on the Westminster Confession in October 1643, a full year

---

[8] The fullest account of Williams's times in London, 1643–1644, seems to be that of Ola Elizabeth Winslow, *Master Roger Williams: A Biography* (New York: The Macmillan Company, 1957) chs. 8–14; see 198–99.

[9] For a recent survey of proposals about sources for the confession, see Jay Travis Collier, "The Sources Behind the First London Confession," *American Baptist Quarterly* 21/2 (June 2002): 196–214.

[10] Barrington E. [sic] White, "The English Particular Baptists and the Great Rebellion, 1640–1660," *Baptist History and Heritage* 9/1 (January 1974): 18.

[11] H. Leon McBeth, *A Sourcebook for Baptist Heritage* (Nashville: Broadman Press, 1990) 45.

before the Baptist confession was published. The Baptists were aware that the assembly was meeting and that it was working on a confession, and it seems highly improbable that while they were themselves working on a confession to build a bridge to Presbyterians and Independents, they would ignore the fact that nearby the Presbyterians and Independents were working on a confession of their own. And, of course, the Baptists who revised their confession in the 1650s would have had access to the finished Westminster Confession.

Another source for the 1644 confession is a book by William Ames, a learned Puritan theologian who had, among other things, attended the Synod of Dort. His book is *The Marrow of Theology*, and it was published in an English translation by order of the House of Commons in London in 1643, the year before the First London Confession.[12] Glen Stassen has called attention to the fact that four articles in the confession of 1644 were drawn from this book.[13] By using Calvinistic sources such as these, Baptists were building bridges to the Presbyterians and Independents.

The Structure and Contents of the Confession

We have been speaking of the confession in general terms; now it is time to give attention to its structure and contents. In what follows most references will be to the text of the original 1644 version as found in *Baptist Confessions of Faith* by William L. Lumpkin; when reference is made to revisions of the original that will be noted.

The confession is composed of fifty-three articles;[14] it was written in English (some contemporary confessions were in Latin) and contains approximately 6,000 words. The articles are numbered rather than titled, and hundreds of scripture references are provided in support of the content of the articles. The grammar, spelling, and style appear quaint to readers today, though presumably they appeared normal to seventeenth-century readers. One

---

[12] William Ames, *The Marrow of Theology*, trans. John D. Eusden (Boston: Pilgrim Press, 1968) 2. There had been two earlier printings of this English translation. The work cited here is the English translation of the third original (1629) edition printed in Latin.

[13] Glen H. Stassen, "Anabaptist Influence in the Origin of the Particular Baptists," *The Mennonite Quarterly Review* 36 (October 1962): 332.

[14] The last two articles are both numbered LII, which explains why it sometimes is said there were 52 articles.

author has spoken of the document as "careful, consistent, profound, and often beautiful,"[15] and another has spoken of its "masterful prose."[16]

The two following passages illustrate that the document was intended to be an exercise in public theology, and they also display how charming the document is:

> Surely, if ever people had cause to speake for the vindication of the truth of Christ in their hands, wee have, that being indeed the maine wheele at this time that sets us awork.
>
> Also we confesse that we know but in part, and that we are ignorant of many things which we desire and seek to know: and if any shall doe us that friendly part to shew us from the word of God that we see not, we shall have cause to be thankfull to God and them.[17]

In the first two articles the authors affirm the most universal and therefore the most ecumenical of all Christian beliefs: there is one true God and "in this God-head, there is the Father, the Sonne, and the Spirit." These affirmations constitute a justification for the recognition of Baptists as orthodox members of the Christian church.

In the third article the authors say that in eternity God decreed all things that are to happen, including the final destinies of each person to be created. In saying this they identified themselves with the Calvinism of the Presbyterians and Independents and, before them, with Synod of Dort and with John Calvin. In the fourth article the authors affirm that all human beings "since the Fall are conceived in sinne." Original sin was also one of the five points of the Canons of Dort.

In the fifth and sixth articles the authors affirm that God judges sinners and gives life to the elect. In the seventh article the authors affirm that the scripture contains the Word of God, which is to guide Christians' worship and service of God. Many Baptists today have become accustomed to confessions in which the first article is about scripture, but the earliest Baptists did not

---

[15] Stassen, "Anabaptist Influence," 327.

[16] William H. Brackney, *A Genetic History of Baptist Thought* (Macon GA: Mercer University Press, 2004) 29.

[17] William L. Lumpkin, *Baptist Confessions of Faith* (Philadelphia: The Judson Press, 1959) 154, 149. The first is from the preface, the second from a conclusion added to the 1646 edition.

routinely put their affirmations about scripture at the beginnings of their confessions.

Beginning with the eighth article and continuing through the twentieth, the authors affirm that Jesus is divine and human, and they elaborate on his work as prophet, priest, and king.

In article 21 the authors say that though "Christ Jesus by his death did bring forth salvation and reconciliation onely for the elect," the gospel nevertheless is to be preached to all people.

Articles 22–24 are about faith. They say that "Faith is the gift of God wrought in the hearts of the elect," that it is received by the elect passively, and that those who receive "this pretious faith" can never finally be lost. These are Calvinistic ideas, all found in the Canons of Dort.

In article 25 the authors say that neither the church nor the state should compel people to accept the gospel. This is an affirmation of the kind of religious liberty with which both General and Particular Baptists had from their beginning been identified. While it contrasts most immediately with the Church of England, it also contrasts with Presbyterian efforts to establish a Presbyterian church in England like that in Scotland.

In articles 26–32 the authors affirm that Christians are united with the Triune God, justified, sanctified, have peace with God, and are engaged in spiritual warfare.

Articles 33–47 are about the church. The church is "a company of visible Saints"; this is in distinction from all national churches. All members of the church are called, separated from the world, profess faith in the gospel, are baptized into the faith, and joined to the Lord and to each other by mutual agreement; this is in contrast to established churches into which infants are baptized.[18] It is to this covenanted church that Christ has given his promises, his covenant, and his blessings, so all Christians ought to come to this church "to lead their lives in his walled sheep-fold and watered garden." All God's servants should bring to this church the gifts God has given them and use their gifts for mutual edification. God gives to this church the authority to choose its own ministers, and "none other have power to impose them"; this is in distinction from churches whose ministers are appointed by the state or by bishops.

---

[18] Not surprisingly, it has been asked if the teaching about predestination in article 3 is consistent with the statement about a profession of faith in article 39. Jaroslav Pelikan and Valerie Hotchkiss, eds., *Creeds & Confessions of Faith in the Christian Tradition*, 4 vols. (New Haven: Yale University Press, 2003) 3:47.

Ministers should do their work faithfully, not out of greed for money. Churches should support their ministers and not expect them to be paid out of tax funds; this is in contrast to established churches. In the revision of 1651 this theme was omitted, "probably owing to Quaker influence"; the Quakers disapproved of paying clergy for their work.[19]

This brings us to the place at which Baptists differed from all other groups, namely, baptism. Only persons who profess faith in Christ should be baptized; this is in contrast to all except Baptist and some Anabaptist churches. Baptism is a prerequisite to taking the Lord's Supper; this may reflect an internal Baptist struggle about whether communion should be open to all Christians or only to those Christians who have received baptism as believers. As the confesson states, "The way and manner of the dispensing of this Ordinance the Scripture holds out to be dipping or plunging the whole body under water." Here there is an interesting note saying that modest garments should be worn during baptism; apparently Baptists were accused of going naked into the baptismal waters. Baptism is a sign of three things, one of which is death, burial, and resurrection (in 1646 the words "of Christ" were added). Any disciple can baptize; this was in contrast to those churches in which only the clergy can baptize, and it probably also reflects a concern of some Baptists about whether their baptism was true baptism if it was not administered by a person who had previously been properly baptized, such persons being hard to find both when Baptists began to baptize only believers (1609) and when they began to baptize only by immersion (1641).[20] Christ has given this church the authority to receive and expel members; members should humbly accept the church's judgment on their conduct, and the church should administer discipline with care and tenderness. In claiming these disciplinary powers for congregations of baptized believers, the authors were denying the powers to the established church and to the state, a move that must have seemed threatening especially to the Presbyterians who were then in the ascendancy. Christ gives leaders to the church, but all members should watch over one another. Those with gifts of preaching should use them in the church. No one should separate

---

[19] Lumpkin, *Baptist Confessions*, 166. George Fox, the founder of the Quakers, began preaching publicly in 1647. Also, in 1651 Roger Williams returned to London, and in 1652 his *Hireling Ministry None of Christs* was published there; like Fox, Williams heaped scorn on men whose income derived from their work as ministers; see Edwin S. Gaustad, *Liberty of Conscience: Roger Williams in America* (Grand Rapids: William B. Eerdmans Publishing Company, 1991) 91–95.

[20] Or 1642 as suggested by Loyd Allen in the preceding chapter.

from the church without having first attempted conscientiously to resolve differences. Each congregation is "a compact and knit Citie in it selfe," but congregations should counsel and assist each other; in creating the confession, members of the seven congregations in London were practicing this principle.

These sections on the church are not only theological; they "provide the basic theological platform for their programme of evangelism, church-planting and organisation of associations for the years down to the Restoration."[21] In forming associations Baptists "were able to create a system of democratic, representative assemblies with no previous parallel, at least in English history."[22]

The remaining articles are about civil society, and in them the authors walked a middle road between Anabaptists and others who have scruples about being loyal to government and the majority of contemporary Christians who believed that civil government should enforce some version of the Christian religion. God sets up civil magistrates, and Christians should obey them in civil laws; they should do this even if, as has often happened, Christians have disobeyed the magistrates in religious laws—by definition all nonconformists did this—and have been persecuted for their disobedience. The authors say that they bless God whenever civil magistrates protect them from persecution by "the Prelaticall Hierarchy," that is, the bishops of the Church of England. However, if the magistrates oppose the Baptist ways, then Baptists "ought to obey God rather than men" and continue to practice their faith as God calls them. In a later revision an article was added affirming that it is lawful for Christians to take oaths. A historian of an earlier generation wrote of this part of the confession that it is "the first publication of the doctrine of freedom of conscience, in an official document representing a body of associated churches.... This is a great landmark, not only of Baptists, but of the progress of enlightened Christianity."[23]

The confession ends with an affirmation that Christians are to give to all people the respect due to them by reason of their place, age, estate, and condition. This is in contrast to the social extremists who refused to defer to

---

[21] B. R. White, *The English Baptists of the Seventeenth Century* (London: The Baptist Historical Society, 1983) 58.

[22] J. F. McGregor, "The Baptists: Fount of All Heresy" in *Radical Religion in the English Revolution*, ed. J. F. McGregor and B. Reay (Oxford: Oxford University Press, 1984) 34.

[23] Henry C. Vedder, *A Short History of the Baptists*, new ed. (Philadelphia: The American Baptist Publication Society, 1907) 212.

their social betters, as when Quakers refused to doff their hats and caps. In conclusion, the authors wrote, "And if any take this that we have said, to be heresie, then doe wee with the Apostle freely confesse, that after the way which they call heresie, worship we the God of our Fathers." They then quoted 2 Corinthians 1:24: "Not that we have dominion over your faith, but are helpers of your joy: for by faith we stand."

Effects of the Confession of 1644

Reference has been made to the fact that the confession was repeatedly revised and republished, and that suggests that it attracted a large readership. Interest in it extended beyond London, for in 1653 a Baptist congregation meeting in Leith and Edinburgh reprinted the confession as a statement of its faith: "This *Confession* [with its later revisions and reprints] was the most influential single document produced by the Particular Baptists during the period 1640–60."[24]

Leon McBeth wrote that "the first London Confession had tremendous influence not only among non-Baptists but was also a formative influence among Baptists."[25] William Lumpkin wrote, "Outside the Baptist fellowship the Confession was received with unequalled surprise. People generally were amazed at the moderation and sanity of its articles."[26]

Late in 1646 an Epistle Dedicatory addressed to Parliament was placed before the preface of a revised version of the confession, and copies were sent to Parliament: "On March 7, 1647, Parliament seems to have given a favorable reply to the appeal of the Baptists; legal toleration was granted them."[27]

In these three senses—exercising influence among Baptists, receiving a favorable response from society, and leading the government to grant toleration to the Baptists—the bridge-building work of the confession of 1644 was a success.

Conclusion

Because Baptists were born at a revolutionary period of English history, the idea of retreat into a sectarian ghetto must have exercised a strong appeal upon them. Nevertheless, Baptists carefully distinguished themselves from

---

[24] B. R. White, "The English Particular Baptists and the Great Rebellion," 18.

[25] H. Leon McBeth, *English Baptist Literature on Religious Liberty*, 85–86.

[26] Lumpkin, *Baptist Confessions*, 147.

[27] Ibid., 148–49.

other contemporary social, political, and religious movements, and they forcefully affirmed their affinities with other Christians. In particular, in 1644 Baptists in London reached out by means of a confession to the Presbyterians and Independents who were then dominant in Parliament and in the Westminster Assembly and described what they had in common with these fellow Christians, while remaining true to those practices and beliefs that set them apart from them.[28]

Therefore, it is appropriate to think of this confession as an early Baptist exercise in public and ecumenical theology and to see it, at least for the period of the Interregnum, as successful and therefore to be appreciated by later Baptists. As Walter Shurden writes, "We should receive it for its historical value, its theological clarity, and its call to serious discipleship."[29]

The confession clearly displays that Baptists engaged in the practice of public theology, and in the following years they continued in that practice. In 1646 the Westminster Assembly completed the Westminster Confession; in 1658 the Independents, now beginning to be called Congregationalists, adopted a statement known as the Savoy Declaration; its doctrinal section comprises "the Westminister Confession of Faith with sundry changes."[30] In 1677 Baptists adopted the Second London Confession of Faith, which, like the Savoy Declaration, was the Westminster Confession with alterations. In the introductory letter to this confession, the Baptists wrote that since they found "no defect in" that "fixed on by the [Westminster] Assembly, and after them by those of the Congregational way, we did readily conclude it best to retain the same order in our present Confession.... making use of the very same words with them both, in those articles (which are very many) wherein our faith and doctrine is the same with theirs. And this we did, the more abundantly to manifest our consent with both, in all the fundamental articles of the Christian religion, as also with many others whose orthodox confessions have been

---

[28] The question that one naturally asks is this: Did the Particular Baptists reach out also to the other Baptists in England, namely, the General Baptists and the Seventh Day Baptists? A survey of this subject is found in B. R. White, "The Frontiers of Fellowship between English Baptists, 1609–1660," *Foundations* 11/3 (July–September 1968): 244–56.

[29] Walter B. Shurden, "The First London Confession of 1644," Center for Baptist Stidies, http://www.centerforbaptiststudies.org/resources/firstlondon.htm (accessed 27 December 2007).

[30] Philip Schaff, *The Creeds of Christendom: The Evangelical Protestant Creeds*, 3 vols., 6th ed. (1931; repr., Grand Rapids: Baker Books, 1983) 1:832.

published to the World."[31]

Half a century later, in 1727, the Baptists, Congregationalists, and Presbyterians of London formed an association for joint political action and were accorded the right of presenting their concerns to the crown; the association is called "The General Body of Protestant Dissenting Ministers of the Three Denominations."[32] The tradition of using confessions that embody public theology came to the new world when, in 1742, the Philadelphia Association adopted a slightly revised form of the Second London Confession.

Today Baptists who have come to the conviction that they share affinities not only with fellow Protestants but also with Roman Catholics and Eastern Orthodox may find it difficult to appreciate the achievement of 1644, but, seen in its historical context, it was an important turning point in Baptist history, such that, in the future, many Baptists were inclined to seek at least as energetically for their common ground with other Christians as for their differences.

Suggested Reading

Lumpkin, William L. *Baptist Confessions of Faith*. Philadelphia: The Judson Press, 1959.

McBeth, H. Leon. *The Baptist Heritage: Four Centuries of Baptist Witness*. Nashville: Broadman Press, 1987).

———. *English Baptist Literature on Religious Liberty to 1689*. London: Arno Press, 1980.

Shurden, Walter B. "The First London Confession of 1644." http://www.centerforbaptiststudies.org/resources/firstlondon.htm.

White, B. R. "The Doctrine of the Church in the Particular Baptist Confession of 1644." *Journal of Theological Studies New Series* 19/2 (October 1968): 209–226.

White, B. R. *The English Baptists of the Seventeenth Century*. London: The Baptist Historical Society, 1983.

---

[31] Lumpkin, *Baptist Confessions*, 245.

[32] *The Encyclopedia Britannica*, 11th ed., s.v. "Baptists," http://encyclopedia.jrank.org/. In 1972 the Presbyterians and Congregationalists merged into a single denomination, The United Reformed Church.

CHAPTER 6

Baptist Associations and the Turn toward Denominational Cooperation: 1640s/1707

Walter B. Shurden

Baptists' practice of congregational church government means that all authority and power in Baptist life is focused in the local congregation of believers, not in any extra-local ecclesiastical body. From their beginnings, especially in America, the Baptist people consistently and repeatedly affirmed the local church as the center of their life together. For that reason there is no "The Baptist Church" in the same sense that there is "The Methodist Church," "The Episcopal Church," or "The Presbyterian Church." There are only "Baptist church*es*." Baptists have formed "conventions" of churches, "unions" of churches, and "associations" of churches, but final authority in Baptist life resides in the local congregation of believers. That authority does not rest in a denomination or any extra-local church body of any kind, civil or ecclesiastical. Baptists' only real "bishops" are local churches.

On the other hand, while local Baptist churches have always been central in denominational life, it is also true that very early in the history of the denomination Baptist churches began to associate together. Although Baptists treasured the independence of the local churches, they quickly sensed the need for the interdependence of the churches. Baptists, therefore, began forming organizations called "associations." Historically, a Baptist association is an organization in which like-minded Baptist churches, usually in a contiguous geographical region, work together on matters of common interest.

The formation of associations initiated the process of organized denominational life among Baptists. Later they would form state or regional conventions and then national conventions. This Baptist turn toward the organization of associations, therefore, marks the beginning of Baptist denominational life, activities in ecclesiastical bodies beyond local churches. When did Baptist churches begin associating together? What were their purposes? If Baptists practiced congregational church polity, how did they justify the formation of associations, extra-local church bodies? How much and what kind of authority have associations wielded in Baptist life? How did associations relate to local churches?[1]

The Historical Origins of Baptist Associations

Given the traditional dates for the first General and Particular Baptist churches in England—1612 for the Generals and as early as 1616 for Particulars—interchurch relationships started early. In other words, the commitment to congregational polity never inhibited Baptists from creating extra-local organizations. The General Baptists began with a more exalted view of the association than the Particular Baptists, but the Particular Baptist model prevailed in America and in most places where Baptists developed associations. It is difficult, if not impossible, to date and/or precisely locate the first Baptist association in the British Isles. Part of the difficulty centers on distinguishing between when informal cooperation between churches became a more formal organization. Even this historical difficulty suggests something very important about the Baptist associations. Early Baptist churches in England and America did not initially come together in order to *form* something; they cooperated together or associated together in order to *do* something. Indeed, Baptist associations could justifiably be called Baptist *cooperations*. Baptist churches did not meet in order to organize; they first met to be of assistance to local churches, to witness to their distinctives, and to preserve and extend that witness.

Informal cooperation among Baptist churches in England began as early as 1626 when five General Baptist churches in the London area joined in communicating with the Waterlander Mennonites of Amsterdam. One of the first examples of Particular Baptists associating together occurred in 1644 when

---

[1] For two treatments of Baptist associational life in England and America, see Hugh Wamble, "The Concept and Practice of Christian Fellowship: The Connectional and Inter-denominational Aspects Thereof, among Seventeenth Century English Baptists" (unpublished doctor's dissertation, Southern Baptist Theological Seminary, Louisville, KY, 1955), and Walter B. Shurden, *Associationalism among Baptists in America* (New York: Arno Press, 1980), which is a reprint of an unpublished doctor's dissertation, New Orleans Baptist Theological Seminary, New Orleans, LA, 1967.

seven churches in London jointly issued a confession of faith. They were seeking to distinguish themselves in the public eye from the Arminian theology of General Baptists and more radical elements of the Anabaptists. In 1651 thirty General Baptist churches in the Midlands of England cooperated in issuing a confession. Interchurch relationships, therefore, existed among Generals and Particulars prior to any formal associational structure.

More formal manifestations of churchly connectionalism emerged among Baptists in the British Isles in the 1650s. On 6–7 November 1650, three churches of South Wales met in a general meeting in what may be called the first Baptist association. The elders and messengers of the three churches gathered "to consult...concerning such businesses as are, through God's assistance, by them now determined." [2] If the General Meeting of the churches in South Wales is not designated as the first Baptist association, the honor maybe should go to the Abingdon Association. Messengers to the 8 October 1652 meeting gathered and concluded that "particular churches of Christ ought to hold a firme communion each with other."[3]

Something very similar to the British Baptist pattern developed in America. Baptist churches in seventeenth-century America were numerically small, geographically scattered, and theologically diverse. Even in light of these mitigating factors, relationships between the churches were not long in developing. Baptists in America, like those in England, manifested no inherent fear of associations, though it is accurate to say that Baptists of America generally manifested a healthy suspicion of any power beyond the local congregation.

In the late seventeenth or early eighteenth century the General Baptists began holding meetings in Rhode Island where churches would send their representatives. These general meetings were referred to interchangeably as "quarterly" or "yearly meetings." This may have been Baptists' earliest experience of interchurch relationships in America.[4] The exact date of the initial Rhode Island meeting is obscure, but John Comer, in his valuable eighteenth-

---

[2] B. R. White, ed., *Association Records of the Particular Baptists of England, Wales, and Ireland to 1660* (London: The Baptist Historical Society, 1971, 1973, 1974) 3.

[3] Ibid., 126.

[4] Richard Knight, *History of the General or Six Principle Baptists in Europe and America* (Providence RI: Smith and Parmenter, 1827) 322. Knight actually said "sixteenth century." He obviously meant seventeenth.

century diary, described the June 1729 meeting as the "largest that ever hath been."[5] Apparently, it had been meeting for several years prior to 1729.

Particular or Calvinistic Baptists organized their first association in America in Philadelphia in 1707. Several years prior to that date, however, churches in the Philadelphia area met informally for Christian fellowship. Because the Philadelphia association remained the only Particular Baptist association until 1751, the Philadelphia Association became a powerful shaping force among Baptists in America. While many variations of associational life would develop among Baptists in the United States, the Philadelphia Association became the dominant pattern throughout the eighteenth century. Indeed, the association became so prominent in Baptist life that some historians refer to "the Philadelphia Tradition."

The Rationale for Baptist Associations

How did Baptists justify interchurch connectionalism in light of their commitment to congregational polity? It may be helpful to distinguish between *why* associations arose and the *defense* of associations after they came into existence. They are not necessarily the same. Without a doubt, the most significant factors in the rise of associations, both in England and America, were practical. Baptists initially formed associations to meet the needs of the churches, to serve the churches, and to benefit the churches. However, if you had asked an eighteenth-century Baptist preacher for the rationale for associations, he probably would have answered with a scriptural citation, a brief statement about the Baptist concept of the church, and an enumeration of practical advantages accruing from associational life. In other words, Baptists justified associations biblically, theologically, and practically. The 1798 Discipline adopted by the Philadelphia Association did precisely this. It declared that associational life was "recommended by the reason of things [practical], the spirit of religion [theological], and apostolic practice (Acts XV) [biblical]."[6]

In forming associations, most Baptists never thought that they were restoring a specific biblical pattern of church order. In other words, the Bible did not mandate organizations called "associations." Baptists did believe,

---

[5] John Comer, *The Diary of John Comer*, ed. with notes by C. Edwin Barrows (Philadelphia: American Baptist Publication Society, 1892) 66.

[6] Samuel Jones, *A Treatise of Church Discipline and Directory* (Lexington: Printed by T. Anderson, 1805) 31.

however, that when their churches associated together, they were being faithful to biblical principles of interchurch cooperation. Acts 15 constituted the most commonly cited biblical text in support of the association. Baptists believed that the Jerusalem Council in Acts 15 established a principle and offered an example of interchurch cooperation worthy of imitation.

While they noted various aspects of the Acts passage, Baptists gave the most focus to the advisory nature of the Jerusalem Council. Baptist churches could imitate apostolic Christianity by gathering to declare and determine the mind of the Holy Spirit, but they also had to follow the apostles' example of not imposing their conclusions upon local churches. Prefacing the decision of the Jerusalem Council was the advisory notice that "it seemed good to the Holy Spirit and to us."[7] Baptists believed the advisory posture to be mandated by the independence of the local congregation. Two ideas formed the theological bases of Baptist associations. Baptists spoke of the church as both local and universal, both visible and mystical. Membership in the universal church was determined solely by one's professing the faith of the gospel and obeying God in following Jesus as Lord. All Christians of all ages belonged to the universal or "mystical" body of Christ.

All Christians of all ages composed the universal church, but only those agreeing in doctrine and practice composed local, individual Baptist churches. Visible churches consisted of Christians who had a common religious commitment and who interpreted that experience similarly. The sense of unity articulated in the concept of the universal church and the doctrinal restrictions placed upon membership in the local church provided the theological footing for Baptist associations.

Baptists viewed their local churches as both independent and interdependent. An individual church could rightly claim the privilege and power of self-government. An individual church should not, however, claim the privilege of living in isolation from other like-minded churches. As the influential Charleston Baptist Association put it, "Although churches formed on the gospel plan are independent of each other with regard to power, yet not so, strictly speaking, with regard to communion."[8] Sharing in each other's gifts and burdens was an indisputable right of the churches.

---

[7] Acts 15:28.

[8] *A Summary of Church Discipline* (1773) in James Leo Garrett Jr., *Baptist Church Discipline* (Nashville: Broadman Press, 1962) 49.

Neither the biblical nor the theological defense of Baptist associations can be properly evaluated apart from the preeminently pragmatic origins of associations. In English Baptist history the earliest experiments of churches associating together arose to confront very practical needs within the churches and Baptist life. The specific reason for the formation of the Philadelphia Association was "to consult about such things as were wanting in the churches."[9]

Pragmatic reasoning echoed repeatedly in associational documents. Associations received "authority from the Light of Nature, and the general laws of society"; associations were "prudent" and "useful," "necessary and useful." They were "advantageous" for the work of the kingdom of God. Newly formed associations faithfully informed the public of the peculiar "uses," "benefits," "advantages," and "utility" of an association of churches. The Charleston Baptist Association enumerated twelve "benefits" coming from associational life. Though blessed with biblical proof texts and having obvious theological implications, most of the "benefits" served very practical ends.[10] The practical origins and nature of Baptist associations have proven beneficial. Those Baptist associations that have been most creative have been the ones who adapted to the specific needs of their geographical regions.

The Changing Purposes of Baptist Associations

If Baptist churches "associated" together primarily for practical issues, what were those issues? Baptists organized the two earliest Baptist associations in America, the Rhode Island Yearly Meeting of General Baptists and the Philadelphia Association of Particular Baptists, for very much the same three reasons. These were fellowship, discipline, and advice.

One needs to remember that the early Baptist churches in both England and America were small, scattered, often without ministerial leadership, and sometimes oppressed by both the civil government and established churches. By 1700, for example, Baptists in America had constituted only twenty-four churches. By 1750, they had formed only 101 churches. These churches desperately needed each other for encouragement, inspiration, and edification.

---

[9] A. D. Gillette, ed., *Minutes of the Philadelphia Baptist Association* (Philadelphia: American Baptist Publication Society, 1851) 25.

[10] See Garrett, *Baptist Church Discipline*, 52. For a more extensive treatment of how Baptists justified the existence of their associations, see Walter B. Shurden, "The Associational Principle, 1707–1814," *Foundations* 21/3 (July–September 1978): 7.

The annual meeting of a Baptist association provided a rare opportunity for needed fellowship between the churches. Today Baptists have many different opportunities for fellowship. Ministers' conferences, state and regional assemblies and conventions, and annual meetings of national assemblies all help to meet the fellowship dimension of Baptist churches. But until the nineteenth century, Baptist associations provided the only opportunity for interchurch fellowship.

The earliest Baptist associations also helped to regularize Baptist life. They helped bring discipline and order to the emerging denomination. Baptists of the Pennsylvania and New Jersey regions, for example, formed the Philadelphia Association "to consult about such things as were *wanting* in the churches, and to set them in order." And the Rhode Island Meeting convened for almost the very same reasons.

Baptists had no powerful bishop, no ultimate national ecclesiastical unit to help them decide how to take care of their life together. How, for example, do you organize a Baptist church? Who is a proper minister of the gospel? How should a church deal with controversy and factionalism? What are acceptable doctrines? Churches would present queries to the annual meetings of associations on many such issues. While the associational answers were not binding, the queries became a kind of unofficial case law for Baptists. The gathered mind of the Baptist community expressed through the association helped bring order to an emerging, struggling denomination of churches.

Eventually, associations adopted official documents that facilitated the regularizing of Baptist life. The Philadelphia Association, for example, adopted "The Philadelphia Confession" and "A Summary of Church Discipline" in 1743. In 1749 the association adopted an "Essay on the Authority and Power of an Association of Churches." Other associations copied the Philadelphia pattern and documents such as these and many others multiplied and helped bring order and discipline to incipient denominational life.

Associations also advised the churches. Indeed, all that has been said above in terms of the regularizing role of an association should be understood as advisory. The association existed primarily to assist churches in their life and witness. One of the primary ways in which an association assisted churches was by encouraging the ministers of the association to preach in churches without pastors. A recurring complaint heard at annual meetings of early Baptist associations was, "We have no preacher." The association would also often assist in organizing a church, in ordaining people to the diaconate and the gospel ministry, and in helping to settle internal conflicts within churches.

As Baptists grew in numbers, their churches multiplied, and as their churches grew in numbers, the associations multiplied. In time the associations became the primary instruments through which Baptists would work for their common interests. For example, associations served as the major denominational mouthpiece for religious liberty. Baptists valiantly struggled for freedom throughout the eighteenth century, and the associations represented the communal voice for a free conscience among the Baptist people. The same was true with ministerial education. The Baptist associations in Philadelphia and Charleston took the lead in establishing schools and providing resources for educating their clergy. Baptist concern for theological education flowed from the ministry of Baptist associations. With William Carey and the beginning of the missionary movement among Baptists in 1792, associations became critical in popularizing and affirming the missionary movement. Until 1814 and the organization of the Triennial Convention in America, Baptist associations, along with societies, became the denominational conduits for the missionary movement.

As organized Baptist life became more complicated, with the presence of state and national bodies, associational life in America declined in influence and power. Where associational life has remained creative and dynamic, it is because the association has sought to address practical issues of ministry in its specific locale. Otherwise, it has often become a conduit for national denominational programs with little concern for its local situation.

The Authority of Baptist Associations

Since the rise of Baptist associations, a recurring question has focused on the extent and nature of associational authority over local churches. What power do associations actually wield over local congregations? Baptists of America have recognized this question to be important for Baptist polity. Associations themselves often addressed the question of association-church relationships, usually with the primary intention of safeguarding local church independence while affirming the value of associational life.[11]

---

[11] To see a list of eight primary documents from eighteenth century Baptist life that address the issue of associational authority, see Walter B. Shurden, "The Authority of a Baptist Association," *Baptist History and Heritage* 40/1 (Winter 2005): 7.

One way of getting at this problem is to describe what Baptists considered to be the exclusive powers of a local church. For Baptists the local church has been the highest spiritual authority upon earth. Ultimate authority, of course, is in God. But God expresses Divine authority, Baptists believed, through the collective mind of the local body of believers as they interpreted Holy Scripture.

When Baptists spoke of "local church independency" and the fact that associations could not interfere in the "internal affairs" of a particular congregation, they meant especially three things. First, local churches were independent in determining their constituency. A local church had the exclusive right to say who could be received as members of the visible church of Christ on earth. Second, local churches maintained the sole authority of disciplining its membership. If associations assumed the power of judging decisively in cases of church discipline, they became usurpers and intruders upon the government of the churches. Associational action could not determine the standing of any member in a local church. Third, local churches maintained sole authority in the selection of church officers. Each church had power from Christ to call and ordain its leadership. Associations may be invited to assist in the ordination of a minister in a local church, but the association was not a churchly body that ordained a Baptist minister. One church requested the Philadelphia Association to appoint the time and ministers to ordain another minister. The association refused because "the appointment of both properly belongs to his church."[12]

Extensive reading in associational documents in America is not required to be convinced that Baptists were far more interested in the freedom of the local church than in extending the powers of the association. Most early associational constitutions, for example, consumed far more space indicating what an association could not do than clearly stating what it could do.

What authority have Baptists attributed to an association? First, an association has the power to determine its own membership. In much the same way that a local church determines which individuals may be members of the church, an association determines which churches may be members of the association. This power of determining its membership has been, without a doubt, the most powerful weapon of an association. However, even the power of an association to withdraw fellowship from a church has never abolished that church's independence. Associations, in other words, can never "dechurch" a

---

[12] See Gillette, *Minutes of the Philadelphia Baptist Association*, 119.

local Baptist church. They certainly can exclude a church form the association's fellowship, however.

Second, most associations maintained the right to advise the churches. No amount of emphasis on local church independency could deny an association the right to advise a church. Associational advice ran the gamut of everything from theological orthodoxy to appropriate church practices to participation in the association. This advice became powerful social pressure on local churches and, if spurned, could certainly end with the church being excluded from the association.

Third, an association had the sole authority to regulate its annual meeting and its internal affairs, much like a local congregation. While Baptist associations claimed legitimate power to control every aspect of their lives, they have usually carried that authority lightly, with a keen eye on the unity of the fellowship of the churches. Associations rarely acted petulantly toward the churches. With the powers they did possess, however, associations brought some unity to Baptist denominational life.

Baptist Associations Today and Yesterday

If you examine Baptist associations among different national Baptist bodies in contemporary America or if you compare Baptist associations in various countries today, you will find a wide divergence in the nature and practice of associations. This leads to the conclusion that Baptists really have no consistent or obvious theology of church order beyond the local church. Baptists do not have an ecclesiology beyond the local church that tells them how they must organize or structure their local churches into a Baptist denomination. For the most part, each group of Baptists has been guided primarily by practical issues, though they usually conscript both the Bible and Baptist theology in making the case for church connectionalism.

In looking back at the history of Baptist associations one can say several things for sure. One, the Baptist association became the earliest and most important factor in the organization and development of the various Baptist denominations around the world. Baptists organized the Triennial Convention, their first national Baptist convention, in America in 1814. Baptist associations played a major role in promoting and supporting the work of the Triennial Convention. Long before the Triennial Convention, however, Baptist associations helped to bring some denominational unity to Baptist life. Two, no amount of emphasis on the independency of local churches blinded early

Baptists to the values of fraternal relationships between the churches. Early Baptists recognized that the associational idea was not opposed to independency but to alienation. Associations were, therefore, embraced with eagerness by most Baptists. Three, while associations assumed and exercised some considerable power within Baptist life, they never sought to become usurpers of local church rights.

Suggested Reading

Shurden, Walter B. *Associationalism among Baptists in America*. New York: Arno Press, 1980. Reprint of unpublished doctor's dissertation, New Orleans Baptist Theological Seminary, New Orleans, LA, 1967.

———. "The Authority of a Baptist Association." *Baptist History and Heritage* 40/1 (Winter 2005) 7. This brief article contains a list of primary documents from eighteenth century Baptist life in American that address the issue of the role of associations in Baptist life.

Wamble, Hugh. "The Concept and Practice of Christian Fellowship: The Connectional and Inter-denominational Aspects Thereof, among Seventeenth Century English Baptists." Unpublished doctor's dissertation, Southern Baptist Theological Seminary, Louisville, KY, 1955.

White, B. R., editor. *Association Records of the Particular Baptists of England, Wales, and Ireland to 1660*. 3 volumes. London: The Baptist Historical Society, 1971, 1973, 1974.

CHAPTER 7

A Turn toward a Doctrinal Christianity: Baptist Theology, a Work in Progress

William H. Brackney

Any serious student of Baptist life and thought recognizes immediately that this is a variegated theological tradition. In the first century of Baptist development, there were at least four "types" defined with reference to Christological, soteriological, and ecclesiological issues: General, Particular, Seventh Day, and Leg of Mutton. In the next hundred years, this typology broadened numerically to another, slightly different four types on both sides of the Atlantic: Calvinistic, General Six Principle, Seventh Day, and Separate. In their third century, Baptists could be categorized theologically as Regular or Missionary, Freewill or General, Primitive or Strict or Old School, Seventh Day, and Scotch or McLeanite.

All of these types were overwhelmed by prevailing Protestant theological trends in the later nineteenth century and the result was a division of the main categories into Regular (missionary) Baptists who were either liberal social activists or conservative evangelicals; Primitive or Strict (hyper-Calvinistic); Freewills and Generals; Black Theology Baptists; and finally Independent Baptists who bear traces of Brethrenite/Dispensationalist genes.

In this essay, I want to trace what I think are turning points in the evolution of Baptist thought that demonstrate clearly the variety of theological perspectives and positions and the watersheds they created. These points include the establishment of an identifiable Baptist theological tradition in the publication of major systematic works like that of Thomas Grantham and John Gill; the rise of the Freewill Baptist movement in New England that broadened the Calvinistic orientation of the group; the emergence of a narrowed doctrine of the church in Landmarkism; the external influences felt in the New

Theology; and the new categories of Baptist theological work in the contemporary milieu.

Particular and General Baptists and the
Differentiation of a Movement

The first theological orientation of identifiably Baptist Christians was in the first decades of seventeenth-century England and produced three theological characteristics. First, Baptists were born in a cradle of Reformed thought. This is beyond doubt, as recent studies have shown, the influence of Puritan-Separatist teaching on the earliest Baptists.[1] But Baptists also struck out on a theological trajectory of their own. Lay theologians like Thomas Helwys and Cambridge-trained former Anglican clergy like John Smyth held to a general view of the atoning work of Christ, earning the sobriquet "General Baptists." Third, these General Baptists espoused the principle of full religious liberty that in turn created openness on other faith and order issues.[2] The General Baptists were a viable collection of congregations and ministers throughout the 1600s, well known through their general assemblies and publications. By the first decade of the seventeenth century, the General Baptists had become much influenced by both unitarian and universalist thinking and lost ground numerically and organizationally.[3]

Clearly, however, the dominant theological stream among seventeenth-century English Baptists was Calvinistic. This stream had its source in the Independent community of the 1630s and reflected a move toward a believer's church ecclesiology and a scriptural understanding of the sacraments/ordinances. Several factors caused this stream to grow steadily in the next sixty years. First, there was little actual differentiation on the major points of doctrine from other mainstream dissenters who were also found in the Reformed tradition, notably those who styled themselves Presbyterians and

---

[1] See B. R. White, *The English Separatist Tradition: From the Marian Martyrs to the Pilgrim Fathers* (Oxford: Oxford University Press, 1971) 42–43; Kenneth Scott Culpepper, "One Christian's Plea: The Life, Ministry, and Controversies of Francis Johnson" (Ph.D. diss., Baylor University, 2006) 48–52.

[2] This actually produced two other sub-types, Seventh Day and Leg of Mutton Baptists. One must take care not to confine the original categories of Baptists in the overall dissenter community to only two types, the Generals and the Particulars.

[3] A. C. Underwood, *History of the English Baptists* (London: Carey Kingsgate Press, 1947) 28–55.

those who were labeled Congregationalists.[4] Second, Calvinistic Baptist life was centered in the urban areas and effectively propagated among divisions of Oliver Cromwell's New Model Army in the 1640s and early 1650s.[5] Third, the Calvinistic community of Baptist congregations was literarily gifted and its spokesmen published an impressive array of literature, including confessions of faith, treatises on various subjects, allegories, hymns, and reports of public disputations in which they were participants.

The emergence of serious and systematic theological discourse reflects the maturity of any denomination of Christians. Both the General Baptists and the Particular Baptists established strong foundations in this regard. Among the General Baptists their most astute early thinker and published theologian was Thomas Grantham (1634–1692). Grantham's most significant work was *Christianismus Primitivus*, published in 1678. Thomas Grantham bequeathed to the making of Baptist theological identity a set of factors that qualified Baptists as a maturing evangelical Protestant tradition.

First and foremost, he set in place the centrality of the doctrine of the church for Baptist theology. His exhaustive discussion of not only the holiness of the Body of Christ, but also its particulars as manifested in the universality of the church, its denominationality among other Christian groups, and its need for a full expression in its internal and external cooperation, stand without peer among his contemporaries. Second, his open and dynamic understanding of scripture as inclusive of canonical books, and more, for the edification of the church, is a healthy and useful position for Baptists of any era.[6] His full and forceful articulation of religious liberty reminds Baptists that this has been a genetic trait found in every generation of the tradition.

Among the Particular or Calvinistic Baptists, John Gill remains the defining figure in published systematic Baptist thought. Gill was a pastor-

---

[4] The distinction between the two was more along lines of church order than theology within a broad Puritanism. Symbolic of the two types were Dr. Daniel Williams among the Presbyterians and Isaac Watts among the Congregationalists.

[5] Robert Torbet, in his *History of the Baptists* (Valley Forge PA: Judson Press, 1963) 44, argued persuasively for this connection, particularly noting the disbanding of Cromwell's army in Ireland in 1653 where Baptist associational life grew up immediately thereafter.

[6] For a fuller exposition of Grantham's contribution, see my essay, "Thomas Grantham, Systematic Theology, and the Baptist Tradition," in *From Biblical Criticism to Biblical Faith: Essays in Honor of Lee Martin McDonald*, ed. William H. Brackney and Craig A. Evans (Macon GA: Mercer University Press, 2007) 199–217.

theologian like Grantham whose brilliant literary productivity was recognized by university divines.[7] Writing in the century after Grantham, Gill produced his magnum opus, *A Body of Doctrinal and Practical Divinity* (1769–1770), on the plan of William Ames, also demonstrating an awareness of Isaac Watts, Thomas Goodwin, Herman Witsius, and John Lightfoot. Gill was exhaustive in his coverage of doctrine and a keen student of ancient and medieval writers in Latin, Greek, Semitic, and European languages. He demonstrated that Baptist clergy were capable of serious theological polemic and were well-versed in classical tradition. His work was influential upon every theologian after him, both as to form and general Calvinistic direction. Those who were not so inclined toward his high Calvinism damned him with faint praise, such as Robert Hall's reference to Gill's work as "a sea of mud."

From these two pioneers would come a wide variety in scholarly Baptist theological literature. Among the Calvinistic breed Robert Hall Jr. and Robert Hall Sr., Andrew Fuller, Abraham Booth, and John Howard Hinton would stand out among English Baptists. Their Arminian counterparts would include Dan Taylor, John Clifford, and Joseph Goadby. In the United States, the evolving Calvinistic (Regular) Baptist community who published were John Leadley Dagg, Hezekiah Harvey, James P. Boyce, and E. Y. Mullins. On the Arminian side could be found John Buzzell, John J. Butler, and Alfred W. Anthony. Well-quoted Baptist systematicians from the "golden age" included E. G. Robinson, A. H. Strong, W. N. Clarke, E. Y. Mullins, W. T. Connor, Dale Moody, James Leo Garrett, Millard Erickson, and Carl F. H. Henry.

The Grip of Calvinism Is Loosened

In the American colonial experience, one can identify four types of Baptists: First Day, Seventh Day, Five Principle Calvinistic, and Six Principle General. If one accepts a basic Baptist premise that ecclesiology, the doctrine of the church, is a legitimate theological category, rather than a matter of "church order," then these divisions reflect theological varieties. The vast majority of the Baptist congregations adhered to the Philadelphia Confession of Faith, a slightly modified version of the Second London Confession of Faith, put forward by the English Calvinistic Baptists. The General Six Principle Baptists

---

[7] Marichal College, University of Aberdeen, conferred the degree Doctor of Divinity upon Gill for his Semitic scholarship. For a helpful introduction, see Timothy George, "John Gill," in *Theologians of the Baptist Tradition*, ed. Timothy George and David Dockery (Nashville TN: Broadman and Holman, 2001) 11–34.

were mostly confined to the coastal regions of Massachusetts and Rhode Island and declined markedly by the eighteenth century. Seventh Day Baptists continued as a small movement of churches, mostly oriented toward the Calvinistic formulae.

Into this community of essentially Calvinistic orientation, surrounded by the Calvinism of the Congregationalist Standing Order and the Regular Baptists, came local preachers like Tozer Lord and Benjamin Randall in New Hampshire. Lord was apparently articulating his own version of "freewillism" in central New Hampshire by the mid-1770s and Randall followed a similar self-taught reaction against determinism. Randall was converted in the context of George Whitefield and read his scriptures without commentary. When confronted by local Calvinistic Baptist ministers in 1779, he dismissed their theology and spoke of his own experience in terms of "Free grace, freewill, and free communion." He soon put together a following of upcountry preachers and preaching points and he became a de-facto bishop of a "connexion" that spanned northern New England and eventually western New York and Michigan.[8] Randall was repulsed by the rigidity and elitism of Calvinism, often appealing to its advocates to prove their positions against his own experience of Christ's love. Randall's movement was a turning point in Baptist theological evolution as it signaled a legitimate alternative to Calvinistic thought. In fact, Randall was a vehement critic of Calvinism and this placed him among other early American century notables such as Hosea Ballou and Elhanan Winchester. Sufficient interest was expressed in Randall's theology to enlarge the connection to the southern states, the Ohio Valley, and the upper Mississippi Valley by the 1880s. The Freewill Baptists also managed to start four colleges, one theological seminary, and several academies before the bulk of the original movement joined the Northern Baptist Convention in 1911. Variously called "Freewill" and "Free" Baptists, a merger of like-minded congregations in upstate New York in 1841, with the "Free Communion Baptists," reduced the collective organizational title to the "Free Baptist General Conference."[9]

---

[8] A major new study of Randall is found in Scott Bryant, "Benjamin Randall and the Rise of the Freewill Baptists: A Reassessment" (Ph.D. diss., Baylor University, 2007).

[9] This movement is only distantly associated with modern Freewill Baptists that have their twentieth-century origins in North Carolina and Tennessee. I use the bracketed Free[will] name to designate the group in the northern and western states from 1841 to 1911.

In the 1820s as a part of the evolving evangelical social consciousness, Free[will] Baptists took an unexpected theological turn that placed them at the forefront of Arminian theological development. Behind activist pastors and educators like Oren B. Cheney, John Buzzell, Ransom Dunn, and John J. Butler, the Free[will] Baptists adopted an unflinching abolitionist, pro-woman, egalitarian social stance that rivaled that of the more liberal Universalists and Congregationalists. Theologically, this meant that Christians were to have a proper regard to their relations and circumstances, those of family, the community, to those more remote, and to all moral beings. This placed them squarely in the stream of Charles G. Finney, the Tappan Brothers, and the Beechers of Connecticut. Unlike other perfectionists of the era, however, Free[will] Baptists were steered away from the holiness tangents of Phoebe Palmer and the Wesleyan Methodists.[10] They were also able to make common cause with the General Baptists in England from the 1840s that created an impressive transatlantic family of non-Calvinistic Baptists.[11] After a little over a century of separate identity, Free[will] Baptist leaders like Alfred W. Anthony saw little continuing distinctive between them and the Calvinistic or Regular Baptists in the northern states and openly courted a possible merger.[12] In the long run, the Northern Calvinistic Baptists had dropped much of their rigid polity, closed communion, and confessionalism while the Free Baptists had embraced a more comprehensive ecclesiology that placed them among the mainstream American denominations. The great contribution of the Free Baptists, thus, was to help open up the Baptist tradition in North America to an evangelical inclusiveness.

---

[10] John J. Butler, *Natural and Revealed Theology: A System of Lectures* (Dover NH: Freewill Baptist Publishing, 1861) 276, 283, wrote, "Sanctification is not a state of absolute perfection, for no being but God is absolutely perfect...." "Sanctification is a progressive work...the growth in grace, so far as we know, may continue forever."

[11] For a fuller accounting of this connection, see William H. Brackney, "Transatlantic Relationships: The Making of an International Baptist Community," in *The Gospel in the World: International Baptist Studies*, vol. 1, ed. D. W. Bebbington (Carlisle, Cumbria: Paternoster Press, 2002) 68–71.

[12] A parallel phenomenon occurred among Free Baptists in the Canadian Maritimes and in Upper Canada Province where they merged with Regular Baptists in 1905 to form a United Baptist Convention.

Establishing the Ancient Landmarks

A turning point of sorts may be seen in the emergence of a local church ecclesiology that swept through Baptist ranks in the 1820s and 1830s and eventually became theologically enshrined as local church protectionism or among Southern Baptists as "Landmarkism." The roots of this theological tradition are found in Jacksonian America and upcountry New England. Following the War of 1812, Baptists grew mightily on the frontiers to the west and south. General Andrew Jackson was the symbol of the era: a self-made rugged individualist who had conquered the Old European powers for the future of North America. Despite his coarse lifestyle and seeming disinterest in religion, Jackson was a heroic figure for many Baptists in every section.[13] Their witness was characterized by itinerant revivalist preachers, self-taught in the English scriptures and dedicated to planting faithful closed-communion congregations. The congregations they established were frequently isolated, and lay preachers were more common than ordained clergy. For Baptists in the era from 1800 to 1880, the local congregation was the center of faith and life.[14] Baptist preachers of the Ohio and Upper Mississippi Valleys inveighed against the hierarchies of Episcopalians, Lutherans, and Presbyterians. They dismissed Alexander Campbell and Barton Stone's connectionalism and sacramentalism. Behind the writings of James R. Graves, Amos C. Dayton, and James Madison Pendleton, local church protectionism took the shape of the Landmarkist tradition from Tennessee to Texas. James E. Tull, the leading student of the movement, called this a form of Baptist "high-churchism" because of its exclusivist and elitist view of the true church of Jesus Christ being associated with an unbroken succession of Baptistic witnesses and martyrs.[15] Again, it would be a mistake to identify Landmarkism only with Baptists in the South and Southwest, for its roots were in the isolated communities of New England

---

[13] See my recent essay, "The Political Ramifications of Being God's People," in *Exiles in the Empire: Believers Church Perspectives on Politics*, ed. Nathan E. Yoder and Carol A. Scheppard (Waterloo: Pandora Press, 2006) 73–74.

[14] Compare Hezekiah Harvey, *The Church: Its Polity and Ordinances* (Philadelphia: American Baptist Publication Society, 1879) 29 and J. L. Dagg, *Church Order: A Treatise* (Philadelphia: American Baptist Publication Society, 1871) 74–77. Both Dagg (southern) and Harvey (northern) agree that the principal usage of the term "ecclesia" is to designate local assemblies, but both also expand the understanding of "church" to include its universal aspects.

[15] James E. Tull, *High-Church Baptists in the South: The Origin, Nature, and Influence of Landmarkism* (Macon GA: Mercer University Press, 2000) 51, 59.

where a fierce antagonism to denominational structures beyond loose associations was present. One can point to Isaac Backus, John Leland, Elias Smith, and the Old School brethren of upstate New York and New Jersey as evidence of the Landmarker proclivity long before its rise in Middle Tennessee.[16]

The doctrine of the church advanced among Landmarkists profoundly influenced the course of Baptist theological development. First, it virtually snuffed out an appreciation for the larger Christian tradition. Other Christians were declared to be part of an evolving "apostate" system. Second, those Baptist ministers who cooperated with persons of other "religious societies" were *persona non grata*. Third, Landmarkers were not convinced of the need for an educated ministry, at least not beyond that of basic bible knowledge. Graves put his support behind Sunday school education and frowned upon the establishment of Southern Baptist Theological Seminary.[17] The turning point one observes in the Landmarkist Movement oriented many Baptists toward a local church ecclesiology and laid the groundwork for later fundamentalism.

New Theology and Its Impact

The next major point of definition for Baptist theology was the impact of the New Theology.[18] By "New Theology" I refer to the development of largely academic theological currents that attracted graduates of mainstream Protestant theological schools and offended many Baptists in the local churches. Characteristic of this movement, which can be traced to German university professors in the Lutheran and Reformed traditions, were methods described as "higher criticism" of the scriptures; identification of comparative religious theological themes;[19] the priority of historical theology over systematic thought; and ideas like the moral influence theories of the atonement, stress upon the humanity of Christ, the fulfillment of the kingdom of God in historical

---

[16] Oliver W. Elsbree, *The Rise of the Missionary Spirit in America, 1790–1815* (Williamsport: Williamsport Printing Co., 1928) was among the first to trace this lineage.

[17] H. Leon McBeth, *The Baptist Heritage: Four Centuries of Baptist Witness* (Nashville: Broadman Press, 1987) 434–36; Tull, *High Church Baptists*, 159–61. McBeth asserts that "the SBSSU [that Graves founded in 1857] helped polarize Southern Baptists, fanning a major theological controversy" (435).

[18] The material in this section first appeared as the 2006 Deere Lectures at Golden Gate Baptist Theological Seminary and is used with their permission.

[19] For example, immortality, salvation, the moral life, myth and ritual.

developments, and the priority of the ethical teachings of Jesus over the miraculous biographies presented by the apostolic writers.[20] Baptist theologians began to discover these new trends as they read in translation several German works. This in turn led to sabbatical trips for study in German universities, and eventually those theologians whose mastery of German or French allowed them to take graduate degrees from schools like Berlin, Halle, Leipzig, and Paris. By 1910 new courses in biblical criticism, historical doctrine, and comparative religion were showing forth in the catalogues at Newton, Rochester, Colgate, and Crozer. Chicago, reorganized under William Rainey Harper, became its own theological graduate school on American soil.

Chicago's stress in its early years was in the humanities and social sciences. This gave it the opportunity to attract a variety of world-renowned scholars in psychology, sociology, history, languages, and religion. Harper and his successors maintained the delicate balance between the skeptics and the faithful in the university by making sure religious ideals were recognized in the rhetorical character of the university and by maintaining the quality of the divinity school on a par with other faculties. The study of theology was not to suffer second place to the other disciplines as was becoming the case at Harvard and Yale and in schools like Cornell, Johns Hopkins, and state universities where it was not even in the curriculum. Ultimately, this meant attracting students from a variety of outlooks that Harper extolled as a truly ecumenical student body. It also meant allowing research and writing in areas foreign to most Baptists and with little practical applicability in the churches. Again, Harper had a plan to keep such forces in check: he and his popular Canadian dean, Shailer Mathews, regularly lectured at Chautauqua and other Baptist ministerial councils in both the North and the South on the benefits of advanced biblical and theological studies for lay people.

Undoubtedly, Harper was a man of faith, but many questioned the faith of one of his leading appointments, George Burman Foster, in the chair in theology. Foster, who had trained under philosophical theologians and was one of the great independent minds of his day, persisted in writing books that pushed the boundary of theological questions into skepticism. His *Finality of Christ* (1909) fueled a conflagration that was not to be easily extinguished.[21]

---

[20] The best introduction to the New Theology is William R. Hutchison, *The Modernist Impulse in American Protestantism* (Durham: Duke University Press, 1992) 76–110.

[21] Hutchison, *Modernist Impulse*, 215–20.

Two millionaire Presbyterian brothers in California were persuaded to underwrite a popular doctrinal series, *The Fundamentals* (1913–1919), and the Chicago Baptist ministerial community held investigations into the continued ministerial status of Professor Foster. Single-handedly, G. B. Foster may have been the catalyst that identified the unifying antagonism among conservative evangelical Baptists in North America to "modernism." Foster's dean, Shailer Mathews, even wrote a thirteen-article "creed" or affirmation of faith for the modernist that began, "I believe in God, immanent in the forces and processes of nature, revealed in Jesus Christ and in human history, as Love."[22]

But the Chicago School should not receive all the credit for igniting the fuse. Two other Baptist universities deserve attention at this context. The University of Rochester (New York), which ceased being church-related in the 1920s, aggressively emphasized the sciences. The city of Rochester had long been well endowed with industrial plants, given the water power in its midst. Flour milling of the 1830s and 1840s gave way to manufacturing machine parts, chemical production, photographic technology, pharmaceuticals, and glass and lens manufacturing.

Rochester leaders had attempted a university under Presbyterian auspices that failed in the 1840s. The local Baptists fared better because they claimed a goodly number of the contemporary captains of industry and promised to be liberal in spirit in the interests of the city. Hence the University of Rochester, born out of First and Second Baptist Churches, always thought of itself as an "open" and ecumenical institution, squarely serving the sciences and technology. Among its great assets by 1900 was Strong Memorial Medical School and the hospital made famous by Henry Strong, brother to A. H. Strong, the leading Baptist theologian of his era, and both sons of one of the wealthiest newspaper publishers in the United States. The University of Rochester, and eventually its sister theological school, Rochester Theological Seminary, developed as centers of creative and scientific modernism. Also like Rochester, was Columbian College, originally the stepchild of the General Missionary Convention; it evolved in the nation's capital to become George Washington University. There the emphasis was upon the political sciences, economics, and corporate management, with growing law and medical schools. George Washington University was a gift to the denomination that it failed to receive and support, and its days as a Baptist-specific school were over in the 1890s. Though often struggling financially, it became a center for the training

---

[22] Shailer Mathews, *The Faith of Modernism* (New York: Macmillan, 1924) 180.

of government personnel and educational administrators, several of whom led Baptist colleges and universities. Other attempts to create this new type of university in a church-relationship included Des Moines University in Iowa, Baylor University in Texas, and Redlands University in California.

In a special way, this rise of the Baptist modern university thus came to symbolize modernism. In fact, the dean of theology of the University of Chicago, Shailer Mathews, coined the term among Protestants. Modernism was the pursuit of religious questions with all the gusto of scientific experimentation. It was the full adoption of critical methods of Bible study, and it was an unveiled program to end "authority" religion and "primitive" ideas like revealed truth. It was also the automatic theological antithesis of where most Baptist laypersons and preachers were in their thought processes and piety.

Modernists, many of whom were trained at Chicago, were soon noticed in many Baptist faculties, usually in the sciences and religion fields.[23] Many were the products of sabbatical studies in German and Swiss universities under the great liberal teachers of their era. Some took degrees in Europe like Barnas Sears at Madison University who went on to succeed the venerable Francis Wayland, who was no less the father of modernity at Brown. The leading Baptist theological schools soon caught the modernist line, employing university Ph.D.s to teach biblical studies and divinity, having specialized in one of the new fields and advocating a literary and theological evolution of biblical literature.

Because of the theological orientation of seminaries, it became their charge to interpret modernism for the churches. In this regard, several schools became known for their modernist stands: Crozer, Chicago, Rochester, and Newton. Rochester was an intriguing case because few theologians had the respect that A. H. Strong enjoyed among traditionalists. As Carl F. H. Henry showed in his Boston University doctoral dissertation, Strong substantially revised his textbook on theology after 1908 to conform to his leanings toward monism in the University of Rochester community.[24]

Crozer Seminary perhaps had the most thorough makeover: in a twenty-year period it went from being a theologically trustworthy school with connections to D. L. Moody's Northfield Bible Conferences, to an epicenter of

---

[23] W. Kenneth Cauthen, *The Impact of American Religious Liberalism* (New York: Harper and Row, 1962) defines Mathews and his role in the Modernist School.

[24] Carl F. H. Henry, *Personal Idealism and Strong's Theology* (Wheaton: VanKampen Press, 1951) 143–49.

angry advocacy of modernism. Professor of Church History Henry Clay Vedder rifled one editorial response to "fundamentalists" after another. Vedder wrote in his oft-quoted book *The Fundamentals of Christianity* (1922), "Religion must not consist of mere vague emotions and aspirations, but must be founded in a definite philosophy of life, corresponding to our scientific knowledge, as well as to our inner experience, or it cannot successfully appeal to a world that more and more demands reality as a basis for its living."[25]

Few schools remained untainted by modernism: even Southern Baptists like E. Y. Mullins were favorably inclined toward Walter Rauschenbush, W. N. Clarke, and the Chicago School, as was William L. Poteat at Wake Forest College who led a virtual modernist crusade in his institution in support of a reasoned faith.[26] It is instructive to read the attendance rosters and papers presented at the autumnal conferences of the pan-denominational Baptist Congress that met from 1880–1911. In those key discussions one finds an amazing variety of Baptist thinkers and leaders who tacitly embraced modernism to one degree or another.

One can also pinpoint the origins of fundamentalism in the fervent reactions to New Theology in both the Northern and Southern Conventions. Here we might well identify another turning point in the establishment of the Baptist Bible Union of America in 1923. This umbrella organization that spanned the Canadian border was in fact a pandemic reaction to modernism. Pastors sympathetic to the fundamentalist position met to hear inspirational speakers and to promote an agenda of theological confessionalism.

In the context of the Northern Baptist Convention, a conservative faction led by William Bell Riley and John Roach Straton brought to a vote in 1922 a proposal to adopt the New Hampshire Baptist Confession of Faith as the convention standard.[27] It was defeated in favor of a statement that read, "The Northern Baptist Convention affirms that the New Testament is the all-

---

[25] Henry C. Vedder, *The Fundamentals of Christianity: A Study of The Teaching of Jesus and Paul* (New York: The MacMillan Co., 1922) 216. Elsewhere in this work he wrote, "There is no man who believes the Bible from cover to cover.... No man can make such profession sincerely unless he has escaped education altogether. Men who say such things are talking buncombe, playing to the galleries (xii).

[26] Poteat's book—*Can a Man Be a Christian Today?*—was a popular expression of the dilemma of the modernists. Clarke's *Sixty Years with the Bible* (1912) remains the autobiographical classic.

[27] On these two characters, see C. Allyn Russell, *Voices of American Fundamentalism* (Philadelphia: Fortress Press, 1976).

sufficient grounds of our faith and practice and we need no other statement."[28] It was defeated by a 2-1 margin of the delegates.

Among Southern Baptists, there was greater success in that the convention approved the essence of the New Hampshire Confession in a document titled Baptist Faith and Message. It was the work of a committee chaired by Southern Baptist Seminary president E. Y. Mullins and it anchored Southern Baptists to their traditional theological moorings for a generation.[29] In the come-outer groups various doctrinal statements bound the affiliate members, all of which followed a pattern set in the New Hampshire Confession with additional content relating to separationism and the pre-millennial interpretation of Christ's return. Clearly, the issues raised in the New Theology of the progressive institutions and urban congregations set in place a watershed that created new Baptist movements defined by theology as well as starting a sharp distinction within the two major conventions between "liberals" and "conservatives."

Different Strokes and Different Folks

In the contemporary era, Baptist theology has been symbolically and substantively volatile. There is more than symbolic name-calling in the designations of the terms "liberal" and "conservative." A liberal tradition among Baptists can be traced to the libertarian thinkers among the General Baptists, through the universalists and unitarians in England and the United States, to those who embraced the New Theology in the latter half of the nineteenth century. Theologically, ideas associated with liberal Baptists first focused upon the nature of the atonement, then the authority of the scriptures, and later the idea of revealed truth. In a conversation that connected with natural and social scientists, liberal thinkers jettisoned verbal plenary inspiration for an historical understanding of scripture and revealed truth was displaced by naturalism and divine immanence. This led to a humanistic Christology and a progressive view of humanity. The Social Gospel, when coupled with these developments, enabled a doctrine of humanity that was progressive and egalitarian.

African-American and feminist thinkers joined the chorus of those who affirmed the theological task as contextual and ecumenical. These included

---

[28] Quoted in William H. Brackney, ed., *Baptist Life and Thought: A Sourcebook*, rev. ed. (Valley Forge: Judson Press, 1998) 358.

[29] Herschel H. Hobbs, *The Baptist Faith and Message* (Nashville: Convention Press, 1971) 13.

Howard Thurman, Benjamin Mays, Mordecai Johnson, Martin Luther King Jr., and Phyllis Tribble. Baptists could be found among the avid readers of Paul Tillich, the Niebuhrs, and the Personalist School. Even among the most radical theologians, the Death of God advocates, William Hamilton, who once held the W. N. Clarke chair in theology at Colgate Rochester, and Harvey Cox, the celebrated author of *The Secular City* (1965), reflect a Baptist ecclesiology. While in a minority, schools in the American Baptist tradition and several Black Baptist institutions could be legitimately identified as theologically liberal.

In contrast, conservative Baptists sought to protect and preserve their tradition. Neo-evangelicals emerged from fundamentalism to converse with those in the Neo-Orthodox camp, demonstrating awareness but not acceptance of that position. These included Edward Carnell, Carl Henry, and Bernard Ramm. Eastern Baptist Seminary, after some adjustments to accommodate losses to the conservative Baptist movement, became a "conservative, but progressive" center featuring voices like Arthur Crabtree, Cuthbert Rutenber, Thorwald Bender, Norman Maring, and Edward Dalglish, who were well beyond conservative, evangelical usage. What these teachers and writers had in common was a nuanced view of biblical authority in a mild form of confessionalism. This allowed the newer schools like Denver, Gordon, and Western Conservative Baptist, plus the once-ethnic institutions like Bethel and North American Baptist Seminary, to articulate a theology that mirrored contemporary evangelical usage: an unequivocally inspired Bible, a well-disciplined ecclesiology, and a mostly pre-millennial eschatology. The most prominent theologians among the latter institutions were Millard Erickson and Stanley Grenz.

It would not be a generation before the same division took place among Southern Baptists. On the conservative evangelical side of theological divide (some would call them fundamentalists) would be Albert Mohler, L. Russ Bush, Paige Patterson, Craig Blaising, David Dockery, and Timothy George. What they share to one degree or another is a high view of revealed truth in scripture with a generally Calvinistic outlook and an absolutist ethical orientation. To the left of a Southern Baptist theological center, one could list Wayne Ward, Molly Marshall Green, E. Glenn Hinson, Dixon Sutherland, James Tull, Morris Ashcraft, Henlee Barnette, and Carlyle Marney. Between the seeming extremes, a moderate cluster of theologians emerged, drawing upon both conservatives and Neo-Orthodox. Included here were theologians like James Leo Garrett and James William McClendon, the former influenced by Harvard and Orthodox scholarship and the latter by Stanley Hauerwas and John Howard Yoder. Bob E. Patterson, long-time theology professor at Baylor University trained at Southern Seminary during its Neo-Orthodox phase, took up the cudgel against Texas Baptist fundamentalists and found himself labeled liberal, while in actuality he has been a moderate.

Unlike their American Baptist cousins in the North, Southern Baptists in various theological traditions have been able to coalesce into institutions that exhibit overall their orientation. Hence, Southern, Southwestern, Beeson, and Southeastern have become epicenters of conservative evangelical Baptist thought; McAfee, Richmond, Wake Forest, and the B. H. Carroll Institute have carried the banner for the more progressive voices, with Truett, Logsdon, Campbell, and Baylor University's Department of Religion clustered in the middle.[30]

Finally, as Baptist fundamentalism has come of age, its theological spokesmen have made noticeable theological contributions. Educated mostly in non-Baptist programs like Trinity Evangelical Divinity School and Dallas Theological Seminary, and/or with secular doctorates from state universities in the US and British doctorates from mostly Scottish institutions, these theologians have basically been defined by their Bible college or theological school doctrinal statements. Exemplary of the wide variety here over half a century are Robert P. Lightner at Dallas Seminary; Elmer Towns and Gary Habermas at Liberty University; George Dollar at Bob Jones University; Warren VanHetloo at Central Seminary; Richard Lovelace, David Wells, and Roger Nicole at Gordon Conwell; Bruce Demarest at Denver Seminary; and Michael Stallard at Baptist Bible College Graduate Seminary. Their doctrinal interests included epistemology, creation, spirituality, classic theism, and, as befits Baptists, ecclesiology.

---

[30] Baylor's Deptartment of Religion stands in a nuanced theological contrast with Truett Seminary. The theologians/ethicists of note in the department have included Bernard Ramm (California), C. Wallace Christian (Vanderbilt), Daniel B. McGee (Duke), John Wood (Baylor), and Bob Patterson (Southern). Of late, Barry Harvey, a Hauerwas protégé, and Ralph Wood, a literary critic trained at the University of Chicago, have attempted to pull the department toward a more definitive evangelical stance under the former watchful eye of Robert Sloan. Truett, in contrast, birthed by Sloan, touted its more conservative profile with A. J. Conyers (Southern Seminary), Millard Erickson (Northwestern), and Roger Olson (Pentecostal background, Rice Ph.D.) teaching theology. Truett's recent identity has been drawn according to its Texas Baptist revivalistic pastor progenitors like B. H. Carroll, L. R. Scarborough, and George W. Truett.

Conclusion

Baptist theology has often been downplayed in the shadow of ordinances, church polity, and order. This is unfortunate because Baptists have a broad interest in theological matters and have made an important contribution. The chief difficulty with solidifying a Baptist theology is its diversity over time and place. The Baptist affirmations of the authority of scripture, the Lordship of Christ, and the relevance of Christian experience have guaranteed diversification because of the flexibility of meanings and applications within these generalities. The development of Baptist theological identity has been affected by internal factors and those of a contextual kind. Only recently, there have been major shifts in theological emphases in North America that will surely create reactions and further developments. Baptist theology is, therefore, a work in progress.

Suggested Reading

Brackney, William H. *A Genetic History of Baptist Thought.* Macon GA: Mercer University Press, 2004.

———. "African American Baptists: Prolegomenon to a Theological Tradition." In *The Quest for Liberation and Reconciliation: Essays in Honor of J. Deotis Roberts.* Edited by Michael J. Battle. Louisville: Westminster John Knox, 2005.

Cauthen, W. Kenneth. *The Impact of American Religious Liberalism.* New York: Harper and Row, 1962.

Cox, Harvey. *The Secular City: Secularization and Urbanization in Theological Perspective.* New York: MacMillan, 1965.

Garrett, James Leo, E. Glenn Hinson, and James Tull, editors. *Are Southern Baptists Evangelicals?* Macon GA: Mercer University Press, 1983.

George, Timothy. "Systematic Theology at Southern Seminary." *Review and Expositor* 82/1 (Winter 1985): 31–47.

Graves, James R. *Old Landmarkism: What Is It?* Memphis: Baptist Book House, 1880.

Henry, Carl F. H. *The Uneasy Conscience of Modern Fundamentalism.* Grand Rapids: Eerdmans, 1947.

Lumpkin, William L. *Baptist Confessions of Faith.* Valley Forge: Judson Press, 1963.

Mullins, E. Y. *The Axioms of Religion.* Philadelphia: American Baptist Publication Society, 1915.

Newman, A. H. "Recent Changes in the Theology of Baptists." *American Journal of Theology* 6/3 (October 1906): 587–609.

Peden, Creighton. *The Chicago School: Voices in Liberal Religious Thought.* Bristol: Wyndham Hall Press, 1987.

Wood, Nathan E. "Movements in Baptist Theological Thought." In *A Century of Baptist Achievement.* Edited by A. H. Newman. Philadelphia: American Baptist Publication Society, 1901.

CHAPTER 8

Baptist Revivals and the Turn toward Baptist Evangelism: 1755/1770

Bill J. Leonard

Baptists began with a commitment to a believers' church. They insisted that all who would claim membership in Christ's church should be regenerated, able to testify to an experience of God's grace in their hearts. The church, therefore, was a believers' church, composed, not of all the baptized in a geographic parish or diocese, but only of those who exercised faith in Christ. Baptism was a public profession of that faith, administered only to believers. The Orthodox Creed (1679) of English General Baptists notes that "those who are united unto Christ by effectual faith, are regenerated, and have a new heart and spirit created in them through the virtue of Christ, his death, resurrection, and intercession, and by the efficacy of the Holy Spirit, received by faith."[1] Regeneration (new birth) was essential for those united to Christ and his church.

While the new birth was required of all church members, the early Baptists had no single method for determining the validity of religious experience. Indeed, many of the earliest Baptists were professing Christians who had come to faith as Anglicans or Puritans and were drawn to Baptist views on baptism and the nature of the church. Conversion was thought to be the work of the Holy Spirit with little uniformity in the salvific process. This was especially true among Particular or Calvinist Baptists who believed that God would bring about conversion in the lives of "elected" individuals who could not adequately believe until grace was "infused" into their hearts. While Baptists preached widely, there was no clear cut strategy for evangelization at home or abroad.

---

[1] William L. Lumpkin, *Baptist Confessions of Faith* (Chicago: Judson Press, 1959) 316.

By the eighteenth century Baptists in America and England turned toward a more explicit form of conversion influenced by the evangelical awakenings that swept across both countries. Divisions over revival methods and the message led to the formation of new congregations and new Baptist denominations including the Separate Baptists in America and the New Connection Baptists in England. In time these groups helped to define the conversion process in ways that set the scene for a new style of evangelism often characterized by mass revivalism and an aggressive effort to bring all persons to faith in Christ. The revivals also led to a greater emphasis on individual free will and the possibility that all who heard the gospel might choose to be saved. This led to significant debates among various Baptist groups regarding such theological issues as election, predestination, and the role of individual free will in the salvation process.

American Awakenings

In this turn to conversionism and a concern for religious awakenings, Baptists were influenced by such pulpit luminaries as Jonathan Edwards (1703–1758) in America and John Wesley (1703–1791) in England. George Whitefield (1714–1770), sometimes known as the Grand Itinerant or the Great Awakener, was a bridge between the two countries and one of the most popular revival preachers of the time. During the early 1730s Edwards, pastor of the Congregational Church in Northampton, Massachusetts, began a series of sermons on justification by faith, calling on persons to repent of their sins and experience the new birth. The result was a rapid increase in conversions, especially among many of the young people of the town. The conversions were frequently accompanied by a variety of "enthusiasms" or "religious affections"—emotional responses to the sermons and to the struggle for conversion. Some conversions occurred rather rapidly; others took more time. Children as young as five years old were known to experience a severe conviction of sin and desire for salvation. During the conversion process many people wept, shouted, and cried for mercy, giving themselves to a variety of enthusiastic outbursts. While many clergy rejoiced at the growth of religious fervor, some were critical of the emotional outpourings as excessive, disruptive, and shameful—inappropriate behavior in the presence of a God who was "not the author of confusion."[2] In a treatise titled *A Faithful Narrative of the*

---

[2] 1 Cor 13:33.

Surprising Work of God (1737), Edwards described the awakening at Northampton and defended the experiences of "religious affections" as evidence of the conversion of the whole person, soul, mind, heart, and emotions. In another work, *A Treatise Concerning Religious Affections* (1746), Edwards wrote, "I know of no Reason, why a being affected with a View of God's Glory should not cause the Body to faint, as well as a being affected with a View of Solomon's Glory. And no such Rule has as yet been produced from the Scripture."[3] As Edwards saw it, the experience of salvation could certainly affect all aspects of spiritual, physical, and psychological life.

Jonathan Edwards promoted what came to be called "evangelical Calvinism" in which preachers declared the word of God to all persons as if all could be saved, knowing that God would use such preaching to awaken the elect. In the *Faithful Narrative*, Edwards set forth the process of conversion he observed in his Northampton church. It reveals the God who seeks out sinners and provides the grace that they are helpless to discover for themselves.

George Whitefield, another evangelical Calvinist, was much less systematic than Edwards. He traveled throughout the colonies preaching spontaneous, unscripted sermons often distinguished by dramatic and emotive calls for conversion. While the leaders of the awakening were primarily Calvinists, their ideas and actions brought significant division to the churches of the New England Way, especially regarding the nature of religious affections. Whitefield's person and methods also sparked controversy. In 1745 the president and faculty of Harvard College labeled him "an Enthusiast, a censorious, uncharitable Person, and a Deluder of the People; which Things, if we can make out, all reasonable Men will doubtless excuse us, tho' some such, thro' a fascinating Curiosity, may still continue their Attachment to him."[4]

Soon divisions arose in New England between New Lights (pro-revival) and Old Lights (anti-revival). Old Lights warned that emotional excesses might be just that and not signs of the movement of the Spirit. They feared the rise of sectarian influence and the loss of "decency and order" in the churches. New Lights generally supported the revival methods while affirming the need for religious liberty, greater church autonomy, and the importance of a regenerate church membership. Many Separates soon rejected infant baptism in favor of

---

[3] Jonathan Edwards, *A Treatise on Religious Affections,*" excerpted in H. Shelton Smith, Robert T. Handy, and Lefferts A. Loetscher, *American Christianity* (New York: Charles Scribner's Sons, 1960) 343.

[4] Ibid., 330.

believer's baptism by immersion to be administered only after the necessary profession of faith. This caused a split among the New England churches, especially in Connecticut, and led to the formation of Separate or New Light Baptist congregations in the late 1740s and 1750s.[5] One critic is said to have remarked, "Whitefield's chickens have all become ducks!"

Awakening Baptists: Separate Baptists

The rise of the Separate Baptists led to controversy and division in the Baptist ranks as the more traditional "Regular" Baptists accused the pro-revivalist Separates of deserting Calvinist orthodoxy. First Baptist Church of Boston divided in the 1743 when the pastor, Jeremiah Condy, was accused of Arminianism because he denied original sin, sought to "intermix" personal regeneration with "free-agency and cooperation," and affirmed a belief in "falling from grace."[6] While the Regular Baptists (as they came to be called) supported the need for a believers' church, they were suspicious of "enthusiastical" religion as a sign of genuine conversion. Likewise, the Regulars preferred more orderly worship, sang only the Psalms as the church's inspired divinely hymnody, and generally called educated ministers who preached from carefully prepared sermon manuscripts. They remained suspicious of the emotions set loose, indeed encouraged, by the Separates.

Separate Baptist worship, on the other hand, was given to boisterous preaching, singing "man-made" hymns, and a call for conversion that could unleash powerful emotions from the sinner fighting against grace or the convert who had received it. They generally rejected confessions of faith, doctrinal statements of human creation, in favor of the sole authority of scripture as the guide for life, faith, and practice. Separate Baptist leader John Leland (1754–1841) described the difference between Separate and Regular Baptist accordingly: "The Regulars were orthodox Calvinists, and the work under them was solemn and rational; but the Separates were the most zealous, and the work among them was very noisy."[7] A 1744 critique of the early Separates set forth some of their most popular practices ("errors") including their belief in a pure church, the recognition of true Christians from false; the power of a call to preach without need for education or special training; a rejection of those

---

[5] William H. Brackney, ed., *Baptist in Life and Thought: 1600–1980* (Valley Forge: Judson Press, 1983) 102.

[6] Bill J. Leonard, *Baptist Ways: A History* (Valley Forge: Judson Press, 2003) 120.

[7] As cited in Leonard, *Baptist Ways*, 122.

churches that differed on these matters; and support for lay preaching.[8] Other accounts confirm their understanding of conversion as a radical departure from one kind of life to another and a direct experience of grace with deep emotional implications.

Two of the best known Separate Baptists from this period are Shubal Stearns (1706–1771) and Daniel Marshall (1706–1784). They helped to found the first Baptist church in the territory of North Carolina in 1755. Known as the Sandy Creek Baptist Church, it became the mother church of over forty congregations on the frontier and helped to establish the Separate Baptist movement across the American frontier.

Shubal Stearns exemplifies Separate Baptist methods and ideology. Born in New England, he was dramatically converted through the influence of George Whitefield. He soon moved toward the Baptists, receiving both immersion and ordination at the hands of Wait Palmer, a Separate Baptist preacher, in 1751. Stearns then headed south to preach the gospel and was joined by his brother-in-law Daniel Marshall. His sister, Martha Stearns Marshall, was also given to public proclamation, a practice that got her into some trouble with those who felt that women were to keep silent in church and elsewhere. The two families moved to Carolina in 1755 and founded Sandy Creek and other Baptist churches. Stearns became pastor of the church and was soon known as a dynamic preacher of the gospel. By 1758 some 900 persons had experienced conversion under the influence of Stearns's preaching.[9]

Morgan Edwards, the colonial Baptist historian, suggested that Stearns's oratorical skills and preaching style illustrated the type of evangelism closely connected to the Separate Baptists. He says of Stearns, "Of learning he had but a small share, yet was pretty well acquainted with Books. His voice was musical and strong, which he managed in such a manner as, one while, to make soft impressions on the heart, and fetch tears from the eyes in a mechanical way; and anon, to shake the very nerves and throw the animal system into tumults and perturbations. All the Separate ministers copy after him in tones of voice and actions of body; and some few exceed him."[10] Edwards also wrote that Stearns's approach bore "the tones, actions and violence which are the Shibboleths of the Separate Baptists" and gave evidence of "the outcries, extacies [sic] and

---

[8] Elder John Sparks, *The Roots of Appalachian Christianity* (Lexington: University of Kentucky Press, 2001) 26–27.

[9] Ibid., 70.

[10] As cited in Leonard, *Baptist Ways*, 121.

epilepsies which are so much thought of among them."[11] Stearns's sermons were apparently preached in a particular vocal form known as the "Holy Tone," a kind of sing-song delivery that became a distinct style of many Separate Baptist preachers.

The first building for the Sandy Creek Church was constructed in 1762 and the church experienced rapid growth. Again, Morgan Edwards described the congregational practices as follows: "Here ruling elders, eldresses, and deaconesses are allowed; also are the 9 Christian rites: baptism; Lord's Supper; love-feast; laying-on-of-hands; washing-feet; anointing the sick; right hand of fellowship; kiss of charity; devoting [dedicating] children." Holy Communion was celebrated at least once a week.[12] When Edwards visited the church during the Revolutionary War he wrote that it had fallen on dark times, noting that after "17 years it is reduced from 606 to 14 souls, and is in danger of being extinct." He believed that British control of the region had a negative impact on the church.[13] Nonetheless, the Sandy Creek Baptist Church survived and continues to this day.

Leon McBeth noted that the earliest covenant produced by the Sandy Creek Church demonstrated a "moderate Calvinism," suggesting "particular election of grace by the predestination of God." Later, he says, the Calvinism "gave way to more emphasis upon human freedom and responsibility to believe the gospel."[14] The Separate Baptists represent one of the great dilemmas for those who support a "moderate Calvinism." The decision to preach as if everyone can be saved may effectively imply that all persons are indeed candidates for salvation and have the free will to choose or reject it. The Separate Baptists continued to use the language of Calvinism, but increasingly gave it a more implicit Arminian interpretation regarding Christ's death for the entire world and the possibility that all individuals could come to salvation. Many continued to use the language of Calvinism but with decidedly Arminian interpretations.

---

[11] Sparks, *The Roots of Appalachian Christianity*, 69.

[12] As cited in Leonard, *Baptist Ways*, 121.

[13] Ibid.

[14] H. Leon McBeth, *The Baptist Heritage: Four Centuries of Baptist Witness* (Nashville: Broadman Press, 1987) 229.

Awakening England: The New Connection Baptists

George Whitefield and John Wesley were catalysts for an awakening that spread across England in the 1740s. The Wesleyan revivals began with clergy in the Church of England who determined to take the gospel directly to the people through a variety of non-traditional tactics such as field preaching—encountering sinners where they congregated outside the churches. These early "seeker-sensitive" approaches took Wesley, Whitefield, and other preachers to mineworkers, farmers, and city dwellers in an effort to call them to salvation. Unlike Whitefield, John Wesley was an Arminian who believed strongly in free grace, free will, and the general atonement of Christ. Methodist societies sprang up within the Anglican Church through small groups organized for prayer and confession as well as Bible study and the cultivation of Christian sanctification (discipleship). The need for personal conversion was a central aspect of Wesley's efforts.

In spite of the religious enthusiasm engendered by the Wesleyan revivals, Baptists were suspicious since it involved persons in the Anglican establishment and a continued emphasis on infant baptism. Likewise, Particular Baptists were hesitant to follow any movement so attached to Arminian theology.[15] While certain Baptists were drawn to the revivals, no significant Baptist attention developed until the appearance of Dan Taylor (1738–1816). Taylor was converted to Christianity under the preaching of Wesley and Whitefield. Largely self-educated, he worked in the mines for a time and then became pastor of a break-away group of Methodists. After contacts with the Particular Baptists he concluded that infant baptism was neither taught nor practiced by the New Testament church. He applied to the Particular Baptists for membership but was rejected because of his Arminian views. Taylor ultimately tracked down a group of General (Arminian) Baptists in Lincolnshire and along with his friend John Slater received immersion from them on 16 February 1763.[16]

Taylor's preaching in his home region of Wadsworth led others to join him, and in conjunction with the General Baptists he founded a congregation there and was ordained as its pastor in 1763. It was not long before he became disillusioned with General Baptist traditionalism and lack of doctrinal clarity.

---

[15] A. C. Underwood, *A History of English Baptists* (London: The Baptist Union of Great Britain and Ireland, 1970) 148.

[16] Ibid., 150–51.

He was particularly concerned that many had moved toward Unitarianism and had compromised a sense of orthodoxy in their view of Jesus Christ.[17]

Although a Baptist, Taylor had significant relationships with a group of revivalists in Lincolnshire generally unrelated to other Protestant groups. Many General Baptists were suspicious of their emotionalism and non-traditional religious practices. Taylor determined to develop a "new connection" between those revivalists and certain General Baptists committed to orthodoxy and religious awakenings. The result was a new denomination, the New Connection of General Baptists, founded on 6 June 1770 in one of London's oldest General Baptist churches. The intent of the New Connection was to retain Arminian theology in order "to revive experimental religion or primitive Christianity in faith and practice."[18] Once again, these Baptists reasserted the need for a conversion experience as required of all who would claim Christianity, and the need for that Christianity to reflect a genuine orthodoxy. New Connection Baptists stressed a kind of congregational egalitarianism, local church autonomy, and discipline of those who stepped outside prescribed doctrinal beliefs and ethical behavior.

New Connection Baptists are important to the Baptist story in England for several reasons. First, they were the clear heirs of the Wesleyan awakenings, reasserting the need for individual conversion through the cooperation of God's saving grace and the prevenient (enabling) grace of free will given to all human beings. Theirs was an experiential religion grounded in faith in Jesus. Taylor wrote that "when I say this salvation is free, I mean that it is freely imparted to the sinner, to every sinner who applies to Jesus for it in the way in which the gospel appoints, that is by faith...without any merits, works, or deservings whatsoever."[19] Second, the concern for conversion led them to work aggressively toward the conversion of all persons, preaching and carrying out evangelical ministry across England. Their earliest confession declared, "We ought in the course of our ministry, to propose or offer this salvation to all who attend our ministry." Salvation, therefore, was to be "held forth to all to whom the gospel revelation comes without exception."[20] Third, they were eighteenth-century "church planters," organizing new congregations with particular attention to cities and working-class regions booming with the rise of the

---

[17] Ibid., 152–53.
[18] Ibid., 153.
[19] Leonard, *Baptist Ways*, 97.
[20] McBeth, *Baptist Heritage*, 163.

industrial revolution. Fourth, their sense of the freedom of all believers led them to develop practices that went beyond the traditional Baptists of their day. These included congregational hymn-singing by both men and women,[21] and a greater sensitivity to the role of women in the church. Nonetheless, church discipline was strenuous and excommunication of recalcitrant church members was not uncommon.[22] Fifth, their concern for conversion was not an exclusive individualism. Their concern for community led to a thriving associationalism among their churches, including "mutual encouragement, fresh ideas, as well as of giving practical support and healthy doctrinal instruction to one another."[23] Taylor turned the small group system of Methodism into Baptist "experience meetings," home gatherings of converts who sang hymns, prayed, encouraged, and critiqued the spiritual life of their brothers and sisters in Christ.[24] In short, they developed new paradigms for evangelization amid the changing social and economic climate of an industrialized nation. Finally, the New Connection Baptists appeared at a time when the other two Baptist groups in England were experiencing significant transition in their denominational identity. General Baptists were moving increasingly toward Unitarian approaches to Christology amid a highly structured system even as their numbers declined rapidly. Particular Baptists were in the throes of controversy regarding the nature of Calvinism, conversion, and the implication of those ideas on world mission. The New Connection movement helped to revitalize Baptist life in England and carry it into a new stage of mission and ministry.

Baptists and Revivals

Baptist participation in evangelical awakenings in England and the American colonies anticipated an important strain of revivalism and conversionism that would stretch from the eighteenth through the twentieth century. The stress on individual conversion and the development of an evangelistic strategy for converting large numbers of persons extended from Jonathan Edwards and John Wesley to multiple generations of Christians who were evangelistic in their desire to spread the Good News of Jesus Christ. By

---

[21] Many Baptists believed that female singing would violate biblical teachings on women's silence in church.

[22] Ibid., 165–68.

[23] Raymond Brown, *The English Baptists of the Eighteenth Century* (London: The Baptist Historical Society, 1986) 111.

[24] William H. Brackney, *Baptists in Life and Thought*, 272.

the early nineteenth century, Baptists on the frontier participated in the camp meeting phenomenon that led to new converts, churches, and theologies as the nation moved west. Camp meetings produced dramatic conversions often evident in certain "exercises" that included shouting, falling, running, jerking, and singing in the Spirit. Preaching and worship often followed spontaneity and hymn-singing of the Separate Baptist style. Leon McBeth reminds readers that the Separates were among the first to use what became the "evangelistic invitation," or the infamous anxious bench, in which the preacher would "extend an invitation to such persons as felt themselves poor guilty sinners, and were anxious by inquiring the way of salvation, to come forward and kneel near the [preacher's] stand."[25]

Charles G. Finney, the New York evangelist of the 1820s and 1830s, carried evangelism from small towns to large cities, softening his Presbyterian theology considerably with an emphasis on conversion for all and Christ's general atonement. His "new measures" for conducting a revival involved preaching for conversion, permitting women to testify in "mixed" gatherings of men and women, and the invitation of sinners to the "anxious bench." His revival meetings were held in churches and public buildings throughout the east. Baptist evangelists Jabez Swan and Jacob Knapp were contemporaries of Finney, who used his new measures in urban and rural evangelism.[26] By the late nineteenth century urban evangelists like Dwight L. Moody extended the influence of revivalism in an effort to reach those outside the church. Moody's campaigns were held in public arenas, used huge choirs and peppy music while calling persons to come forward to register their Christian commitments on "decision cards." This tradition was continued by innumerable twentieth century evangelists, especially Billy Graham and his evangelistic association. Baptists were heirs of this revivalistic tradition, with many churches holding seasonal revivals (protracted meetings) aimed at calling persons to conversion, rededication of life, and "full-time Christian service." Many of these revivals reflected the exuberance and enthusiasm of the Separate Baptists with shouting, weeping, and dramatic struggles with grace. In fact, revivalism became one of the chief vehicles of Baptist evangelism in a tradition that stretches from Shubal Stearns and Dan Taylor to Charles Haddon Spurgeon and Billy Graham.

---

[25] McBeth, *Baptist Heritage*, 231, citing Robert I. Devin, *A History of Grassy Creek Baptist Church* (Raleigh: Edward Broughton and Company, 1880) 69.

[26] Leonard, *Baptist Ways*, 217.

Suggested Reading

Edwards, Jonathan. *The Works of Jonathan Edwards*. Volume 9, *A History of the Work of Redemption*. Edited by John F. Wilson. New Haven: Yale University Press, 1989.

Leonard, Bill J. *Baptist Ways: A History*. Valley Forge: Judson Press, 2003.

Sparks, Elder John. *The Roots of Appalcahian Christianity*. Lexington: University of Kentucky Press, 2001.

Sweet, W. W. *Religion on the American Frontier: The Baptists*. Chicago: University of Chicago Press, 1931.

CHAPTER 9

Baptist Missions and the Turn toward Global Responsibility: 1792

Rosalie Beck

In the England of the 1700s, Baptists were in decline because of infighting, theological disagreements, and a general religious malaise. They did not give much thought to evangelism or missions. This indifference to missions changed slowly throughout the century until 1792 whe a handful of Particular Baptist ministers in Kettering organized the first modern Protestant foreign missionary society. From this small beginning, the modern mission movement grew. At the center of this turning point was William Carey, a man who called himself a "plodder for Christ."[1]

Carey's Background

Born in Northamptonshire, William Carey (1761–1834) was the oldest of two sons and two daughters born to the Edmund Careys. Mr. Carey wove wool for a living, but he opened a school when the production of wool cloth as a cottage industry became unprofitable. William, who loved reading adventure books like the *Journal of Captain Cook's Last Voyage*, was largely self-educated because he left school at the age of twelve to become a gardener's apprentice. William quickly realized he was sensitive to the sun and left the job market until his father found Clarke Nichols, a shoe cobbler, who took the sixteen-year-old boy as an apprentice in 1777.[2] This apprenticeship altered Carey's life.

John Warr, Carey's roommate and fellow apprentice of Nichols, was a Dissenter, and Carey found his arguments for a different form of church

---

[1] "A Baptist Page Portrait: William Carey." *The Baptist Page* June 2006. http://www.siteone.com/religion/baptist/baptistpage/Portraits/print/print_Carey.html.
[2] Leon McBeth, *Men Who Made Missions* (Nashville: Broadman Press, 1968) 70–73.

persuasive. Carey embraced Warr's understanding of the gospel and became a dissenting Christian. When Nichols died, Carey became the apprentice of Thomas Old, a relative of Nichols who lived in Hackelton. Either at the Dissenters meeting or through the wife of his master, Elizabeth Plackett Old, Carey met and married Dorothy Plackett. When they married in 1781, he was nineteen, and she was twenty-five. Dorothy used an "X" to sign her name because she was illiterate, but she learned to read and write after they were married. As Carey finished his training, he and Dorothy began their family, which eventually included five sons and two daughters.[3]

As Carey studied the Bible, he concluded that Particular Baptists were closest to his understanding of baptism and the church. So in 1783 John Ryland Jr., a Particular Baptist minister, baptized Carey, recording in his journal, "This day baptized a poor journeyman shoemaker."[4] Little did Ryland know how important that "poor journeyman shoemaker" would be to the history of missions.

In 1786 Carey moved his family to Olney where he spent the summer making shoes and preaching at the Baptist church. At the end of his "try-out," the congregation decided not to ordain Carey because he was not a good speaker. The Baptist church in Moulton called him to be their pastor, and with the blessing of the Olney church, they ordained Carey in 1787.[5] Carey supplemented his meager church income by teaching school. For the geography lessons, Carey created a globe of scrap leather, etching countries and information on the surface. Daily, he reminded himself of the multitudes of non-believers around the world. Coupled with his interest in travel, nature, and history, his concern for the souls of non-Christians grew with each passing year.[6] But as a Particular Baptist, he had little or no opportunity to pursue his growing concern for souls.

When William Carey became a Particular Baptist minister, these Baptists already embraced hyper-Calvinism. Particular Baptist theologians like John Gill presented arguments against evangelism and missions. An overemphasis on election and predestination caused pastors to assert that believers should not

---

[3] James R. Beck, *Dorothy Carey: The Tragic and Untold Story of Mrs. William Carey* (Grand Rapids: Baker Book House, 1992) 27–35.

[4] Galen B. Royer, "William Carey: The Father of Modern Missions," http//www.wholesomewords.org/missions/bcarey3.html June 2006.

[5] McBeth, *Men Who Made Missions*, 74.

[6] "A Baptist Page Portrait: William Carey," http://www.siteone.com/religion/baptist/baptistpage/Portraits/print/print_Carey.html June 2006.

"address the gospel to the unsaved." They lost their zeal for "evangelism and vital church life." The leaders refused to offer Christ "to unregenerate sinners and taught others to make the same refusal."[7] Particular Baptists accepted the argument that rejection of the gospel by non-believers made them liable to judgment by God, and the assertion that the Great Commission of Matthew 28:19–20 applied only to the early church.[8]

Andrew Fuller played a key role in the reversal made by Particular Baptists as they embraced missions. Fuller, who was a little older than Carey, served as pastor of the nearby Kettering Baptist Church. Fuller questioned the hyper-Calvinist refusal to invite the lost to be saved. Through Bible study and analysis, he concluded that preaching the gospel was a scriptural imperative that continued even to this day. In his book *The Gospel Worthy of All Acceptation* (1785), Fuller proved that one can hold to God's sovereignty as a good Calvinist, yet still preach the gospel in response to the command of God. Carey agreed with Fuller, but John Ryland Sr., the moderator of the Ministers Fraternal of the Northampton Association of which they were members, refused to listen to the younger pastors.[9] In 1787 Carey challenged Ryland when asked what question the ministers should discuss at their meeting. He said, "Whether the command given to the apostles to teach all nations was not binding on all succeeding ministers to the end of the world, seeing that the accompanying promise was of equal extant?"[10] Ryland Sr. did not allow the discussion to occur, but other ministers became convinced that missions were a central responsibility of the church, and they refused to keep silent.

Carey took two actions in 1792 that have become missionary lore. The first was his publication of *An Enquiry into the Obligations of Christians to Use Means for the Conversion of the Heathens, in Which the Religious State of the Different Nations of the World, the Success of Former Undertakings, and the Practicability of Further Undertakings Are Considered.* A friend of Carey's, Thomas Potts, encouraged him to put his ideas on missions in a booklet, and the *Enquiry* was born.[11] Carey based his arguments on scripture and contemporary

---

[7] H. Leon McBeth, *The Baptist Heritage: Four Centuries of Baptist Witness* (Nashville: Broadman Press, 1987) 170–76.

[8] Beck, *Dorothy Carey*, 61.

[9] Ibid., 60.

[10] Donald Alban Jr., Robert H. Woods Jr., and Marsha Daigle-Williamson, "The Writings of William Carey: Journalism as Mission in a Modern Age," *Mission Studies* 22/1 (2005): 89–91.

[11] Ibid., 89–91.

information. He argued for the eternally binding nature of the Great Commission and refuted all arguments against missions and evangelism. The *Enquiry* proved to be "the charter of the modern missionary movement.[12]

Carey's second important action in 1792 took place at the May meeting of the Ministers Fraternal. It was Carey's turn to preach, and he chose Isaiah 54:2–3 as his text: "Enlarge the site of your tent, and let the curtains of your habitations be stretched out; do not hold back; lengthen your cords and strengthen your stakes. For you will spread out to the right and to the left, and your descendants will possess the nations and will settle the desolate towns" (NRSV). Carey argued that this passage commanded that the gospel be preached. How could the tents be enlarged or the cords lengthened unless proclamation of the gospel occurred? His presentation became known as "The Deathless Sermon" because his two key points—attempt great things for God; expect great things from God —grabbed the imaginations of the ministers present. They resolved to "form a Baptist society for propagating the gospel among the Heathen" at the next meeting. In October 1792 a dozen or so ministers met in the parlor of Mrs. Beebe Wallis's house in Kettering and formed the Particular Baptist Society for the Propagation of the Gospel among the Heathen, known as the Baptist Missionary Society (BMS). They collected 13 pounds, 20 shillings and 6 pence in their first offering, and placed the money in a snuff box that had a picture of the conversion of St. Paul on the lid.[13]

William Carey soon volunteered to serve as the society's first missionary. The members of the BMS, however, could not decide exactly where he should go or how they could fund the trip. They found an answer in Dr. John Thomas, a surgeon who served on the ship the *Earl of Oxford* when he first sailed to India in 1783. While in port, he worked as a medical missionary among the people of Bengal and learned something of their language. Later, at the request of George Udney, an official of the East India Company, Thomas returned to India to practice medicine in 1786. The leaders of the BMS heard of Thomas when he arrived in England to raise money for the translation of the Bible into Bengali. He immediately offered himself as a missionary, and the society accepted his offer. The BMS leaders then asked Carey to go with Thomas to

---

[12] McBeth, *Baptist Heritage*, 184–85.
[13] "October 2, 1792: Baptist Missionary Society Formed in England," http://chi.gospelcom.net/DAILYF/2003/10/daily–10–02–2003.html June 2006. This is a daily calendar for Christian events.

save money.[14] Carey agreed, and he and Thomas planned their trip as the first Baptist missionaries to India.

Carey as a Missionary

The East India Company controlled entry to all areas of India controlled by the British and did not welcome anyone whom they thought would create difficulties that diminished their profits. The East India Company especially suspected missionaries, fearing they would cause a disturbance among the nationals and threaten the company's control. The company made it almost impossible for missionaries to obtain the required special license for entry into India. If someone tried to enter illegally, they were deported as soon as they were discovered. [15]

Carey faced another problem: his wife Dorothy refused to go to India. They had buried their daughters Ann and Lucy in England, her large family was there, and Dorothy was five months pregnant. Nonetheless, Carey intended to go to India and made plans to take his oldest son, Felix, with him. Carey planned to work for a year and then return to convince Dorothy to go back with him to India.[16] Dorothy remained adamant in her refusal.

Without proper papers, the Careys and the Thomas family sailed in spring 1793 to the Isle of Wight to join a convoy bound for India. While there, someone informed the authorities of their illegal status and they were placed off the ship. They went to another port and booked passage on the Danish vessel *Kron Princessa Maria*, bound for Calcutta. While waiting for the ship to depart, Carey decided to go home to convince Dorothy to come with him. Either he or Thomas proved persuasive, because Dorothy chose to join Carey, along with their sons Felix, William, Peter, three-week-old Jabez, and her sister Catherine.

The new missionaries arrived in Calcutta in November 1793, and they almost immediately found themselves in financial difficulty. They had no regular income and Thomas proved to be a miserable financial manager. Within a month, Carey moved to Bandel, a nearby Portuguese colony where it was cheaper to live. Eventually, he applied for and received free land in the Ganges River delta, called the Sunderbunds, to establish a plantation. Carey escaped deportation before his final move to the Danish colony of Serampore

---

[14] Beck, *Dorothy Carey*, 68–69.
[15] Stephen Neill, *A History of Christian Missions*, 2nd ed., The Penguin History of the Church Series (New York: Penguin Books USA Inc., 1990) 223.
[16] Beck, *Dorothy Carey*, 67ff.

by avoiding British officials and by listing himself as a planter rather than a missionary.[17]

For five months the Careys lived in the Sunderbunds, trying to build a plantation. All this time he studied the languages of the Indians, especially Bengali, because he believed translation of the Bible into the indigenous language was a priority. Thomas eventually contacted Carey about an indigo plantation, owned by George Udney, that needed a manager. Carey took this job because it gave him more time to learn languages and work with the people than he had while building a plantation. In mid-1794 the Carey household, minus Catherine Plackett who had married a local planter, moved hundreds of miles to Mudnabati where they lived for almost six years.

With a job at the indigo factory, Carey applied legally for a permit to stay in East India Company territory. He had time, after supervising the 400–500 workers, to study languages and to preach to both Europeans and the indigenous people. He bought a printing press and began publishing portions of scripture and gospel tracts in Bengali. Carey's work absorbed him. However, when his five-year-old son Peter died from fever and dysentery in 1794, Carey's world changed. Dorothy, unable to adjust to life in India, began to go insane. She blamed Carey for Peter's death. She eventually developed delusions about Carey being unfaithful, and she created public scenes by screaming at him and any woman she thought was having an affair with him. After their move to Serampore in 1800, she became uncontrollable and was confined to a single room in their home at the request of the local police. Carey felt great sorrow and guilt over her mental deterioration, but he continued his work. H. Leon McBeth rightly observed, "Somewhere in missionary history a word of compassion should be written for Dorothy Carey, who paid a high price for Baptist missions and never knew why."[18]

Carey in Serampore

In 1799 English Baptist missionaries Joshua Marshman, William Ward, William Grant, David Brundsdon, and their families arrived in Calcutta, but moved on to Serampore when the company officials would not allow them to stay in Calcutta. They took a Danish ship sixteen miles up the Hooghly River to Serampore, and the missionary families settled there. Serampore proved a good

---

[17] McBeth, *Men Who Made Missions*, 80.
[18] McBeth, *Baptist Heritage*, 186; Beck, *Dorothy Carey*, 103, 153.

place for them because the Danish governor, Colonel Ole Bie, wanted them in his territory. He offered them inducements to stay. They could use the church he was building, they could install a printing press for the publication of scripture, and he would issue them Danish passports so they could travel to British-controlled areas with no trouble. After settling his family, Ward visited Carey to persuade him to move to Serampore. Ward, a trained printer, met Carey years earlier when Carey had encouraged him to become a missionary to India. Carey weighed the matter seriously and decided to move because in Serampore he could preach more openly, he would have more freedom to operate his printing press, and the city provided a strategic center from which to reach the Bengali people.[19] In January 1800 he and his family moved the 200 plus miles to Serampore.

It was in Serampore that the first national convert, Krisha Pal, became a believer in 1800. By 1821 more than 1,400 persons had been baptized by the missionaries and national leaders in and around the city. With multiple printing presses, Carey and the others produced more than 210,000 portions of the Bible and books important for the development of India's own publication business—dictionaries and grammars for languages like Bengali. Carey translated daily and preached twice a week at the local church. In 1801 he published his first edition of the Bengali New Testament, the Sanskrit New Testament came out in 1808, and the Bengali Old Testament in 1809. Even after a fire destroyed the print shop in 1813, Carey and his helpers salvaged what they could and within days began to publish again. In 1813 they had five presses, and by 1820 they possessed twenty presses for publishing their own work as well as Bengali documents for the government. Carey died in 1834, but by 1837 he and his associates had translated portions of the Bible into more than forty languages.[20]

Carey believed indigenous Christians made the best leaders and needed a good education to be effective. While in Mudnabati and through his years in Serampore, he established grade school for boys and girls. In 1819 Carey helped establish Serampore College "for the instruction of Asiatic, Christian, and other youth, in Eastern Literature and European Science." Thirty-seven students formed the first class, half of whom were non-Christians. This school still exists and has trained hundreds of indigenous leaders, both within the

---

[19] McBeth, *Men Who Made Missions*, 84; Beck, *Dorothy Carey*, 151.
[20] Alban, Woods, and Daigle-Williamson, "The Writings of William Carey," 97; "A Baptist Page Portrait."

Christian faith and within the larger world of an India emerging from British control.[21]

Believing that missionaries should be self-supporting, Carey accepted a job in 1801 with the British government teaching Bengali at Fort William College, the East India Company civil servant training school in Calcutta. For the next thirty years, Carey went to Calcutta several days a week to teach Bengali, Sanskrit, and Marathi. As a "missionary," he received about one-half the salary the other professors earned, but he still earned a substantial salary for India. He earned 1,200 pounds a year, from which he drew 60 pounds for living expenses and put the rest into the common fund from which all the missionaries could draw. The missionaries lived as one large family to keep expenses down. Each family had a small allowance, but most of the money earned by members of the mission went into a common fund. Because they feared tensions could arise within any closely-knit group, they set aside a time each Saturday for folks to air their grievances and work out differences. This family way of doing mission work succeeded until the mission grew so large that it was no longer practical.[22]

From time to time, problems assailed Carey and the others. Dorothy Carey's two attempts on his life made work and home life very difficult for Carey. He warned the BMS that they should send only those missionary wives who were "as hearty in the work as their husbands." He was not a disciplinarian, and his coworkers complained about the wild behavior of his sons. In a letter to his siblings in England, Carey announced Dorothy's death in 1807 and his plans to remarry within a few months. The other missionaries also knew and advised against it, but he needed a wife for himself and a mother for his four sons so he married Charlotte Rumohr in 1808. Charlotte Rumohr came to Bengal for her health in the early 1800s and was baptized into the Baptist church by Carey. A Danish woman of means and family, Rumohr proved to be a talented linguist who helped Carey with his translations. They enjoyed thirteen years together before her death in 1821. Although devastated by Charlotte's death, Carey married Grace Hughes in 1822. She was an English widow seventeen years his junior who cared for him during his final years.[23] Carey did what he thought he had to do to find comfort and companionship.

---

[21] Neill, *History of Christian Missions*, 5; Royer, "William Carey."

[22] Ruth A. Tucker, *From Jerusalem to Irian Jaya* (Grand Rapids: Academie Books, 1983) 118–20.

[23] McBeth, *Men Who Made Missions*, 83; Beck, *Dorothy Carey*, 157–67.

It pained Carey greatly when the BMS and Serampore mission split in 1827 (the breach ended three years after Carey's death). As society secretary, Andrew Fuller set a precedent by letting the missionaries conduct their work as they chose. When Fuller died, control shifted to people in London who did not know Carey, Ward, or Marshman personally. The Londoners wanted control of the mission's daily life, a careful accounting of all funds, and all funds processed through the BMS rather than a fund on the mission field. New missionaries arriving at Serampore after 1815 did not like the dictatorial methods of Marshman, thought Carey needed to quit translating and preach more, and disliked the living style of the mission. Miscommunication between India and London exacerbated the problems until the missionaries in Carey's group at Serampore split from the BMS and formed their own missionary society in 1827. Carey sided with his coworkers. Those who wanted to remain connected to the BMS formed the Calcutta Missionary Union.[24] Carey grieved over this division, but he believed missionaries needed the freedom to make their own decisions.

At the end of his life, William Carey suffered from several serious illnesses. He resigned from his teaching position at Fort William College and spent his limited energy on translation work. At his death in 1834 Carey was one of the most honored citizens of India. The Danish governor and his wife attended the funeral and provided a military escort and salute. All the government flags flew at half-mast for this "poor journeyman shoemaker." Carey chose his own epitaph, lines from a hymn by Isaac Watts: "A wretched, poor, and helpless worm, On Thy kind arms I fall." One young missionary attending the funeral service wrote, "With our departed leader all is well. He had finished his course gloriously. But the Work now descends to us."[25] William Carey inspired, challenged, and supported the missionaries with whom he worked. The young missionary understood the example set by Carey and knew the amount of work ahead.

Carey's Legacy

Carey's influence extended far beyond India to the United States and Britain where he breathed new life into both English and American Baptists, giving them a "new sense of purpose and solidarity." This influence is seen in

---

[24] H. Leon McBeth, *A Sourcebook for Baptist Heritage* (Nashville: Broadman Press, 1990) 192–94; Tucker, *From Jerusalem*, 118–20.

[25] Galen B. Royer, "William Carey"; "A Baptist Page Portrait."

the 1814 formation of the first nationwide Baptist convention in America. Ann Hazeltine and Adoniram Judson began their missionary careers as Congregationalists. They sailed to India as Congregational missionaries two weeks after they were married in 1812. Knowing they would encounter William Carey, the Judsons studied the Greek New Testament to develop arguments in favor of infant baptism by sprinkling, as opposed to believer's baptism by immersion as taught by Carey. From their study, they became Baptists, and upon landing at Calcutta, they made their way to Serampore where they were baptized by William Ward. William Carey financially supported these young people when they resigned from the Congregational missionary society, and he urged Thomas Baldwin, a Baptist pastor in Boston, to gather support for the Judsons. The Judsons' friend Luther Rice, also a Congregational missionary who became Baptist on the voyage to India, returned to America to raise money for their support. With Baldwin, Rice, and others urging American Baptists to organize for missions, Baptist leaders met in Philadelphia in May 1814 and formed the "General Missionary Convention of the Baptist Denomination in the United States of America for Foreign Missions."[26] American Baptists formed their first national organization at the urging of William Carey, even though he knew that his financial support would decrease as Americans shifted their money to the Judsons. His selflessness speaks well of his character and his commitment to missions.

The General Missionary Convention (GMC) also supported the work of Johann Gerhard Oncken (1800–1884), the father of Continental Baptists. Oncken, born in Germany, grew up in Scotland where he served an apprenticeship with a merchant. He moved to London, married, and became an evangelical Christian. Oncken devoted his life to distributing Bibles and gospel tracts in Germany. He reported in 1879 that since 1823, he had given away more than 2,000,000 Bibles. Oncken became a Baptist in the mid–1820s as a result of his study of the Bible. When someone told him he should baptize himself, he said he would wait for a "Philip" to come and baptize him. At a GMC meeting Professor Barnas Sears heard about Oncken, and when he went to Germany on a study leave, he sought out and baptized Oncken, his wife, and five others in 1834, forming the first Baptist church in Hamburg and the oldest surviving Baptist church in Germany.[27] Carey influenced the formation of the

---

[26] Wiliam H. Brackney, *The Baptists* (Westport CT: Praeger Publishers, 1988) 14–15; Leon McBeth, *Women in Baptist Life* (Nashville: Broadman Press, 1979) 81–82.

[27] McBeth, *Baptist Heritage*, 471–72; McBeth, *A Sourcebook*, 347.

GMC, which in turn provided spiritual and financial support for Oncken's work in Germany.

William Carey had a powerful influence on the course of missions and on the lives of Indians. The East India Company's charter came up for renewal in 1813 and encountered obstacles in the House of Commons as a result of Carey. From India, he stimulated a letter-writing campaign in which some 1,000,000 letters went to members of Parliament supporting proposed changes in the company's charter that favored missionaries. When the issue came up in the House of Commons, the restrictive measures relating to missionaries were stricken down by a two-to-one vote. Carey made it possible for missionaries to work in India without fear of deportation or governmental persecution.

William Carey showed his love and concern for the peoples of India by what he did as well as by what he preached. One cultural practice that sickened Carey, and that he helped to end, was *sati*—the act of a widow being burnt to death in her husband's funeral pyre. Carey witnessed his first *sati* in Mudnabati in 1799, and he immediately began his work to end the practice. By writing letters and speaking with government officials, Carey kept the issue on the minds of people. When Lord William Bentinck became governor general of British India in 1828, he outlawed *sati* and honored William Carey by commissioning him to translate the order into Bengali and publish it quickly. Carey received the commission on a Sunday and dismissed church, saying, "If I delay an hour to translate and publish this, many a widow's life may be sacrificed."[28] William Carey left a legacy of active social and spiritual concern and established missionary methods for generations.

It is difficult to measure Carey's influence on missions. With his friends Ward and Marshman, the Serampore trio, he established the way missions would be done for generations. Through his correspondence, Carey enlisted the imagination and support of Baptists in Europe and America. He worked hard to identify and train indigenous leaders so the church would be truly theirs. He founded educational and medical facilities to enhance the physical lives of the people, and he started churches and preaching points to deal with their spiritual well-being. He worked hard to understand and appreciate the culture of India. With his translation work, he pioneered a vital function of contemporary missions. Carey persevered in the more traditional forms of gospel proclamation, but his greatness lies in the importance he placed on

---

[28] Beck, *Dorothy Carey*, 170–71; Alban, Woods, and Daigle-Williamson, "The Writings of William Carey," 87–108; Royer, "William Carey."

biblical translation and the publication of religious literature to help support the indigenous church. McBeth was doubtless correct when he noted that William Carey "ranks as one of the most versatile and effective Christian missionaries of all the ages."[29]

Suggested Reading

"A Baptist Page Portrait: William Carey." *The Baptist Page.* http://www.siteone.com/religion/baptist/baptistpage/Portraits/print/print_Care y.html.

Beck, James R. *Dorothy Carey: The Tragic and Untold Story of Mrs. William Carey.* Grand Rapids MI: Baker Book House, 1992.

McBeth, Leon. *Men Who Made Missions.* Nashville TN: Broadman Press, 1968.

Royer, Galen B. *William Carey: The Father of Modern Missions.* http://www.wholesomewords.org/missions/bcarey3.html.

Tucker, Ruth A. *From Jerusalem to Irian Jaya.* Grand Rapids MI: Academie Books, 1983.

---

[29] McBeth, *Men Who Made Missions*, 72.

CHAPTER 10

Baptist Missions and the Turn toward National Denominational Organizations: The Baptist Missionary Society and the Triennial Convention: 1792/1812

Carol Crawford Holcomb

The Founding of the Baptist Missionary Society

On the morning of 2 October 1792 a small group of men from the Northamptonshire Baptist Association gathered in the back parlor of Mrs. Martha Wallace's home in Kettering, England for a business meeting. Their ears were still ringing with the force of the words proclaimed in a sermon by a young pastor the night before. The preacher had declared, "Expect great things. Attempt great things." With these words William Carey had presented the ministers with an astounding challenge. He insisted that Christians were obligated to share the gospel with the entire world.

In spite of Carey's powerful words, no one attending the next morning's session would venture to make a motion concerning world missions. As the meeting was about to adjourn, Carey reached for the hand of the moderator, Andrew Fuller, and tugged in desperation. "Oh sir," Carey cried, "is nothing to be done? Is nothing again to be done?"[1] The final plea rallied the group into action. Thirteen pledged to support the Particular Baptist Society for Propagating the Gospel among the Heathen, commonly referred to as the Baptist Missionary Society (BMS). This first modern society for foreign

---

[1] Leon H. McBeth, *The Baptist Heritage: Four Centuries of Baptist Witness* (Nashville: Broadman Press, 1987) 185.

missions served as a major turning point in Baptist life. "On that day," quipped one historian, "Baptists were leading the whole Church of Christ."[2]

The events that led to this business meeting in 1792 have their roots in a spiritual awakening that began over fifty years before. The First Great Awakening, swept along by the preaching of John Wesley and the hymns of Charles Wesley, proclaimed the message of salvation by grace to a new generation. The revival that flowed from the preaching of the Wesleys invigorated and restored the branch of Baptists known as General Baptists or Arminians due to their belief that Christ died for all people. Because they placed a stronger emphasis on free will, the Wesleys' preaching dovetailed with the theology of the General Baptists. The infusion of Wesleyan theology from the revivals strengthened their flagging churches and gave rise to a "New Connection" of General Baptists in 1770.

Yet even as the revival strengthened the Arminian wing of English Baptists, it placed the more Calvinistic "Particular" Baptists on the defensive, compelling them to cling more fiercely to the doctrines of election and predestination. Many of these Particular Baptists became convinced that the divine decree of election and damnation occurred before the creation and before the fall of humanity. Therefore, they concluded that since Christ died only to redeem those whom God had previously chosen, then preaching to sinners was useless. Baptist preachers such as John Skepp and John Brine practiced this "non-invitation, non-application scheme." [3] Basically, these ministers dedicated themselves to teaching doctrine to the elect and encouraging the non-elect to behave until the Lord returned. One of London's most influential pastors, John Gill, believed that it made no sense to issue "Gospel invitations" to the non-elect.[4] "Evangelism," as one historian pointed out, "was not so much forgotten as ruled out of court as an attempt to usurp God's prerogative of salvation."[5] Leon McBeth insists that this system "brought the kiss of death to the Particular Baptists."[6] The churches—in decline and drained of evangelistic fervor—soon fell into a "winter of hyper-Calvinism."[7]

---

[2] A. C. Underwood, *A History of the English Baptists* (London: Carey Kingsgate Press, 1961) 165.

[3] Underwood, *A History*, 133–34.

[4] McBeth, *Baptist Heritage*, 177.

[5] Brian Stanley, *The History of the Baptist Missionary Society, 1792–1992* (Edinburgh: T&T Clark, 1992) 3.

[6] McBeth, *Baptist Heritage*, 178.

[7] Underwood, *A History*, 160.

The first visible signs of a thaw appeared in 1770 when the Northamptonshire Baptist Association sent a letter to the member churches that said, "Every soul that comes to Christ to be saved...is to be encouraged." In that same association a few years later, Robert Hall Sr. preached a sermon characterizing hyper-Calvinism as a "stumbling block" that hindered sinners from coming to Jesus.[8] Hall's sermon was so popular that he later expanded it into a lengthier work called *Help to Zion's Travellers*. The sermon had the "effect of a bombshell" upon the churches of the Midlands—shaking the foundations of hyper-Calvinism.[9]

In 1784 a young Particular Baptist pastor in Northampton, John Ryland Jr., opened a parcel of books sent to him by a friend. In these books he discovered a little pamphlet by the New England theologian Jonathan Edwards. Ryland found hope for revival in the words of the American pastor. Edwards balanced his Calvinism with a fervent evangelical spirit and allowed room for human responsibility. Ryland shared the ideas he found with his circle of friends in Northamptonshire, including John Sutcliff and Andrew Fuller. The enthusiasm of these young ministers soon began to shape their Baptist association as they called the churches of the Midlands to pray for a "revival of religion."[10]

When Andrew Fuller's well reasoned rebuttal to hyper-Calvinism appeared in 1785, it dealt the system a "mortal blow." Fuller went after hyper-Calvinism, claimed one historian, with a "terrier-like tenacity." He sank his teeth into his opponent's argument and "shook it to death."[11] Fuller's treatise, *The Gospel Worthy of All Acceptation*, presented a twofold argument. First, sinners are capable of responding to the gospel. He explained that:

> No one in his senses would think of calling the blind to look, the deaf to hear, or the dead to rise up and walk; and of threatening them with punishment in case of their refusal. But if the blindness arise from the love of darkness rather than light; if the deafness resemble that of the adder which stoppeth the ear, ...and if the death consist in

---

[8] Underwood, *A History*, 160.
[9] McBeth, *Baptist Heritage*, 180.
[10] Stanley, *Baptist Missionary Society*, 3–4.
[11] Underwood, *A History*, 166.

alienation of heart from God and the absence of all desire after him, there is no absurdity or cruelty in such addresses.[12]

Secondly, Fuller castigated his fellow ministers for having "lost the spirit of the primitive preachers" and warned them that they neglected preaching the gospel to their own peril.[13] By refocusing the Particular Baptists on their obligation to call sinners to repent, Fuller helped restore the balance between God's sovereignty and human responsibility. Furthermore, Fuller's theology tilled the soil for the missionary zeal of his dear friend William Carey.

On 5 October 1783 John Ryland Jr. wrote in his journal, "Baptized today poor journeyman shoe cobbler."[14] The "poor" cobbler was named William Carey. Carey had been raised in the Anglican tradition, but he began attending Bible studies with Dissenters as a teenager. In 1779 Carey had become convicted that he must identify himself fully as a Dissenter. Over time Carey's views fell in line with the Particular Baptists and he submitted himself to baptism by immersion. His spiritual journey pulled him into a circle of committed young Baptist ministers who had been praying with their churches for revival since June of the previous year. After Ryland baptized Carey, John Sutcliff recommended him for his first pastorate, and Andrew Fuller became his life-long supporter.[15]

Not long after his baptism, Carey began preaching bivocationally and studying biblical languages. Although he was a determined student and a gifted linguist, Carey never proved to be a particularly talented preacher. His physical characteristics did little to recommend him to a congregation. "Slight of stature, prematurely balding, and wearing an ill-fitting red wig," Carey presented a "distinctly unimpressive personal appearance."[16] In fact, his preaching was received so poorly by his congregation that they at first refused to ordain him. In spite of these setbacks, Carey persevered.

During his early ministry Carey encountered Robert Hall's *Help to Zion's Travellers*. Carey later commented, "I do not remember to have read any book

---

[12] Andrew Fuller, "The Gospel Worthy of All Acception," in *Baptist Roots: A Reader in the Theology of a Christian People*, ed. Curtis W. Freeman, James Wm. McClendon Jr., and C. Rosalee Velloso da Silva (Valley Forge: Judson Press, 1999) 146.

[13] Fuller, *Baptist Roots*, 147.

[14] McBeth, *Baptist Heritage*, 184.

[15] Stanley, *Baptist Missionary Society*, 7–8 passim.

[16] McBeth, *Baptist Heritage*, 184.

with such raptures."[17] The tales of Captain James Cook's voyages to the South Seas stirred his imagination. Though his students may have benefited little from his geography lessons, Carey's vision profited enormously as he contemplated the vast regions of the globe that had never received the gospel. The passion for world conversion "welled up in Carey's soul" and became the central focus of his life.[18]

In 1788 Carey met with his friends Fuller, Sutcliff, and Ryland at the latter's home in Northampton. Carey urged his more established colleagues to publish pamphlets asserting that "something should be done for the heathen." The older three agreed that Carey should write instead. So he poured his heart into a little book called *An Enquiry into the Obligations of Christians to Use Means for the Conversion of the Heathen*. In this work Carey detailed his conviction that Christians were commanded to take the gospel to all the nations. Furthermore, the failure of believers to act upon this command rested not in their *impotence* but in their *disobedience*—a willful act of negligence. After tracing the history of missions and sketching a portrait of the world's geography and population, Carey enjoined Christians to join him in "fervent and united prayer." "We must not be contented however with praying," concluded Carey, "without exerting ourselves in the use of means for the obtaining of those things we pray for."[19] For any who lacked the imagination to enumerate the means, Carey outlined how Christians might establish a society to send missionaries around the world.

When the ministers of the Northamptonshire Baptist Association gathered again in 1791, Carey urged them to form a society. By this time, most of the ministers present were "sympathetic in principle" to Carey's proposal.[20] But the enormity of what he was suggesting gave them pause. Sutcliff, in particular, counseled them to proceed with caution. Another year passed. In 1792 Carey preached the associational sermon. His text was Isaiah 54:2–3: "Enlarge the place of your tent, stretch your tent curtains wide, do not hold back; lengthen your cords, strengthen your stakes." His message had two points: Expect great things and attempt great things. These incisive words represented more than a single inspiring sermon; they were the culmination of seven years of unwavering, dogged, perseverance on the part of William Carey. The men

---

[17] Underwood, *A History*, 161.
[18] McBeth, *Baptist Heritage*, 185.
[19] William Carey, *An Enquiry*, in *A Sourcebook for Baptist Heritage*, ed. Leon McBeth (Nashville: Broadman Press, 1990) 137.
[20] Stanley, *Baptist Missionary Society*, 10.

brought seven years of reflection and discussion with them to the business meeting the next morning. Ultimately it was not impulse or emotion, but long deliberation and reasoned persuasion that undergirded the formation of the Baptist Missionary Society (BMS).

The BMS chose Andrew Fuller to serve as the first secretary of the society, a post he held until his death. The society became aware of a doctor named John Thomas who had experience working in India and who wished to return. After a discussion of his theology, the BMS appointed Thomas as their first missionary and William Carey as the second.[21]

The pain of leaving family, friends, nation, and culture was exacerbated by financial difficulties. Thomas proved to be an impulsive and erratic personality. He "squandered" an entire year's stipend in the first few weeks on the field. Andrew Fuller commented that Thomas "seldom walked an even path." He vacillated between despair and hope. "His sorrows bordered on the tragical," observed Fuller, "and his joys on the ecstatic."[22] The crushing poverty, culture shock, and uncertainty took its toll on Dorothy Carey and after five-year-old Peter died from dysentery, she never recovered. She fell into a "debilitating depression" and spent the next thirteen years of her life confined to her home.[23]

The family tragedies and financial troubles convinced Carey that they should establish a mission based on the Moravian pattern, basically a free standing commune where missionary families would live according to a common rule. The arrival of William Ward in 1798 and Joshua Marshman the following year brought new resources and talents to the mission enterprise. Ward, a printer by profession, helped Carey place his translations of the scriptures into the hands of the people. Marshman's training as an educator would bear fruit in the development of an extensive educational program from primary schools to a missionary training institution called Serampore College.

---

[21] Carey hurried home to inform his wife, Dorothy, who was pregnant with their sixth child, that they were moving across the world. She refused at first. Carey took their oldest son, Felix, and boarded a ship bound for India. The ship experienced some difficulties that delayed the voyage for six weeks. During the interim, Dorothy had a change of heart. So, on 13 June 1793, Dorothy joined William aboard ship along with their four boys, Felix, William, Peter, and baby Jabez (for further discussion, see chap. 9). The Careys lost their firstborn, Ann, to a fever when she was two. Their second girl, Lucy, died before her second birthday.

[22] Fuller quoted in F. A. Cox, *History of the Baptist Missionary Society from 1792 to 1842*, 1 (London: T. Ward & Co., 1842) 73.

[23] McBeth, *Baptist Heritage*, 186.

Meanwhile Carey continued his most important contribution to the mission: Bible translation. In his forty years in India, Carey translated the scriptures into Bengali and provided linguistic aids for the Mahratta, Sanskrit, Telinga, Punjab, and the Bhotanta languges. One historian noted that Carey translated the scriptures for "one third of the world's population."[24] This great triumvirate of Baptist missionaries—Carey, Ward, and Marshman—shaped the Baptist mission in India and blazed the trail for a generation of missionaries who would follow them.

The founding of the BMS marked a major turning point not only for Baptists, but also for the history of Protestant missions. Carey's *Enquiry* combined with his letters from India stimulated the growth of a host of voluntary missionary societies. Congregationalist leaders formed the London Missionary Society in 1795. Anglican clergy organized the Church Missionary Society in 1799. These were followed by the Wesleyan Methodist Missionary Society, the mission boards of the Church of Scotland, and many others. Voluntary societies began sending European missionaries into "heathen lands" in tandem with the forces of imperialism that were beginning to restructure global politics. By the end of the nineteenth century the Protestant missionary movement transmitted the Christian religion to a "greater area of the world's surface than had taken place in all the preceding Christian centuries put together."[25] Consequently, when William Carey's ship dropped anchor off the coast of Calcutta in 1793, a new chapter opened, "not just in Christian history, but in the history of the relations between the Western and non-Western world."[26]

The Origins of the Triennial Convention

As British Baptists were organizing a society for world missions, Baptists in America were celebrating the ratification of the Bill of Rights. When William Carey set sail for India there were roughly fifty Baptist associations cooperating together in the United States, but no national organization. The emergence of the first national organization for Baptist work, the Triennial Convention, proved to be the major turning point for American Baptists in the first third of the nineteenth century.

---

[24] Brackney, *The Baptists*, 141.

[25] A. Dakin, *William Carey: Shoemaker, Linguist, Missionary* (Nashville: Broadman Press, 1942) 9.

[26] Stanley, *Baptist Missionary Society*, 1–2.

The importance of the development of the Triennial Convention cannot be exaggerated. At the turn of the nineteenth century Baptists in America were a common-folk frontier religion, suspicious of elitism and institutions. Even the best educated Baptist clergy expressed concern over "prepared" sermons and insisted that real preaching should be extemporaneous, spirit-led, and passionate. "Delivery without notes," said Francis Wayland, "was alone called preaching." If a minister used a manuscript, "it was called merely *reading*."[27]

In 1792 with the ink on their guarantee of religious liberty barely dry, Baptists were leery of institutions and denominational control. A profound individualism born out of their struggle for religious liberty—their desire to be free to worship God according to the dictates of their own consciences—made Baptists an unwieldy lot. Therefore, it is remarkable that this fiercely independent group of believers could have been compelled to cooperate at all. However, there were threads of unity. Revival fires that swept across the country before and after the American Revolution were stoked and tended by the Baptists. Revivalism helped create a common commitment to Christian experience, regeneration, and evangelism. The struggle for liberty both religious and political sparked a denominational consciousness. Thus, the successes of the battles for religious liberty, the bonds forged in military victories, and the afterglow of revival left Baptists ripe for the growth of missionary efforts.

About this time, reports began to circulate among Baptists in America of the thrilling work that Carey had undertaken to "convert the heathen." David Benedict wrote that churches received frequent reports "of the successful operations of our British brethren in India under Carey, Marshman, Ward and others." These reports "excited a generous sympathy among our brethren...which led them to make liberal collections for that age."[28] Support for the cause of foreign missions grew with each subsequent letter received from Carey. Meanwhile, the crest of a great new wave of revivals was about to break on American soil.

The first stirrings of a Second Awakening began in New England in the 1790s. Unlike the First Great Awakening, the colleges of New England played a central role in the progress of the Second Awakening. Timothy Dwight, the grandson of Jonathan Edwards and president of Yale, sparked a revival at that

---

[27] Francis Wayland, *Notes on the Principles and Practices of Baptist Churches* (Boston: Gould and Lincoln, 1856) 24.

[28] Benedict, *Fifty Years*, 112.

university with his determined defense of the gospel. When the revivals swept through Yale in 1801, a third of the students professed conversion. Soon the revival spread across New England fostering a sober spirit of devotion and moral reform.

On a sultry August afternoon in 1806 in a maple grove near the campus of Williams College in Massachusetts, a group of Congregationalist students gathered for prayer. Just as a freshmen named Samuel Mills was about to convene the meeting, torrential rains began to pour from the dark clouds above. Five young men sought shelter underneath the sheaves of a haystack and continued to pray. Protected by the roof of hay, these five all committed themselves to take the gospel to a "dark and heathen" land. Many historians identify this legendary "Haystack Prayer Meeting" as the birth of the foreign mission movement in America.[29]

After graduating from Williams College, Samuel Mills continued his education at Andover, a Congregational seminary in Massachusetts. There he was introduced to two other men passionate about missions, Adoniram Judson and Luther Rice. All three of the men were dedicated to serving as foreign missionaries. But there was a major obstacle to their goal. No foreign mission society or sending agency existed in America at the time. The students began to seek counsel from older ministers, and then finally they drafted an appeal to the governing body of their denomination. Judson read the appeal to the General Association of the Commonwealth and named the students who were offering themselves as foreign missionaries. The appeal was met with great emotion "as tears began to roll down the faces of the people in the audience." Some spectators "covered their faces with their hands and sobbed."[30] The next day, 29 June 1810, the convention established the American Board of Commissioners for Foreign Missions, the first foreign mission board in the United States.

One evening during the convention, Judson had supper in the home of a prominent deacon named John Hasseltine. Judson's biographer insists that he was "struck dumb" by the sight of the deacon's youngest daughter, a "beautiful creature" with "jet-black curls, clear olive complexion and dark, lustrous eyes." Ann Judson, whom people usually called Nancy, was not as immediately impressed by the visitor whom she deemed "a little too short and slight" with a

---

[29] McBeth, *Baptist Heritage*, 344. See also Courtney Anderson, *To the Golden Shore: The Life of Adoniram Judson* (Valley Forge: Judson Press, 1987) 61–62.

[30] Anderson, *To the Golden Shore*, 70.

nose that was "somewhat too prominent." [31] However, Judson apparently wooed her to a more favorable view and they were married on 5 February 1812. A few days later, Judson, Rice and three others were ordained as foreign missionaries. As the men knelt to be commissioned, Nancy slipped from her pew and knelt not far from them, publicly demonstrating that she too felt called to the service of foreign missions.

Because of the conflicts of the War of 1812 and the potential natural hazards of sea travel, the missionaries set sail on separate ships for India where they planned to meet William Carey. Knowing that they would be meeting with Baptists, the Judsons used the many idle hours aboard ship to study baptism in their Greek New Testaments. To their dismay, they could find in the Bible no record of the form of baptism they had been taught from infancy in the Congregational Church. They continued their studies in Carey's library after they arrived in India. Nancy commented in her journal, "I...must acknowledge that the face of Scripture does favour Baptist sentiments. I intend to persevere in examining the subject, and hope that I shall be disposed to embrace the truth, whatever it may be."[32] Within a few days after arriving at the Serampore mission, Adoniram was convinced. Nancy struggled a bit longer, but finally agreed with him. They crafted a letter to Serampore insisting that "the immersion of a professing believer is the only Christian baptism" and requesting baptism by immersion from the British Baptist missionaries.[33] When Luther Rice arrived he vigorously attempted to draw the Judsons into a debate on the matter. Adoniram refused to engage him and merely directed him to study the scriptures for himself. About a month after the Judsons were baptized, Rice confessed that he too had become convinced that the Baptists were correct in the matter. On 1 November 1812 Luther Rice followed the Judsons in baptism, giving American Baptists three missionaries on a foreign field before the first mission board was ever formed.

The first challenge these three fledgling Baptists faced was procuring financial support. Honor prohibited them from continuing to seek aid from their Congregationalist investors. The three decided that Adoniram and Nancy must press on to establish a mission while Rice headed back to America to rally the Baptists to their cause. After numerous conflicts with the East India Company, the Judsons finally managed to settle in Burma, a terrifyingly hostile

---

[31] Ibid., 72.
[32] Ibid., 144.
[33] McBeth, *Sourcebook*, 206.

land with despotic local governors known for proscribing harsh, cruel punishments for any that defied them. On the last leg of the journey to this dangerous new land, Nancy gave birth to a stillborn child—without a nurse, doctor, or even another woman to aid her. Nancy's first sight of Burma was from a stretcher as she was carried ashore, still exhausted from labor and grief.

Rice returned by the first possible ship to America. With eloquence and vision, he quickly began to rally the Baptists with the news of the Judsons' work. Existing missionary societies expressed interest in supporting the mission and Rice persuaded still others to organize. In a day before railroads with few steamboats and when stagecoaches were expensive, Rice "generally traveled in his own one-horse light conveyance and he often astonished his brethren with the rapidity of his movements and the suddenness of his transitions from one place to another."[34] By 1813 he identified seventeen local and regional societies willing to "hold the ropes" for the Judsons. But Rice had greater plans for the Baptists than loosely organized societies. "The plan which suggested itself to my mind," wrote Rice, was to form "one principal society in each state, bearing the name of the state." Furthermore, he envisioned that "by these large or state societies, delegates be appointed to form one general society."[35] On 18 May 1814 the vision of Rice came to fruition with the establishment of the General Missionary Convention of the Baptist Denomination in the United States for Foreign Missions, commonly referred to as the Triennial Convention. The convention elected Richard Furman of Charleston president and William Staughton of Philadelphia corresponding secretary. Rice's basic purpose in returning to America was thus accomplished. Baptists now had a united organization to support missionaries overseas.

Meanwhile in Burma, Nancy and Adoniram Judson had established a permanent mission. For the first two years Adoniram labored to master the Burmese language and began writing tracts to share the gospel. Seven years passed before a single convert professed faith in Christ. During a military conflict between the British and the Burmese, Adoniram was imprisoned. Though nursing a newborn baby, Nancy struggled to take food and supplies to the prisoners. Tragically, the effort ruined her health. Nancy died in 1826 and the baby died soon after. Her death sent shockwaves of grief throughout Protestant circles. The name of Ann Judson, her formal name, became a synonym for faith and sacrifice in the cause of missions.

---

[34] Benedict, *Fifty Years*, 116.
[35] McBeth, *Baptist Heritage*, 346.

In 1834 Judson published his first edition of the Burmese Bible. This edition was followed by numerous other books in Burmese. Repeatedly Judson wrote to Luther Rice urging him to return to Burma. However, the officers of the Triennial Convention insisted Rice remain in the United States to continue his efforts on behalf of the mission.[36]

Rice also believed more needed to be done. If Baptists were going to commission missionaries, then they needed to be able to train missionaries sufficiently. He wrote to Adoniram Judson that it had become "obvious that a Theological Institution was indispensably necessary."[37] So, Rice hastily purchased a piece of land in Washington, DC, for a college, began raising money for a building, and then persuaded the Triennial Convention to expand its mission to include support of theological education. With foreign missions secure and theological education underway, the indefatigable Rice soon began to develop a strategy for reaching the Missouri Territory. On one of his many tours around the country in June 1815, Rice stayed in the home of John Mason Peck. The two men stayed up most of the night dreaming of the possibilities for home missions. At Rice's urging, Peck petitioned the Triennial Convention for appointment as a home missionary and was commissioned in May 1817.

In 1818 the Triennial Convention launched its first paper, *The Latter Day Luminary*. This publishing venture allowed the convention to promote missions and education among Baptists and soon had a circulation of about 8,000 copies per month. Thus, in the span of three years under the influence of Luther Rice, Baptists in America had progressed from virtually no organization to supporting a national organization with major investments in foreign missions, home missions, theological education, and publications. Benedict remarked that "Mr. Rice, in a few years after he commenced his agency for the foreign cause, had his hands full of appendages to his main employment."[38]

But the blitz of institutional development came with a cost. For all of his vision, vigor, and charisma, Rice had very few administrative skills. His bookkeeping skills were poor and he was apparently tardy in fulfilling his contracts. "All parts of Mr. Rice's complicated machinery seemed to work well," commented one historian wryly, "until an empty treasury stared the whole denomination in the face."[39] The New England managers became frustrated

---

[36] William Brackney, *The Baptists* (Westport CT: Greenwood Press, 1988) 203–204.
[37] Luther Rice in McBeth, *Sourcebook*, 212.
[38] Benedict, *Fifty Years*, 118.
[39] Ibid., 119–20.

with Rice's erratic management style and his propensity for committing the board to projects without their permission. In 1826 the board launched a formal inquiry into Rice's behavior. The report found "nothing affecting the moral character of Mr. Rice," nor did they find any hint of "corruption" or "selfish design." However, they did charge Rice with being generally "imprudent" and "too loose in all his dealings."[40] Even though the report essentially exonerated Rice from any wrongdoing, the inquiry damaged Rice's reputation and his influence on the denomination continued to diminish.

In the same year the convention leadership investigated Rice, they embarked on a dramatic downsizing program, casting off every commitment save foreign missions. The move shifted the basic character of the Triennial Convention. It had been born as a society for foreign missions, then ballooned into a full convention with multiple ministry goals, and finally returned to a society with a sole focus on foreign missions—all within a span of twelve years. The other interests, released from the orbit of the convention, spun off to become independent societies for home missions, publications, and education.

The passion for missions dragged American Baptists into the depths of denominational organization, perhaps before they were fully prepared to swim. The growing pains suffered by the Triennial Convention resulted from the frenetic pace of institutional development. In the ensuing years Baptists would struggle with cognitive dissonance as they attempted to harmonize their need for a unified organization with their suspicion of hierarchy. Whether or not they were ready, when this fiercely independent, unwieldy group of Baptists inherited a devoted cast of missionaries in Burma, they responded with a national organization to meet their needs with remarkable speed. Thus, the birth of the Triennial Convention marks a pivotal turning point for Baptists because it catapulted them from the rural margins of American religion into the mainstream of the "Great Century" of world missions.

Suggested Reading

Anderson, Courtney. *To the Golden Shore: The Life of Adoniram Judson*. Boston: Little, Brown, 1956.

Babcock, Rufus. *A Discourse Commemorative of the Life and Labors of the Rev. Adoniram Judson*. New York: E. H. Fletcher, 1851.

---

[40] "Committee on the Conduct of Mr. Rice," in McBeth, *Sourcebook*, 213–14.

Brumberg, Joan J. *Mission for Life: The Story of the Family of Adoniram Judson, the Dramatic Events of the First American Foreign Mission, and the Course of Evangelical Religion in the Nineteenth Century.* New York: Free Press, 1980.

Brackney, William H. "The Legacy of Adoniram Judson." *International Bulletin of Missionary Research* (22 July 1998): 122–27.

Carter, Terry G., editor. *The Journal and Selected Letters of William Carey.* Macon GA: Smyth & Helwys Publishing, 2000.

Drewery, Mary. *William Carey: Shoemaker and Missionary.* London: Hodder and Stoughton, 1978.

George, Timothy. *Faithful Witness: The Life and Mission of William Carey.* Birmingham: New Hope Publishers, 1991.

Potts, E. Daniel. *British Baptist Missionaries in India, 1793–1837: The History of Serampore and Its Missions.* Cambridge: Cambridge University Press, 1967.

William Carey. *Christian History and Biography*, volume 11, number 4, issue 36 (November 1992).

CHAPTER 11

Baptists Turn toward Education: 1764

William H. Brackney

The Baptist pilgrimage in higher education has been an impressive struggle against the odds of an unlearned ministry, too many experiments for a fledgling denominational tradition, and inadequate financial resources. Yet, overall the Baptist accomplishment is without question and worthy of comment. There are five critical points, including the establishment of the College of Rhode Island, the beginning of Newton Theological Institution, the creation of Spurgeon's Preacher's College, the establishment of the University of Chicago, and the conservative/evangelical resurgence at Southern Baptist Seminary. In this chapter we will look at each as a turning point in the history of the denomination.[1]

Brown: The First Institution

As numerous historical accounts have already demonstrated the roots of the College of Rhode Island in 1764 are variegated. One might point to the tradition that Edward Terrill established in 1679 at Bristol, England, where for the first time in Baptist history funds were set aside for the education of ministers of the gospel. This led to a mentoring program at Broadmead Baptist Church in the city of Bristol and eventually to the establishment of Bristol Baptist Academy and Bristol Baptist Education Society.[2] From this strong taproot came a succession of able pastors and missionaries who influenced the

---

[1] Much of this material was originally presented as the 2006 Derwood Deere Memorial Lectures at Golden Gate Baptist Theological Seminary.

[2] The Bristol story is covered in Norman S. Moon, *Education for Ministry: Bristol Baptist College 1679–1979* (Bristol: Bristol Baptist College, 1979) 1–9. The shadow that the college cast is the subject of Roger Hayden, "The Contribution of Bernard Foskett," in *Pilgrim Pathways: Essays in Baptist History in Honour of B.R. White*, ed. William H. Brackney and Paul S. Fiddes (Macon GA: Mercer University Press, 1999) 189–206.

enlarging Baptist tradition worldwide. Surely a second root was to be found in the grammar school that Isaac Eaton established at Hopewell, New Jersey, in 1756. Eaton was ahead of his time among Baptists, but he was following a clear direction set by William and Gilbert Tennent of Great Awakening fame in the Middle Colonies. From Eaton's school came, among others, James Manning, who would lead the College of Rhode Island as its first president.[3] One must also note the indirect influence upon the Baptists of other Protestant denominations in establishing their schools, again largely for the training of clergy in the colonies.[4]

The College of Rhode Island was from its outset a Baptist institution in the best sense of the words. It was sponsored by the oldest association of Baptists in continual existence in the colonies, the Philadelphia Association, and it carried the local approbation of the prominent Baptists of the colony of Rhode Island, like Governor Daniel Jenckes and the Brown family. Its charter was secured with the assistance of Congregationalists and Seventh Day Baptists and its governance was as cooperative as the Baptists of that era were egalitarian.[6]

Moreover, under the wise tutelage of James Manning who had been shaped by the classical tradition at the College of New Jersey (later Princeton), Manning was a professional pastor who led the congregations at Warren, and

---

[3] Samuel Jones, David Jones, Hezekiah Smith, and Isaac Skillman were all standout pastors in the Philadelphia Association.

[4] Harvard (Congregationalist/Massachusetts), Yale (Congregationalist/Connecticut), Dartmouth (Congregationalist/New Hampshire), Kings (Church of England/New York), Princeton (Presbyterian/New Jersey), Queens (Reformed Church/New York, New Jersey), William and Mary (Church of England/Virginia), St. Johns (Church of England/Maryland), and Pennsylvania (Church of England/Pennsylvania). In the Academy of Philadelphia, later the University of Pennsylvania, it was the indirect link with George Whitefield, an erstwhile Anglican priest under partial support from the Society for the Propagation of the Gospel that gave some denominational flavor to the school. The school actually served several Christian traditions through its open admission policy.

[5] In the Academy of Philadelphia, later the University of Pennsylvania, it was the indirect link with George Whitefield, an erstwhile Anglican priest under partial support from the Society for the Propagation of the Gospel that gave some denominational flavor to the school. The school actually served several Christian traditions through its open admission policy.

[6] See Reuben Aldridge Guild, *The Early History of Brown University Including the Life, Times and Correspondence of President Manning 1756–1791* (Providence: Snow and Farnham, 1896) 534.

later, at Providence, Rhode Island. He was a classicist himself (fluent in the languages) and mentored several generations of Baptist leaders, both lay and clergy. What he established in the college was ratified in 1804 by a generous gift from the Nicholas Brown family of Providence and the institution evolved across the nineteenth century as Brown University.

Brown's great value to the Baptists was that it signaled that a hole-in-the-wall sect had serious designs upon becoming a permanent and leading part of the American religious landscape. It presidents were a distinguished lot: Jonathan Maxcy, Asa Messer, Francis Wayland, Barnas Sears, Alexis Caswell, E. B. Andrews, Ezekiel G. Robinson, and finally William H. P. Faunce.[7] Faunce was, sadly, the last president of Brown as a denominationally connected school. In 1922 he sought to sever ties with the Northern Baptist Educational Board over his desire to protect Brown's charter rights to be free of ecclesiastical interference and potential control. In addition to having an impact upon the later Baptist colleges, Brown's presidents had a profound influence upon curricular developments in American higher education, the development of philanthropic agencies, and the cause of religious liberty.

Newton: The First Post-Graduate Theological Seminary

If the establishment of Brown signaled a serious intent to build a learned ministry and make a contribution to the intellectual life of a new nation, the beginnings of Newton Theological Institution were likewise of inestimable importance to Baptists. Once again, Newton was not a fresh beginning, but an important turning point for the denomination. Its parent, Andover Theological Seminary, is well-acclaimed as a new departure among theological faculties in the United States. Established in 1807, Andover is always seen as a reaction to Harvard on theological matters, particularly the Unitarian stance of the older divinity professors. Andover was founded to be Trinitarian in perpetuity and accountable to its church constituency. It was also a freestanding theological seminary, unattached to a college or university, and thus the precursor to all

---

[7] Maxcy, who was awarded an honorary degree from Harvard in 1801, had a second career in the South where he helped to found South Carolina College and was well-known in the Baptist community in that state; Caswell was a key figure at Columbian College in Washington, DC, in establishing the Baptist movement in Nova Scotia and charting the direction of Newton Theological Institution; Robinson was associated with Western, Rochester, and Chicago theological schools, and Wayland is considered one of the pioneers of higher education in the US as well as authoring the principal textbook of the era for college students on moral philosophy.

graduate, professional theological schools.[8] In the decade or so of Andover's history it marked a new course in the training of ministers and in 1825 Baptists in the greater Boston region sought to imitate it. In the prosperous community of Newton Centre they established a post-undergraduate theological seminary of their own. Its curriculum imitated Andover's, and some of the professors lectured at each school, notably Moses Stuart, the biblical theologian. The Baptist pastors behind the founding of Newton had already marshaled their support in favor of voluntary societies for mission and education as well as producing a national periodical of wide popularity, the *Massachusetts Baptist Missionary Magazine*.

Under the direction of the Rev. Irah Chase, Newton Theological Institution became the training ground for a new breed of pastors, urbane in outlook, schooled in the contemporary categories of biblical studies, ecclesiastical history, systematic theology, and homiletics.[9] Newton's graduates were soon found in all sections of the United States and its elite were selected to lead both colleges and seminaries around the Baptist world. Eventually, the prevailing pattern for Baptist theological education came to be the underpinning of a bachelor's degree, followed by a degree or diploma from a recognized theological seminary. Sometimes referred to as the "New England Pattern,"[10] this was Newton's gift to the Baptist community, and its influence was soon realized at Western Baptist Theological Institute, Southern Baptist Theological Seminary, Rochester Theological Seminary, and Crozer Theological Seminary.

As we shall note in a succeeding discussion of turning points in Baptist theology, Newton reconnected with its early New England roots at Andover and entered into an affiliative arrangement in 1930–1931 that led eventually to a merger of what became Andover Newton Theological School in 1965. Situated on the historic Baptist hill outside Newton Centre, Andover Newton

---

[8] On Andover's development, see Daniel Day Williams, *The Andover Liberals: A Study in American Theology* (New York: Octagon Books, 1970).

[9] Chase was a graduate of Middlebury College in Vermont. He joined William Staughton's Theological School in Philadelphia and moved with Staughton to become an inaugural faculty member at Columbian College in Washington DC. In becoming the head faculty member at Newton in 1825, Chase was an incalculable loss to Columbian.

[10] See Howard Williams, *History of Colgate University 1819–1969* (New York: Van Nostrand, 1969). Williams notes the differentiation in Colgate's model (that of a mixed literary and theological institution) from the New England region where colleges were more numerous than on the frontier.

followed a direction of liberal theology in the Reformed tradition among American Baptist theological schools. To its credit academically, it was a founding partner in the Boston Theological Institute that included several denominations and Harvard Divinity School and Boston University School of Theology.

Spurgeon's: An Alternative Pattern

A third turning point came in the establishment of the Pastor's College by Charles Haddon Spurgeon, one of the most highly-regarded Baptist ministers of all time. To understand the peculiar importance of this institution, one must place Spurgeon himself in context. As a young man, Charles had applied to Stepney College, the Baptist school in the London area (later to become Regents Park College). Through a mishap, he was denied an interview and he set about to train himself for possible ministry. He was immersed in the Puritan Classics and portrayed a lifelong disinclination toward university-based ministerial education. When the Evangelical Alliance was formed in 1846, Spurgeon was a charter member and held tenaciously to a confessional basis for denominations, notably his own. Through the 1860s and 1870s the pastor of Britain's largest Protestant church, London's Metropolitan Tabernacle, noticed troubling evidences of doctrinal slippage. Spurgeon and a small group of like-minded pastors referred to the course of doctrinal expression and teaching, plus an alarming openness to cooperation with Arminian groups,[11] as a "downgrade," using a familiar railroad motif.

To counter what Spurgeon thus considered unwholesome theological education, in 1856 he founded the Pastor's College. At first the "college" was merely lectures that he or a revered colleague gave to willing students. But as his lectures were widely published and "the school that met at Mr. Spurgeon's Church" became known for its ardently evangelical witness, the college became much more formal. In the 1880s and 1890s principals George Rogers and David Gracey defined the school as a center of evangelical Calvinism and Scottish Common Sense Philosophy, pushing it toward an official recognition parallel to the status of London University.[12] In the mid-twentieth century under strong

---

[11] This was a veiled reference to the long-proposed merger of the General and Particular Baptist families into the Baptist Union of Great Britain and Ireland.

[12] See Brackney, *Genetic History of Baptist Thought*, 190ff and David Bebbington, "Spurgeon and British Evangelical Theological Education," in *Theological Education in the*

principial leadership, Spurgeon's College edged its way into being a recognized school of the Baptist Union and eventually its leading institution in terms of enrolled students. The pilgrimage of Spurgeon's College demonstrates the validity of alternative educational institutions among Baptists in spite of the strength and academic reputation of older denominational schools. It also signaled the parallel, and some would argue, new paradigm of conservative evangelical denominational education. This paradigm would entail conformity to doctrinal statements, accountability to the evangelical wing of the denomination, and emphases on missions and evangelism. Both Bible colleges and theological seminaries would spring forth in the Baptist community built upon the same foundations laid by Spurgeon.

Chicago: The First Modern Baptist University

The fourth critical juncture in the evolution of Baptists in higher education is the University of Chicago. The Baptist communities North and South had spawned several institutions from the 1830s to the 1870s that presumed to the title "university." These included Furman University, Madison University (later Colgate), Mercer University, the University at Lewisburg (Bucknell), Baylor University, University of Rochester, and Des Moines University. None of these schools had graduate programs on the European model, yet most had multiple faculties of theology, medicine, education, or law. In 1857 Chicago Baptists won a charter for a university in their city that had high expectations. Fostered by the venerable Stephen A. Douglas, the school took shape with buildings and curricula.[13] Over the decade or so of its first manifestation, it enrolled several hundred students and held tenaciously to a credible faculty. Before long, however, overextended credit and a poor economy forced the foreclosure of the school by 1885.[14] Distantly attached to the first University of Chicago was the Baptist Theological Seminary at Morgan Park, which had attracted a fairly distinguished faculty.

Evangelical Tradition, ed. D. G. Hart and R. Albert Mohler Jr. (Grand Rapids: Baker Books, 1996) 217–34.

[13] Richard J. Storr, *Harper's University: The Beginnings* (Chicago: University of Chicago Press, 1966) 3–4.

[14] On the original institution, see Thomas W. Goodspeed, *A History of the University of Chicago, Founded by John D. Rockefeller, the First Quarter Century* (Chicago: University of Chicago Press, 1916) 30–32.

Like a phoenix in ancient mythology, out of the ashes of the failed project came forth a renewed attempt at a second university of Chicago that was destined to survive. William Rainey Harper, a Yale Ph.D. in Semitic languages and faculty member at Morgan Park in its early development, assumed the provisional presidency of the new scheme, and he built upon the German models. Harper created an institution that gave priority to graduate education with appendages of professional schools and a network of feeder and affiliate colleges.[15] His intent was to instate a new design for American higher education that would bring research and publication into focus and supply a battery of professors for other schools. He would rival the older New England colleges and compete with Cornell, Clark, and Johns Hopkins. All of this was to be accomplished in the clothing of a church-related institution, whose capstone was a divinity school composed of the best scholars available. Harper sincerely believed the maturing Baptist character could provide the space for untrammeled research and yet fidelity to the Christian religion. His first faculty included Eri Hurlburt, George W. Northrup, and Ernest D. Burton, with later additions of George Burman Foster, Shailer Mathews, Shirley Jackson Case, and Harry Pratt Judson.

Despite deep suspicions about Chicago's liberal spirit, under Harper's regime, the University of Chicago did set new standards and set a pace for all other Baptist schools. His successors were less successful in maintaining harmony in the Baptist community, and deep rifts opened first in Chicago and later across North America over the new departures of Chicago. In light of Chicago's energetic advocacy of a new definition of university, most of the older Baptist universities reduced their programs to undergraduate education, many dropped their professional schools, and one, Colby, restored its title to college. Chicago's all-out pursuit of international status ultimately surpassed the needs of its denomination and by the mid-twentieth century, its Baptist ties were severed, except for the divinity school.[16]

In addition to the worthy and energetic accomplishments educationally seen in the University of Chicago, it was a landmark in Baptist philanthropy as well. Recognizing the failed efforts of the local Baptists in the Midwest to support the first University of Chicago, Harper pursued a new source of

---

[15] The feeder schools included Kalamazoo College, Stetson University, Butler University, and Des Moines University.

[16] See William H. Brackney, "Secularization of the Academy: A Baptist Typology," *Westminster Studies in Education* 24/2 (2001): 117–19.

funding for his university. He enlisted the work of Frederick Gates, an entrepreneurial pastor from Minnesota and the well-worn Thomas J. Goodspeed who knew the older university very well, and the trio approached one of the wealthiest American industrialists of the era for his generous support. John D. Rockefeller was the leading oil industrialist in the United States and a Baptist. Not only did Rockefeller give generously to Chicago, but he was personally committed to the establishment of the American Baptist Education Society in 1888 to assist other worthy institutions in the denomination as well. Those who claimed substantial grants from the society included Bucknell, Brown, Colgate, Rochester, Wake Forest, Stetson, and Des Moines universities, plus numerous black colleges under the auspices of the American Baptist Home Mission Society.

Under New Management: Southern Seminary

One final turning point is worthy of attention. The resurgence of conservative evangelical (some would call it fundamentalist) theology among Southern Baptists provided a significant turning point in Baptist higher education. By the 1960s Southern Baptists had built the largest network of Baptist higher education in the history of the denomination and were energetically providing necessary funds to sustain their schools. There were over fifty accredited institutions listed in the 1960 Southern Baptist Convention (SBC) *Annual.* Apparently Southern Baptists had not read carefully the tragic history of Northern Baptist educational losses in the era 1920–1950 or they reasoned the cultural binding that held them together was impervious to those same forces. In any case, the takeover, reorganization, or evolution to fundamentalist control of institutions related to the Southern Baptist Convention or its state affiliates is one of the significant turning points in Baptist history. I have selected Southern Baptist Theological Seminary in Louisville, Kentucky, to illustrate this turning point because it was among the first to be transformed, and it has been considered the parent of Southern Baptist seminaries and thus exceedingly symbolic.

Conservative evangelical writers of the history of Southern Seminary depict it as a school with definite evangelical roots in a Calvinistic tradition from its inception. They generally point to James P. Boyce's theological orientation and the "Abstract of Principles" that safeguarded the seminary's identity. Others find in writing about Southern that it was a national rather than a regional school with intentions of becoming the leading graduate center for

Baptist theological education and that many Southern Baptist leaders earned doctoral degrees at the school, attesting to its breadth and faculty resources.[17] E. Y. Mullins becomes the heroic figure of this interpretation.[18] Still others assert that Southern has always been a school with a certain degree of tension in its theological makeup, tilting from time to time in either direction.[19]

It is clear that the faculty of post-World War II Southern Seminary had intentions of becoming a world-class institution. The sharp rise in its enrollment, its new campus facilities, the expansion of its faculty, low-cost additional graduate degrees available to the entire Baptist family, and an extensive library collection all spoke to its robust identity. Theologians like Dale Moody and James Leo Garrett openly sought relations with other than Baptist Christians and led a chorus of Southern graduates to take additional graduate work beyond Southern Baptist schools.[20] By the 1960s there was a widespread impression that Louisville had become a Neo-Orthodox school, if not for many observers, plainly in the theologically liberal camp. Only the statesmanship qualities of President Duke McCall for over four decades maintained a balance in Southern's image. With McCall's presidential retirement in 1982,[21] and the election of a succession of conservative evangelical Southern Baptist Convention presidents, it seemed the oldest Southern Baptist seminary was over-ripe for change from a conservative perspective and newly-elected fundamentalist trustees gradually began to demand curricular and staff changes.

The most dramatic change took place in 1993 when R. Albert Mohler, editor of *The Christian Index*, the Georgia Baptist newspaper, succeeded Roy Honeycutt as president of the school.[22] Skilled in his use of the national media,

---

[17] William A. Mueller, *A History of Southern Baptist Theological Seminary* (Nashville: Broadman Press, 1959).

[18] Russell Dilday, "Mullins the Theologian: Between the Extremes" *Review and Expositor* 96/1 (Winter 1999): 75–86.

[19] Brackney, *Genetic History*, 406, 414.

[20] Moody studied with Karl Barth and Emil Brunner and took a second doctorate at Oxford, while Garrett took a second doctorate at Harvard.

[21] He remained chancellor, the first in the seminary's history, until 1990.

[22] Honeycutt, a theologically conservative Old Testament teacher, made numerous efforts to compromise with fundamentalists and preserve Southern's heritage by appointments like David Dockery and Craig Blaising, noted exponents of conservative evangelicalism. The two presidential succession finalists were Mohler and Timothy George, dean at Beeson (Samford) Divinity School. Mohler, whose doctoral studies were

a close confidante of the new Christian right, and possessed of deep convictions about his place in history, Mohler made it clear that he intended to create a new faculty at Southern that would reflect his preoccupation with the Reformed (Calvinistic) tradition. Numerous tenured Southern faculty left for other more theologically open institutions,[23] new faculty recruits came from schools outside the SBC, and Mohler set new standards for publications[24] and the curricula of the several divisions.[25] By 1995 the changeover at Southern was complete and President Mohler was a national figure in the media, often called upon to reflect the opinion of the 16 million-member Southern Baptist Convention.[26]

The turning point reflected in Louisville had profound impact upon other seminaries and schools. In 1994 Southwestern Baptist Theological Seminary President Russell Dilday was fired from his post, to be succeeded by Kenneth Hemphill, a pastor from Virginia. Perhaps most theologically dramatic was the transition at Southeastern Baptist Seminary where Randall Lolley in 1988 stepped down as president in favor of Lewis Drummond, who was himself after only four years succeeded by Paige Patterson, the former president of Criswell Bible College.[27] Similar presidential changes occurred in due course at

---

in systematic and historical theology, is a devotee of the work of Carl F. H. Henry. He had also served previously in the Southern Seminary administration.

[23] Actually, the exodus from Southern began in the previous decade as Bill J. Leonard went to Samford University and Walter Shurden went to Mercer University, while later departures continued with John Jonsson and Alan Culpepper to Baylor University, Raymond Bailey to a pastorate in Texas, and Glenn Hinson eventually to the Baptist Theological Seminary at Richmond.

[24] Supporters of the *Review and Expositor*, long published by the faculty at Southern, pulled it away from seminary control and Mohler created a new periodical, *The Southern Baptist Journal of Theology*, of which he is the publisher and editor.

[25] The Carver School of Social Work, with strong ties to the Woman's Missionary Union, was closed and the dean, Diana Garland, was fired. Mohler saw the social work track as a "back door for women in ministry" and Garland went to Baylor University to recreate its department of social work in the tradition of Carver (personal interview with David and Diana Garland, n.d.).

[26] The seminary website quotes the news media in dubbing Mohler the "reigning intellectual of the evangelical movement in America." Southern Baptist Theological Seminary, Al Mohler biography page (accessed 10/24/06).

[27] Drummond had previously been the Billy Graham Professor of Evangelism at Southern Seminary and taught from time to time at Spurgeon's College in London. Patterson, who received his doctorate from New Orleans Baptist Seminary when that faculty included Clark Pinnock and Samuel Mikolaski among others, stepped down from his position at Criswell under pressure from trustees because of his full engagement of the plan to reorganize the SBC.

Midwestern, New Orleans, and Golden Gate seminaries and again at Southwestern, completing the sweep. The initial resurgence was skillfully carried forth by Paul Pressler and Paige Patterson, aided by prominent pastors like W. A. Criswell, Adrian Rogers, and Charles Stanley. As conservative evangelical influence reached to control the SBC seminaries, a new generation of hard-line conservatives rose to the fore, including Albert Mohler, L. Russ Bush, Paige Patterson, Craig Blaising, David Dockery, and Timothy George.

As if to signal a turn toward a new future of defining Baptist identity in the traditional South, what began at Southern spawned a series of new theological seminaries or programs independent of Southern Baptist controls, and this has produced a broadened definition of the overall Southern Baptist educational culture. The perspective is wide: with Wake Forest University Divinity School, a reorganized Central Baptist Seminary, and the Baptist House at Duke University Divinity School catering to the needs of the most progressive to the Baptist Theological Seminary at Richmond, McAfee School of Theology at Mercer, Truett Seminary at Baylor, and Logsdon School of Theology at Hardin-Simmons reaching centrist to conservative moderates to Beeson at Samford University, Campbell University Divinity School, and Gardner Webb Divinity School identified with more conservative constituencies. Outside the listed institutions is the B. H. Carroll Institute in Dallas/Fort Worth, Texas, a distance education program without residential students that carries the old Southwestern heritage.[28]

The turning point initiated at Southern Seminary in 1993 also cast a shadow over colleges and universities related to the Southern Baptist Convention. As charges of uncooperative leadership or unsavory social trends in several schools reached toward the real possibility of interference in institutional governance, the older institutions began to place distance between their respective state conventions and their trustees. With the passage of revisions to the Baptist Faith and Message in 2000, which became a landmark standard for compliance with the new directions of Southern Baptist institutions and agencies, a succession of colleges and universities actually severed ties with their state Baptist bodies. These included Wake Forest University, Furman University, Stetson University, Meredith College, Mercer University, and Georgetown College. In some cases, angry struggles occurred

---

[28] Russell Dilday has been a prime mover in the institute, in some ways a reaction to the course charted at at Baylor's Truett Seminary under former president Robert Sloan and dean Paul Powell.

among trustees over charter interpretations that led to wrenching administrative changes or threats of litigation as at Belmont University, Louisiana College, or Carson Newman College or a court challenge as at Shorter College. Some smaller colleges capitulated in the face of potential loss of funds, like Southwest Missouri Baptist University or Brewton Parker College in Georgia, while other historically Southern Baptist schools like Averett University in Virginia took advantage of the opportunity to move away from church-relatedness.

Conclusion

The historic pilgrimage of Baptists in higher education represents more than it may appear at first glance. The establishment of schools, colleges, universities, and theological schools are marks of maturity of the tradition or denomination. The capability to sustain permanent institutions in the early republic reflected well on mainstream Baptists in America in spite of vocal opposition from the anti-missionary or Old School churches. Further, the religious values and traditions of a denomination are conserved in such institutions from one generation to the next. Following patterns of other Protestant groups gave Baptists a sense of commonality with the emerging evangelical traditions of the later nineteenth century. Baptists valued an educated ministry, as well as religious experience and the personal gifts of a preacher, for instance. In establishing Brown, Baptists made a signal contribution to New England and later American culture, worthy of inclusion with the elite colleges of the colonial era.

From their humble origins within English Dissent, Baptists were a work in progress. Their attempts at creating institutions of higher education were not always successful or desirable across the entire constituency, but as we have seen in this brief survey, there were signal accomplishments that moved the denomination along the path of greater sophistication in the articulation of their own views and increased public acceptability of Baptists in the Christian family. We have also noted two turning points that, seemingly regressive from a mainstream Baptist perspective, initiated new departures in Baptist-related higher education.

Suggested Reading

Brackney, William H. "Secularization of the Academy: A Baptist Typology." *Westminster Studies in Education* 24/2 (2001): 111–28.

Guild, Reuben A. *Early History of Brown University, including the Life, Times, and Correspondence of President Manning 1756–1791*. Providence RI: Snow and Farnum, 1896.

Moon, Norman S. *Education for Ministry: Bristol Baptist College 1679–1979*. Bristol: Bristol Baptist College, 1979.

Moss, Lemuel, editor. *The Baptists and the National Centenary: A Record of Christian Work: 1776–1876*. Philadelphia: American Baptist Publication Society, 1876.

Mueller, Walter. *A History of Southern Baptist Theological Seminary*. Nashville TN: Broadman Press, 1959.

"A Typology of Baptist Theological Education." *American Baptist Quarterly* 18/2 (June 1999).

Woolley, Davis C., editor. *Baptist Advance: The Achievements of the Baptists of North America for a Century and a Half*. Nashville TN: Broadman Press, 1964.

CHAPTER 12

Baptist "Anti" Movements and the Turn toward Progressivism: 1820/1832/1845

Michael E. Williams, Sr.

By the end of the second decade of the nineteenth century, Baptists were on the march. Due to the work of individuals like William Carey and the Judsons on the foreign fields; Andrew Fuller and the Baptist Missionary Society in Britain; and the Triennial Convention, Luther Rice, and John Mason Peck in the United States, Baptists were more interested and involved in promoting missions in a systematic and collaborative fashion than ever before. Baptists had created a national university in the US capital, and advocates for missions fanned out across the frontier, spreading Baptist ideas about cooperative missions and promoting the work of the American Baptist Foreign Missions, Home Missions, and tract societies. However, during the early nineteenth century other Baptists opposed centralized or coordinated action. Some Baptists believed mission efforts were unbiblical. Others resented educated ministers, either because of the lack of their own education or because they saw education as dampening spiritual and evangelistic zeal. Due to this opposition, many Baptists were forced to consider their own support of progressive cooperation in missions and institutional and organizational development and to reaffirm the biblical and theological basis for such organizations. In order to understand more fully this turn away from individualistic approaches to missions and the rejection of missions organizations, understanding the cultural climate in the United States and Britain in the early decades of the nineteenth century is important.

In the United States, Americans described the years that followed the end of the War of 1812 as the Era of Good Feelings. Nationalism surged in the wake of the war, especially after Andrew Jackson's victory at New Orleans in

January 1815. Subsequent years saw the creation of a legislative program named the American System. Promoted by Henry Clay, Daniel Webster, and others, the program was designed to protect emerging manufacturing, aid the development of the West, create a national market, and bind the country together with a system of roads and canals. Likewise, Congress chartered the Second Bank of the United States in 1816. Following in the footsteps of the First Bank, the Second Bank served as a repository for federal funds and also helped to manage the government's fiscal affairs. Congressional leaders believed these progressive arrangements were necessary due to the nation's rapid growth, particularly the dramatic growth that occurred in the American West. Between 1812 and 1852 the population of the United States grew from approximately 7 million to about 23 million. The country quickly added new states, mainly in the West. From 1816 to 1821, five new "western" states, Indiana, Mississippi, Illinois, Alabama, and Missouri, joined the Union. During the four decades after 1821, new western states like Arkansas, Texas, Iowa, and Wisconsin achieved statehood as the land available for settlement grew from 1.7 million to nearly 3 million square miles.[1]

By the 1820s, however, the Era of Good Feelings was coming to an end. Two major issues arose: the economic crisis known as the Panic of 1819 and the political crisis known as the Missouri Question. These issues generated sectional sentiments that created tensions between the East and the West and between the North and the South. The Missouri Question and the subsequent Missouri Compromise raised for the first time the ugly specter of slavery's divisive power. The panic re-energized western suspicions of the eastern banking and political structure, producing a generation of westerners who resented control of their region's political futures by the political establishment in Washington, DC, and despised the manipulation of their own economic futures by the financial establishment of the eastern seaboard. The survival of the US Bank in the midst of the Panic of 1819 while smaller western banks closed seemed to prove that the US Bank existed to protect the moneyed classes and the political elite. John Quincy Adams's selection in the disputed election of 1824 during which the presidency was "stolen" from western hero Andrew Jackson appeared to westerners to confirm that the corruptness of the political structure. The bank and Adams became the targets of the People's Revolution

---

[1] From Revolution to Reconstruction, "An Outline of American History," http://odur.let.rug.nl/~usa/H/1954uk/chap4.htm.

or the rise of Jacksonian democracy that swept Jackson into the White House in 1828 and led to the elimination of the bank in his second term.

In some ways, the British context was similar to that of the United States. Great Britain emerged victorious from the Napoleonic Wars in the first decades of the nineteenth century with its international prestige higher than ever before. The British navy ruled the high seas, and due to the origins of the Industrial Revolution, the world sought British manufactured goods. Many Britons believed that these developments ushered in an era of Pax Britannia, and in the following years, many Britons fondly declared that "the sun never set on the British Empire." Yet the nation had a myriad of problems. A conservative reaction rejected the reform impulse that had begun in response to the French Revolution, causing the government to reduce dramatically the individual liberties of British citizens. In the aftermath of the Napoleonic Wars both public finances and private business struggled. Considerable tension existed between the poor and wealthy Britons over the controversial Corn Laws. However, when reform began in the early 1820s, rampant financial speculation took place that ultimately resulted in an economic crash in 1826. The hardships that followed led to the death of old line Toryism. A poor harvest in 1829 contributed to civil unrest. Some parliamentary reform took place in this era, but "rotten boroughs" remained a consistent problem that allowed unequal representation to exist. The need for parliamentary reform contributed to the creation of the Great Reform Bill of 1832. These conditions also contributed to the rise of a popular movement known as Chartism. The Chartist movement originated as a populist style reform movement seeking democratic reforms in Parliament and in the British political structure.[2]

Reform elements touched British religion as well. The Act of Toleration in 1689 relieved Presbyterians, Congregationalists, Baptists, and other British dissenters from persecution, but it did not give British dissenters full political rights. Nor did it include Catholics, Jews, and Unitarians. Officially, the British government still discriminated against those not a part of the Church of England. The introduction of the Emancipation Bill granting Roman Catholics certain rights generated a crisis of church and state regarding the favored status of the Anglican Church and allowed Catholics entry to Parliament.

---

[2] William B. Willcox, *The Age of Aristocracy: 1688–1830* (Lexington: D. C. Heath, 1976) 256–77 and Walter L. Arnstein, *Britain Yesterday and Today: 1830 to the Present* (Lexington: D. C. Heath, 1976) 4–17, 30ff.

Generally, British Baptists prospered in the period from 1792 until the 1830s. The creation of the New Connection of General Baptists re-energized General Baptist life, and the Baptist Missionary Society reinvigorated Particular Baptist life. The creation of the Baptist Union in 1813 furnished Particular Baptists the opportunity of a national organization that they had historically rejected. Even in 1813, some Particular Baptists rejected involvement in a national association. Some, like Andrew Fuller, feared that it would compete with the Baptist Missionary Society for allegiance.[3]

By the early 1820s the series of revivals in the United States that had begun around 1800 and that were known as the Second Great Awakening began to slow. However, these revivals experienced a rebirth in the North and West because of the influence of the revivalist Charles Finney and the incorporation of his "New Measures." Likewise, the Second Great Awakening stimulated a plethora of reform movements as well as para-church and denominational mission and reform agencies that solidified the influence of the Awakening and institutionalized its missions. The Second Great Awakening had also planted the seeds of conflict with the birth of an organized abolitionist movement in the North.

In America, Baptists, more than any other denomination besides the Methodists, benefited from the Second Great Awakening. The Baptist emphasis on the priesthood of believers and the autonomy of the local church contributed mightily to the growth of Baptists among the independent-minded frontiersmen who flooded the frontier. Likewise, the fact that Baptist polity allowed anyone who felt called and was endorsed by his church to preach, thereby facilitating the planting of small Baptist churches throughout the West. Other Baptists, stimulated by the magnificent work of English Baptists William Carey and Andrew Fuller, felt led to establish American Baptist efforts in foreign missions. Lesser known foreign mission activity by black Baptists like David George and George Liele [or Lisle] in places like Nova Scotia, Sierra Leone, and Jamaica preceded Carey's work and laid the foundation for later African-American Baptist mission work. The establishment of the Triennial Convention in 1814 to support foreign mission work and the subsequent creation of the American Baptist Foreign Mission Board and the Home Mission Board served as rallying points for these efforts. But as these efforts expanded, and as individuals like Luther Rice traveled throughout the West to promote

---

[3] H. Leon McBeth, *The Baptist Heritage: Four Centuries of Baptist Witness* (Nashville: Broadman Press, 1987) 289–92.

the causes of missions and education, they found that the same currents that flooded across the frontier politically and economically also flowed across the religious landscape.

The American Anti-Mission Baptists

Three of the most interesting and controversial Baptists of the early nineteenth century led the anti-missions movement. Their names were John Taylor, Daniel Parker, and Joshua Lawrence. Yet another Baptist who led this anti-missions movement eventually no longer called himself a Baptist but preferred the nomenclature "Christian." His name was Alexander Campbell.

When Baptists formed the Triennial Convention and subsequently sought to expand the cooperative work of Baptists, one of the first individuals to oppose them was John Leland. While Baptists generally laud Leland for his tenacious support of religious liberty and separation of church and state, they tend to ignore the fact that he was an outspoken critic of creeds, mission societies, formal religion, educated and professional clergy, and anything else that he believed approached coercion or pretense. In fact, one recent scholar calls Leland "a grandfather to the primitivist movement." Among those with whom Leland corresponded was John Taylor.[4]

Taylor grew up along the Virginia frontier in the late colonial time period. He later moved to Kentucky where he became one of the key leaders of the anti-missions movement. While H. Leon McBeth identifies Taylor as more moderate than Lawrence, Parker, or Campbell, the damage that Taylor did to cooperative missions was significant nonetheless. In 1820 Taylor published a pamphlet titled *Thoughts on Missions* in which he recounted the story of two young members of the Presbyterian Board of Missions. Taylor recalled that they were "respectable looking young men, well informed, and zealous in the cause in which they were employed." They shared with him the story of Adoniram Judson and Luther Rice while recalling that ever since the people of New England had been "stirr[ed] up," that the lifestyles of New England ministers had greatly improved. The young Presbyterians insisted that if Taylor and other frontier Baptist ministers would "stir up the people to Missions and

---

[4] Nathan O. Hatch, *The Democratization of American Christianity* (New Haven and London: Yale University Press, 1989) 95–101 and Michael A. Dain, "The Development of the Primitivist Impulse in American Baptist Life, 1707–1842" (Ph.D. diss., Southwestern Baptist Theological Seminary, 2001) 111.

Bible Society matters" a magnificent "change in money affairs in favor of the preachers" would occur.[5]

This conversation led Taylor to believe that he could "smell the *New England Rat*," apparently his nickname for Luther Rice. While he criticized Adoniram and Ann Judson, Taylor saved his most brutal criticism for Rice. Taylor heard Rice speak at the Elkhorn Association in Kentucky in 1815. While acknowledging that he "admired the art of this well-taught Yankee," Taylor considered Rice a modern Tetzel, saying "that the Pope's old orator of that name was equally innocent with Luther Rice, and his motive about the same." For Taylor, Rice's pleas for the support of missions and Tetzel's pleas for indulgences were all about "MONEY."[6]

Taylor also believed that mission societies violated traditional Baptist polity. He argued that "the missionary society was really an aristocracy." Moreover, the actions of John Mason Peck and others in the Home Mission Society (HMS) incensed Taylor. Peck and other HMS representatives implied that the West lacked qualified and educated ministers which may have generated at least some of Taylor's criticism.[7]

Joshua Lawrence served as another leader of the anti-missions movement. The same year that Taylor published his *Thoughts on Missions*, Lawrence published a pamphlet that proved influential, particularly in North Carolina. In fact, McBeth states that this pamphlet "helped turn the Kehuckee Association against missions and made 'Kehuckeeism' a synonym for anti-missions." Seven years later, this "large and influential" association produced "A Declaration against the Modern Missionary Movement and Other Institutions of Men" in which the association "discard[ed] all Missionary Societies, Bible Societies and Theological Seminaries." Participants at the association's annual meeting voted to exclude from fellowship those who supported any of these "man-made institutions." One recent scholar indicates that Lawrence feared that such organizations imitated the institutionalization that occurred in the aftermath of the Constantinian legalization of Christianity in the fourth century. Lawrence compared professional ministers to Roman Catholic priests, who he denounced

---

[5] John Taylor, *Thoughts on Missions*, 1820 as cited in Robert A. Baker, *A Baptist Source Book* (Nashville: Broadman Press, 1966) 79–80. See also McBeth, *Baptist Heritage*, 374.

[6] H. Leon McBeth, *A Sourcebook for Baptist Heritage* (Nashville: Broadman Press, 1990) 232 and Baker, *Baptist Source Book*, 80, 81.

[7] William Warren Sweet, *Religion on the American Frontier: The Baptists, 1783–1830, A Collection of Source Material* (New York: Cooper Square Publishers, 1964) 68 and McBeth, *Baptist Heritage*, 374.

for "I dread the tyranny of an unconverted, men-made, money making...factoried" clergy. In this manner he utilized arguments similar to those used by Leland.[8]

The most vociferous opponent of the mission societies was Daniel Parker, the rough frontier preacher. McBeth describes Parker as a "man of slight build and unkempt appearance, his beard often streaked with tobacco stains" who also "had a keen mind and piercing blue eyes." A man of little formal education, Parker opposed mission societies, theological seminaries, and other institutions that he viewed as man-made. A relatively successful church planter, Parker served churches in Tennessee and Illinois before planting in Texas what some regard as the first Baptist church there. In order to get around Mexican government rules, Parker actually formed the church in Illinois and transplanted it to Texas where his congregation settled on a land grant in Stephen F. Austin's colony.[9]

Parker's primary objection to mission societies was theological. While serving as a pastor in northern Tennessee, he combated Methodists and Baptists who he felt had muted the Calvinist theology he believed. Parker promoted a doctrine of extreme Calvinism that insisted upon "two seeds in the spirit." According to Parker, God chose those who were of "woman's seed" as his elect, while those of the "serpent's seed" were the non-elect. This unusual interpretation of predestination insisted that Satan's seed designated a "covenant of works," while Christ's seed in Eve ordained a "covenant of grace." Parker and his followers then taught that the non-elect could not be redeemed; therefore, mission societies were unnecessary and unbiblical. In 1820 he issued a widely distributed pamphlet that harangued the foreign mission society. In subsequent years he published a newspaper titled the *Church Advocate*, in which he disseminated his ideas. This newspaper demonstrated that local loyalties dominated Parker's thoughts and that he rejected anything that smelled of ecclesiastical organization as did Taylor. Parker's primary concern was that Baptists founded missionary societies based on elitist control rather than on a sound biblical theology. McBeth acknowledges that Parker's "opponents may

---

[8] McBeth, *Baptist Heritage*, 372–73, 375; Dain, "Development of the Primitivist Impulse," 110–11, 123; and Lawrence as cited by Bertram Wyatt-Brown, "The Antimission Movement in the Jacksonian South: A Study in Regional Folk Culture," *The Journal of Southern History* 36/4 (November 1970): 518.

[9] McBeth, *Baptist Heritage*, 373 and H. Leon McBeth, *Texas Baptists: A Sesquicentennial History* (Dallas: Baptistway Press, 1998) 22.

have seen more anti-mission implications in his two-seeds doctrine than Parker intended." His followers eventually became known as Primitive Baptists, or as they were sometimes called, "Hardshell Baptists," and have remained most pervasive in rural areas of the southeast and southeastern Texas.[10]

Perhaps the greatest summary of Primitive Baptist beliefs may be found in the Black Rock Address issued by a group of Maryland Old School Baptists. In this 1832 address, these Baptists attacked tract societies, Sunday school, Bible societies, mission societies, colleges and theological education, and "protracted meetings"(revival meetings). They considered all these recent innovations as unbiblical and man-made creations.[11]

As damaging as the opposition of Taylor, Lawrence, and Parker was, the ruckus raised by Alexander Campbell had the longest lasting consequences among Baptists in the South. Along with his father, Campbell emigrated from Scotland and later migrated from the Presbyterian ministry into Baptist life. After his first child was born, Campbell rejected infant baptism, requested believer's baptism by immersion from a Baptist pastor, and led the church he served to become an independent immersionist church. Due to its similar beliefs on baptism, Campbell's congregation joined a Baptist association in Pennsylvania. Campbell remained a Baptist only seventeen years, but during those years and those that followed he wreaked havoc on Baptist churches and associations, especially in Kentucky and Tennessee. A popular religious debater and writer/editor of a widely read religious newspaper originally named the *Christian Baptist* and then renamed the *Millenial Harbinger*, Campbell began a Primitivist movement in which he and others styled themselves as "Reformers" and lauded a "return" to New Testament ways. Like Taylor, Lawrence, and Parker, Campbell believed that mission societies and Bible societies were "unbiblical." As McBeth observes, Campbell also attacked "associations, confessions of faith, use of the title *reverend*, and many other things he

---

[10] Sweet, *Religion on the American Frontier*, 68–69; McBeth, *Baptist Heritage*, 373–74; Pamela R. Durso and Keith E. Durso, *The Story of Baptists in the United States* (Nashville: The Baptist History & Heritage Society, 2006) 209–10. The author also gratefully acknowledges his use of an unpublished paper by Brian Franklin, "The Antimission Movement and the Authority of Church and State" for insights on the anti-missionists' concerns regarding authority and their links with Jacksonian Democrats.

[11] McBeth, *Baptist Heritage*, 373; McBeth, *Sourcebook*, 236–39; and Bill J. Leonard, *Baptist Ways*, (Valley Forge: Judson Press, 2003) 182.

considered nonbiblical" and "sought to cleanse the churches of all 'human traditions' and return to 'primitive order.'"[12]

Campbell's movement tapped into some of the same reservoirs of resentment that other opponents of missions did. His bitter accusations against mission societies cast a long shadow. As McBeth records, "He accused some societies of greed, dishonesty, embezzlement, and outright stealing." As harmful as the attacks of Parker and others had been, Campbell's attacks reached far beyond missions and resulted in entire churches and associations across the frontier leaving Baptist life to join Campbell's "restorationist" movement. Other congregations, like First Baptist Church of Louisville, Kentucky, experienced bitter splits. McBeth agrees with historians who contend that "fully half the Baptist churches of Kentucky switched" to the new movement begun by Campbell and his followers that was labeled as the Disciples of Christ or the Church of Christ. Bill Leonard notes, "Hundreds of Baptist churches experienced similar schisms" to that of the Louisville church. Battles between Baptists and those they labeled "Campbellites" spanned generations across the American South and Southwest in numerous small towns and communities.[13]

The British Anti-Mission Baptists

At approximately the same time that the anti-mission movement originated in the United States, a similar movement arose in Great Britain. While no apparent direct link between these two movements exists, the two movements were founded on similar ideas. Some of the British anti-missions Baptists held ideas similar to those of Daniel Parker and to the Primitive Baptists with regard to atonement. Generally speaking, these British Baptists called themselves Strict and Particular Baptists. They saw themselves in the tradition of John Brine, John Skepp, and John Gill as they resisted "Fullerism." Fullerism was the evangelical Calvinism adopted by Andrew Fuller and William Carey that resulted in the expansive support of the Baptist Mission Society. Strict and Particular Baptists rejected Fullerism and the support of the Baptist Mission Society on the basis that it contradicted the High Calvinism that they held. Later opponents identified themselves as Gospel Standard Baptists due to Christological conflicts. Some of these Strict and Particular Baptists, especially

---

[12] McBeth, *Baptist Heritage*, 375, 377–78.

[13] Ibid., 375, 377–80; Leonard, *Baptist Ways*, 182–83; and Jesse C. Fletcher, *The Southern Baptist Convention: A Sesquicentennial History* (Nashville: Broadman and Holman Publishers, 1994) 39.

the Gospel Standard Baptists, anticipated or agreed with Landmark Baptists in America as they refused communion to those who were not of like mind. In England men such as William Gadsby, John Warburton, and John Kershaw led the anti-missions Baptists in their reaction against "Fullerism." Gadsby's influence was felt especially in East Anglia and in the Suffolk and Norfolk Association in England and in Scotland. Some of their ideas spread to Canada and Australia as well. As Kenneth Dix demonstrates, some of these Strict and Particular Baptists to a large extent were not necessarily anti-missions. They were more literally an anti-mission society. Generally, they were divided on issues like Sunday schools and other man-made institutions unlike the Primitive Baptists and the supporters of Alexander Campbell in the United States who opposed these institutions.[14]

However, the Strict and Particular Baptists clearly held a different viewpoint than the followers of Fuller and Carey. While some Strict Baptists dedicated themselves to evangelism and missions and urged people "to repent and believe," others rejected the concept "that it is the duty of every person to repent and believe," arguing that human beings are incapable of doing so and thus they typically avoided "exhorting their hearers" in any fashion that they believed might mislead them. The Gospel Standard Baptists tended even more toward hyper-Calvinism in that they believed preachers should not "offer the gospel of Christ to all without discrimination, nor to call all in their audience to repentance and faith."[15] In this sense, these Strict Baptists considered themselves the true heirs of the Brine, Skepp, and Gill, eighteenth-century Baptists who completely rejected the teachings of Andrew Fuller. The Gospel Standard Baptists identified with the London Confession of Faith from 1689 and earlier Particular Baptists.

---

[14] McBeth, *Baptist Heritage*, 521; Leonard, *Baptist Ways*, 236–37, 296; A. C. Underwood, *A History of the English Baptists* (1947; repr., London: The Baptist Union of Great Britain and Ireland, 1970) 185–89; and Kenneth Dix, *English Strict and Particular Baptists in the Nineteenth Century* (Northampton: Baptist Historical Society, 2001) 37–38, 269–70, 275–78. See Dix also on the Gospel Standard movement, 93–104 and S. F. Paul, *Historical Sketch of the Gospel Standard Baptists* (Croydon: Farncombe and Sons, 1961).

[15] "Who Are the Strict Baptists?", http://www.strictbaptisthistory.org.uk/. See also Dix, *English Strict and Particular Baptist.*

Conclusion

The anti-missions movement in the United States clearly tapped into a "Jacksonian bias against elites and aristocracy" and also into a "Jacksonian egalitarianism" that resented "educational elitism" that existed especially on the frontier and in the South.[16] Likewise, British Baptists most likely responded to the growing unrest in British life by suspecting any movement toward institutionalization as that demonstrated by the Baptist Missionary Society and the Baptist Union. In both cases, Baptists rejected anything that seemed to take away local autonomy or might somehow compromise what they viewed as historic Baptist beliefs. Anti-mission leaders reflected the growing sense of independence in American frontier life and the increasing egalitarianism of British life. How did "Missions" or "Missionary" Baptists respond to these various attacks on their support of the missions endeavor? Some Baptists, especially on the frontier, abandoned the missions societies and institutional Baptist life and moved into either Primitive Baptist or various expressions of the Churches of Christ in the United States, and some British Baptists aligned themselves with the Strict and Particular Baptists. Yet, by and large Baptists rallied in response to Taylor's anti-mission diatribe in 1820 and the Black Rock Address of 1832 by a defense of cooperative efforts to support missions and other institutional endeavors. By 1845 in the United States, Baptists like R. B. C. Howell assessed the damage wrought by the anti-missions movement and urged Baptists to move forward. Associations like the American Baptist Association in Kentucky and the Beaver Baptist Association in Pennsylvania responded clearly and boldly to "Campbellism."[17] These responses became critical in subsequent years as a new "anti" movement, Landmarkism, emerged, and among other things, Baptists found themselves once again defending cooperative missions. Also in Britain by 1845, Baptists more closely aligned themselves to the Baptist Union and rallied to support the Baptist Missionary Society. In the long run the anti-missions movements forced Baptists in both the United States and Great Britain to defend their principles, reject hyper-Calvinism and anti-institution Baptists, and affirm that the cooperative support of missions was indeed biblical and part of the greater calling that God had placed upon Baptists. The more progressive of Baptists agreed that in order to

---

[16] Wayne Flynt, *Alabama in the Twentieth Century* (Tuscaloosa: The University of Alabama Press, 2004) 185, 220.
[17] McBeth, *Sourcebook*, 239–46.

propagate the gospel into the "uttermost parts of the world," they would have to work together to accomplish it.

Suggested Reading

Durso, Pamela R., and Keith E. Durso. *The Story of Baptists in the United States* Nashville: The Baptist History & Heritage Society, 2006.

Hatch, Nathan. *The Democratization of American Christianity*. New Haven and London: Yale University Press, 1989.

Leonard, Bill J. *Baptist Ways: A History*. Valley Forge: Judson Press, 2003.

McBeth, H. Leon. *The Baptist Heritage: Four Centuries of Baptist Witness*. Nashville: Broadman Press, 1987.

———. *A Sourcebook for Baptist Heritage*. Nashville: Broadman Press, 1990.

Wyatt-Brown, Bertram. "The Antimission Movement in the Jacksonian South: A Study in Regional Folk Culture." *The Journal of Southern History* 36/4 (November 1970): 501–29.

CHAPTER 13

Baptist Freedom and the Turn toward Separation of Church and State: 1833

J. Bradley Creed

Discussions about the separation of church and state, whether in casual conversation, the classroom, or the courtroom, inevitably center on the First Amendment of the United States Constitution. This is the supreme law of the land and the final legal basis for arbitrating disputes and conflicts on such matters. Baptists and other dissenting groups that advocated religious liberty for all citizens can rightfully claim an influential role in ratifying the Constitution in 1789. This was a major turning point in the history of the nation and in the struggle for legal safeguards against religious tyranny. The Bill of Rights is fundamental to our nation's understanding and practice of democracy. The issue of church-state separation relative to the Constitution, however, is a prime illustration of the difference between *de jure* and *de facto* implementations of the law. Even though the Constitution prohibited a legal establishment of religion (*de jure*), disestablishment did not become a reality (*de facto*) for another four decades. States within the new nation carried laws and institutions that existed prior to 1789, and several resisted the new statutes by maintaining that the provisions of the Constitution applied only at the national level. The struggle for full religious liberty continued for nearly half a century after the ratification of the Constitution, and Baptists worked diligently to erase the last vestiges of legally established religion in the young republic as they gained influence.

During the American Revolution, Baptists identified political liberty with religious liberty, so most of them supported the patriot cause. The American Revolution not only severed political ties with the nation of England but also legal ties to an established church. This created the possibility for a social structure unprecedented in history. Even though there were serious debates on the issue and proposals for a state-approved arrangement among the churches, political realities mitigated against the creation of a national church.[1] The two religious traditions that dominated the colonies prior to the Revolution were Congregationalism in New England and Anglicanism in the South. Because of its ties to the Church of England, the American Anglican Church suffered a loss of position and control after the war. The Congregational Church was a regional church having no strong basis outside of Connecticut and Massachusetts. There was no other single candidate for the position of national church, and Baptists and other Free Church groups opposed this on the principle that there should be no national church.

There would not be a Church of America as the moral guardian of the new nation, but vestiges of establishment persisted and ideas that bolstered the idea of a state church were pervasive and powerful. At the time of Cornwallis's surrender at Yorktown, most of the colonies still supported some concept of state-sponsored religion. It was generally believed that the civil peace and moral health of the nation depended on the firm maintenance of religious faith and of the institutions of religion by the state. Also, there were legal measures in most of the states that provided financial support for the established churches. Authorities compelled colonial dissenters to pay taxes for supporting churches that they in good conscience could not support, and some were persecuted for their dissent and acts of conscience. The exceptions were Maryland, New Jersey, Delaware, and Pennsylvania, which provided some measure of toleration for dissenters but not full religious freedom. Rhode Island alone guaranteed full religious freedom for its inhabitants.

The Struggle for Religious Freedom after the Revolution

During and immediately after the Revolution, Baptists continued the struggle for religious freedom by seeking the dismantling of religious establishments, particularly in New England and Virginia. As early as 1773, Baptists sent petitions to the Massachusetts legislature along with a memorial to the delegates to the Continental Congress. Four years later, they joined the battle over the state constitution of Massachusetts. Under the capable leadership of Isaac Backus, Baptists protested that the proposed document offered no significant changes in the laws prohibiting religious freedom. Backus served as the chair of the influential Grievance Committee of the Warren

---

[1] Edwin Scott Gaustad, ed., *Religious Issues in American History* (New York: Harper Forum Books, 1968) 64–67.

Association. In his role as elder statesman among Baptists in New England and through the publication of his pamphlets and petitions, he addressed the situation in Massachusetts by comparing it to the colonists' struggle for liberty during the Revolution. In his writings, Backus located the struggle for freedom on two fronts: a struggle against the British government for civil liberty and a struggle against the state-sponsored established church of Massachusetts for religious liberty. In his arguments, he drew parallels between the colonial struggle against British authority regarding taxation without representation and the Baptists' struggles against the religious taxes imposed by the state of Massachusetts.[2] Backus believed that the struggle for religious liberty was the fundamental issue of the American Revolution. Because of their efforts, Baptists witnessed the defeat of the proposed constitution in 1788, but during the following year, establishment leaders in Massachusetts made another attempt to frame a new constitution and prevailed. Massachusetts maintained an official establishment of religion for another forty-four years.

In reviewing these events, Leon McBeth states that Backus and others formed their positions gradually and that in the initial stages of the struggle for full religious liberty and disestablishment in Massachusetts, they accepted a *de jure* religious establishment as long as all religious groups were treated fairly. In time, however, Backus "came to see that Baptists would fare better on their own and what began as a matter of pragmatic preference gradually matured over the years to embody a principle of religious liberty for all."[3] Even though Isaac Backus and the Baptists of Massachusetts did not prevent the ratification of the state constitution, they were able to experience religious liberty in practice if not always in the full measure of the law.

In the South, particularly in Virginia, it was the Anglican Church and not the Congregational Church that the Baptists struggled against. From the earliest colonial days in the seventeenth century, Virginia enacted laws providing for the punishment of dissenters, but such measures were not always strictly enforced. After the First Great Awakening, as Separate Baptists grew dramatically in number, opposition to dissenters increased and escalated to persecution in some cases. Authorities publicly whipped and jailed several notable preachers and levied heavy fines on others. Under the provisions of the

---

[2] Isaac Backus, "An Appeal to the Public for Religious Liberty," in *A Sourcebook for Baptist Heritage*, H. Leon McBeth (Nashville: Broadman Press, 1990) 173–78.

[3] H. Leon McBeth, *The Baptist Heritage: Four Centuries of Baptist Witness* (Nashville: Broadman Press, 1987) 262.

English Act of Toleration, Baptists were eligible for relief from this punishment as long as they registered their meeting houses. This proved to be a problem since many of the dissenting groups had no official meetinghouses and met in homes, barns, or outside in groves. To compound their difficulties, local authorities often refused to recognize the validity of the marriages of Baptists and other dissenters.

Baptists in Virginia addressed these injustices as their brethren in New England did. They launched a petition campaign directed to the House of Burgesses and drew parallels between their struggles with oppressive religious establishments and the American colonists' battles against an oppressive British monarchy. In 1784 the Baptists in Virginia created the General Committee made up of delegates from each of the local associations, and from this point forward, the committee coordinated and centralized the petition efforts. The petitions addressed a variety of issues such as taxation to support Anglican clergy, requirements to register their meeting houses, the refusal of the government to acknowledge the validity of their marriage ceremonies, and the Anglican Church's control over the glebe lands, which were tracts of property deeded to the church from the public domain. The General Committee secured the services of John Leland as its representative in opposing these laws.

Because the membership rolls of Baptist churches swelled and local politicians depended upon their support, the authorities in Virginia had no choice but to address their complaints. One proposal for resolving the conflict was a compromise in the form of a "general assessment" bill for religion. This arrangement essentially kept Christianity as the officially-established religion of Virginia but provided that all denominations would enjoy equally the privileges of establishment. Respected leaders such as Patrick Henry and George Washington supported this measure as being fair to all concerned. Seen as a skillful move to bring peace, Henry's proposal proved to be popular and moved toward certain approval until Baptists, with assistance from other dissenting groups and joined by the statesman James Madison, launched countermeasures to defeat it.[4]

It was during this legislative struggle that James Madison composed his landmark treatise "A Memorial and Remonstrance on the Religious Rights of Man." Echoing the sentiments of Baptists such as Roger Williams and Isaac Backus who earlier had advocated religious liberty, Madison in his "Memorial and Remonstrance" insisted that temporal authorities had no business making

---

[4] Ibid., 278–79.

laws about spiritual matters. Only one authority could rule these affairs—the Supreme Lawgiver of the universe. The Christian religion did not depend on the support of the state for its justification. The general assessment bill along with an act granting special privileges to the clergy of the Anglican Church were defeated in 1784. McBeth comments that Madison's "Memorial and Remonstrance" is a magnificent statement that "gathers up the best American thinking on church-state relations to that time." Madison's arguments "sounded the death knell for general assessment in Virginia and probably in several other states as well."[5] Madison's "Memorial and Remonstrance" paved the way in the next year for the Virginia Assembly to consider a bill on religious freedom that had been introduced by Thomas Jefferson ten years earlier. After several amendments, the assembly passed in January 1786 the Bill for the Establishment of Religious Freedom, which effectively counteracted the efforts of Anglicans to maintain an established church. Even though other matters such as the disposition of the glebe lands had to be worked out, this bill settled the issue of religious liberty in the state of Virginia.

The next battle for church-state separation joined by the Baptists of Virginia was the Federal Constitution. When the proposed document first appeared in 1787, Baptists were dismayed that there was no guarantee for religious freedom. The document, in fact, had little to say about the subject of religion at all. When the General Committee of Virginia Baptists met in 1788, their first order of business was the proposed Federal Constitution. They appointed John Leland as their representative, and as with the petition movement earlier, he became a tireless advocate for redressing this deficiency. On behalf of the Baptists of Virginia, Leland addressed the issue with numerous constituents including George Washington and especially James Madison who stood with the Baptists during the struggle over general assessment. As a candidate to represent his district at the Constitutional Convention, Madison soon realized that unless he could assure his constituents that he would work diligently for a Bill of Rights when the next Congress convened, the proposed Constitution would most likely fail in his state. Baptists even mounted a campaign opposing ratification, and Madison became the focus of their lobbying efforts.

The events that followed are not always clear from the historical records. Some accounts indicate that the Baptists, recognizing their growing political influence, decided to run their own candidate, possibly John Leland, against

---

[5] Ibid., 279.

James Madison in the election for delegates to the Constitutional Convention. An alleged meeting between Leland and Madison in a grove of trees to broker a deal has taken on the aura of legend. Some historians indicate that this day-long meeting swayed the election and subsequently determined the course of American history on the issue of church-state separation. Other versions describe Leland and Madison meeting in Leland's home where the two discussed the Constitution for several hours. Regardless of where, when, how, or if these two met, Leland and the Baptists of Virginia, with assurance from Madison that he would work for a Bill of Rights that guaranteed religious liberty, pledged their political support to Madison, and he was elected as the representative to the Constitutional Convention. While it might be a slight exaggeration to claim that John Leland and the Baptists of Virginia were responsible for the Bill of Rights and the First Amendment, it is fair to state that the Leland's caucusing and the support of the Baptists was crucial in determining the outcome of Madison's election. McBeth assesses these developments by saying, "Baptists provided many of the ideas undergirding religious liberty, and they spearheaded the public agitation which led to the Bill of Rights."[6]

Madison delivered on his political promises. In 1789 he introduced and championed the proposed amendments to the Constitution that became known as the Bill of Rights. The first of these amendments, which Congress eventually approved, reads, "Congress shall make no law respecting an establishment of religion, or prohibiting the free exercise thereof; or abridging the freedom of speech, or of the press; or the right of the people peaceably to assemble, and to petition the Government for a redress of grievances."[7] Aside from the First Amendment, however, the Constitution scarcely mentioned religion, and after its passage, religious establishments supported by public tax revenues continued for another forty years. The framers of the Constitution were political realists who realized the difficulty of ratifying of such a document in a fledgling nation of divided religious loyalties, so they said as little about the subject as possible. The prevailing assumption was that religion and in particular Christianity should be able to flourish without governmental interference, so politically

---

[6] Ibid., 283.

[7] "About the First Amendment," First Amendment Center, http://www.firstamendmentcenter.org/about.aspx?item=about_firstamd (accessed 5 November 2006).

dominant and established churches, especially in New England, continued to enjoy special privileges.

The Demise of State-Established Religion

Connecticut was one of the states where the Standing Order of Congregationalists, ruled by a small group of elite families, still stood. Non-Congregationalists did not enjoy the same freedoms as Americans in other states. Baptists and other dissenters were able to claim exemption from religious taxation, but the process for exemption involved a confusing and humiliating process of obtaining certificates whose stipulations often changed upon the passage of every new bill of legislation. The state church controlled the upper house of the legislature in which none but Congregationalists could serve, and Congregationalist ministers operated the schools and through them the church-state system that benefited their churches. Establishment clergy were not reticent in ridiculing dissenters and denouncing Jeffersonian democracy as invidious threats to true religion and civilized society.

John Leland, who had successfully served as a leading opponent of established religion during his fourteen years of residence in Virginia, returned to his native New England in 1791. He settled with his family in Connecticut and continued the fight that he championed in the South. Known for his quick-witted and popular preaching, he also wielded a sharp pen and with other dissenters launched into a pamphlet war to assault the remaining vestiges of state-controlled religion in Connecticut. The titles of Leland's pamphlets were as colorful as the language he employed in making his arguments. In tracts such as *The High-Flying Churchman, Stript of His Legal Robe, Appears a Yahoo*, and *The Dissenter's Strong Box*, Leland, in his inimitable folksy and rustic manner, appealed to the growing ranks of Jeffersonian Republicans, middle-class farmers, and mercantile shopkeepers who resented the high-handedness of the establishment caste. Leland's *Strong Box* became his tool box in hammering away at the establishment. With it, he provided sample petitions that dissenters could use as missiles in firing at the General Assembly and citations of extracts from the constitutions of sixteen states and territories that had already conformed their laws and practices to the Federal Constitution. Through his writings, he was effective in making the case that Connecticut should ratify a new state constitution that conformed to federal laws.[8]

After launching the pamphlet war, momentum shifted to the side of the dissenters. During this political skirmish, President Thomas Jefferson wrote his famous letter to the Baptists of Danbury, Connecticut, in 1802 in which he coined the phrase "building a wall of separation between church and state."[9] One year later the Supreme Court issued the *Marbury vs. Madison* decision that determined that a state had no legal justification for violating the provisions of the Federal Constitution. Dissenters buried their sectarian and doctrinal differences to unite as one against the common foe of the Standing Order, and the party of Jefferson gained ground by winning key state elections. In a supreme irony illustrating that politics often makes strange bedfellows, the leaders of the Episcopal Church, the same church that had resisted the efforts of the Baptists in Virginia, closed ranks with the Baptists, Methodists, Quakers, Unitarians, and disaffected "New Light" Congregationalists to vote Republican and bring down the last remnants of state-sponsored religion in Connecticut. By 1818 the state had capitulated to a full acceptance of the provisions of the First Amendment.

The most eloquent and ardent supporter of the establishment in Connecticut was Lyman Beecher. Beecher and members of his powerful family were the instantiation of establishment and the old order of religion in New England. With imploring sincerity, Beecher throughout the pamphlet war argued for the necessity of a state church as the very foundation for good government, sound morals, societal stability, and true religion. Within a few years, however, he dramatically reversed his unflinching position and confessed that what he thought would be the worst thing to happen in Connecticut turned out to be the best. He relented, "Before we had been standing on what our fathers had done, but now we were obliged to develop all our energy." He confessed that the new order of things threw the churches "wholly on their own resources and God" and thereby enabled churches to exercise a greater

---

[8] For the works of Leland, see *The Writings of the Late Elder John Leland, Including Some Events in His Life, Written By Himself, With Additional Sketches*, ed. L. F. Greene (New York: Arno Press and New York Times, 1969).

[9] "Jefferson's Wall of Separation Letter," The US Constitution Online, http://www.usconstitution.net/jeffwall.html (accessed 15 March 2006).

influence through voluntary efforts.[10] Beecher's "conversion" was emblematic of the force of progress toward legal disestablishment in the new nation.

Only Massachusetts held fast and was the last to surrender. As a colony founded by the Puritans, Massachusetts had been entrenched in its opposition to religious dissent for nearly 200 years. After the Revolution, amendments to the state constitution ameliorated harsh penalties such as physical punishment and banishment, yet main articles of the document still clearly provided for the support of a state church. Massachusetts allowed for taxes levied against dissenters to be used in supporting teachers of their own churches provided that these groups were able to maintain a regular minister. But if this condition were not met, then these tax revenues were transferred for the support of the teachers of the established church in the parish or precinct in which the funds had been collected. Invariably, this meant that dissenters were still being taxed to support the local Congregational church and its minister. The law stipulated that the dissenting congregations that appealed for the use of tax funds must first apply to the public treasurer. In some instances treasurers escrowed the payments and forced dissenters to file lawsuits to obtain their funds. To further compound their difficulties, the Massachusetts Supreme Court in 1810 ruled that preachers of unincorporated religious societies were not considered public teachers within the strict interpretation of the law. Subsequent developments in Massachusetts, however, mirrored the pattern of other states. While members of the Standing Order temporized, they gradually lost their majority status because of the growth in numbers of Baptists and other members of dissenting churches.

John Leland again entered the fray for full religious freedom as he had in Virginia and Connecticut. After spending only a short time in Connecticut, Leland relocated to the village of Cheshire in Western Massachusetts. As he had done in Virginia and Connecticut, Leland served a local Baptist church as pastor, engaged in an itinerant evangelistic ministry, and prosecuted with fervor his pamphlet and tract writing against the religious establishment. The "frontier" of Western Massachusetts, remotely removed from the commercial and cultural hub of Boston, was known as a stronghold for Baptists and other dissenters. In opposition to the prevailing federalist sentiments in the state, the Republicans of this region wielded their rising influence and overwhelmingly won elections during the fermentative period of contention over state-

---

[10] Winthrop S. Hudson, *The Great Tradition of the American Churches* (New York: Harper and Row, Publishers, 1953) 65.

established religion. A vignette from American political lore illustrates the shifting political tide in this area of the state known for its agrarian base. Dairy farmers from Western Massachusetts sent a half-ton block of cheddar cheese as a gift to President Thomas Jefferson. A delegation of local voters authorized Leland to dispatch a letter of appreciation to the president to accompany the cheese on its journey to Washington. In the communiqué Leland bragged that not a drop of milk from a federalist cow had been used in molding the mammoth cheese.[11]

The dissenters were persuasive in accomplishing their objectives, but other events proved to be just as decisive in bringing down the last bastion of the state church system in America. An internecine skirmish between Trinitarian and Unitarian parties within the Congregationalist Church led to a decision that gave the Unitarians the right to control properties of the church when they held the majority. Once dispossessed, Trinitarian Congregationalists, like the dissenters, considered it reprehensible to pay taxes to a church that violated their doctrinal tenets and that, in good conscience, they could not support. Economic issues also factored into the shifting tide of affairs. The burgeoning New England industrial order depended upon immigrant laborers, many of whom were Roman Catholic. It was no longer financially pragmatic or economically feasible to marginalize groups that were essential to manufacturing, trade, and commerce. Massachusetts's belated surrender of its religious establishment, characteristic of Yankee thrift, was desirable only when it became profitable.[12]

In 1833 the Massachusetts legislature proposed annulling the contested provisions of the state constitution, and when it put the matter in a referendum to the people, the citizens of the state voted ten to one to remove the statutes that provided for state-sponsored religion. The year 1833, then, is one of those landmark turning points in the history of Baptists and other dissenters who had born witness, sometimes with the price of their own blood, to the ideal of religious liberty and church-state separation. In that year, the last remnant of the standing order of state-established religion in the United States fell, never to rise again. During the meetings of the First Continental Congress when Baptists had gained a brief hearing to protest their mistreatment and to lay

---

[11] C. A. Browne, "Elder Leland and the Mammoth Cheshire Cheese," *Agricultural History* 18 (1944): 145–53.

[12] Joseph Martin Dawson, *Baptists and the American Republic* (Nashville: Broadman Press, 1956) 135.

claim to fundamental religious rights, they were dismissed as "enthusiasts" with little cause for complaint. Reportedly, John Adams of Massachusetts in a parting shot commented sourly that the Baptists "might as well expect a change in the solar system as to expect they would give up their establishment." As McBeth observes, "Thus far the solar system has endured, but religious establishment in Massachusetts gave way in 1833, over forty years after the adoption of the First Amendment."[13]

The Impact of Disestablishment

Disestablishment, which now carried with it the force of law in every state of the nation, not only altered the relationship of churches to the government but also impacted the structure of churches as ecclesiastical bodies. Some of the churches, such as the Anglican Church, reorganized on national patterns. Others, like the Presbyterians regrouped, and the Congregationalists suffered further polarization between Old Order, "New Light," and Unitarian parties. The older communions increasingly lost ground to newer groups, such as the Baptists and Methodists, and the era gave rise to innovative religious expressions not previously seen in the history of Christianity. When disestablishment altered the sphere of influence of the churches, religious leaders gave their energies to new forms of ecclesial expression. The developing construct for understanding the identity and mission of the church in the wake of church-state separation was the denomination that Martin Marty describes as the most significant ecclesiastical invention of the era and that "imposed itself as if its logic were irresistible and its scope predestined on all churches."[14] With denominationalism also came the demise of the parish system and a growing focus upon the local church.

In the midst of what Nathan Hatch called "the most centrifugal epoch in American church history"[15] when churches of the old order no longer stood at the center of culture, there was nevertheless the centripetal development of a broad, evangelical consensus. While theological and ecclesiastical differences existed among groups formally at odds over church-state issues, Christians as "co-belligerents" often united for strategic, benevolent, and political purposes.

---

[13] McBeth, *Baptist Heritage*, 266.

[14] Martin E. Marty, *Righteous Empire: The Protestant Experience in America* (New York: Harper Torchbooks, 1977) 68.

[15] Nathan Hatch, *The Democratization of American Christianity* (New Haven: Yale University Press, 1989) 15.

The hope of realizing a Christian civilization remained undaunted in the aftermath of legal disestablishment. The watershed of church-state relations in 1833 signaled that the matrix of ideas had shifted to a Jeffersonian emphasis on separation and a fundamental evangelical conviction that the realm of authentic religion lay beyond the reach of government, but certain vestiges of state religion persisted nonetheless. A majority of evangelical Christians held firmly to the belief that Christianity was indispensable to the moral and social health of the nation. Robert T. Handy in *A Christian America: Protestant Hopes and Historical Realities*, states that "the passing of the patterns of colonial establishment did not at all mean that the Christian hope for the triumph of Christian civilization was being given up, but that voluntary ways of working towards it were being extended."[16] Beyond 1833 the efforts to extend a renewed vision of Christian civilization focused less on theological and denominational differences and more on the broader issues of true religion, morality, and education.

Baptists, people of missionary zeal and voluntary religion, were in a prime position to migrate from outside of the stream of religious influence to the center as they contributed to and capitalized upon this broad, evangelical consensus. Before the reality of full legal disestablishment, Isaac Backus in his work titled *History of New England, With Particular Reference to the Denomination of Christians Called Baptists*, proclaimed bright millennial hopes for the progress of Christianity and its transformation of American society. Unlike his opponents from the Standing Order of New England, however, Backus believed that the path toward realizing a post-millennial order of peace, justice, and morality was the Baptist way of voluntary religion and freedom for the progress of the gospel without either the sponsorship or constraints imposed by the government. A generation later, Francis Wayland, president of Brown University and leader among Baptists in America, echoed the hopes voiced by Backus. With confidence, he averred that voluntary societies are "to be the great moral means by which the regeneration of the world is to be effected."[17]

When state-established denominations faded, volunteerism came to the front. Philip Schaff concluded that voluntarism was, in fact, the necessary

---

[16] Robert T. Handy, *A Christian America: Protest Hopes and Historical Realities* (New York: Oxford University Press, 1971) 25.
[17] Francis Wayland, *The Limitations of Human Responsibility* (Boston: Gould, Kendall and Lincoln, 1838) 90–91.

consequence of the separation of church and state.[18] As a result, a new surge of spiritual vitality brought a profusion of voluntary societies with specific missions. These societies comprised of individuals drawn from multiple denominations pursued moral concerns beyond the confessional and liturgical traditions of the churches. Operating beyond the supervision and control of bishops, synods, judicatories, and associations, the voluntary societies spent their moral energies on such wide-ranging causes as literature, Sunday schools, colleges, hospitals, charitable foundations, temperance, and the abolition of slavery.

One particular issue that served as an index of the power of volunteerism in the wake of disestablishment and an unabated commitment to the achievement of a Christian civilization was the crusade to prohibit the delivery of mail on Sunday and to promote the observance of the "Christian Sabbath." Most Protestant leaders and clergy during this period, including Baptists, weighed in behind the crusade. A notable exception was John Leland, who feared that organizing voluntary societies to protect the Sabbath was a harbinger of regression towards a reestablishment of state religion that would reverse the hard-won gains made for full religious liberty. Leland's voice on the subject, though strong, principled, and sometimes shrill, was in the minority. The irony of this expression of voluntarism is that Baptists and other former dissenters who vehemently opposed taxation to support public religious activities nevertheless teamed up with the "theocrats" of the former Standing Order, such as Timothy Dwight and Lyman Beecher, to push for public and legal restrictions on the Sabbath as a noble effort to secure a Christian society.[19]

Volunteerism revealed that the methods but not the goals of Protestant leaders had changed. The effects of Enlightenment thought, the contributions of the Great Awakening, and the tensions among diverse and multiplying churches all played a role in the erosion of the religious establishment, but the idea of cultivating and protecting a Christian society was deeply embedded in the culture. Leaders associated with the formerly established churches generally accepted the new plurality of denominations and with it the influence that Baptists and other groups exerted. Even though they abandoned the theocratic project, they sought to maintain Protestant hegemony by the power of spiritual

---

[18] Philip Schaff, *Church and State in the United States* (New York: G. P. Putnam's and Sons, 1888) 78.
[19] Brad Creed, "John Leland and Sunday Mail Delivery: Religious Liberty, Evangelical Piety, and the Problem of a 'Christian Nation,'" *Fides et Historia* 33/2 (Summer/Fall 2001): 1–11.

persuasion and volunteerism. Winthrop Hudson asserts that the great tradition of the American churches is the voluntary principle and resulted in "one of the most successful penetrations of culture by a religious faith that the world has ever known."[20] Instead of leading to the demise of true religion, as some had warned, these developments brought about renewed growth to Christianity in America and extended the influence and scope of the churches in society.

Since their inauspicious beginnings in England in the early part of the seventeenth century, Baptists had faithfully contended for complete religious freedom. What began as a testimony about a religious conviction rooted in their understanding of scripture and the nature of God found fruition in landmark changes in law and government over 200 years later. The separation of church and state is the logical and necessary corollary of the witness of religious liberty for all people. Historically, it was both cause and effect in the maelstrom of monumental religious and cultural changes sweeping through a new nation. The year 1833, a denotation of time when the last legal establishment of religion in America crumbled, was a turning point for Baptists who had battled for centuries through adversity, marginalization, and persecution. It was also a turning point in the history of church-state relations since nothing of this magnitude had occurred in 1,400 years, and a watershed in the history of democracy and the human quest for freedom.

Suggested Reading

Dawson, Joseph Martin. *Baptists and the American Republic*. Nashville: Broadman Press, 1956.

"About the First Amendment." First Amendment Center. http://www.firstamendmentcenter.org/about.aspx?item=about_firstamd.

Gaustad, Edwin Scott. "Responsible Freedom: Baptists in Early America." *Baptists in the Balance*. Edited by Everett C. Goodwin. Valley Forge: Judson Press, 1997.

———, editor. "Subsidy or Separation." Chapter 5 in *Religious Issues in American History*. New York: Harper Forum Books, 1968.

McBeth, H. Leon. "Baptists in Colonial America: The Struggle for Religious Liberty." Chapter 8 in *The Baptist Heritage: Four Centuries of Baptist Witness*. Nashville: Broadman Press, 1987.

[20] Hudson, *Great Tradition*, 20.

CHAPTER 14

Baptists and Racism and the Turn toward Segregation: 1845

Terry Carter

The year 1845 stands out as one of the most significant in the history of Baptists and especially those in the United States. In that year white Baptist leaders of the South separated from Baptists of the North and formed the Southern Baptist Convention (SBC) in Augusta, Georgia, primarily in defense of slavery. Slavery laid the groundwork for attitudes and actions that would plague the Southern Baptist Convention for more than a century and a half. While it may be true, as some historians have argued, that other issues influenced the formation of the SBC, one must stress that the major point of contention between white Baptists of the North and those in the South centered on attitudes toward slavery and the black population in America. The defense of slavery was not only the major factor in the organization of the SBC, but it also set the stage for a racial prejudice that exists to the present day.

English Baptists and Slavery

Slavery and the negative attitudes toward African Americans were not unique to Baptists in the United States. British Baptists also faced the issue, but they overcame it more quickly due to the abolitionist work of William Knibb and the anti-slavery attitudes that developed in the British government. England had an active slave trade based in its colonial empire, and in the early 1700s some English Baptists accepted it and even defended it. In 1711 the First Baptist Church of Charleston, South Carolina, inquired of the Western Baptist Association in England as to whether to discipline a slaveholding member who had severely punished a runaway slave. The English association replied with a proslavery statement stating that slavery was lawful, the buying and selling of slaves was not scripturally forbidden, and that slave owners must have the right to enforce discipline.[1] Not all British Baptists agreed, however, and eventually the anti-slavery voices became the loudest among the Baptists of England. After the mid 1700s many British Baptist associations opposed slavery, and some even formed abolition societies and raised money to end the slave trade. One influential Baptist leader, Robert Robinson of Cambridge, preached and wrote against slavery. In 1788 Robinson even helped write a resolution to Parliament condemning slavery.[2]

One of the strongest and most outspoken Baptist voices of the eighteenth century against slavery was Abraham Booth. Booth published a treatise in 1792, *Commerce in the Human Species, and the Enslaving of Innocent Persons, Inimical in the Laws of Moses and the Gospel of Christ*, condemning slavery. He claimed that slavery not only violated the Holy Scripture of both Old and New Testament but also that it deprived the rights of humans. For Booth the whole business was "barbarous and savage."[3]

English Baptists' condemnation of slavery and slave trade increased in the early nineteenth century. The British Parliament abolished slavery in 1833 and much of the impetus came from vocal and active Baptists. Even one of William Carey's colleagues, William Ward, started out his ministry speaking and writing against slavery. However, one of the most influential opponents to slavery and slave trade was William Knibb, who served as a missionary in the British colony of Jamaica. He defended the human rights of blacks enslaved there. In England Knibb's speeches aroused the British against slavery. After 1833 Knibb followed up by helping released slaves find their way with their newly granted freedom. In Jamaica Knibb performed a funeral service depicting death for slavery by burying a coffin filled with leg irons and shackles at midnight. He declared that the monster—slavery—was dead.[4]

English Baptists desired to spread the call for freedom. They were distressed that slavery in America seemed to be of the worst kind, entrenched and cruel. In 1833 British Baptists sent a letter to Baptists in America opposing slavery and promoting abolition. The letter condemned the slave system in America as sin and suggested that it be abandoned as evil. They encouraged Baptists in America to do all they could to "effect its speedy overthrow."

---

[1] Leon McBeth, *The Baptist Heritage: Four Centuries of Baptist Witness* (Nashville: Broadman Press, 1987) 197–98.

[2] Ibid.

[3] Ibid.

[4] Ibid., 300–301.

American Baptist leaders in the Triennial Convention replied that they could not interfere in this area. Despite the convention's response, some American Baptists sent other letters agreeing with the English. The English Baptists persisted, sending two representatives—Francis A. Cox and James Hoby—to visit America to promote the emancipation of the Negro slaves. Cox and Hoby, prominent English pastors, traveled throughout the United States for several months with their anti-slavery message. Although dissatisfied with their efforts, Cox and Hoby stirred up tensions among Baptists in the United States over the issue of slavery. It helped inflame the circumstances that eventually led to the schism of 1845.[5]

American Baptist Attitudes Concerning Slavery

Slavery and prejudice against blacks among American Baptists were not always clearly Northern or Southern issues. Prior to 1800 some Baptists in the South opposed slavery and even organized abolition organizations. However, as is often the case, social and economic circumstances influenced beliefs and prejudices. Increased industrialization impacted the larger cities of the northern United States resulting in a decreased need for any kind of slave labor. This shifted Northern attitudes against slavery because it was no longer profitable. In the South the invention of the cotton gin by Eli Whitney in 1792 made it possible for cotton to become king. Cotton became more profitable because it could be separated more easily and cheaply from the seeds. However, planting and harvesting cotton required manual labor and the African slave met that need. Slavery became an economic necessity in the eyes of Southerners including Baptists of the South. No doubt many Baptists in the South who at one time opposed slavery changed their minds after 1800.

American Baptists defended the idea of slavery on several accounts. Emmanuel L. McCall listed at least six negative attitudes toward African Americans.[6] Two of the reasons seem to be especially racist. Hamitic Determinism, or reference to the curse of Ham regarding black humans, became a common argument among pro-slavery Christians in the South. According to this view, when Noah got drunk after the flood and laid naked on his bed, his son Ham saw him. Ham became the father of Canaan, and Noah cursed Canaan with slavery because of the sin. White Southerners used this text

---

[5] Ibid.

[6] Emmanuel L. McCall, "Slave or Free: Baptist Attitudes toward African Americans," *Baptist History and Heritage* 32/3–4 (July/October 1997): 48–53.

to attribute the idea of slavery to God himself and believed it singled out the Negro for a life of slavery. This curse was endowed with even more racism when some argued that Ham's real sin was "racial amalgamation." He contaminated the race by marrying into Cain's family, which according to the theory was stricken with black skin because of his sin of killing Abel.[7] Although these theories are ridiculous in more ways than one, no doubt many Baptists in the South bought into them with other Southern Christians. Accepting such ideas would have made it easy to support slavery. Fortunately, most Baptist leaders who wrote in support of slavery did not use these arguments.

Richard Furman, pastor of the prestigious First Baptist Church of Charleston and first president of the Triennial Convention, presented a milder but still racist approach to the defense of slavery. In his 1822 *Treatise on Slavery*, directed to the governor of South Carolina, Furman argued against general emancipation because of the chaos that would result from releasing one-sixth of the population from slavery. He warned that rebellion might occur and that then even those in favor of the emancipation would join with fellow-citizens to quell the resulting carnage. He argued further that the right to hold slaves was "clearly established in the Holy Scriptures, both by precept and example."[8]

Furman added that slavery in America possessed some positive elements for African slaves. While explicitly rejecting cruelty in slavery, Furman believed that the slaves were helped spiritually and physically because of slavery. It is a means of saving lives because their living conditions improved when sold to humane masters. These slaves also benefited spiritually because coming to the United States "has been the means of their mental and religious improvement, and so of obtaining salvation, as many of themselves have joyfully and thankfully confessed."[9] Setting them free would not result in their happiness or that of the nation according to Furman. However, he stated that if a time arrived when emancipation would be best for slaves and the nation, Baptists would gladly allow it. Furman did not argue that slaves were less human or cursed and therefore deserving of the state of slavery. However, as humane as

---

[7]H. Shelton Smith, *In His Image, But...: Racism in Southern Religion, 1780–1910* (Durham: Duke University Press, 1972) 130–31. The story of the Hamitic curse is located in Genesis 9:20–25.

[8] Leon McBeth, *A Sourcebook for Baptist Heritage* (Nashville: Broadman Press, 1990) 252–53.

[9] Ibid.

his argument is in comparison to the Hamitic conclusions, it still kept blacks in a subservient role believing that best for all concerned.

American Baptists' Reactions to Slavery Issues

It should be noted that slavery and beliefs concerning the state of the African slave were not the only reasons that Baptists in the North and South struggled to get along. Along with cultural differences they disagreed over the type of organizational structure needed to carry out missions. From the formation of the Triennial Convention in 1814, controversy continued over convention versus society types of organization. Originally, many Baptists favored a society approach similar to that of the Baptist Missionary Society formed to support William Carey. Based in the North, the Triennial Convention formed in 1814 in Philadelphia followed the society approach, and its northern location was popular with Baptists in the North due to the ease with which they could attend its meetings.

Baptists in the South tended to support the more complex convention style of organizational structure. The Triennial Convention originally appeared more like a convention when it supported both foreign and home missions, and education. When the convention eventually dropped the two latter endeavors and moved the foreign missions headquarters further north to Boston in 1826, structure became more societal and also less accessible to Southerners. This caused dissension.

Home missions provided another reason for dissension among Baptists. In 1832 Baptists established the Home Mission Society in New York City designed to focus on the ministry that the Triennial Convention gave up. Baptists in the South supported the society but issues developed. Southerners believed that, despite their financial support, the HMS was dispensing monies or assigning missionaries inequitably. The statistics don't fully support the reality of the complaint. In fact, the Southern states may have received more missionary aid than they gave from 1832 to 1841. Records also demonstrate that in terms of missionary personnel, most mission volunteers came from Northern states and were distributed primarily in the upper Midwest. However, the Home Mission Society tried to be sensitive and equitable and solve the problem. They issued special appeals to Southerners for mission volunteers and even offered higher salaries for those who would go south. Even with their efforts Northern volunteers showed reluctance for southern fields for reasons like slavery, distance, and the climate. Undoubtedly, the hot southern summers with insects and humidity didn't help their efforts. This problem added to the Southern desire to form a separate convention in 1845.

Even though organizational concerns and the perceived imbalances in home mission efforts added fuel to the flames of Southern frustration with the Triennial Convention and the Home Mission Society, these stood as secondary issues to the main point of contention—slavery. As the Baptists in the North grew more vocal about the moral evil of slavery and promoted abolitionism, Baptists in the South defended slavery more vigorously. The major question centered upon how the two mission sending organizations should handle the problem of mission appointments. Pressure mounted in the North to exclude slaveholders from mission service. Naturally, this worried Baptists in the South.

Both organizations reacted by distancing themselves from the slavery issue. As far back as 1834 the Triennial Convention had issued a statement to English Baptists that it could not interfere with the issue of slavery since it was not "among the objects for which the Convention and the Board were formed."[10] Their first reaction was one of neutrality. As tensions grew in the 1840s, both boards restated that approach. Leaders on both sides wanted to avoid division if possible. Some Baptist groups in the South called for a separate convention as early as the 1830s. The Charleston association voted in 1840 to consider a Southern Baptist Foreign Mission organization. Hoping to allay Southern and Northern anxieties, the Triennial Convention adopted an official policy of neutrality on slavery. They reaffirmed foreign missions as the one object of the convention and recalled the origin of the convention where no obstruction was laid which would hinder anyone from giving or being involved.[11] The Home Mission Society took the same tack in its 1841 meeting voting that "cooperation in this body does not imply any sympathy either with slavery or anti-slavery."[12] These efforts did not calm either side. Prompted by Richard Fuller of Charleston, the Home Mission Society repeated their neutral stance in 1844.

A Test of Neutrality

Neutrality is easily stated but some Baptists in the South doubted its reality. Two separate groups decided to test it by forcing the hands of both boards. Georgia Baptists, not convinced that the Home Mission Society would actually appoint a slaveholding volunteer, submitted James E. Reeve as a

---

[10] McBeth, *Baptist Heritage*, 301.
[11] McBeth, *Sourcebook*, 255.
[12] McBeth, *Baptist Heritage*, 385.

missionary candidate and raised the money for his support. Reeve owned only a few slaves. The Home Mission Society found itself in a difficult situation. To approve his application would have caused concerns with abolitionist Baptists in the North. To reject it meant problems with Baptists in the South. Georgia Baptists orchestrated this dilemma. They openly stated that it was a test to close the mouths of "gainsayers." The Home Mission Society attempted to remain neutral on the issue. This proved a hard task. In their opinion, acting on a test case would violate the society's neutrality. They informed Georgia Baptists that they did not feel at liberty to entertain Reeve's application. In this way the society did not appoint or reject. Georgia Baptists saw it another way. They believed that this test case offered proof that a slaveholder would not be welcomed as a home missionary. Such an action eliminated many Baptists in the South from active home missionary service.

Alabama Baptists addressed the question directly to the Triennial Convention. Like Georgia Baptists, Alabama Baptists also had doubts that a slaveholder could be appointed. Alabama Baptists passed strongly worded resolutions asking outright if a slaveholder could be appointed. The Triennial Convention faced the same difficult decision the Home Mission Society faced with the Reeve case. They could offend either Southerners or Northerners with their decision. The convention's board chose to remain neutral but added a revealing statement. While restating neutrality, they added, "One thing is certain; we can never be a party to any arrangements which would imply approbation (approval) of slavery."[13] Alabama Baptists received this word as a definite "no" to their question. In their minds, slaveholders and those who supported slavery were eliminated from mission service with the boards.

A Decision to Separate Prompted by Support of Slavery

Virginia Baptists reacted first to the outcome of the Alabama Resolutions. The *Religious Herald* in March 1845 complained that society's boards had violated the rights of Baptists in the South and called for a quick withdrawal from the convention. The Virginia Baptist Missionary Society had already passed resolutions calling for a meeting to decide the best way to promote foreign missions as a Baptist convention in the South and designated a meeting time and place. They called for a meeting in Augusta, Georgia, two months

---

[13] Ibid., 387.

later. Not everyone agreed with such hasty and rash action, but the meeting took place.

On 8 May 1845, 293 male Baptist delegates representing various churches and organizations from Southern states met in Augusta. All but twenty of the delegates were from Georgia, South Carolina, and Virginia. Even one Northern organization, the American Baptist Publication Society, sent a representative. A key figure in the deliberations was William Bullien Johnson of South Carolina. Johnson had been an important part of the Triennial Convention organization and the South Carolina Baptist Convention. He served as president of the Triennial Convention in 1844. Undoubtedly, he would have been reelected had he not declined to run for health reasons. It is possible that he chose not to stand for re-election in an effort to ease the tension between abolitionists and slaveholders. His views concerning slavery and missions prompted him to take an active role in the formation of a new convention in the South.

Some say W. B. Johnson arrived at the Augusta meeting in May 1845 with a draft of a constitution for a new convention in his coat pocket. Despite divisive issues such as finances and Landmarkism, delegates approved Johnson's proposal for the new convention with only minor changes. The constitution's organizational structure was convention-oriented rather than societal. The constitution focused on foreign and home missions. The convention elected board managers to administer its business. Delegates elected Johnson as the convention's first president. The new Domestic Mission Board, with a focus on the United States, was initially headquartered in Marion, Alabama, and later moved to Atlanta, Georgia. The Foreign Mission Board settled in Richmond, Virginia, where it still resides.

The division was final. The issues of slavery and attitudes toward African slaves in the South proved so important that the Baptists in the South were unwilling to give them up. They chose to form their own organization and keep slavery rather than compromise in order to be involved in missions. Some Northerners understood the action, but believed it a temporary arrangement and hoped for eventual reconciliation. That did not prove to be the case. The division was permanent. Although slavery was the central issue for the separation, the new Southern Baptist Convention preferred to cite Northern violation of the mission societies' constitutions as the division's cause.

Secondly, the new convention claimed to restore the original basis of Baptist missionary work, which did not consider slavery in its deliberations. Finally, in an apparent attempt to deemphasize the role of slavery in its creation cause, the Southern Baptist Convention stated that its purpose was not to defend slavery but to extend the "Messiah's Kingdom." Perhaps they wanted to avoid the designation as the "slave convention." Statistically the Southern Baptist Convention started well. It numbered 4,126 churches with 351, 951 members and recorded 23,222 baptisms in its first year of existence.[14] Missions played a key role in the new convention from that time on.

The Vestige of Racism and Segregation

With such origins the attitudes of Baptists in the South regarding African Americans proved slow to change. Even after defeat in the Civil War and slavery's abolition, Southern Baptists retained long-entrenched ideas concerning race and segregation. Before the war, converted black slaves either worshiped in the white churches or were allowed to form their own churches under white supervision.[15] Following the Civil War, blacks left the white churches *en masse* as an expression of freedom and their uniqueness as a race. Many of the white churches encouraged them and some helped organize and train leaders for black churches.[16] Although beneficial for black leadership, it established a pattern of segregated churches that continues to exist. Any biracialism exhibited by white Southern Baptist churches was often the result of paternalism, a desire to counter the effect of Northern missionaries, or a form of white control. Southern Baptists often explained the segregation by saying that blacks preferred it.[17] No doubt racism and negative attitudes toward the former slaves prompted much of their separation from former masters' churches.

After Reconstruction, Southern states began to institute the so-called "Jim Crow Laws" that legalized segregation and further entrenched racism. These segregationist laws were upheld by the Supreme Court in its infamous *Plessy v. Ferguson* decision that declared "separate but equal" the law of the land. During this time leading Baptist clergymen promoted a belief in the inferiority of the Negro and encouraged segregation to avoid racial mixing. Jeremiah Jeter, who wrote for the *Religious Herald*, put forth the argument that God put within man the instinct to keep the races (black and white) separate and social mingling violated God's plan. Jeter believed that such mixing would eventually lead to a

---

[14] Ibid., 391.
[15] McCall, "Slave or Free," 51.
[16] Ibid., 55.
[17] Smith, *In His Image*, 226–27.

degrading of the "noble saxon race." On this premise he argued black Baptist churches should organize separately from white churches.[18] Southern Baptists generally affirmed the racial attitudes that had divided Baptists in 1845 in arguments for universal segregation and encouraged a Southern culture of segregation and racism that continued well into the twentieth century.

The Apology—1995

Fortunately, the legacy of racism eventually caused embarrassment for Southern Baptists whose origins were steeped in its defense. For much of the twentieth century racism's legacy was such a part of Southern culture that very few apologized for it and most regarded it an accepted way of life. However, with the success of the civil rights movement in the 1960s and with continued efforts on behalf of racial equality, tolerance, and reconciliation, Southern Baptists felt the need to express regret over such questionable beginnings. The Southern Baptist Convention had accomplished phenomenal things in the 150 years of existence up to 1995 in areas of missions, education, and evangelism. However, the shadow of its racist origins hung over the denomination.

In June 1995, 20,000 Baptists gathered in the Georgia Dome in Atlanta for the annual convention. At this convention they passed a resolution attempting to remedy a long-standing problem—the stigma of racism and the defense of slavery connected to the origins of the SBC. A resolution "On Racial Reconciliation on the 150th Anniversary of the Southern Baptist Convention" overwhelmingly passed. The resolution theologically connected all races as part of God's world from one mother (Eve) and declared no partiality on God's part. It admitted to past sins of defending slavery, opposing civil rights for African Americans, and racism. Condemning these things, the convention resolved to denounce all racism as sin and lament and repudiate the past actions of the convention that supported it. A statement of apology to all African Americans boldly confessed the sins of the past and asked for forgiveness.[19]

Such an apology and confession grew out of the conviction that the year 1845 was a pivotal turning point in Baptist history. Despite the accomplishments of 150 years of ministry the convention admitted that Southern Baptists were founded upon the twin concepts of slavery and racial

---

[18] Ibid., 228–29.

[19] "Resolution on Racial Reconciliation on the 150th Anniversary of the Southern Baptist Convention," *SBCNet*, http:/sbc.net/resolutions/amResolution.asp?ID=899 (accessed 3 January 2006).

inferiority for African Americans. The year 1845 marked the occasion that Baptists in the South decided that the African slave deserved the state of bondage and was inferior to whites, and that provided reason enough to form a separate and distinct convention. The legacy of that decision lingered for more than a century both as part of the convention and Southern culture. There may be much of which to be proud in Southern Baptist history, but the reasons for its formation that were grounded in slavery and racism cannot be included in that list.

Suggested Reading

Fletcher, Jesse C. *The Southern Baptist Convention: A Sesquicentennial History* (Nashville: Broadman & Holman Publishers, 1994).

Mathisen, Robert R. *Critical Issues in American Religious History: A Reader* (Waco: Baylor University Press, 2001).

McBeth, H. Leon. *The Baptist Heritage: Four Centuries of Baptist Witness* (Nashville: Broadman Press, 1987).

———. *A Sourcebook for Baptist Heritage* (Nashville: Broadman Press, 1990).

Smith, H. Shelton. *In His Image, But...Racism in Southern Religion, 1780–1910* (Durham: Duke University Press, 1972).

CHAPTER 15

Baptists and Landmarkism and the Turn toward Provincialism: 1851

Stephen Stookey

Dateline: Cotton Grove, Tennessee, 24 June 1851. "Baptists Claim Exclusive Rights to the Kingdom of God." Such a headline could have appeared as the Landmark movement was officially launched in western Tennessee. Landmarkism introduced an exclusionist ecclesiology into Baptist life, creating an increasingly isolationist stance among Southern Baptists. The Landmark movement, in Leon McBeth's assessment, "anticipated the modern 'independent' Baptist movement."[1]

As 1851 approached Baptists on both sides of the Atlantic used theology as a means of exclusion and isolation. Fearful of the progressive religious climate of the early nineteenth century, Landmarkism in the American South developed a dogmatic ecclesiology. Frustrated by the advance of Fullerism, high Calvinist English Baptists advanced separation as a means to protect and preserve a pure soteriology.[2]

---

[1] H. Leon McBeth, *The Baptist Heritage* (Nashville: Broadman Press, 1987) 460.
[2] While Landmarkism pulled at the fabric of Baptist connectional life in the United States, high Calvinists among English Baptists advocated separation as the only sure means of preserving and protecting a presumed authentic, biblical theology of salvation. Reacting to the popular embrace of Fullerism, acceptance of open communion and open baptism, and the growing partnerships between the New Connection of General Baptists and the Particular Baptists, the Strict and Particular Baptist movement maintained a faith and practice that would have made John Gill proud. The Strict and Particular Baptist movement lacked a strong, charismatic leader similar to Landmarkism's J. R. Graves. By mid-nineteenth century the Strict and Particular Baptist movement was a collection of small regional associations defending high Calvinism through a series of periodicals. See Earnest A. Payne, *The Baptist Union: A Short History* (London: Carey Kingsgate Press, 1958) and J. H. Y. Briggs, *The English Baptists of the 19th Century* (Didcot: Baptist Historical Society, 1994) for a summary of the interaction between the Strict and

An earnest desire to discern and practice New Testament Christianity birthed and nurtured the Baptist movement. While Baptists have traditionally held their beliefs open to the scrutiny and witness of scripture, some segments of the Baptist family have claimed final, dogmatic understandings of New Testament teachings. Emboldened by a sense of proprietary ownership of New Testament Christianity, these Baptists have used their peculiar theological affirmations as points of division and exclusion. Landmarkism stands as the supreme example of such tendencies in the nineteenth century.

Cotton Grove and the Genesis of "Old Landmarkism"

Landmarkism reflected the reactionary, high church, and creedal retrenchments experienced by Protestant denominations amid the religious progressivism in early nineteenth-century America.[3] Presbyterians, Lutherans, and Episcopalians all experienced attempts to turn their respective denominations inward by reclaiming creedal and/or apostolic authority. The American frontier was the scene of intense denominational competition as Methodist circuit riders crisscrossed the countryside and Campbellism swept through Kentucky, Tennessee, and surrounding states, dividing Baptist churches and associations. By mid-century Baptists had endured the anti-missions backlash, defections to Campbellism, and the break-up of the Triennial Convention. Beleaguered Baptists in the mid-South found refuge in the dogmatic ecclesiastical assertions and historical assurances of Landmarkism.

"Old Landmarkism" derived its name from two principal Old Testament passages, Proverbs 22:28 and Job 24:2. Its purpose was to defend and preserve "historic" Baptist doctrines under attack from enemies of the faith or neglected by ill-informed Baptists. J. R. Graves observed that acceptance of alien immersions, pulpit affiliation, and recognition of non-Baptists at associations and conventions were all too common within Baptist life.[4] Graves took his

---

Particular Baptists and the Baptist Union. The Strict Baptist Historical Society maintains a useful Internet site at www.strictbaptisthistory.org.uk. See also, Geoffrey Breed, *Particular Baptists in Victorian England* (Didcot: Baptist Historical Society, 2003). This chapter utilizes Landmarkism as a case study of the mid-nineteenth-century turn inward among doctrinaire Baptists.

[3] For a concise summary of early-nineteenth-century American religious culture, see Winthrop S. Hudson and John Corrigan, *Religion in America* (Upper Saddle River: Prentice-Hall, 1999) 143–85.

[4] J. R. Graves, *Old Landmarkism: What Is It?* (Memphis TN: Baptist Book House, Graves, Mahaffy & Company, 1887) xi–xv.

concerns to the public as editor of *The Tennessee Baptist.*[5] His popularity grew, as did the subscriber base for *The Tennessee Baptist*, with his aggressive, dogmatic assertions on the preeminence of Baptist understandings of New Testament faith and practice to the exclusion of other Christian sects.

Landmarkism's public introduction came in June 1851 at Cotton Grove, Tennessee. Seizing the momentum of a running three-year newspaper debate over the validity of non-Baptist immersions and pulpit affiliation, Graves called for a meeting "of all Baptists willing to accept and practice the teachings of Christ and his apostles in these matters" at Cotton Grove, Tennessee, on 24 June 1851. Alien immersion and pulpit affiliation were the paramount issues of concern for those gathered at Cotton Grove. Per the meetings' minutes, Graves posed five questions to the assembled brethren, framing the theological agenda of Landmarkism and setting Southern Baptists on a course toward exclusivism and isolationism:

> 1st. Can Baptists, consistently with their principles or the Scriptures, recognize those societies not organized according to the pattern of the Jerusalem Church, but possessing different *governments*, different *officers*, a different class of *members*, different *ordinances*, *doctrines* and *practices*, as churches of Christ?
>
> 2d. Ought they to be called gospel churches, or churches in a religious sense?
>
> 3rd. Can we consistently recognize the ministers of such irregular and unscriptural bodies as gospel ministers?
>
> 4th. Is it not virtually recognizing them as official ministers to invite them into our pulpits, or *by any other* act that *would or could be* constructed into such a recognition?
>
> 5th. Can we consistently address as *brethren* those professing Christianity, who not only have not the doctrine of Christ and walk not according to his commandments, but are arrayed in direct and bitter opposition to them?[6]

---

[5] The antecedents of the Landmark movement are traced to an intense debate between Graves and fellow editor John Waller found in the pages of *The Tennessee Baptist* and the *Western Baptist Review* beginning in 1848. Graves defended the exclusive validity of Baptist immersion and attacked Waller's position of qualified acceptance for Pedobaptist immersions.

[6] As found in Graves, *Old Landmarkism*, xi–xii.

Setting the theological agenda for Landmarkism, these resolutions were all answered in the negative, with the exception of the fourth, and gained hearty approval from the assembled brethren. Individual Baptists and associations across the South and Southwest endorsed these statements.[7]

As declared at Cotton Grove and clarified by 1855 in articles and texts, Landmarkism rejected the validity of non-Baptist ordinances, ministers, and churches.[8] Exalting Baptists as the sole heirs of New Testament Christianity, Landmarkism scrutinized all religious entities according to the movement's peculiar interpretation of the New Testament ecclesiology. In *Old Landmarkism: What Is It?*, Graves outlined seven distinguishing marks present in all true gospel churches:

1. The church and the kingdom of Christ is a divine institution;
2. The church is a visible institution;
3. The locality of the church is upon this earth;
4. The church is a local organization, a single congregation;
5. The church is composed of a regenerate membership;
6. The church's baptism is the profession, on the part of the subject, of the faith of the Gospel by which he is saved;
7. The Lord's Supper is a local church.[9]

---

[7] The Big Hatchie Association at its July 1851 meeting in Bolivar, Tennessee, unanimously adopted the Cotton Grove Resolutions, becoming the first of many associations to do so. James E. Tull, "A Study of Southern Baptist Landmarkism in the Light of Historical Baptist Ecclesiology" (Ph.D. diss., Columbia University, 1960) 132.

[8] Tull, "Southern Baptist Landmarkism," 127, contends that "by 1855, [Landmarkism's] characteristic emphases had been advanced, and had been welded into a compact, hard-hitting ecclesiology." The Landmark Triumvirate of J. R. Graves, J. M. Pendleton, and A. C. Dayton dictated mid-nineteenth-century Baptist ecclesiological dialogue in the South through *The Tennessee Baptist*, pamphlets, books, and sermons. Pendleton provided the movement with a compact theological system, while Dayton popularized the movement through prose. The core of Landmark ecclesiology was in place by the mid-1850s, but some theological "fine-tuning" is evident in the post-Civil War years.

[9] These seven marks are enumerated and clarified in Graves, *Old Landmarkism*, 29–130. James E. Tull, *High-Church Baptists in the South: The Origin, Nature, and Influence of Landmarkism* (Macon GA: Mercer University Press, 2000) 43–44; Tull, "Southern Baptist Landmarkism," 258–59, adds an eighth mark: continuity of the kingdom of Christ. This is a valid addition as it was a prominent piece of Graves's ecclesiological construct, and it received separate treatment within *Old Landmarkism*.

Graves concludes that a true church, local and visible, is scripturally and historically a Baptist church, though not always identified with the Baptist moniker, and it will always be a Baptist church.[10] Christ, according to Graves, enjoined his apostles and ministers to organize all churches "according to the pattern and model he 'built' before their eyes." Those who establish religious groups outside the model and mandates of Christ form religious "societies," mere expressions of "human *opinion*."[11]

Landmarkism positions each New Testament church as a complete, independent ecclesiastical entity capable of fulfilling all of Christ's commands apart from all other religious bodies. Graves proclaimed that the local church is "the highest and only source of ecclesiastical authority on earth, amenable only to Christ, whose laws alone it receives and executes."[12] The local, visible church—"isolated and independent"—meets, under Christ's authority, to administer his ordinances and to transact kingdom business.[13] Utilizing a strained hermeneutic, Graves asserted that the New Testament usage of *ecclesia* strictly establishes the church as a local, independent body.[14]

---

[10] J. R. Graves, "Communion: or The Distinction between Christian, and Church Fellowship," in *The Southern Baptist Almanac, and Annual Register, for the Year of Our Lord, 1851* (Nashville: Graves & Shankland, 1851) 9, as quoted in Smith, *In His Image*, 261.

[11] Graves, *Old Landmarkism*, 30–31. Dayton and Pendleton concur with Graves in identifying non-Baptist groups as "societies." A. C. Dayton, *Theodosia Earnest: Heroine of Faith*, 2 vols. (Philadelphia: American Baptist Publication Society, 1903) 2:93, 168; J. M. Pendleton, *An Old Landmark Re-set* (Nashville: South-Western Baptist Publishing House, 1854).

[12] Graves, *Old Landmarkism*, 38.

[13] Dayton, *Theodosia Earnest*, 2:93, 168.

[14] Graves, *Old Landmarkism*, 39, claimed that of the 110 appearances of *ecclesia* in the New Testament at least ninety-eight directly refer to the church as a local organization. J. R. Graves, *The Intercommunion of Churches, Inconsistent, Unscriptural, and Productive of Evil* (Memphis: Baptist Book House, 1882) 128, acknowledged that advocates for a universal or invisible church theory point to at least nineteen usages of *ecclesia* as figurative. These passages are Matthew 16:18; Acts 9:31; 1 Corinthians 12:28, 15:9; Galatians 1:13; Philippians 3:6; Hebrews 12:23; 1 Timothy 3:15; Ephesians 1:22; 3:10, 21; 5:23–25, 27, 29, 32; and Colossians 1:18,24. Graves conceded that as many as twelve of these appearances of *ecclesia* are figurative, but he asserted that a proper interpretation of the figure intends a local meaning. Graves used metonymy and synecdoche to interpret these usages of *ecclesia*. The twelve passages in question are: Matthew 16:18; Ephesians 1:22; 3:10; 5:23–25, 27, 29, 32; Colossians 1:18, 24; 3:15. See Graves, *Intercommunion*, 115–39.

Graves's strictly defined church-kingdom theory equated God's kingdom on earth with the aggregate of Baptist churches and negated any kingdom concept that accorded official churchly status to non-Baptist churches or affirmed the existence of the universal/invisible church. Graves's Landmark ecclesiology rejected all theories allowing for a catholic/universal church and a proliferation of denominations, and argued instead for the *"Baptist, or scriptural theory; viz.*, the church is a *local* organization." "The *ecclesia* of the New Testament," according to Graves, "could, and was required to assemble in one place."[15] To grant churchly status to the present redeemed in aggregate denigrated the local church's authority over and sole proprietorship of all "gospel acts": ordination, preaching, baptism, and communion.[16] An invisible, universal church/kingdom concept allows for meaningful cooperation in missions and preaching, acceptance of ordinances from non-Baptist churches, and validation of non-Baptist minister—all of which Landmarkism could not tolerate. Separation from such heresies, according to Landmarkers, is necessary to preserve and advance New Testament churches.

Landmarkism's limiting of the church to a local expression runs contrary to previous Baptist theological affirmations of both a universal, spiritual church and a local, visible church. The Philadelphia Confession, much in vogue in the South during the nineteenth century, supported the doctrine of an unorganized, universal, spiritual church, composed of the redeemed throughout the ages.[17] Several prominent Baptists defended the Philadelphia ecclesiology, including P. H. Mell, John Leadley Dagg, J. B. Jeter, and Richard Fuller.[18] Graves, however, challenged this viewpoint, arguing that the concept of an invisible church

---

[15] Graves, *Old Landmarkism*, 40.

[16] Graves, *Intercommunion*, 293–95.

[17] William Lumpkin, *Baptist Confessions of Faith*, rev. ed. (Valley Forge: Judson Press, 1983) 347–53.

[18] James E. Tull, *Shapers of Baptist Thought* (1972; repr., Macon GA: Mercer University Press, 1984) 142–43; Tull, "A Study in Southern Baptist Landmarkism," 265–66. P. H. Mell, *Baptism in Its Modes and Subjects* (Charleston: Southern Baptist Publication Society, 1853) 173, mentions "the whole body of the redeemed people in heaven or in earth." John Leadley Dagg, *Manual on Church Order* (Charleston: Southern Baptist Publication Society, 1857) provides a substantial discussion on the existence of the universal church. Richard Fuller, *Baptism, and the Terms of Communion* (Charleston: Southern Baptist Publication Society, 1859) 220–21, equates all the redeemed with Christ's spiritual, universal Church.

cannot be found in the pages of the New Testament. He identified this concept as a device designed to support erroneous ecclesiology.[19]

Graves waged war against Roman Catholics, Methodists, "Campbellites," Presbyterians, and Protestants in general.[20] His early writings contain vicious attacks against anyone who dared oppose his theological system, establishing a pattern of invective rhetoric in Baptist life. His assaults against Alexander Campbell during an 1854 newspaper debate brought Graves notoriety and accolades as a "Baptist gladiator."[21] He justified the use of personal attacks, saying, "We are compelled to be personal for our enemies make it a personal matter. We break the force of many articles by showing that their writers are irresponsible, men of the least credit."[22]

Truth was to be aggressive, and Graves was sure that the controversy he created would issue forth in God's bountiful blessings. The aggressive, combative nature of Landmarkism, while subdued in the post-Civil War Graves, became a foundational feature of non-cooperative Landmarkism.

The high church exclusivism of Landmarkism erected a wall between Landmark Baptists and non-Baptists. This same scrutiny that ejected non-Baptist churches from the kingdom of God and virtually negated all ecumenical activity would eventually be applied by Landmarkers to Baptists. Any Baptist group who practiced open communion, practiced open baptism, or participated in ecumenical activities was deemed apostate and not worthy of the title Baptist.[23]

---

[19] Graves, *Old Landmarkism*, 32.

[20] These groups bore the brunt of Graves's fury as expressed in the *Tennessee Baptist* and through his many books. Graves targeted Methodism in *The Great Iron Wheel: or, Republicanism Backward and Christianity Reversed* (Nashville: Graves & Marks, 1855); Graves derided Presbyterianism in, *The Trilemma: Or, Death by Three Horns* (Memphis: J. R. Graves & Son, 1890) first published in 1860; J. R. Graves's *Campbell and Campbellism Exposed: A Series of Replies* (Nashville: Graves & Marks, 1854) was a compilation of his 1854 literary debate with Alexander Campbell.

[21] Tull, "Southern Baptist Landmarkism," 233.

[22] J. R. Graves, "To Our Readers," *The Tennessee Baptist*, 5 July 1849, 2. In "No Small Matter," *The Tennessee Baptist*, 3 December 1853, 2, Graves further justified utilizing personal attacks: "We *love* all men but we *hate* all error, if we wound it is to heal, if we kill it is to save." Also see Graves, "Special Addresses," *The Tennessee Baptist*, 15 February 1851, 2.

[23] Stephen M. Stookey, "The Impact of Landmarkism upon Southern Baptist Western Geographical Expansion" (Ph.D. diss., Southwestern Baptist Theological Seminary, 1994) demonstrates the separationist mind-set present among Landmark-oriented Southern Baptists in the western United States. R. E. Milam, the driving force

Landmarkism's exclusive claims of local church prerogative in ministerial and ecclesiastical matters beg the question as to the exact relationship a Baptist may have with a Christian member of a religious society. Landmarkism acknowledges the existence of Christians outside of the Baptist realm.[24] While strictly forbidding the practice of "church fellowship" with non-Baptist Christians, Landmarkism did permit limited Christian fellowship.[25] A Baptist believer in Christian fellowship could participate privately in prayer groups, social groups, and other religious ventures so long as these activities do not involve ministerial or ecclesiastical matters belonging solely to New Testament churches. Graves defined Christian fellowship as a "spiritual communion, or religious enjoyment" believers share under a common Lord. Union meetings, ecumenical alliances, and joint evangelistic efforts were all rejected by Landmarkers as a violation of the strictures for church fellowship. Landmarkism's elitist ecclesiology and vitriolic condemnations of other denominations left Christian fellowship a belief minimally observed.

Graves's strict church-kingdom theory negated any kingdom concept that accords official church status to either non-Baptist congregations or the invisible church. To afford church status to the present redeemed in aggregate would denigrate the local church's claim to authority over and sole proprietorship of all "gospel acts." An invisible, universal church/kingdom concept would allow for meaningful cooperation in missions and preaching, acceptance of ordinances from non-Baptist churches, and validation of non-Baptist ministers—all of which Landmarkism could not tolerate.

Graves's American edition of G. H. Orchard's *History of Foreign Baptists* provided Landmarkism with a historical justification for its exclusivistic claims

---

behind SBC expansion into the Pacific Northwest, claimed "Southern Baptists, and they alone, have a sound New Testament ecclesiology." Milan advocated separation as the means necessary for preserving and advancing true New Testament churches. R. E. Milam, *The Fortress of Truth, the New Testament Church* (Portland OR: n.p., 1954) 222–23.

[24] J. R. Graves, "Querist," *The Baptist*, 3 May 1884, 6. Graves states: "The *family* of God and the church of Christ are two very different nations. We are all the children of God by faith in Christ, but the children of God are not members of Christ's church until baptized into it. For in one spirit we are all baptized into one body, i.e., a local church" (J. R. Graves, *Christian Baptism, The Profession of Faith of the Gospel* [Memphis: Baptist Book House, 1881] 6).

[25] Graves, *Old Landmarkism*, 131–39; J. R. Graves, "The Lord's Supper a Symbol of Church, Not Christian Fellowship," in *Reasons for Becoming a Baptist*, ed. William L. Slack (Nashville: South-Western Publishing House, 1857) 60.

through an emphasis upon the historical succession of Baptist churches.[26] While not an entirely new theory, Baptist succession provided ecclesiastical battle-weary frontier Baptists with a pedigree that affirmed their status as the true heirs of the New Testament church, countering Campbellite claims of apostolic antiquity.[27]

A strict application of emerging Landmark ecclesiology called into question the organizational structure of the fledgling Southern Baptist Convention. At the close of the 1850s, drawing upon a wave of support generated by a contentious public conflict with R. B. C. Howell, then president of the SBC, Graves rallied Landmark adherents to challenge the connectional ministry structure of the SBC and its mission boards.[28] At the 1859 SBC

---

[26] Barnes, *Southern Baptist Convention*, 104–105 asserts that with the publication of Orchard's history, Landmarkism "gained momentum and proved a fiercely fighting force." Numerous authors adopted and advanced the Baptist theory of church succession. D. B. Ray, *Baptist Succession: A Handbook of Baptist History* (Cincinnati: G. E. Stevens, 1870) set the pace for post-war books on church succession. Other works in the late nineteenth century that echoed Graves include: W. A. Jarrell, *Baptist Church Perpetuity, or, The Continuous Existence of Baptist Churches from the Apostolic to the Present Day Demonstrated by the Bible and by History*, 3rd ed. (Fulton: National Baptist Publishing House, 1904); John T. Christian, a Southern Baptist Theological Seminary faculty member during the Whitsitt Controversy, produced *Did They Dip?* (1896) and *Baptist History Vindicated* (1899) in opposition to William Whitsitt's *A Question of Baptist History* (1896). J. M. Carroll, *The Trail of Blood* (Lexington KY: Ashland Avenue Baptist Church, 1931) is still a popular booklet in the Southwest.

[27] Thomas J. Brown, "Origins of the Prophets," *The Baptist*, 12 September 1846, 45–46. See W. Morgan Patterson, *Baptist Succession* (Valley Forge: Judson Press, 1969) for an extended discussion of Baptist successionist views.

[28] The Graves-Howell conflict stemmed from Graves's anger over Howell's opposition to Landmark theology and the Landmark-dominated Southern Baptist Sunday School Union and quickly spread beyond First Baptist Church, Nashville, polarizing Baptists in the South, as Graves stoked the flames of controversy in *The Tennessee Baptist*. See Tull, "Southern Baptist Landmarkism," 399–451, and *Encyclopedia of Southern Baptists*, "Graves-Howell Controversy," 2 vols., ed. Norman Cox (Nashville: Broadman Press, 1958) 1:580–85. Hereafter cited as *ESB.* for summaries of the Graves-Howell controversy. The Little River Association of Texas passed a resolution during its 1859 annual meeting in support of Graves in his fight with Howell; Little River Association of Baptists, *Minutes* (Anderson TX: Texas Baptist Book and Job Establishment, 1859) 9. It is interesting to note that the moderator of the Little River Meeting was Elder B. Carroll—father of B. H. and J. M. Carroll. The action taken by the Little River Association is indicative of numerous associations that addressed the Graves-Howell controversy. It displays the rapid spread of Landmarkism and Graves's popularity.

biennial meeting, Graves and his Landmark faction attacked the convention and its boards as unscriptural, usurping the authority of the local church. Following a raucous, day-long debate messengers rejected Graves's attempt to dismantle the Foreign Mission Board (FMB). The SBC, however, adopted a compromise mission-funding plan, allowing churches and associations the option of appointing missionaries and sending funds to designated missionaries through the FMB.[29] While Graves and his supporters accepted the compromise package as a minor victory, a fierce anti-convention strain of Landmarkism had been unleashed and would manifest itself through small schismatic groups in the late nineteenth and early twentieth centuries. The Civil War effectively ended further attempts by Graves to take over the SBC.[30]

Graves emerged from the Civil War years "a sobered and chastened man."[31] Graves refrained from attempting an overt takeover of the SBC in the post-war period. The pre-war denominational combatant emerged as an elder-statesman within the SBC.[32] Graves's new strategy in promoting Landmarkism was to make the movement appear less combative. The marketing plan, reflected in the advocacy tone of Graves's newspaper, worked.[33] A cooperative,

[29] Barnes, *Southern Baptist Convention*, 109–13; *ESB*, 1:580–85.

[30] The harsh realities of the Civil War quenched Graves's appetite for denominational infighting. Graves lost his business and home, as he and his family fled Nashville in 1862. Graves also witnessed the horrific battle at Shiloh, serving as Confederate chaplain. Graves, "The Battle of Shiloh," *Biblical Recorder*, 28 May 1862, 1. A family tradition claims Graves is the person who retrieved the lifeless body of General Albert Sidney Johnston from the field of battle at Shiloh, sheltering the news of the General's death from the soldiers until the battle was finished. Oren L. Hailey, *J. R. Graves: Life, Times, and Teachings* (Nashville: n.p., 1925) 79–80; Harold Stewart Smith, "A Critical Analysis of the Theology of J. R. Graves" (Th.D. diss., Southern Baptist Theological Seminary, 1966) 95.

[31] Tull, "Southern Baptist Landmarkism," 455.

[32] This new approach is exemplified in his appointment to a 1868 committee commissioned to present the SBC's pleas for southern geographical integrity to the ABHMS. Robert A. Baker, *Relations between Northern and Southern Baptists* (Fort Worth: Evans Press, 1948) 97–98.

[33] Graves's newspaper reemerged after the Civil War under the title *The Baptist*, enjoying a wide readership. By 1860 R. B. C. Howell recognized Landmarkism's influence upon state papers in Arkansas, Mississippi, Louisiana, and Alabama. James Tull, "Southern Baptist Landmarkism," 526 notes: "Landmarkism was fortunate in finding itself most strongly entrenched in the very field which exercised a controlling influence in the making of the denominational mind—the denominational paper." For a discussion of Landmarkism's influence upon Baptist periodicals in the South see, Tull, "Southern Baptist Landmarkism," 455–58, 498–500, 526–27. Newspapers and journals,

Convention Landmarkism emerged and infiltrated Southern Baptist life. Graves and Landmark Southern Baptists came to identify the SBC as the repository of true New Testament churches, helping foster an intense denominational loyalty among Southern Baptists. The result was an ever-vigilant segment of Southern Baptists standing guard for pure theology and separation from non-Baptists. Leon McBeth succinctly summarizes the long-term impact of Landmarkism upon Southern Baptists, resulting from Graves's post-Civil War marketing plan:

The continuing Landmark legacy can be seen in several contemporary Southern Baptist traits and practices. These include an exaggerated emphasis upon local church autonomy, continuing tensions over alien immersion and closed communion, a suspicion of other denominations, refusal to participate in organized ecumenical conferences, SBC representation that is now limited to messengers from churches, and a continued emphasis among a few Southern Baptists upon a successionist view of Baptist history.[34]

Non-Cooperative, Schismatic Landmarkism

Shortly before Graves's death in 1893, Landmark factions arose and sought to recover the movement's combative, anti-board spirit. Taking their cues from Graves's pre-Civil War application of Landmark ideals, schismatic Landmarkism surfaced in three separate controversies, each questioning the scriptural legitimacy of convention/board structures and including segments of the Baptist family to the growing list of illegitimate churches. Southern Seminary was the site of an additional Landmark-oriented controversy in the late 1890s, and the issue was church succession. It produced no schism, but it

---

in addition to *The Baptist*, disseminating Landmark ideology included: *Western Recorder*, under editor T. T. Eaton; S. A. Hayden's *The Texas Baptist and Herald*; J. B. Cranfill's *Baptist Standard*; and *Baptist Record*, under editor J. B. Gambrell. Landmark papers and periodicals were prevalent in the lower Midwest: in Missouri D. B. Ray established and edited *The Battle Flag and Church Historian*, later known as *The American Baptist Flag* and *The Baptist Flag* (1905) under J. N. Hall; J. B. Moody and Hall published *The Baptist Gleaner* in Fulton, Kentucky; W. P. Throgmorton's papers in Illinois included *The Baptist Banner*, *The Baptist News*, and *The Illinois Baptist*; Memphis and St. Louis, in turn, served as home for S. H. Ford's *The Christian Repository and Home Circle*, later known simply as *The Christian Repository*. An intricate web of friendships and alliances existed behind the presses as editors learned their skills from one another, joined forces during tough economic periods, and contributed articles to one another's publications.

[34] McBeth, *The Baptist Heritage*, 461.

did demonstrate the extent to which Landmark ideology had infiltrated Southern Baptist thinking, especially in the Southwest.

T. P. Crawford's "Gospel Missionism" gave voice to a quiescent anti-board Landmark sentiment. From 1888 to 1892 Crawford waged a war against the SBC and its Foreign Mission Board, seeking to dismantle both in favor of direct missionary initiative through the local churches or associations.[35] A small faction of churches adopted Crawford's Gospel Missionism and separated from the SBC, but the majority of Landmark sympathizers remained within the SBC, following the cooperative example of J. R. Graves.[36] Convention Landmarkers, now in key SBC leadership roles, attacked Gospel Missionism's non-cooperative spirit as contrary to New Testament teachings.[37]

S. A. Hayden began a concerted effort in 1894 to shift the Baptist General Convention of Texas (BGCT) away from a messenger basis of representation to a delegate system. Delegates, according to Hayden, protected the autonomy of the local church by giving it a direct voice in BGCT actions. A delegate system, however, subjected churches to the delegates' majority-rule, thereby violating local church autonomy—a fact recognized by Hayden's Convention Landmark opponents, including J. B. Cranfill, J. B. Gambrell, B. H. Carroll, and J. M. Carroll.[38] Hayden and his followers separated from the BGCT in 1899, forming

---

[35] See Tull, "Southern Baptist Landmarkism," 569–77 for a summary of Crawford's activities. T. P. Crawford, *Churches to the Front!* (China: n.p., 1892) stands as the definitive text for Gospel Missionism.

[36] E. E. Folk, "Shall Southern Baptists Divide?," *The Baptist Argus*, 12 January 1899, 8, surmised: "A large majority of Southern Baptists, Landmarkers and anti-Landmarkers, believe in the board system of doing work, but some do not. These are called Gospel Missioners. Nearly all Gospel Missioners are Landmarkers, but not all Landmarkers are Gospel Missioners by a great deal." George Lofton, "Gospel Methods," *Baptist and Reflector*, 15 August 1895, 3. Landmark adherent George Lofton defended the SBC board system against Gospel Mission attacks. Lofton argued that the board approach was just as scriptural as the missionary enterprises of independent churches or associations "and a hundred times more systematic, expedient, effective and fruitful."

[37] J. B. Gambrell, *Ten Years in Texas* (Dallas: Baptist Standard, 1910) 165–66 affirms the New Testament principle of inter-church cooperation or comity while still holding to basic Landmark ecclesiology, citing the examples of Antioch, Jerusalem, and Paul in 2 Corinthians 8. Gambrell accuses the Gospel Missions movement of a faulty hermeneutic, which only considered portions of the New Testament supportive of their anti-convention agenda and ignored passages contrary to their beliefs.

[38] Gambrell, *Ten Years*, 160–61 states: "A council composed of messengers from churches can never be invested with the slightest degree of church character.... It is altogether within the power of the sovereign church to send messengers to a council, as

a rival state convention, which later merged with Ben Bogard's Landmark faction.[39]

Ben Bogard spearheaded a strict, schismatic Landmark movement in Arkansas, consolidating growing opposition to convention/board approaches to missions and a paid state missions secretary.[40] Before arriving in Arkansas in 1899, Bogard promoted Gospel Missions, succeeding in recruiting a number of Primitive Baptists to the movement.[41] Bogard's group split from the Arkansas Baptist State Convention in 1902 and the SBC in 1905 after it failed to shift either body to an anti-board mission structure.[42]

Southern Seminary President William Heth Whitsitt created a Landmarkist controversy from 1896 to 1899 with his anti-church succession views.[43] In *A Question of Baptist History* (1896), Whitsitt academically dismantled church succession and asserted that Baptists emerged as a new Christian movement from seventeenth century English Separatism. Landmarkers throughout the SBC, enraged over Whitsitt's historical treatment of Baptists, demanded his removal. Trustee meetings over the next three years were contentious as efforts to fire Whitsitt escalated. Whitsitt defused the situation in 1899, resigning as seminary president. The Whitsitt controversy displayed the extent to which Landmark ideology had infiltrated the Southern Baptist psyche. James Tull sees the Whitsitt controversy as indicative of a SBC power-shift from the non-Landmark Southeast to the pro-Landmark Southwest.[44]

---

the Antioch church did send messengers to Jerusalem. But no church can claim anything of their messengers in council on score of church sovereignty, because the transaction is carried entirely beyond the limits of independent churches, out on the open field of inter-church or denominational comity."

[39] *ESB* 2:1374–90.

[40] See Tull, "Southern Baptist Landmarkism," 618–28.

[41] Ibid., 573; Ben Bogard, "A Glorious Success," *Western Recorder*, 8 July 1897, 5.

[42] *ESB*, 1:72–81; *Arkansas Baptist State Convention, Annual* (n.p., 1903) 15–27 records the terms of peace mandated by Bogard's rival state convention. *The American Baptist Flag*, 23 February 1905; *Southern Baptist Convention, Annual*, (n.p., 1905).

[43] For a detailed analysis of the Whitsitt controversy, see Rosalie Beck, "The Whitsitt Controversy: A Denomination in Crisis" (Ph.D. diss., Baylor University, 1984); Charles B. Bugg, "The Whitsitt Controversy: A Study in Denominational Conflict" (Ph.D. diss., Southern Baptist Theological Seminary, 1972). Also see Tull, "Southern Baptist Landmarkism," 577–618.

[44] Tull, "Southern Baptist Landmarkism," 616–17. State conventions—Kentucky, Mississippi, Arkansas, Louisiana, and Texas—in the Landmark belt officially registered their opposition to Whitsitt, passing resolutions calling for his immediate resignation. The two leading anti-Whitsitt trustees, T. T. Eaton (Kentucky) and B. H. Carroll

Gospel Missions, Haydenism, and Bogardism represent extreme expressions of Landmarkism. These factions claimed Graves, Pendleton, and Dayton as their spiritual godfathers. Each adhered to a literal interpretation of the Landmark triumvirate's writings, carrying Landmark ecclesiology to its logical conclusion—Baptist isolation and localism. Their separation from SBC left a cooperative Convention Landmarkism present among Southern Baptists.

Landmarkism's Regional Identity

Landmark ideology, while an integral mix in the Southern Baptist milieu, did not infiltrate the entire SBC. Landmarkism became the dominant Baptist identity in western Tennessee, Arkansas, Oklahoma, Texas, Louisiana, western Mississippi, Oklahoma, Texas, northern Alabama, western Kentucky, southern Illinois, and portions of Missouri—the Landmark belt. Tull chronicles the genesis of Convention Landmark influence as the center of SBC power shifted from the southeastern and eastern seaboard states to the south-central and southwestern United States.[45]

Several studies have recognized the influence of Landmarkism upon the synthesis of Southern Baptist identity. Walter Shurden identifies a Tennessee (Landmark) tradition as one of four identity traditions within the SBC mosaic. Expanding Shurden's discussion of regional identities H. Leon McBeth, John Loftis, and Robert Dale each detail an additional Landmark-influenced tradition centered in the Southwest.[46] The Southwest/Texas tradition exhibits a

---

(Texas), were representative of the emerging Southwest leadership—moderate Landmarkers, yet supportive of SBC cooperation.

[45] Tull, "Southern Baptist Landmarkism," 486–692.

[46] Walter B. Shurden, "The Southern Baptist Synthesis: Is It Cracking?" *Baptist History and Heritage* 16/2 (April 1981): 2–11. Shurden identifies four traditions in Southern Baptist life: (1) the Charleston Tradition, (2) the Sandy Creek Tradition, (3) the Georgia Tradition, and, (4) the Tennessee (Landmark) Tradition. Robert D. Dale, "An Identity Crisis: Southern Baptists Search for Heroic Leaders," *Faith and Mission* 1/2 (Spring 1984): 36–47 accepts Shurden's four original designations while suggesting the possibility of a fifth tradition in the Southwest. John Loftis Franklin, "Factors in Southern Baptist Identity as Reflected by Ministerial Role Models, 1750–1925" (Ph.D. diss., Southern Baptist Theological Seminary, 1987) utilizes Shurden's thesis of a synthesis of traditions to delineate five distinct traditions in Southern Baptist life: (1) the Regular Baptist Tradition, (2) the Separate Baptist Tradition, (3) the Southern Orthodox Baptist Tradition, (4) the Landmark Baptist Tradition, and (5) the Evangelical-Denominationalist Baptist Tradition. H. Leon McBeth, centers a fifth identity tradition in Texas in "The Texas Tradition: A Study in Baptist Regionalism, Part I," *Baptist*

strong Convention Landmark base. The Carroll brothers, B. H. and J. M., promoted Convention Landmarkism in the Southwest. J. M. Carroll's Landmark leanings are displayed in his defense of church succession in *The Trail of Blood*. B. H. Carroll praised the genius of Graves, Pendleton, and Dayton, and he disseminated Landmark ecclesiology to ministerial students at Baylor and Southwestern Baptist Theological Seminary. A devoted denominationalist, B. H. Carroll's Convention Landmark leanings are evident in his opposition to Gospel Missionism, Haydenism, and Bogardism.[47] The influence of Graves and Landmarkism within Texas was so strong that B. H. proclaimed, "In Texas the spirit of J. R. Graves goes marching on."[48]

Convention Landmarkism in the Southwest stood ready to defend Baptist "orthodoxy" as well as SBC missionary methods. While not as doctrinaire as Schismatic Landmarkism, Convention Landmarkers were on the guard for doctrinal decay. The Southwest, with its moderate, Convention Landmarkers, served as the staging ground for Southern Baptist migrant families as America moved west. McBeth observes that "as early Texas was largely an extension of the Tennessee tradition, so Baptist expansion westward has been an extension of the Texas tradition."[49] The theological character of Southern Baptist western expansion is reflective of Convention Landmarkism—holding to the old Landmarks, yet progressive in missionary spirit.

An earnest desire to discover and practice New Testament Christianity birthed the Baptist movement in the seventeenth century. This same desire created a schismatic, separationist impulse within Baptist life as segments of the

---

History and Heritage 26/1 (January 1991): 37–47; H. Leon McBeth, "The Texas Tradition: A Study in Baptist Regionalism, Part II," *Baptist History and Heritage* 26/1 (January 1991): 48–57.

[47] B. H. Carroll spoke in glowing terms of the Landmark triumvirate, especially J. M. Pendleton and his *Church Manual*. Carroll referred to Pendleton as "a Prince of Israel" and spoke of Graves, Pendleton, and Dayton as "the great Baptist trio of the South." B. H. Carroll Collection, file 208:1, Texas Baptist Historical Collection, Dallas, Texas. Carroll's indebtedness to the Landmark triumvirate is evident during his teaching days at Baylor. E. P. Alldredge's lectures notes from Carroll's course on ecclesiology reflect a healthy affirmation of Pendleton, Dayton, and Graves. These notes also contain a direct reference to the errors of William H. Whitsitt. E. P. Alldredge class notebook, E. P. Alldredge Collection, Southern Baptist Historical Collection and Archives, Nashville, Tennessee.

[48] As cited in McBeth, "The Texas Tradition, Part II," 49.

[49] Ibid., 53. See Stookey, "The Impact of Landmarkism upon Southern Baptist Western Geographical Expansion" for a detailed discussion of Landmarkism's influence upon Southern Baptists in the western United States.

Baptist family have claimed final, dogmatic understanding of New Testament teachings. Feeling a sense of proprietary ownership of New Testament Christianity, some Baptists claimed to be the sole heirs to the New Testament church to the exclusion of all other Christian denominations and sects. Landmarkism stands as the supreme example.

Conclusion

Baptists, from their seventeenth-century beginnings, believed their understanding of Christian faith and practice most closely aligned with New Testament ideals. However, they did not so define their ecclesiology to exclude non-Baptist churches from the kingdom of God or to advance a doctrine of separation from non-Baptists. J. R. Graves and Landmarkism introduced an elitist, exclusivist ecclesiology into Baptist life. As a dogmatic theological system, Landmarkism runs against the stream of traditional Baptist understandings of ecclesiology, leaving its adherents no choice but to move toward positions of separation/isolation and localism. Leon McBeth provides an apt summary of Landmarkism's contrarian ecclesiology: "The evidence confirms that the movement was more nearly a 'new stake' than an 'old Landmark.'"[50]

Suggested Reading

Tull, James E. *High-Church Baptists in the South: The Origin, Nature, and Influence of Landmarkism*. Macon GA: Mercer University Press, 2000.

Patterson, W. Morgan. *Baptist Successionism: A Critical View*. Valley Forge: Judson Press, 1969.

Graves, J. R. *Old Landmarkism: What Is It?* Memphis: Baptist Book House, 1881.

---

[50] McBeth, *The Baptist Heritage*, 460.

CHAPTER 16

Baptists and Race and the Turn from Slavery to Greater Institutionalization among African-American Baptists, 1850–1880

Sandy Dwayne Martin

This chapter explores one of the most momentous and fascinating periods of African-American Baptist and American history, the decades from 1850 to 1880. These years constitute an important turning point among African-American Baptists, the move from freedom to greater institutionalization of their churches, associations, and conventions. While this chapter focuses mainly on institutionalization, it also reflects many changes and developments: the last decade of enslavement, the emancipation of 4 million African Americans from slavery, increased organizational unity among African-American Baptists, their embrace of citizenship and suffrage, and the active participation of Southern black and white progressives in political affairs.[1]

This period covers the final decade of enslavement, inaugurated by the passage of the Fugitive Slave Law of 1850, which placed the full force of the American government behind the recapture of escapees from slavery. It is punctuated with the Supreme Court's Dred Scott Decision, which called into question the rights of even free blacks; the Civil War, which brought freedom; and the Reconstruction era (ca. 1867–1877), which witnessed African-American political participation and movement toward freedom in all areas of life. This chapter extends to 1880, which was the year the Baptist Foreign Mission Convention appears and becomes a very critical development in the march toward true national unity among black Baptists. In the decades after 1880 and sometimes simultaneous with the above developments are establishment of non-

---

[1] John Hope Franklin and Alfred A. Moss Jr., *From Slavery to Freedom: A History of African Americans*, 8th ed. (Boston: McGraw-Hill, 2000). For this period, see 138–291.

religious or quasi-religious African-American institutions of various types, disenfranchisement of the majority of African Americans in the South, racial segregation fostered by local and national government bodies, renewed acts of racial terrorism (such as lynching), increased involvement of black Baptist in overseas missions, and serious debates and even divisions among black Baptists over the manner in which they should cooperate with their white counterparts. This writer does not contend that this was the most important era in African-American Baptist history. Perhaps it is; maybe it is not. It is definitely a turning point.

Background and Overview

Before commencing with a more in-depth study of the 1850–1880 period, let us dispel some commonly held myths regarding African-American Christianity. First, black Christians, including Baptists, were not mere imitators of white Christians but held their own identities and pursued their own goals. Second, contrary to a common belief, African peoples in the United States were not by and large forced or tricked into accepting Christianity. Third, the African-American Baptist presence did not begin in the post-Civil War period but dates back to the Colonial age. Fourth, black Baptists, despite the discrimination they often faced, were not isolated in a world to themselves but were active members of the worldwide fellowship and activities of Baptistdom. Fifth, when it came to overthrowing slavery, African-American Christians in general and Baptists in particular were not passive objects of concern, but active agents of their own liberation by means of escape from slavery, engaging in abolitionist activities, working through independent black churches to aid others in securing freedom, and continuously protesting against the system.[2]

The Last Decade of Chattel Slavery, 1850–1860:
Southern Black Baptists

Proslavery advocates, including clergy of various denominations, often spoke of the supposed benign character of slavery, how it introduced blacks to "civilization" and Christianity, and how blacks were really content with their lot

---

393 For a historical introduction to African American religion, see Albert Raboteau, *Canaan Land; A Religious History of African Americans* (New York: Oxford University Press, 2001) and Carter G. Woodson, *History of the Negro Church*, 3rd ed. (Washington, DC: Associated Publishers, 1972).

in life. Yet the narratives of ex-slaves, including that of the Baptist Peter Randolph, give a different, vivid, even heart-rending portrait of the institution: enslaved people's yearning for freedom, the abuse of the slave driver, beatings and other acts of cruelty, break up of families through the selling of even one's closest relatives, the gross inconsistency of white preachers who extolled a gospel of love and forgiveness but defended and even participated in the brutality of the slave system, etc.[3]

Nonetheless, a Baptist presence among enslaved African Americans existed and in some places flourished through three major vehicles of corporate worship and fellowship. First, there was the "invisible institution." This was the practice of religion among the enslaved beyond the eyesight and earshot of whites—"invisible" to them. When blacks could "steal away to Jesus" in cabins, creeks, forests, and other places, they could speak more boldly about the hunger for freedom; the sins of the slaveholders; the confidence that God would eventually overthrow the system; and in general preach, pray, and sing in their own way without interference from whites.[4]

Second, there were many biracial churches, some of which had overwhelming black majorities. To be sure, these churches were firmly under the control of whites, and blacks suffered discriminatory and segregated treatment in the house of God. Still, separate worship services for blacks, often led by black preachers or exhorters (whether officially ordained or not), and other activities provided opportunities for fellowship even amid these trying circumstances. Third, there existed independent black congregations in the South, especially in the larger towns and cities. It is true that no black institution could be completely free in slavocracy. Especially after the slave plot of Denmark Vesey, a Methodist, in South Carolina in 1822 and the actual uprising of Nat Turner, a Baptist, in Virginia in 1831, these churches fell under even closer surveillance and scrutiny. Technically, they often had to have white clergy for pastors. This often turned out to be a mere formality. Yet even when surveillance was more than a formality, the independent status of the

---

[3] Peter Randolph, *From Slave Cabin to the Pulpit: The Autobiography of Rev. Peter Randolph: The Southern Question Illustrated and Sketches of Slave Life* (Boston: James H. Earle, Publisher, 1893). Available electronically at http://docsouth.unc.edu/neh/randolph/randolph.html as part of the Documenting the American South Collection of the University of North Carolina at Chapel Hill.

[4] Albert J. Raboteau, *Slave Religion: The "Invisible Institution" in the Antebellum South*, updated ed. (New York: Oxford University Press, 2004) 211–321.

congregations provided, if not freedom, at least a considerable degree of autonomy compared to the situation in the white controlled biracial churches.

Northern Black Baptists, 1850–1860

Ninety percent of African Americans in the US during the 1850s lived in the South. Ninety percent of these Southern blacks were enslaved. Only 10 percent resided in the North in free states. Of course the terms "free state" and "free black" are relative. Nevertheless, living in New York was far better than living in Alabama, and being "free" in either the North or South was clearly superior to being held as a chattel slave. Just as enslaved Christians made the most of their situation, so did many free blacks in Northern states. Some Northern free black Baptists were members of biracial churches and generally suffered the same indignities in those bodies as blacks in the South. Some Baptists were members of black congregations that were part of predominantly white associations. Hence, they had freedom at the local level, which for Baptists was most important. Most black Baptists were members of predominantly black congregations, such as Abysinnian Baptist Church in New York City and a host of First African Baptist churches in various locales. But black Baptists in the North had another option not available to their Southern kin: blacks in the North often formed their own black associations and conventions. The Wood River, Providence, and Union Baptist Associations organized in the 1830s and 1840s continued their existence into the 1850s. The Amhertsburg Association in upper Michigan and Canada also continued its influence as did perhaps the earliest attempt at a national organization of black Baptists, American Baptist Missionary Convention, founded in 1840 in New York.

These independent groups—congregations, associations, and conventions—generally had as their objectives missions and evangelism (sometimes with aspirations for overseas work), racial uplift, and dismantling slavery. Like their white counterparts, black Baptists expressed interest in the spiritual and temporal needs of people on the western frontier and in other lands (Canada, Liberia, and Haiti). In various ways independent black groups supported the abolitionist cause: making their churches available for use by abolitionist speakers, distributing antislavery literature, passing resolutions against slavery and in favor of civil rights, and providing haven and other necessary assistance to those escaping slavery.[5]

Civil War and Reconstruction Era, 1860–1880: Freedom Comes

H. Leon McBeth, in his very fine collection of Baptist documents, says the years 1845–1900 were a time when Baptists in the US were "Going Separate Ways." Black Baptists also experienced sectional, theological, and philosophical tensions that sometimes eventuated in the formation of new groups or the failure of current groups. Nonetheless, this era for the most part witnessed moves toward greater consolidation and unity among African-American organizations. More specifically, the Civil War and Reconstruction era, as well as the prior period of sectional tensions, pulled white Baptists and many other white Christians apart. Conversely, these events drew black Baptists and other black Christians into greater unity and solidarity. From the perspective of white Northerners, including Baptists, the conflict raging from 1861–1865 was a Civil War, a horrendous rebellion threatening to tear the nation asunder. For Southern white Christians, including Baptists, the fight was a noble War for Southern Independence. Black Christians, including Baptists, certainly understood that this was a Civil War and an attempt to establish a Southern nation. Beyond these realities, however, the conflict for blacks and their white antislavery sympathizers soon became a War of Black Emancipation. For white Christians, North and South, God was on their respective sides, preserving the Union or creating a new Confederacy. For African-American Christians, North and South, God was on their side, acting in human history in answer to centuries of prayers and hard work to dismantle the evil system of slavery.

The Civil War brought emancipation. Emancipation refers not simply to the Emancipation Proclamation, promulgated as a wartime measure, but also the subsequent constitutional change and official actions that permanently and unconditionally freed African Americans from chattel bondage. Of course it meant physical freedom: liberty of movement, cessation of grinding but unrewarded labor, release from sexual and verbal assaults, escape from physical

---

[5] For a historical overview of the emergence of black Baptist organizations at all levels, see Leroy Fitts, *A History of Black Baptists* (Nashville: Broadman Press, 1985) 41–106. James M. Washington provides a more focused, in-depth account of the persons, organizations, and factors leading to the establishment of the National Baptist Convention in 1895. See his *Frustrated Fellowship: The Black Baptist Quest for Social Power* (Macon GA: Mercer University Press, 1986).

abuse, opportunities to reunite with family members or at least search for them, and regularization of marriage and development of family life. Furthermore, this physical freedom carried with it deep theological meaning. Enslaved Christians and their black and white sympathizers saw emancipation as their exodus from an Egyptian slavery far greater than the one experienced by the ancient Hebrews. This emancipation-exodus vindicated their faith in a God who would not forever allow God's people to live in bondage. In many ways that freedom was incomplete and even uncertain at times, but it was a very long way from chattel bondage.

In addition to physical freedom, this exodus brought with it the opportunity of greater religious freedom to practice their faith openly, for full religious freedom cannot operate within a system of chattel slavery. Enslaved Christians who once worshiped secretly could now join the membership of officially recognized churches and be more open about their religious convictions and objectives. Black Baptists who were members of white-controlled churches seceded and formed their own fellowships. Thus, a particular date given for the organization of a black congregation in many instances tells only part of the story, for long before 1867, for example, there existed a fellowship that with the coming of emancipation was able to formalize its existence as a separate body.

How did white Baptists feel about black members seceding from biracial churches? In some instances white Baptists were probably very happy that blacks were leaving, a voluntary departure that saved whites the inconvenience or embarrassment of requesting them to do so. Quite possibly the response most of the time was a bit more nuanced. McBeth provides documentation that apparently captures sentiments of the majority of white Southern church people, including Baptists. White Baptists said to their black counterparts (colloquially paraphrasing McBeth's documents), "Well, we like the *idea* of your remaining a part of one bi-racial fellowship of Christians. But *practically speaking* if you are not going to stay in your subordinate place and refrain from being a nuisance by demanding the same respect and courtesy that we white people show each other, then we certainly wish you well and will gladly take time to instruct you about the true meaning of Christian charity and leadership." [7]

---

[6] H. Leon McBeth, *A Sourcebook for Baptist Heritage* (Nashville: Broadman Press, 1990) 270–91.

[7] H. Leon McBeth, *A Sourcebook for Baptist Heritage* (Nashville: Broadman Press, 1990) 270–91.

But black Baptists had absolutely no intention of being second-class citizens in the house of their first-class Savior. Various historical records consistently point out that black Baptists could not understand how whites could actually see themselves as Christians given their track record in defending slavery and advocating what was often termed as caste Christianity. Additionally, black Christians, including Baptists, believed they had a God-given mission to evangelize and uplift the race throughout the world and provide a clear example to all peoples of true Christianity.[8] Many Southern and Northern African-American Baptists, both the formerly enslaved and those free at the time of emancipation, wished to form one racial fellowship among themselves, in spirit if not in actual organization. Furthermore, they hoped for a wider fellowship of cooperation and mutual respect between black Baptists and white Baptists. There were a number of hindrances to this twofold goal. Many Northern black and white Baptists who journeyed to the South to work among the freed people came with the impression that the Christians among them had a degraded Christianity polluted by white slaveholding teachings. As time progressed, many of the newcomers gained a greater appreciation for the intensity and commitment of Southern black faith, though differences over certain worship practices continued in some instances.

Formation of Black Baptist Institutions, 1860–1880

Organization and reorganization of Baptist life proceeded at all levels: local, regional, state, and national.[9] Locally, pre-Civil War black congregations continued. Sometimes white members left biracial churches and turned over the property to the remaining black members. At other times black members left and built new church structures. Very often these new structures were "brush arbors." African-American Christians in these instances built churches with tree limbs, poles, and bushes because they lacked the funds and/or means to secure the lumber and bricks necessary for more durable, permanent structures. Black Baptists also did remarkably well in the organization of intra-state associations. Over the decades associations have provided assistance and guidance to local churches and persons on a host of matters, such as founding churches and

---

[8] See Leonard I. Sweet, *Black Images of America, 1784–1870* (New York: W. W. Norton & Company, Inc., 1976).

[9] See Fitts, *History*, 64–106; Washington, *Fellowship*; and particularly for a treatment of foreign mission interests, see Sandy D. Martin, *Black Baptists and African Missions: The Origins of A Movement* (Macon GA: Mercer University Press, 1989).

gaining official recognition, settling disputes, resolving issues relating to doctrine and practice, ordaining ministers, and helping to secure pastoral leadership. Prior to the Civil War, many black Baptist congregations belonged to white-controlled associations. During and immediately after the Civil War, African Americans began establishing their own associations at the same time that they were establishing local congregations.

A third area of organizational success was the founding of state Baptist conventions. About ten years after emancipation there emerged conventions in practically every state with a sizable black population. North Carolina, Virginia, Alabama, and Arkansas were among the earliest established. These state conventions had the typical objectives: home missions or evangelism, foreign missions (especially to Africa and to places in the Americas with significant black population), and education. State bodies played crucial roles in founding or supporting persons, institutions, and movements striving to concretize active interest in the uplift of the race in all areas of life: religious, political, social, and economic. State conventions also paved the way for and/or gave support to regional and national organizations.

Regional and National Conventions, 1860–1880

The fourth area of organization during the period of 1860–1877, regional and national conventions, met with mixed success. Even prior to the conclusion of the Civil War black Baptists from a number of southern and western states, representing two conventions, assembled in 1864 in St. Louis, Missouri, to form the regional Northwestern and Southern Baptist Convention. For two years this successful merger lasted. Then in 1866 there was an even more ambitious move toward the national organizational unity of African-American Baptists. Convening in Richmond, Virginia, the pre-Civil War organized American Baptist Missionary Convention, strongest in the northeastern and midwestern states, combined forces with the Northwestern and Southern Baptist Convention to produce the Consolidated American Baptist Convention (CABC). Between 1867 and 1871 the CABC met in both Southern and Northern states and counted among its leadership distinguished Baptists such as William Troy of Virginia and R. L. Perry of New York. The organization met for the final time in Kentucky in 1878.

Why did this national organization among black Baptists not ultimately survive? First, many black Baptists, like many white Baptists, were very committed to the principle of local autonomy and saw convention formation as

201

a threat to local governance. One might say that African Americans were influenced by Landmark thought. One could also posit, however, that many black and white "mainstream" Baptists, like their Primitive and Landmark siblings, simply retained ideals, such as a fierce commitment to strong local autonomy, that had roots in earliest Baptist history. Perhaps, second, large geographical distances combined with associated travel expenses greatly hindered the operations of the group and participation of poorer delegates and leaders. A third factor, related to the preceding, was the existence of North-South sectional tensions even among black Baptists. To be sure, these tensions were seldom, if ever, as powerful as those between white Baptists; after all, black Baptists during these years did unite temporarily and then more permanently before the close of the century, unlike their white counterparts. Nonetheless, these sectional frictions among blacks were sometimes quite strong and influenced by Northern and Southern black Baptists respective perceptions of each other's worship style and sometimes by socio-economic class differences.

Even before the demise of the CABC in 1878, we see the rise of two regionally based conventions. In 1873 the Baptist General Association of Western States and Territories (BGAWST) emerged. By the 1880s this convention had missionaries, such as T. E. S. Scholes, stationed in central Africa. It eventually united with the National Baptist Convention in the 1890s. Like other black Baptist groups it encountered difficulty in its attempt to have equitable cooperative arrangements with the largely white American Baptist Missionary Union in conducting African missions. Many Baptists involved in the CABC continued their activities in the New England Baptist Missionary Convention, founded in 1874. Indeed, the convention, despite its name, covered other states, including New York and New Jersey. It has been active in domestic and foreign missions, support of education, and predated many other Baptist groups in the formation of a Women's Auxiliary in 1892. Unlike the BGAWST, it has continued in existence as a very strong and influential regional body.

Conclusion

The era from 1850 to 1877 was a critical one in the history of African-American Baptists. During this epoch black Baptists moved from slavery to freedom, vastly expanded membership roles, maintained existing churches and established new ones, and founded associations and regional and national bodies above the congregational level. It is true that national organization of black

Baptist forces during this time was short-lived. Yet for a people who highly prized local church autonomy, faced great geographical distances separating mainly impoverished and former slaves, and dealt with sectional tensions, black Baptists laid important organizational groundwork that would produce far stronger institutional unity in the decades to come. Three years after the "official" ending of Reconstruction in 1880, the Baptist Foreign Mission Convention would organize in Montgomery, Alabama, and later unite with two subsequently formed organizations, the American National Baptist Convention and the Baptist National Educational Convention, to form in 1895 the National Baptist Convention. This convention itself would suffer secessions and divisions, but black Baptist national unity would continue with its existence and in the truly national character of at least two of its succeeding bodies, the National Baptist Convention of America (1916) and the Progressive National Baptist Convention (1961). The contributions of these local, regional, state, and national organizations were not limited to "spiritual" matters. In addition, these groups founded, fostered, promoted, supported, and encouraged political involvement, businesses, schools and colleges, and a continuing sense of mission to a people who for many decades would have for the most part only the family and the church to serve those needs. Yes, the period 1850–1877, from slavery to greater institutionalization, is indeed a turning point in African-American (and American) Baptist history.

Suggested Reading

Boothe, Charles Octavius. *The Cyclopedia of the Colored Baptists of Alabama*. Birmingham: Alabama Publishing Company, 1895.

Carter, E. R., editor. *Biographical Sketches of Our Pulpit*. 1888. Chicago: Afro-Am Press, 1969.

Dwelle, J. H. *A Brief History of Black Baptists in North America*. Pittsburg: Pioneer Printing Company, n.d.

Higginbotham, Evelyn Brooks. *Righteous Discontent: The Women's Movement in the Black Baptist Church, 1880–1920*. Cambridge: Harvard University Press, 1993.

Jordan, Lewis Garnett. *Negro Baptist History, U.S.A., 1750–1930*. Nashville: Sunday School Publishing Board, National Baptist Convention, USA, [1936?].

Pius, N. H. *An Outline of Baptist History*. Nashville: National Baptist Publishing Board, 1911.

Whitted, J. A. *A History of the Negro Baptists of North Carolina*. Raleigh NC: Edwards & Broughton Printing Company, 1908.

CHAPTER 17

Baptists and Women and the Turn toward Gender Inclusion

Karen Bullock

Introduction

A traveler is sometimes pleasantly surprised, while rambling along footpaths through English meadows or wandering Oxford's ancient lanes, to find the passage barred by a "kissing gate," intricately designed and often perplexing to use. In order to move ahead, one turns a lever to close the opening, slides the body sideways into a narrow space, turns the spokes and slides again, then breaks free on the other side. This chapter title may suggest that, like the "kissing gate," there has been indeed such a turning point in Baptist life *toward* gender inclusion—perhaps a singular point in time, or a series of events when, after complexities were resolved and toiling ceased, the narrow trail gave way to a broad expanse and a sense of belonging settled.

Instead, the story of women's inclusion in "the Baptized Way" has been perhaps more like a latch-less gate banging wildly in the wind, a constant fluctuation of motion—ever-widening, abruptly narrowing, and flying open yet again—all along the span of four centuries. In this story, both official statements and long-held practices on a number of key issues seem paradoxical and confusing, sometimes creating enough tension to set brother against brother and sister against sister, and each against the other, all within the span of a single lifetime. At the same time, steady and encouraging thoroughfares have continued to invite where the whispers of exclusion have never yet been breathed. This chapter traces the erratic movement of women's inclusion in

Baptist life across the ten generations in which women and men have lived, worked, and served Christ together.[1]

Living with Circles and Gates

Women have experienced inclusion in Baptist life in varying degrees in different eras, roles, and regions of the world. To even the casual historian the complexities of this topic are obviously deep and conflicting; however, the broadest historical sweep suggests three overarching themes by which observations regarding inclusion may be identified. These themes are the specific categories of being, service, and expression, and perhaps may be best considered as concentric circles flowing outward from the center of one's deepest and most closely patterned concerns. Because these circles operate both chronologically along a life's (or a denominational) spectrum, and simultaneously, as any given person (or entity) operates in many roles in relationship to others, the circles represent for Baptist women, both individually and corporately, a most intricate and contextual matrix with each aspect of the whole conveying its own nuances of inclusion.

The Circle of Being: Women Included as "Fellow-Heirs"

Across the centuries, like the generations of Christian brothers and sisters before them, Baptist women have shared the grace of God. Jesus demanded that women make their own personal commitments to him, even if that loyalty sometimes required that she countered prevailing notions of family solidarity.[2] The underlying theological reality for women in the kingdom of Christ is that

---

[1] This chapter is a panoramic and thematic look at specific aspects of Baptist life regarding the concept of "inclusion" across the spectrum of four centuries of Baptist witness. As such, it focuses upon *inclusion* rather than its logical corollary of *exclusion*, although the latter will be addressed when evidence and space permit. This chapter obviously cannot incorporate the history and development of gender studies in conjunction with Baptist women; however, it must be noted that a comprehensive research study in this area is sorely needed in Baptist life. Neither will it thoroughly explore the nuances associated with the specific positions on marriage and/or ministry roles in current debate (for example, egalitarianism and complimentarianism; pastoral office; deaconate). Official statements regarding the exercise of public ministry, except as they pertain to the historical record, will not be analyzed in this brief overview for lack of space and focus. Please see Pamela Durso's "Baptists and the Turn toward Baptist Women in Ministry," chapter 22 in this book, for more of this discussion.

[2] Mt 10:32–9; Lk 12:51–3.

Jesus is the Savior who gives himself especially to the lowly and oppressed and "calls all without distinction to the freedom of the Kingdom of God." [3] This is why Paul declared in his exquisite Christocentric expression of faith, that "there is no 'male and female;' for you are all one in Christ Jesus."[4]

Baptist women have also received gifts of the Spirit, alongside those of men, in order to serve others and edify the Body of Christ.[5] These gifts have been given as the he has determined.[6] Women have also received the Holy Spirit's empowering and indwelling so that they may fulfill the assignments to which God has called them—daughters who have their living, moving, and being in him.[7]

From the beginning, then, Baptist women, like men, have known the joy of salvation through Christ Jesus, have been gifted by the Holy Spirit, and have been equipped and empowered to serve him. In all of these ways they have shared equally in the spiritual inheritance of faith as they have received forgiveness of sin and new life in Christ and worshiped the One who made that redemption possible through his own death, burial, and resurrection. In Jesus, the Gate of Life stands wide open and accessible (John 10:9), for he himself is the Way and no one, who comes to him in faith, is excluded. Is there inclusion for Baptist women in Christ? Without hesitation this Gate, boundless and eternal, welcomes all who will enter in to become his disciples. The next circle embraces persons nearest to the heart.

Circles of Service

It was to the solitary male as "incomplete" creation[8] that God brought the woman to complete him and, by her coming, to create the first home.[9] From the dawn of humankind, mothers and aunts and grandmothers and sisters, married, unmarried, or widowed, have shared along with the corresponding men in their lives the significant responsibilities associated with rearing and instructing children in both religious and secular matters, influencing future

---

[3] Albrecht Oepke, "Female," in *Theological Dictionary of the New Testament*, 10 vols., ed. Gerhard Kittel (Grand Rapids: William B. Eerdmans, 1964) 1:784.
[4] Gal 3:28.
[5] 1 Cor 12:7–10; 14:12; 1 Pet 4:10.
[6] 1 Cor 12:11.
[7] Acts 1:8; 17:27–8; Col 1:9–12.
[8] Gen 2:18a, 22.
[9] Gen 2:24.

generations and shaping society in their roles as makers, keepers, and guardians of home, family, and societal structures.

That women's inclusion in family life is a given fact hardly warrants discussion; yet, Baptist families were in turbulence early in the seventeenth century as England was poised for civil war. Family life was torn between two models of societal structure: (1) familial, political, and royal patriarchy; and (2) dissent. A somewhat enlarged status for women, brought about by the independent actions of laywomen, traced back to the time of the Henrician Reformation (1534–1547), had been in place for almost a century. In this somewhat more permissive era, women spoke, wrote, and worked in public spheres with greater acceptance.

In both conforming and dissenting families, fathers and mothers reared children together after the earliest years of a child's life. In Baptist homes parents taught their children along Puritan lines, where daughters were trained to read, keep financial records, and enter into political spheres as wives, widows, or the *femme sole* (single life), even if their roles were primarily traditional in other respects and formal education outside the home would elude them for another two centuries.[10]

At the Restoration of the Monarchy in 1660, however, the crackdown against dissent, with the adoption and implementation of the harsh Clarendon Code (1661–1679), reversed the prevailing winds of moderation when patriarchal forms were reinstated and women's voices suppressed.[11] Despite

---

[10] For discussions of political versus religious dissent and the differences between perceived "authority" versus "power" in this period, see Christopher Hill, *The Century of Revolution 1603–1714: A History of England*, ed. Christopher Brooke and Denis Mack Smith (London: Thomas Nelson and Sons, Ltd., 191) 167; and Sharon L. Jansen, *Dangerous Talk and Strange Behavior: Women and Popular Resistance to the Reforms of Henry VIII* (New York: St. Martin's Press, 1996) 141–46. For the suppression of agitators, see Sara Mendelson and Patricia Crawford, *Women in Early Modern England: 1550–1720* (Oxford: Clarendon Press, 1998) 418–20; and Kirsten Timmer, "English Baptist Women under Persecution (1660–1688): A Study of Social and Religious Conformity and Dissent" (Master's thesis, Southwestern Baptist Theological Seminary, 2004) 9–41, especially the discussion regarding women's roles in this era. During this period, a Baptist woman could marry only within the Baptist fold; therefore, because the number of men in Baptist churches was lesser than that of women, her chances of finding a mate were reduced; Timmer, "English Baptist Women," 20–23.

[11] The Clarendon Code was a series of statutes (1661–1679) passed by the "Cavalier Parliament" of Charles II (1660–1685) reestablishing the Anglican Church and ending the Cromwellian toleration of sects and independent congregations, among whom Baptists were counted. For a fuller discussion, see Christopher Haigh, ed., *The Cambridge*

these restrictions, even as they resisted such impediments to self-expression, Baptist women continued to find measures of fulfillment as they tended to the well-being of those closest to them—parents, spouses, children, extended family members, and friends. The response of strong stewardship of home and family by Baptist women has been consistent throughout the ages and across the globe since these circles closest to the heart operate sequentially, concurrently, and congruously.[12] However, beyond the family unit, Baptist women have also

---

Historical Encyclopedia of Great Britain and Ireland (Cambridge: Cambridge University Press, 1990) 203, 234; and Elaine Hobby, *Virtue of Necessity: English Women's Writing 1649–1688* (London: Virago Press, 1988) 11, 199; and Mendleson and Crawford, *Women in Early Modern England*, 418–20.

[12] To date, there has been no candid, comprehensive study conducted that would measure Baptist women's attitudes, perspectives, or behavior in order to demonstrate their stance on the issues of life that affect them (for example, personal faith; theology; marriage; motherhood; their roles at home, church, and community; balancing work responsibilities with home and church life; feminism; violence against women; Christian witnessing or reticence to witnessing; activism and women's rights; and the challenge to live in the world but not be dominated by it). A recent study, however, gives such a perspective into the broader scope of evangelical Christian women as they discuss their lives.

In "Book Review of *Shared Beliefs, Different Lives: Women's Identities in Evangelical Context*," *Journal of Religion and Society* 2 (2000) par. 3, http:/muses.creighton.edu/JRS/toc/2000.html, William Lyons of Florida State University takes an objective view as he reports on this new study by Lori G. Beaman, in *Shared Beliefs, Different Lives: Women's Identities in Evangelical Context* (St. Louis: Chalice Press, 1999). Beaman identified three primary streams of thought among the group of women who participated in her study, labeling these categories as: traditionalist, moderate, and feminist evangelicals: "Traditionalists object to women's participation in the paid labor force outside the home, interpret biblical passages more literally than women in the other categories, and adhere to the traditional division of labor between men and women. They are also the smallest of the three groups. Feminist evangelical women form a sharp contrast to the traditionalists. They reject all rhetoric of submission and call for an articulation of male-female relationships as partnerships. They embrace women's equality and advocate for increased roles for women within church hierarchy. Moderates, as distinct from the other two categories, accept biblical teachings on submission and male leadership, but live and interpret them from the perspectives of partnership and equality within their own marriages and churches. They readily accept feminist notions of equality, but are outspokenly cautious about any form of feminist activism. This latter group comprises the largest group of women in the study."

The diverse responses to Beaman's study indicate that for these women, evangelical ideology is descriptive rather than prescriptive," says Lyons. In an era when many voices are speaking for and about Baptist women, such a study of Baptist women, in particular, could help to identify Baptist women's own self-perceptions within their denominational

contributed significantly to community life in their broader circles of marketplaces and churches.

Baptist women have worked outside the home in all times and places. Women have added value to community life, served in churches, cared for others, and contributed in varied ways to family sustenance whether of economic necessity, biblical response, or societal or ecclesiastical expectation and whether offered voluntarily, dutifully, or upon demand. Gender studies of the recent two decades demonstrate, for example, that the earliest Baptist women in the seventeenth century worked in the marketplaces of their era as writers, book publishers or traders, nurses, midwives, shopkeepers, and toilers of the land alongside their men in agricultural contexts.[13] In that day business practice in a woman could be seen as an extension of her role as the mainstay of her household, and women's "productivity and talents" depended on "the domestic conditions that fostered them or precluded them."[14]

Rarely have there been times and places where Baptist women have not worked to supplement family income. One remembers the women who endured the unspeakable injustice of eighteenth- and nineteenth-century slavery in Africa, the Caribbean, and America; the abject poverty of the Welsh mining system of the late nineteenth century; the global sharecroppers who scratched out their livings in the early twentieth century; the bare subsistence of communism-controlled Europe; the Mexican and European workers who cross national borders to find employment and asylum; and the poorest who inhabit the known world even today, so many of them Baptists.[15] Along with the men in

---

contexts and gauge whether they correspond with, and may differ from, this larger group of evangelical Christian women.

[13] Alice Clark, ed. *Working Life of Women in the Seventeenth Century*, ed., Miranda Chaytor and Jane Lewis (repr., London: Routledge, Taylor and Francis Books, Ltd., 1982) 31.

[14] Clark, *Working Life of Women*, 31. See also Antonia Fraser, *The Weaker* Vessel (New York: Alfred A. Knopf, 1984) 333–417; and Timmer, "English Baptist Women," 28–41. See also the story of Baptist church planter, Dorothy Hazzard of Bristol, for example, who kept her shop open on Christmas Day to protest what she believed to be "pagan practices" that had crept into the Anglican Church in H. Leon McBeth, *Women in Baptist Life* (Nashville: Broadman Press, 1979) 27.

[15] Sandy D. Martin, *Black Baptists and African Missions: The Origins of a Movement, 1880–1915* (Macon GA: Mercer University Press, 1998) 12–39, 107–35. See also the histories of people groups arranged by geographic region in Albert Wardin, *Baptists Around the* World (Nashville: Broadman & Holman Publishers, 1995); McBeth, *Women in Baptist Life*, and William R. Estep, *Whole Gospel, Whole World* (Nashville: Broadman & Holman Publishers, 1994) 50–58.

their lives, these women provide daily sustenance and, in some places where violence has left its wounds most poignantly visible, they fulfill roles of both father and mother in their homes and communities.[16] Other women labored for different reasons.

In the United States and across Great Britain and Europe, particularly, middle-class women, along with their poorer sisters, began to consider emancipation, educational and voting opportunities, and work outside the home in greater numbers as the nineteenth century closed. The catastrophic wars, political upheavals, advances in technology and commerce, and sweeping social transformations gave birth to a new era in all phases of life.[17] Baptist women remained committed to Christ, family, their communities, and their churches even as their roles within the world changed.

---

[16] Martin, *Black Baptists and African Missions*, 129–35. See also the work of the Baptist World Alliance Women's Department, which, with the leadership of Lauran Bethell (recipient of the Baptist World Alliance Human Rights Award, fights to eradicate the exploitation of women and children across the globe. Bethell lives in Prague, where she serves as an international consultant to encourage and facilitate Christ-based ministries. Her vision is to bring together Christians from around the world to equip and empower them to work with exploited women and children. Her vision became reality at the International Christian Conference on Prostitution called Living Hope, held 22–27 April 2006. There were 200 participants from 36 countries. Leaders included representatives of the regional ministries from Europe, North America, Africa, Asia, and Latin America. Several decades ago, a leading American theory purported that, since fewer women worked outside the home, these women spent more time involved in "religious activities." The corollary of that concept was that if women worked outside the home, they would be less inclined to volunteer in such numbers in their local churches. This has been proven to be a misconception. According to Mark Alan Chaves, a sociologist at the University of Arizona, Tuscon, most women have careers—and they continue to be more active in the church. "It's a mystery, really," Chaves said. "Any way you measure it women are more religious than men." See Gary Soulsman, "In Church, Women Lead the Way," *Delaware News Journal*, 20 April 2003.

[17] See Marie R. Griffith, *God's Daughters: Evangelical Women and the Power of Submission* (Berkeley: University of California Press, 1997), and Lori G. Beaman, *Shared Beliefs, Different Lives: Women's Identities in Evangelical Context* (St. Louis: Chalice Press, 1999). Beaman challenges popular misconceptions about modern evangelical Christian women in two areas. Beaman notes that evangelical Christian women are "endlessly diverse and vibrant in the expression of their faith within their own worlds" and that Christian women who choose to live in a patriarchal context are not "mindless doormats" or "submissive servants" (Beaman's words, 138). Instead, they are "purposeful agents negotiating the implications of their faith within their daily lives," neither resisting traditional patriarchal dogma outright nor accepting it at face value" (Beaman, 138).

Women Included as Churchwomen

For almost 400 years, including the earliest years of Baptist life, women have served in all aspects of church life. It seems surprising, when the proper role of women is the topic of weighty discussion in the current climate, that women held such prominent leadership roles in the seventeenth, eighteenth, and early nineteenth centuries and that so many of their churches fully encouraged them to do so. The earliest Baptist women served regularly as deaconesses, eldresses, teachers, missionaries, committee members, and preachers. They cooked church suppers, visited the sick, received ordination, and helped to conduct baptisms. As the years progressed and women consistently comprised more than 55 percent of the membership of Baptist churches, they contributed funds to Baptist missions, orphanages, and colleges; instructed children, men, and other women in religious matters; and wrote theological treatises. They voted in church decisions; helped to call and support pastors; witnessed the conversions of their family and neighbors; gave public testimony of God's work in their lives; and shared in church discipline, worship, and praise. From the earliest Baptist church records evidence abounds that women exercised spiritual giftedness in a variety of ministry roles, buy much of this ministry was conducted while running from the law.

As was true of women in the early church, English Baptist women endured persecution for their strong convictions. During the reign of Charles II (1660–1685), the English Parliament's Clarendon Code persecuted "Dissenters," including Baptists, for meeting together to worship, holding any form of service other than Anglican, or refusing to baptize their infants. Women took extreme measures to remain faithful to scriptural teachings. For example, Thomazine Stott was ordered to jail for her stance on believer's baptism. Katherine Peck of Abingdon Church, Berkshire, was persecuted with her husband and, upon his death, excommunicated, arrested, and taken to London for trial.

Baptist women provided "birthing" homes outside the parish boundaries for new mothers who refused, on biblical grounds, for their infants to be baptized. Still others served as lookouts, posted in stairwells, with children gathered round, so that their Baptist brothers and sisters could worship in attics or back rooms. If discovered, these brave women would sound the alarm and sometimes, at great peril to themselves, block the route of soldiers who were intent upon arrest, affording others the chance to escape across adjoining rooftops.

Today, Baptist women in some regions of Africa, Asia, Latin America, and Eastern Europe suffer as well. The sometimes explosive conditions that accompany political and social chaos provide little security for the daughters, mothers, and grandmothers who live under the constant threat of violence, human atrocities, and religious persecution. Historically speaking, persecution has held little regard for gender, and so women have experienced death for their faith.

The first Baptist woman in America was Catherine Scott, made famous by the journal entry of Governor Winthrop of Boston. In 1639 Winthrop wrote that this wonderful woman had persuaded Roger Williams to profess Baptist views and that he had "formed a thing like a church" in Providence, Rhode Island, the first Baptist Church in America.[18] For the first hundred years in American Colonial life, Baptist women's roles were not uniformly defined. Some Baptist churches excluded "all women whomsoever from all degrees of teaching, ruling, governing, dictating, and leading the church of God." Other churches encouraged the offices of "eldress," "deaconesses," and "widows."[19] These latter roles seemed to be separate offices based on New Testament passages, yet there seemed to be no real difference in their respective function within the church. These women prayed, taught in their assemblies, consulted with sisters about concerns of the church, represented the women to the body, and attended the sisters in matters of baptism and sickness. In Colonial America, as is still true today, leadership roles seemed to relate strongly to women's and children's ministries.

Baptist women in the Southern Colonies fared somewhat differently than their Colonial or Middle Colony sisters. After the First Great Awakening of the 1740s, Separate Baptists planted churches in the South. Led by Shubal Stearns and Daniel Marshall, these Baptists were characterized by spontaneous worship styles, fervent evangelism, emotional conversions, and women leaders. Regularly ordained as deaconesses and eldresses, Separate Baptist women also made a name for themselves as preachers. Perhaps the most popular woman preacher was Mrs. Martha Stearns Marshall, sister of Shubal Stearns and wife of Daniel Marshall, who was described as "a lady of good sense, singular piety and

---

[18] Her sister, Anne Hutchinson, later massacred with her family by Indians, was probably the first woman preacher in America, although she was not a Baptist. Material in this section excerpted from Karen Bullock, "Women in Baptist Life Series," *Missouri Baptist Word and Way*, 23 March 1995, 3.
[19] 1 Tim 5:2; Rom 16:1; 1 Tim 5:9.

surprising elocution, in countless instances [she] melted a whole concourse into tears by her prayers and exhortations."[20] Daniel Marshall credits Martha's witness in his decision to become a Baptist, but this was not unusual. In many areas of the South, a woman was the first to bring to rural areas the Baptist faith.[21]

Despite sharp differences in faith and practice, Regular and Separate Baptists felt increasing pressure to unite, even though the obstacles seemed almost insurmountable. Regular Baptists with their urban churches, Calvinistic theology, educated clergy, and orderly services did not readily encourage leadership of non-ordained men or women. Separate Baptists lived in mostly rural areas, were less Calvinistic, were uninhibited, more structured denominationally, and favored a shared ministry. To the Regular Baptists, the most grievous aspect of the decision to merge was how Separate Baptists viewed the role of women in church life. In 1787 both groups of Baptists in the South overcame their opposition and merged, dropping the Regular and Separate designations, and the new United Baptists then became the family from which much later Baptist work in America evolved. The Separate Baptist women of this era must have agreed that uniting for greater effectiveness was more critical to the Baptist family than the exercising of their own more prominent roles.[22]

---

[20] George W. Purfoy, *A History of the Sandy Creek Association* (New York: Sheldon and Company Publishers, 1859) 63.

[21] In 1783, for example, McBeth notes that two women in Westmoreland County, Virginia, planted the Nomini Baptist Church, and in Louisa County two other women began Baptist work there in 1788. Margaret Meuse Clay was another remarkable Separate Baptist woman whose home was a center for Baptist life in Virginia. She was among eleven who were arrested, found guilty for unlicensed public preaching, and sentenced to public whipping. Still another leader was the educated Hannah Lee, whose aristocratic family was shocked when she became a Baptist. She was subsequently arraigned for her absence from Anglican parish services and disinherited from her family, but after her first husband died, she remarried Dr. Richard Hall, and the two of them started a center for Baptist preaching from their Virginia home (H. Leon McBeth, *Women in Baptist Life* [Nashville: Broadman Press, 1979] 27–73).

[22] Although a matter for conjecture as to why these Separate Baptist sisters stepped back from accepted roles as preachers, the actual historical record is deafening in its silence. Interestingly, the same action took place on the other side of the Atlantic during the nineteenth century when various groups of English Baptists merged and the sisters took less prominent roles in public worship there as well. See McBeth, *Women in Baptist Life*, 37, 46.

By the mid–1800s and for the next century, Baptist churches in both England and America generally abolished the office of deaconess,[23] restricted the vote in church matters to men, and silenced women's voices in church life.[24] The Separate Baptist tradition of women preachers virtually disappeared, except for some opportunities afforded Free Will Baptist sisters. Only a very few geographic regions retained the office of deaconess. The gap through which women had been moving was narrowed and then closed. Not until the twentieth century would these matters again be addressed in Baptist polity. Meanwhile, some Baptist women sensing a special call to ministry turned to the mission fields to find places of expression. This gate still stood ajar for women.

Women Included in Missions: Societies and Service

During the nineteenth century Baptist women formed organizations where they could speak, be heard, and work together to support ministries that extended the gospel. Women joined the early Baptist mission, undergirding the enterprises prayerfully, financially, and in sacrificial cross-cultural service.

In America the energetic twenty-one-year-old Mary Webb formed the "first women's missionary society" in 1800 and called it the Boston Female Society, which became fully Baptist twenty-nine years later. From her wheelchair, Miss Webb wrote letters and reports, prepared financial statements, helped to start similar societies among other denominations, and conducted business conferences for the groups. Many other Baptist women's mission societies organized before the Triennial Convention took shape in 1814 in

---

[23] See Charles W. Deweese's excellent discussion of the difference between "women deacons" and "deaconesses," and the development of both patterns in Baptist life, in "Baptist Women Deacons and Deaconesses: Key Developments and Trends, 1609–2005," *Baptist History and Heritage* 40/3 (Summer/Fall 2005) 65–79.

[24] The question of woman's suitability to vote in church conference rocked the Southern Baptist Convention in 1885 when Mrs. J. P. Eagle, wife of speaker of the Arkansas House of Representatives, and Mrs. M. D. Early, wife of a prominent pastor, registered as messengers. After many lengthy sessions, and a constitutional change specifying that henceforth messengers should be "brethren," the issue was finally settled. Women were officially excluded from membership in the SBC, a status that would last thirty-three years. In the pivotal year 1918, two years before the United States passed the nineteenth amendment extending the right of vote to women citizens, the SBC overwhelmingly voted to extend to women voting privileges, together with "tardy recognition to the good women who are doing such noble work in carrying out all the tasks undertaken by Southern Baptists." See J. W. Frost, Southern Baptist Convention, Hot Springs, Arkansas, May 15," *Religious Herald*, 23 May 1918, 4.

order to bring together the work of Baptists on a national level.[25] In 1817, for example, there were at least 187 known Baptist missionary societies in the United States alone, 110 of them solely operated and staffed by women.[26]

The first single missionary woman sent from this society was Charlotte H. White, a widow who had long sensed a call to missions. She arrived in Serampore in 1815 and met the unmarried English missionary Joshua Rowe. When they married, they opened new work in Digha. She was followed by Sarah Cummings and Caroline Harrington, sent to Burma (Myanmar) in 1832 to help the teams of British and American missionaries already there (Serampore Trio and the Judsons).

British Baptist women had numbered among the first missionaries appointed by the Baptist Missionary Society in 1792 to India. In fact, in 1796 William Carey indicated the acute need for women missionaries to communicate the gospel in places where men were not allowed to enter. Among those places were the high-caste *zenana* dwellings of Indian women, from which all males, except for immediate family, were barred. In 1854, however, Baptist missionary Elizabeth Sale was invited to enter the prohibited spaces and, a dozen years later, Marianne Lewis published an account of the need for Baptists to form a society to fund a specific ministry to these women. The Ladies Aid Society for the Support of Zenana Work and Bible Women of India was formed in 1867 in London by the women of the Baptist Missionary Society and was later called the Baptist Zenana Mission (BZM). These British Baptist women sought ways to better the lives of women trapped in the most appalling living conditions with no hope of receiving the gospel, educational opportunities, or kindly treatment.[27] The BZM later expanded to include work among women in China as women's mission societies continued to flourish.

After the American Civil War, the mission centers in Asia and the Orient called persistently for women missionaries, particularly single women, to join the fields. The American Baptist Missionary Union (formerly the Triennial Convention of 1814) answered the pleas.[28] In 1871 Mrs. Ann Baker Graves of

---

[25] Estep, *Whole Gospel, Whole World*, 34–37.
[26] McBeth, *Women in Baptist Life*, 81.
[27] See Karen E. Smith, "Women in Cultural Captivity: British Women and the Zenana Mission," *Baptist History and Heritage* 40/1(Winter 2006): 30–41.
[28] Louise Celestia Fleming, valedictorian of her class at Shaw University, was the daughter of a slave and Civil War veteran who became the first black person appointed to career missions by the Woman's American Baptist Foreign Mission Society of the West. After sailing for Africa in 1887, she returned home to earn a degree from the

Baltimore formed Woman's Mission to Woman, a financial and prayer support group for women missionaries that the Foreign Mission Board of the Southern Baptist Convention (SBC) heartily endorsed. Dedicated mission-minded women of South Carolina, Georgia, and Virginia also formed mission societies and sent the Moon sisters (Edmonia and Lottie) and others to China. In fact, these societies broadened their purposes to include buildings for schools and chapels, igniting an explosion of mission interest and support. Women responded so fervently that a convention-wide organization soon took shape, resulting in the formation of the Woman's Missionary Union (auxiliary to the Southern Baptist Convention) on 11 May 1888 in Richmond, Virginia. Visionary leaders like Annie Armstrong and Martha McIntosh provided strength and wisdom, helping to train and encourage Southern Baptists toward regular support of missionaries and special offerings. Soon Southern Baptist missionaries sailed to Italy, Mexico, Brazil, Japan, and Africa.

By 1900 women's societies had appointed 113 women missionaries and supported 284 indigenous "Bible women."[29] Women have remained steadfast in their positive responses to missions whether home or international mission fields; in fact, until recently, missionary service has continued to be the most inviting avenue for Baptist women's diverse vocational callings.[30]

The circles of service have been, with few exceptions, open for women. Families, communities, and marketplaces have welcomed the ministries of women. Churches, too, have depended on the service of women for their very existence. Except for the role of pastor and public denominational roles, women have found support. Beyond the circles of being and service, however, lies the circle of expression, wherein women have found the most controversial of all spaces related to living as Baptists.

Pennsylvania Woman's Medical College. She then returned to the Congo where she poured out her life in pioneer medical missions.

[29] Robert G. Torbet, *Venture of Faith* (Philadelphia: Judson Press, 1955) 199.

[30] During the twentieth century, for example, among Southern Baptists alone, appointed single and married women missionaries consistently totaled well more than half of all missionaries for both Home and Foreign Mission Boards. In 2005 women numbered 31 percent (3,096) of the North American Mission Board missionaries appointed to full-time service. For the International Mission Board, 53 percent (2,695) of the total 5,050 workers were women. Cited from Hannah Elliott's article titled "Survey finds 60 Baptist Women Ordained for Ministry in 2005," Associated Baptist Press, 6 July 2006. The statistics are part of a larger Baptist Women in Ministry report compiled by authors Eileen Campbell-Reed and Pamela Durso, called *The State of Women in Baptist Life*, and given at the organization's annual meeting in summer 2006 in Atlanta.

The Circle of Expression

The opening days of the twentieth century witnessed remarkable changes in the roles of Baptist churchwomen across the globe. They began once again to vote in church conference; represent their churches at conventions; and organize more strategically for the specific purposes of global evangelism, missions, education, stewardship, and human rights. They shouldered leadership responsibilities alongside the men in church life, demonstrating vast resources of spiritual giftedness and effective ministry in a variety of ways. Despite often overwhelming pressures to be embroiled in other crusades, women of the Baptist heritage remained resolutely focused, keeping their priorities fixed on kingdom issues. As they did so, they joined other women in finding a voice for expressing such concerns. For some women, the gates began to swing open; for others, they slammed shut again, demonstrating the ever-equivocal nature of Baptist opinion on the public role of women in the church.

Women Included in Pastoral Ministry and Denominational Leadership

Old debates about women's roles in church life resurfaced and ran the gamut of views. In some places women received ordination, like Freewill Baptist Ruth Bixby who was ordained in 1846, Seventh-Day Baptist Experience Burdick who was ordained in 1885, or American Baptist Edith Hill Booker who was ordained in Kansas in 1894. Other women preached to "Separate Baptists, American Baptists, Freewill Baptists, German Baptists, and Swedish Baptists, while Baptists in the South resisted the practice."[31] In England some Baptist women had served as pastors and deacons for centuries, both with and without official ordination. They generally performed the full work of ministers, from baptizing to performing weddings and funerals, to preaching sermons and counseling, to administering the Lord's Supper. Some women were accepted wholeheartedly to preach; some held with skepticism unless "miraculously inspired"; still others were silenced.

---

[31] From the time Southern women were granted the right to vote in the SBC in 1918 until 1964, there were no ordinations until Addie Davis became the first woman to be ordained. Even though she was reared and ordained among Southern Baptists, no SBC church would call her as pastor. She eventually became the pastor of the FBC of Readsboro, Vermont, and the Second Baptist Church of East Providence, Rhode Island, both American Baptist congregations. See Carolyn D. Blevins, "Diverse Baptist Attitudes toward Women in Ministry," *Baptist History and Heritage* 37/3 (Summer/Fall 2002): 73.

Early in the twentieth-century America, some Baptist women enjoyed the opportunities to pursue theological education, participate fully in seminary classes, and develop personal leadership skills. As the century progressed and the gates widened incrementally, women joined the faculties of Baptist colleges and seminaries in the fields of music, religious education, and theological and biblical studies. Baptist women at all levels shared increased spheres of influence beyond the home afforded them by their involvement in community, careers, mission-travel, and global causes. One such outstanding American Baptist woman was Helen Barrett Montgomery, licensed minister, social activist, author, and lecturer. Montgomery published a translation of the Greek New Testament and was the first president of the Northern Baptist Convention in 1921 and 1922. Her life's work was dedicated to the Woman's American Baptist Foreign Mission Society as president, world travel on behalf of ecumenism, and her involvement in establishing what is now called the World Day of Prayer.

The last quarter of the twentieth century, however, was one of significant shifting for many Baptist women across the world. In Japan, China, Africa, and Western Europe, for example, women found greater freedom to minister. Indeed, 11 percent of the pastors in the Japanese Baptist Convention were women in 1995.[32] In 1984, however, messengers to the Southern Baptist Convention meeting in Kansas City passed a resolution against women's ordination, and in 2000 the same body adopted a new confession of faith that clarified the role of pastor as it applied to men only.[33] Ironically, at the same time that greater numbers of women were being ordained to the ministry, opportunities for these women to serve in churches narrowed, even in Baptist groups that publicly supported such roles. Thus, women continued to serve in increasing numbers as chaplains, co-pastors, associate pastors, student ministers, and counselors.

As the twenty-first century dawned, opportunities for women to teach men students in theological disciplines classrooms in SBC seminaries closed, and women divinity students found their courses different from those of their brothers.[34] On the other hand, among European Baptists, ordained women

---

[32] Nancy Ammerman, *Baptist Battles: Social Change and Religious Conflict in the Southern Baptist Convention* (New Brunswick: Rutgers University Press, 1990) 96.

[33] See the SBC's *Baptist Faith and Message 2000*. It was during this decade that the organization Women in Ministry formed in Pittsburgh in 1983.

[34] For example, women Master of Divinity degree students take a different set of both courses and content in specific areas, such as sermon preparation, preaching lab, and

serve as pastors and deaconesses, and in fact the latter role has stood for generations. Women also serve on the boards of denominations with regularity. There are many such examples. Regina Claas, who serves the Baptist World Alliance as chairman of the Freedom and Social Justice Study Commission, is also the general secretary of the Union of Evangelical Free Churches in Germany, and Birgit Karlsson, who serves as the general secretary of the Baptist Union in Sweden. In Italy women are ordained as pastors, such as Anna Maffei, president of the Baptist Evangelical Christian Union of that country. In Latin America, in countries like Brazil, Cuba, and Mexico, Baptist women preach and serve as deaconesses and professors in theological education. Dr. Dinorah Mendez, professor of Theology and History at the Mexican Baptist Theological Seminary represents a growing number of women who serve at the denominational level, as does Carla Gay A. Romarate-Knipel, who serves in the College of Theology and the Religion and Ethics Department of the Central Philippine University, Iloilo City, Philippines. At the same time, the numbers of Baptist women who hold positions of leadership in Baptist congregations in Romania, Siberia, for example, are almost negligible.

Among General Association of Regular Baptists (GARB), Conservative Baptists of America (CBA), Baptist Missionary Association (BMA) and Primitive Baptists, ordination of women has not been common, although in a few of these churches women deacons serve. Most ethnic Baptists do ordain women deacons but not women preachers. Some of the black Baptist groups do ordain women to preach and often to be deacons, but not all do so. There seems never to have been an overall consensus regarding the role of women in Baptist life, although spiritual stewardship and care of familial needs have not been proven to be inconsistent with being in Christ, service to Christ, or the *expression* of one's gifts and callings from Christ.

Conclusion

From the beginning Baptists have stood firmly entrenched in the belief that the Bible is authoritative for faith and practice. Throughout the almost four centuries of Baptist life, different generations of Baptists have struggled with passages relating to women's roles within the body of Christ and attempted to interpret and apply these correctly. As a result, women all along

---

hermeneutics; taken from curriculum comparison study from the Master of Divinity degree in the six SBC seminaries in 2006.

the spectrum have found their "inclusion status" in a storm of constant upheaval. Yet this uncertainty has never daunted women.

In the new millennium Baptist women are heavily involved in kingdom work. Included? Absolutely. Like their English and American Baptist grandmothers and mothers throughout four centuries, Baptist women today visit the sick; bring the gospel to migrant camps; teach, guide, and disciple new converts; nurture children in the faith; work with family ministries; champion the rights and dignity of society's outcasts; seek protection for the innocent; minister to the families of missionaries through prayer and support; pack boxes of clothing and food for prisoners and the needy; administer healing in Christ's name; preach from pulpits or street corners or flag poles; distribute Bibles and literature; raise money for Baptist causes; and weep, laugh, and encourage, serving all with willing hearts. Some women are ordained; others are not. Some are licensed; many more are not. Some function in prominent leadership roles, while the vast majority of them continue to do the work of ministry unseen. Through these actions of everyday life, as the decades have rolled on and on, Baptist women have consistently modeled faithful obedience, sometimes in the face of formidable obstacles and at times with the cries of condemnation from their own brothers and sisters in Christ ringing in their ears.

Have women been recognized publicly, consistently, and professionally for this service that has benefited the cause of Christ in such immense measure? Not yet. As A. T. Robertson so wistfully stated, "The point is that, 'in Christ Jesus' race or national distinctions do not exist, class differences vanish, sex rivalry disappears. This radical statement marks out the path along which Christianity was to come in the sphere and spirit and power of Christ. Candor compels one to confess that this goal has not yet been fully attained. But we are on the road, and there is no hope on any way than on 'The Jesus Road.'"[35]

Across the globe, Baptists have yet more work to accomplish in order for the voices and gifts of women to be valued, consulted, and expressed. The Baptist gate still fluctuates as the twenty-first century begins. In the current climate in which most Baptists seek unity while celebrating diversity, search for authentic models of servant-hearted leadership, and champion protection for the worlds' most vulnerable in both the name and the spirit of Christ, there is room to affirm, invite, and encourage Baptist women's contributions of being, service, and expression. As ever-increasing members of the Baptist family

---

[35] A. T. Robertson, "The Epistles of Paul," *Word Pictures in the New Testament*, 6 vols. (Nashville: Broadman Press, 1931) 4:299.

choose to stand in welcome to open the gate these brothers and sisters will usher in a new turning point in Baptist life that may at last engender inclusion.

Suggested Reading

Briggs, John H. Y. "She-Preachers, Widows and Other Women: The Feminine Dimension in Baptist Life since 1600." *Baptist Quarterly* 31/7 (July 1986): 337–52.

Campbell-Reed, Eileen, and Pamela Durso. The *State of Women in Baptist Life—2005*. Atlanta: Baptist Women in Ministry, 2006.

Lynch, James R. *"Baptist Women in Ministry through 1920." American Baptist Quarterly* 13/14 (December 1994).

McBeth. H. Leon. *Women in Baptist Life*. Nashville: Broadman Press, 1979.

Timmer, Kirsten. "English Baptist Women under Persecution (1660–1688): A Study of Social and Religious Conformity and Dissent." Master's thesis, Southwestern Baptist Theological Seminary, 2004.

"Baptist Women in America." *Baptist History and Heritage* 40/3 (Summer/Fall 2005).

"Baptist Women around the World." *Baptist History and Heritage* 41/1 (Winter 2006).

"Women and the Church. "*Review and Expositor* 72/1 (Winter 1975).

CHAPTER 18

Baptists and Global Unity and the Turn toward the Baptist World Alliance

Glenn Jonas

The BWA allows Baptists to pool their resources to do large tasks. It provides inspiration, especially for the smaller Baptist groups, to see they are part of a vast world movement of Baptist faith. It allows Baptists to speak more effectively to world issues, especially in religious liberty. It provides Baptists from over 125 countries, with their cultural and theological variety, a moving demonstration that their common ties in Jesus Christ are more important than their various doctrinal and social differences.[1]

H. Leon Mcbeth used these sentences to summarize the significance of the Baptist World Alliance (BWA), an organized fellowship of 214 Baptist denominations that represent more than 80 million Baptists worldwide.[2] Now more than a century old, the BWA provides fellowship, promotes evangelism, cares for the dispossessed and needy, and advocates human rights (especially religious freedom) around the world. The headquarters were located in London, England, until 1940, when due to the threat of the Nazi bombing of London, they were moved to the United States. The transfer was made permanent in 1947 and the headquarters today are located just outside of Washington, DC, in Falls Church, Virginia.

The idea for a worldwide Baptist union was not new in 1905 when the Baptist World Alliance was constituted. As early as 1678 English General

---

[1]H. Leon Mcbeth, *The Baptist Heritage: Four Centuries of Baptist Witness* (Nashville: Broadman Press, 1987) 525.

[2] "About BWA," Baptist World Alliance, http://www.bwanet.org/AboutUs/WhatIs-BWA.htm (accessed 12 June 2006).

Baptist leader Thomas Grantham said, "I could wish that all congregations of Christians in the world, that are baptised according to the appointment of Christ would make one consistory, at least sometimes, to consider of matters of differences among them."[3] A century later, around 1790, John Rippon, another popular English Baptist and editor of *The Baptist Annual Register*, expressed hopes that within a short period of time, Baptists from other parts of the world would be able to meet "to consult the ecclesiastical good to the whole."[4]

In 1904 *The Baptist Argus*, a periodical edited by J. N. Prestridge of Louisville, Kentucky, began to give attention once again to the idea of a world gathering. A. T. Robertson, a professor at the Southern Baptist Theological Seminary, suggested that an issue of the periodical should be devoted to the theme of "Baptist World Outlook," and focus attention on Baptist work around the world. The following issue (January 1904) contained an editorial by Robertson titled "Why Not a World's Baptist Conference?" He said, "We suggest, for what it may be worth, that next summer…in London, the Baptists of the World send some of its mission and education leaders for a conference on Baptist world problems."[5]

Robertson and Prestridge worked together to generate interest. Robertson later recalled that he had shown the editorial to both E. Y. Mullins, the president of the Southern Baptist Theological Seminary, who was enthusiastic, and to Prestridge, and "Dr. Prestridge pushed the matter vigorously." The editorial was well-timed as indicated by the fact that "the responses came thick and fast from all over the world and great interest was aroused."[6]

In summer 1904 the Baptist Union of Great Britain and Ireland issued an invitation for the meeting to take place in London 11–18 July 1905. Delegates from twenty-three countries gathered at Exeter Hall in London, England, and formally organized the Baptist World Alliance. The seventy-nine-year-old Rev.

---

[3] Richard Knight, *History of the General or Six Principle Baptists in Europe and America* (Providence: Smith and Parmenter, 1827) 120–21. There are several noteworthy histories of the Baptist World Alliance. Richard V. Pierard, ed., *Baptists Together in Christ 1905–2005: A Hundred-Year History of the Baptist World Alliance* (Falls Church: Baptist World Alliance, 2005) 1; F. Townley Lord, *Baptist World Fellowship: A Short History of the Baptist World Alliance* (Nashville: Broadman Press, 1955); Carl W. Tiller, *The Twentieth Century Baptist: Chronicles of Baptists in the First Seventy-five Years of the Baptist World Alliance* (Valley Forge: Judson Press, 1980).

[4] Horace O. Russell, "Early Moves in the Direction of Greater Cooperation," in Pierard, *Baptists Together in Christ*, 1–2.

[5] Cited in McBeth, *Baptist Heritage*, 523.

[6] Lord, *Baptist World Fellowship*, 3 quoting Robertson.

Alexander MacLaren was selected to be the first presiding officer. MacLaren gave the opening address in which he invited the participants to stand and repeat the Apostles' Creed, for the purpose of showing the world that Baptists considered themselves to be unified with the mainstream of the historic Christian tradition.[7]

The Baptists at London drafted a constitution and approved it on the second day of the gathering. It provided for a general meeting or "congress" to be held every five years; an executive committee to be elected by the messengers at the congresses; and a group of officers including a president, a vice-president from each country represented in the Alliance, and a treasurer and two secretaries (one each from Great Britain and the United States). The famous London preacher John Clifford was elected as the first president with J. H. Shakespeare and J. N. Prestridge chosen as the first secretaries.[8] A portion of the constitution called "Nature and Functions" spelled out in detail the function of the Baptist World Alliance:

> Have as one of its primary purposes the safeguarding and maintenance of full religious liberty everywhere, not only for our own constituent churches, but also for all other religious faiths.
>
> 1. Serve as an agency for propagating Baptist principles and tenets of faith, objectives and distinctive principles throughout the world.
>
> 2. Serve as an agency to make surveys throughout the world with a view to furnishing facts to the various Baptist groups and counseling with them in establishing work in new fields when such service is requested.
>
> 3. Serve as a world-wide agency in making such use of the radio and press as may be practicable in preaching the Gospel, propagating Baptist principles, and promoting common tasks of Baptists throughout the world.
>
> 4. Arrange and conduct preaching missions throughout the world.

---

[7] For the complete text of the address see Walter B. Shurden, ed., *The Life of Baptists in the Life of the World: 80 Years of the Baptist World Alliance* (Nashville: Broadman Press, 1985) 16–18.

[8] Carl W. Tiller, ed., *The Twentieth-Century Baptist: Chronicles of Baptists in the First Seventy-Five Years of the Baptist World Alliance* (Valley Forge: Judson Press, 1980) September 1905, 1:1. Since 1928 the alliance has had only one secretary, elected each five years at the congress, rather than a secretary from both the United States and Great Britain.

5. Co-operate with Baptist groups in instituting and administering relief funds as occasion may require.

6. Gather news by means of correspondents in the various Baptist groups, and disseminate it by use of bulletins, Baptist and other papers, and radio; and, when feasible, by a Baptist world publication.[9]

How did the idea for a world Baptist fellowship suddenly take root in the early twentieth century when previously there had been little interest? Several forces came together at the beginning of the twentieth century that led to the organization of the Baptist World Alliance. Advances in communication and travel made the logistics of such a meeting a greater possibility. The growing emphasis on ecumenism among various Protestant denominations in the late nineteenth century had an impact on Baptists and serves as an important factor leading to the Baptist World Alliance as well. Movements with emphases on social justice and world evangelism such as the Second Great Awakening, the Christian Socialist Movement, the Social Gospel, and the modern missionary movement all served to unite concerned Christians from various denominations in the nineteenth century. Furthermore, in addition to the Baptist World Alliance, Christians from six other denominations constituted world denominational fellowships, indicating the concern of many Christians for church unity at the beginning of the twentieth century. Though an interest in ecumenism permeated many sectors of the Christian world at the end of the nineteenth century, the Baptist World Alliance would have never been constituted had it not been for the efforts of British Baptists in Great Britain and both Northern and Southern Baptists in the United States.[10]

The primary influence on the rise of the Baptist World Alliance contributed by Northern Baptists was the Baptist Congress that met from 1882–1915. These meetings were open to all Baptists and allowed for open discussion of a variety of issues of the day. The Baptist Congress began among Northern Baptists, but eventually Southern, Canadian, and British Baptists participated. In many ways, the Baptist Congress served as a precursor to the

---

[9] McBeth, *Baptist Heritage*, 524.

[10] Craig Alan Sherouse, "The Social Teachings of the Baptist World Alliance, 1905–1980" (Ph.D. diss., The Southern Baptist Theological Seminary, 1982) 12–23. The other world denominational fellowships cited by Sherouse are the Old Catholic Congresses, the World Presbyterian Alliance, the Anglican Lambeth Conference, the Ecumenical Methodist Council, the International Congregational Council, and the International Council of Unitarian and Other Liberal Religious Thinkers and Workers.

Baptist World Alliance. It captured a measure of international flair and the Baptist World Alliance later modeled its structure after that of the Congress.[11]

Southern Baptists also provided an important impetus for the subsequent creation of the Baptist World Alliance. Craig Sherouse argues that Southern Baptist leaders such as William Warren Landrum, R. H. Pitt, A. T. Robertson, and J. N. Prestridge provided the momentum for the formation of a world Baptist organization. In short, Southern Baptists were the influential cheerleaders "by generating American Baptists,' north and south, interest in such an international body."[12]

Finally, Sherouse indicates that British Baptists contributed to the creation of the Baptist World Alliance by adding their maturity and expertise, especially their interest in ecumenism, regarded as more mature than that of Southern or Northern Baptists. The most important name to illustrate the influence of British Baptists was John Clifford, "one of the most outstanding nineteenth century British ecumenists."[13] Along with Clifford, other British Baptists such as F. B. Meyer, J. H. Shakespeare, and Alexander MacLaren became strong supporters of the Baptist World Alliance because they saw in the alliance a first step toward their hope that eventually all Christians would be able to unite around the world. While Northern and Southern Baptists in America were interested in Baptist unity, many British Baptists were interested in moving further toward total Christian unity. Through the influence of particularly Clifford and Shakespeare, the British Baptist Union (October 1904) invited all Baptists to London for the congress and appointed a thirty-two-member committee to make the necessary organizational plans.[14]

J. H. Shakespeare was the prime mover of the Baptist World Alliance in its first two decades. He served as general secretary from 1905 to 1925. He was succeeded by J. H. Rushbrooke who served in the role from 1928–1939.[15]

---

[11] Sherouse, "Social Teachings," 27–33.

[12] Ibid., 33. Sherouse believes that the Whitsitt Controversy had an important effect of causing many Southern Baptists to look beyond themselves toward other Baptists in the world, particularly British Baptists. The interest generated by the Whitsitt Controversy in Baptist origins in the seventeenth century and the realization that the Baptist movement originated among the British produced a desire to connect with British Baptists. See 33–44 for a more complete discussion.

[13] Ibid., 45.

[14] Ibid., 44–48.

[15] Successors in the role of general secretary have included: Walter O. Lewis, (United States) 1939–1948; Arnold T. Ohrn, (Norway) 1948–1960; Josef Nordenhaug (Norway) 1960–1969; Robert S. Denny (United States) 1970–1980; Gerhard Class (West

There have been nineteen Baptist World Congresses since the first 1905 meeting in London.[16] The meetings are usually marked by fellowship, discussion of relevant doctrinal or political issues, and rousing sermons and speeches. One of the most impressive events that occurs at each congress is the roll call of the nations represented. This event is usually highly emotional and inspiring, given that Baptist life in some countries during the last century has been far from easy or comfortable. For example, at the second Baptist World Congress in Philadelphia in 1911, a noteworthy presence was a contingent of thirty representatives from Russia. One Russian, Ivanoff-Klishnikoff, had baptized more than 1,500 converts, had been imprisoned thirty-one times for his faith, and had been exiled twice. Other Russian Baptists spoke to the delegation about persecutions they had endured.[17]

Although all of the nineteen Baptist World Alliance Congresses have been significant in their own right, two deserve particular attention. In 1934 the Baptist World Congress met in Berlin. The political climate in Germany under Adolf Hitler created a tense environment for this congress as thousands of delegates gathered. It must have been a surreal experience for the delegates as they entered the Kaiser-Damm Hall and noticed the display before them. A large Nazi flag hung at the front of the hall on the left and just behind the speaker's platform. In the center behind the podium was a large painting of a cross that showed a dove descending from heaven above the cross and the figures of Charles Spurgeon, William Carey, and Johann Gerhard Oncken (regarded by many as the "Father of German Baptists") below it. In front of the

---

Germany) 1980–1988; Denton Lotz (United States) 1988–present. After Lotz announced his retirement in 2006, the BWA nominated Neville Callum to succeed him. The formal election occurred in the summer of 2007. See McBeth, *Baptist Heritage*, 524–25; Pierard, *Baptists Together in Christ*, 325; "Lotz Congratulates Callam, New BWA General Secretary Nominee," Baptist World Alliance, http://www.bwanet.org/default.aspx?pid=457 (accessed 10 January 2008).

[16] The World Congresses have met in the following locations: London (1905); Philadelphia (1911); Stockholm (1923); Toronto (1928); Berlin (1934); Atlanta (1939); Copenhagen (1947); Cleveland (1950); London (1955); Rio de Janeiro (1960); Miami Beach (1965); Tokyo (1970); Stockholm (1975); Toronto (1980); Los Angeles (1985); Seoul (1990); Buenos Aires (1995); Melbourne (2000); Birmingham, England (2005).

[17] Lord, *Baptist World Fellowship*, 27–30.

[18] Lord indicated that one of the reasons for delaying the gathering of the world congress for one year was to observe the 100th anniversary of the death of William Carey, the beginning of the Baptist movement in Germany under Johann Gerhard Oncken, and the birth of Charles Spurgeon. See Lord, *Baptist World Fellowship*, 79–80.

pulpit was a portrait of German President Paul von Hindenburg draped in black. Hindenburg had died two days before the congress opened and the Nazis were creating a spectacle of his state funeral that week.[19]

The political climate surrounding this congress deserves special attention. Hitler had been in power for eighteen months. Although he was still consolidating his power, the effects of his brutal regime were already obvious in Germany. Just weeks before Hitler had launched a bloody purge throughout Germany eliminating his political rivals by imprisonment or forced emigration. The press had been muzzled and the secret police lurked in the shadows creating an environment of suspicion and fear. A systematic purging of the Jews from German society was underway. The *Kirchenkampf*, a conflict for control of the state church in Germany, was also in progress. The pro-Hitler "German Christians" (*Deutchen Christen*) sought to purge the German church of all Jewish influences, including abolishing the use of the Old Testament and demanding the dismissal of all clergy with Jewish ancestry. Opposing them was the "Confessing Church" (*Bekennende Kirche*) with leaders Martin Niemöller and Dietrich Bonhoeffer. Given the circumstances, it is no surprise that many Baptists believed that the congress should be held in Zurich rather than Berlin.[20]

In spite of the tense circumstances, the Nazi regime seemed willing to court the Baptist visitors. Official greetings were brought by various people including the mayor of Berlin. Hitler sent the delegates a telegram thanking them for their resolution of sympathy regarding Hindenburg's death. Leaders of the Baptist World Alliance were invited to a reception at city hall. Perhaps most telling was a personal invitation from Reich Bishop Ludwig Müller to a delegation of Baptist World Alliance leaders, which included J. H. Rushbrooke, George W. Truett, L. R. Scarborough, Louie D. Newton, and Arnold T. Ohrn, where he assured the Baptist leaders that his objective was to secure the freedom for the gospel to be preached in Germany, that he harbored no ill feeling toward the free churches such as Baptists, and that he had no desire to force them into unity with the *Deutchen Christen*. The German press seized the

---

[19] Lord indicated that one of the reasons for delaying the gathering of the world congress for one year was to observe the 100th anniversary of the death of William Carey, the beginning of the Baptist movement in Germany under Johann Gerhard Oncken, and the birth of Charles Spurgeon. See Lord, *Baptist World Fellowship*, 79–80.

[20] Erich Geldbach, "The Years of Anxiety and World War II," in Pierard, *Baptists Together in Christ*, 80–88.

occasion to promote the significance of the BWA Congress visitors as well. At the congress Baptists felt free to speak out against racism and the attention to militarism and nationalism of the Nazis. But within eighteen months, German Baptists discovered they had no freedom under Hitler, and that they were expected to conform to Nazi orders. In short, the German Baptists "and the BWA had been victims of massive self-deception."[21]

The BWA World Congress of 1934 saw the introduction of study commission reports for the first time. Three years prior, five topics (nationalism, racialism, moral standards connected with marriage and family, temperance, and economics and the mind of Christ) were chosen and 155 members from forty-five countries were appointed to the study commissions. These five commissions presented their reports to the congress and in particular the reports on nationalism and racialism were strongly worded and probably caught the Nazis' attention.[22] The congress passed several resolutions. The first protested the suppression of religious dissent in Russia and expressed concern and sympathy for those who suffer for their faith. The second resolution addressed reports of starvation and famine in Russia. The third indicated the congress's belief that war is incompatible with the mind of Christ. Racial repression of Jews and Africans was the topic of the fourth resolution urging respect for all humans regardless of race. The final resolution declared that any interference with the freedom of the church is an obstruction of the relationship between God and God's people and called for complete religious liberty for all people.[23]

Historian Loyd Allen states that while Baptists spoke their minds on issues such as militarism, racism, and separation of church and state at the Berlin congress, some were essentially duped by the Nazi propaganda. Various Baptists from the United States returned from the congress actually praising Hitler and the Nazis. Although this may seem bizarre today, Allen argues that three factors caused this to happen: emphasis on personal piety that had a blinding effect on their ability to see the larger social sins of the Nazis; a two-pronged doctrine of salvation that tended to see evangelism and the political

---

[21] Ibid., 83.
[22] Ibid., 84–88.
[23] Tiller, 7:4 (September 1935).

world order as existing in two different realms; and fear of communism that caused them to support any ruler who was opposed to Russia.[24]

The Baptist World Alliance celebrated its 100th anniversary in Birmingham, England, 21–27 July 2005. General Secretary Denton Lotz greeted the attendees and indicated that a paradigm shift had occurred in the Baptist world. In 1905 85 percent of the Baptists in the world were in Europe and North America. However, by 2005, 65 percent of Baptists were in the two-thirds world. He indicated that the "Southern Hemisphere may lack money, political freedom or clout, but they are going to evangelize the world."[25] The delegates at the opening assembly also followed the lead of actor Eric Petrossian who, like Alexander MacLaren a century before, led in repeating the Apostles' Creed.

While observing the centennial anniversary of the Baptist World Alliance at the 2005 World Congress was a festive, celebratory occasion, events preceding it were not so festive. For the first time in a century Southern Baptists were not an official participant in a Baptist World Alliance Congress. The controversy surrounded the application in 2001 from the Cooperative Baptist Fellowship (CBF) for membership in the BWA. The fellowship was formed in 1990 by moderate Southern Baptists weary from a decade of fighting with fundamentalists who had captured control of the Southern Baptist Convention through a series of presidential elections beginning in 1979. By 1990 the SBC was firmly in fundamentalist hands and they were unwilling to share governance.

When the Cooperative Baptist Fellowship applied for membership in 2001, the initial response from the Membership Committee of the General Council was that it could not recommend membership due to the fact that a clear delineation between the CBF and SBC did not exist. In 2002, over the objections of Southern Baptists, the General Council accepted a special report from the Membership Committee on the matter. The report spelled out specifically what the CBF needed to do before it could be approved for membership.

Several months later, the Southern Baptist Convention Executive Committee appointed a study committee to look into the matter and to

---

[24] Wm. Loyd Allen, "How Baptists Assessed Hitler," *Christian Century* 99/27 (1–8 September 1982): 890–91.

[25] Greg Warner, "Baptist Congress Today," Baptist World Alliance, www.bwanet.org/Congress/index.htm (accessed 27 June 2006).

rship in the BWA. In February 2003 the SBC reduced
to the BWA from $425,000 to $300,000. It also
of creating another world Baptist fellowship to rival
the Membership Committee for the General Council
led membership for the CBF. Reaction from the SBC
nd soon a recommendation came to sever ties between
n action was formalized by vote of the messengers at the
Indianapolis in June 2004. After ninety-nine years of
uthern Baptist Convention was no longer a part of the
6

:ontroversy between the SBC and BWA probably can be
)f the SBC fundamentalists to control the BWA. Unable
to do so, the SBC claimed that there were three reasons for the withdrawal:
perceived anti-Americanism in the BWA, theological liberalism, and the
Cooperative Baptist Fellowship. General Secretary Denton Lotz responded to
the charges by indicating his belief that the charges "are laced with
generalizations, second hand information, guilt by association, and a
misinterpretation of the facts of what actually happened."[27]

Denton Lotz, who retired from his position as general secretary in 2006,
wrote an essay for the centennial history of the Baptist World Alliance that
provides a good retrospective look at the work of the organization and
recognizes seven prominent developments. He first noted the tremendous
growth of the BWA. In 1905 there were only about 7 million Baptists
worldwide. Now, a century later, that number has climbed to 48 million. If the
total number of people in Baptist households were counted (in addition to those
who were baptized members of Baptist churches) along with those Baptists who
do not affiliate with the BWA, the number would climb to 150 million.[28]

The internationalization of the BWA is another hallmark of the
organization during the last century. In 1905 most of the BWA leadership came
from Europe and North America. In 1960 João Filson Soren from Brazil
became the first president who was neither from North America nor the United

---

[26] Ken R. Manly, "Forward into the New Century, 1995–2005," in Pierard, *Baptists Together in Christ*, 295.

[27] Denton Lotz to BWA General Council members, committee, commission members, 23 February 2004, http://www.mainstreambaptists.org/mob4/lotz.htm (accessed 27 June 2006).

[28] Denton Lotz, "Afterword," in Pierard, *Baptists Together in Christ*, 300–17.

Kingdom. Baptist World Alliance presidents and officers now routinely come from other parts of the world. Furthermore, regional headquarters are now located in Africa, Asia, the Caribbean, Europe, and Latin America. Although the BWA Congress is held every five years, the General Council meets annually. It meets on a different continent each year to insure inclusiveness of the world Baptist family.[29]

Regionalization has been a third significant development in the Baptist World Alliance over its first century. In 1975 the BWA established a Long Range Planning Committee that recommended establishing six regions. The concept was modeled on the idea of the European Baptist Federation that began in 1949 as the first region of the BWA. The All-Africa Baptist Fellowship, Asian Baptist Federation, Caribbean Baptist Fellowship, Union of Baptists in Latin America, and the North American Baptist Fellowship were all added to the European Baptist Federation to create the six regions. The idea behind creating regions was to foster better communication between Baptists in each region. It also provided for less expensive travel and better relations. Member bodies of each region have dual membership in both the alliance and the local region.[30]

One of the hallmarks of the Baptist World Alliance through the years has been its attention to freedom and justice issues. The Baptist World Alliance has never hesitated to speak out clearly and forcefully in areas where religious persecution exists and to lend its resources where relief efforts are needed. As previously seen in 1934, the Baptist World Alliance spoke out against racism in Germany. It has spoken against apartheid in South Africa and has championed religious liberty in Russia and the former Soviet states. Its Freedom and Justice Commission has been active throughout the years in speaking for the poor and underprivileged. The BWA has recognition as a nongovernmental organization at the United Nations and it has used that status to promote religious liberty.[31]

The BWA also has created study commissions throughout the years to provide a forum for the free exchange of ideas on a variety of topics of interest to Baptists. The study commissions have meetings each year at the General Council meetings and the sessions are usually well-attended. The BWA evaluates the study commissions every five years and decides whether any should be deleted or new ones added. Currently, there are six study commissions actively working: Baptist Heritage and Identity, Christian Ethics,

---

[29] Ibid., 301–302.
[30] Ibid., 302–303.
[31] Ibid., 304.

Church Leadership, Doctrine and Interchurch Cooperation, Freedom and Justice, and Worship and Spirituality.[32]

Another important theme that permeates the first century of BWA work is Baptist identity. In areas of the world where there is tremendous growth, the question of Baptist identity is particularly relevant. Lotz argues that whereas many North American and European Baptists have deemphasized their identity, in the two-thirds world where most of the new Baptist growth is located, Baptist identity is tremendously important. How should a Baptist church function? What is the role of the pastor and laity? What does the word Baptist mean? These are all questions that Lotz considers important for the BWA to reflect upon as it seeks to assist Baptist churches around the world.[33]

A final theme that the Baptist World Alliance has emphasized concerns its attention to missions. Missions is one of the most important elements of Baptist World Alliance work. The tremendous growth of Baptists around the world during the last century is directly attributed to the importance Baptists have placed on missions. The BWA sponsors conferences around the world for Baptists to dialogue about how best to carry out their mission endeavors. Whereas in 1905, most of the mission efforts were carried out by Baptists in western countries, that is no longer the case. Missions have now become the focus of Baptists worldwide largely because of attention from the Baptist World Alliance.

As the Baptist World Alliance looks toward a new century, one observer has noted that at least three challenges lie ahead: the majority of Baptist Christians now live below the Equator; there is a theological education crisis worldwide on the horizon for Baptists; and Baptists are struggling to preserve their identity worldwide.[34] Another observer noted that he was most impressed by "the energy and vitality from Baptists in what is often called 'the developing world'" and that Baptists in North America and Europe have much that can be learned from Baptist sisters and brothers in Latin America, Asia, and Africa.

---

[32] See Baptist World Alliance, http://www.bwanet.org/Ministries/study/main.htm (accessed 28 June 2006).
[33] Lotz in Pierard, *Baptists Together in Christ*, 305.
[34] Bruce Gourley, "Reflections from the Baptist World Alliance Congress," *The Baptist Studies Bulletin* 4/8 (August 2005), http://www.centerforbaptiststudies.org/bulletin/2005/august.htm#Resources (accessed 27 June 2006).

The next century of the Baptist World Alliance will most certainly be influenced by these Baptists.[35]

Suggested Reading

Lord, F. Townley. *Baptist World Fellowship: A Short History of the Baptist World Alliance*. Nashville: Broadman Press, 1955.

Pierard, Richard V., editor. *Baptists Together in Christ 1905–2005: A Hundred-Year History of the Baptist World Alliance*. Falls Church VA: Baptist World Alliance, 2005.

Sherouse, Craig Alan. "The Social Teachings of the Baptist World Alliance, 1905–1980." Ph.D. dissertation, Southern Baptist Theological Seminary, 1982.

Shurden, Walter B., editor. *The Life of Baptists in the Life of the World: 80 Years of the Baptist World Alliance*. Nashville: Broadman Press, 1985.

Tiller, Carl W. *The Twentieth Century Baptist: Chronicles of Baptists in the First Seventy-five Years of the Baptist World Alliance*. Valley Forge: Judson Press, 1980.

---

[35] Daniel Vestal, "Reflections on the Baptist World Alliance," *Cooperative Baptist Fellowship*, 5 August 2005, http://www.thefellowship.info/News/050802BWA.icm (accessed 27 June 2006).

CHAPTER 19

Baptists and the Social Gospel and the Turn toward Social Justice: 1898–1917

E. Glenn Hinson

It may be more accurate to speak of a "re-turn" toward social justice, for Baptists started their journey with a two-sided Puritan concern for heart religion manifested in transformation of life and society. In *The Pilgrim's Progress* John Bunyan panned Talkative for making religion a matter of "talk" rather than "walk." "The soul of religion is the practical part," Christian insists, proceeding to quote James 1:22 and 27. "This Talkative is not aware of; he thinks that *hearing* and *saying* will make a good Christian; and thus he deceiveth his own soul...let us assure ourselves that at the day of doom men shall be judged according to their fruits (Matt. xiii.23); it will not be said then, 'Did you believe?' but 'Were you *doers*, or *talkers* only?' and accordingly shall they be judged."[1]

This sense of social responsibility suffered some diminishment and impairment during the Great Awakening (1720–60) and Frontier Revival (1790–1820) as Baptists, like other Protestants, shifted from a concern for a more full-orbed spiritual formation to a preoccupation with conversion.[2] The "awakenings" enabled Baptists to burst the bonds of hyper-Calvinism and to launch an aggressive missionary movement to take part in Christianity's "great century" of missionary expansion, the nineteenth, but they seem also to have diverted attention from social issues as the industrial revolution burst forth in the eighteenth century.

---

[1] John Bunyan, *The Pilgrim's Progress*, in *The Doubleday Devotional Classics*, ed. E. Glenn Hinson, 2 vols. (Garden City: Doubleday & Co., 1978) 2:384.
[2] On this see E. Glenn Hinson, "Baptist Approaches to Spirituality," *Baptist History and Heritage* 37/2 (Spring 2002): 12–18.

The revolution erupted in England in the 1700s and spread from there to other parts of Europe and to North America in the 1800s, transforming the northern hemisphere from a largely rural and agricultural society into an essentially urban and industrial one. Indicative of the radical change, whereas in 1685 Liverpool and Birmingham numbered about 4,000 and Manchester about 6,000, in 1881 Liverpool tallied 552,425, Birmingham 400,757, and Manchester 393,676. More significantly, the shift to an industrialized urban society effected a radical change in human lifestyle and magnified conventional human problems or introduced a mind-boggling array of those not faced in an agrarian age—grinding poverty, fifteen-hour workdays, frequent unemployment, women and child labor for sub-survival wages, industrial accidents, inadequate housing, and a host of other ills. Readers of Charles Dickens's mid-nineteenth-century novels such as *Bleak House* (1853) and *Hard Times* (1854) will have no difficulty envisioning the horror of those sooty factories and urban wastelands.

In both England and America Baptists drew their constituency heavily from among the working masses and obviously experienced firsthand the plight of people toiling in "those dark satanic mills." For an educationally challenged group, however, experience may neither translate into understanding nor understanding into meaningful action. Indeed, Baptist privatistic piety and preoccupation with evangelism and missions tended to act as brakes against impulses toward a social Christianity. In time, however, pastors and other leaders could no longer turn blind eyes toward the suffering of their own as a result of the industrial revolution. From Baptist ranks came two of the most perceptive and eloquent visionaries and prophets for a "social gospel"—John Clifford in England and Walter Rauschenbusch in the United States.

John Clifford

John Clifford got a firsthand taste of the hellishness of the industrial revolution in childhood. He was the first child of Samuel and Mary Stenson Clifford, born 16 October1836 in Sawley. His father worked on a warp machine in a local lace factory, which often experienced strife and, as steam power displaced manpower, unemployment. Not surprisingly, Samuel, like many Baptists in the Midlands, joined the Chartists. This working class movement's 1838 charter espoused universal human suffrage, a secret ballot, no property qualifications for members of parliament, salaries for members of parliament, annual elections, and equal electoral districts. Mary Clifford tatted lace at home to supplement the family income. The family belonged to the General Baptist

Church of Sawley, which had come under Methodist influence. Samuel Clifford, although a Particular Baptist at this time, had some Methodist background, but Mary stemmed from a long line of Baptists.

When John was four the family moved to Beeston, where John attended a Wesleyan school. During a brief move to Lenton, he went to a Baptist school and then, for a short time, the Baron-lane National School in Beeston. Just before he turned eleven, however, his schooling ended, for, like many other children of the working class, he had to take a job in the local lace factory, an event that would give shape to his social views from then on. He opened his autobiography, written when he was eighty, with this statement: "I began life in a factory and I have never forgotten the cruel impressions I received there of men and work. Ebenezer Elliott's prayer was on our lips daily—'When wilt Thou save the people?' Chartists were alive and eloquent.... So I came to have sympathy with the working classes, of which I was one—and I have still—and I have never lost it after eighty years, and I feel it stronger to-day than ever."[3] His father roused him from bed at 4:00 a.m. He worked from 5:00 a.m. until 7 or 8 p.m. six days a week as a "jacker-off" or "piecer" whose job was to make sure the lace machine had an unbroken supply of thread. Mercifully, workers got a half hour for breakfast and an hour for dinner during their fifteen hour day. A good worker, at age twelve John was promoted to "threader" and at thirteen to assistant to a man charged with taking care of two big machines. He secured the reluctant consent of his supervisor to read while he worked. After a breakdown of his health at age sixteen, he returned to the factory as a bookkeeper and supervisor of the lace-making department.

Sunday was welcomed by the Clifford family, as it was by most other working families. On a Sunday evening in November 1850, John experienced forgiveness and liberation from a burden of guilt accompanied by a realization of the wonder and beauty of nature that evoked effusive love for God. On 16 June 1851 he received baptism in the Baptist Chapel at Beeston at the hands of Richard Pike, the minister. The baptism made a deep impression, which he remembered each anniversary. Near the end of his life, he wrote in a letter to someone about the receive baptism, "Year by year, as the day comes round, I like to get alone and look into my spirit, to review the year just closeing [*sic*],

---

[3] Quoted by G. W. Byrt, *John Clifford, Fighting Free Churchman* (London: Kingsgate Press, 1947) 18.

and to give myself again with a fresh enthusiasm to the work God has set me to do."[4]

Two years later John Clifford felt an inward urge to preach and presented himself for a trial sermon at Nether-street Baptist Chapel, Beeston. After two years of local preaching he applied for admission to the Baptist Academy at Leicester, entering in September 1855. There he received an education that enabled him to relate a well-rooted biblical faith to the questions swirling around him in Victorian society. Thomas Goadby, later principal of the academy, impressed upon him a responsibility "to familiarise the minds of Christian men [and women] with the idea and results of the study of Biblical doctrine in its origin and historical development" and not to think of biblical criticism as "wholly negative and destructive" but rather "essentially, though slowly, constructive and quickening."[5] That instruction put John Clifford at the eye of the storm when his longtime friend and fellow minister Charles Haddon Spurgeon, fearing that liberalism was creeping into Baptist life, launched the Downgrade Controversy in 1884.

One could hardly credit anything with as much effect on the social perceptions of John Clifford as the church he was called to serve on 29 August 1858, the Praed Street Baptist Church, Paddington, in London. He accepted the call on 17 October and, as it turned out, stayed nearly sixty years. There was nothing impressive about the sixty or seventy poor and lowly souls who attended then. From the start Clifford strained to find ways to minister to them in their poverty, which he had amply experienced in his life to that point. Fortunately, his quest coincided with the gain non-conformists had made toward religious liberty and their corresponding development of a conscience and determination to serve the working class. In such ministry John Clifford soon took a leading role.

Praed Street Church was probably the first "institutional" church in London, that is, a church that fostered multiple ministries to meet the needs of its members. In 1861 Clifford established a Mutual Economical Benefit Society, a great novelty at the time. Members paid fourpence dues a week. When they fell ill, they received twelve shillings a week and medical care.[6] Shortly after this, he started a Mutual Improvement Society, which offered free lectures

---

[4] In Byrt, *John Clifford*, 28.

[5] Ibid., 37.

[6] Sir James Marchant, *Dr. John Clifford, C. H.: Life, Letters and Reminiscences* (London et al.: Cassell & Co., Ltd., 1924) 42.

during the winter and a Wednesday night study class. He also organized a weekly social gathering for music, singing, brief speeches or lectures, conversation, and refreshment. Explosive growth at Praed Street Chapel forced a move to more extensive grounds and the building of a larger sanctuary at Westbourne Park, a mile West of Praed Street. The church opened at its new location on 30 September 1877, with C. H. Spurgeon preaching the dedicatory sermon. Meantime, Clifford, ever eager to expand his own learning, took a BA degree in the University of London in 1861, a B.Sc. in logic, moral philosophy, geology, and paleontology in 1862, an MA in 1864, and a degree in Principles of Legislation in 1866. He was elected a fellow of the Geological Society in 1879.

As his own pursuit of education would indicate, John Clifford looked to education to supply a ladder out of poverty and social degradation. From his work among young men and women, which began in 1858, emerged in 1885 the Institute that set forth as its purpose "the establishment and carrying on of such agencies as shall afford legitimate recreation and contribute to the social and intellectual well-being of our members."[7] In pursuit of that objective the Institute sponsored scientific and literary lectures; geological excursions; archaeological visits; concerts by the Choral Association; classes in French, German, Spanish, Italian, mathematics, elocution, shorthand, building construction, dressmaking, and geometry; a reading room and library; and the literary and debating society.

John Clifford played such an active role in Baptist life that it is a wonder he had time to support so many diverse social programs. He held the offices of secretary (1876–1878) and president (1879) of the London Baptist Association. He served as president of the General Baptist Union in 1872 and led in effecting a union of General and Particular Baptists in 1891; in 1900 he was elected president of the merged union. He was vice-president of the Baptist Union of Great Britain and Ireland in 1887 and 1888 when it had to deal with Spurgeon's charges in the Downgrade Controversy. He had an active role in forming the Baptist World Alliance in 1905 and his Baptist colleagues of the world elected him as the alliance's first president. Notwithstanding all of these demands, he gave his heart and soul to issues that confronted the working people among whom he labored: alcoholism, women's rights, housing, arbitration in disputes with business, and a "living wage."

---

[7] Quoted by ibid., 63.

He joined enthusiastically into the Temperance movement. In 1885 his congregation created Westbourne Park Home for Servants to offer short term care for young women who found themselves temporarily unemployed in London without a respectable home. The home lasted nineteen years.[8] Concern for adequate housing aroused Clifford's interest in the Christian Social Brotherhood and to speak out against exorbitant rents for substandard apartments. He lobbied for a "living wage" on behalf of miners. In 1919 he became president of the World Brotherhood Federation, which honored him with a lectureship named for him. He delivered the first series of lectures under the title *The Gospel of World Brotherhood according to Jesus*.

Jesus, he argued, taught reverence for humanity, the right to personal freedom, and equality of opportunity. Under the third Clifford laid out an indictment of his society:

> The social order must be based on relations of equal justice for all or it cannot be brotherly. Brotherly love will set itself definitely and strenuously to get rid of the injustices created by the "inhumanity of man to man." The handicap of circumstance must be lifted. Thousands of our fellows never get a chance to make the best or even a moderate good of life. All doors are closed. Every avenue is fenced in. They are born poor, live poor, and die poor. It is a dwarfed life they lead. Some of them heroically fight for a chance to get out of their early surroundings, and at immense cost they succeed; but where one rises from the deeps, and "breaks his birth's invidious bar," thousands are drowned. Brotherhood ought not to rest except as it is toiling to secure an equal chance for all; for the poor in the slums; for the children in the gutters, for women in chains, for men crushed beneath loads they never created. All our collective action in village and town, city and State, should be directed to equalising the opportunities of education and training of ethical and spiritual development of the manhood and womanhood of the world.[9]

---

[8] Charles T. Bateman, *John Clifford: Free Church Leader and Preacher* (London: National Council of the Evangelical Free Churches, 1904) 178–79.

[9] John Clifford, *The Gospel of World Brotherhood According to Jesus* (London: Hodder & Stoughton Ltd, 1920) 59–60.

Later he gave a graphic summary of the effects of greed run rampant on the lives of children. He depicted "children crushed and crippled by the industrial machine, huddled together in a jumble of sheds called houses; slaving in factories without any limits to their hours, and often toiling for fifteen hours; paid their pittance on the truck system, crawling in the darkness of coal mines; punished by transportation if they resisted their masters; and if they stole anything, likely to be hanged by the neck till they were dead." He went on to put his finger on the underlying evil. Possessions supplanted persons; "the industrial revolution said property was sacred, human beings were mere tools to be worked for the increase of property and then flung to the scrap heap. Life was wholly subordinated to property. Nobody cared. The spirit of fellowship was dead. Men had not caught sight of the Ruskinian doctrine that 'There is no wealth but life.'"[10] Jesus, Clifford insisted, "set moral limits to accumulation of property; taught that the possession of it is a solemn trust for the use of others; insisted on absolute rectitude in the methods of making wealth, and made men feel that an ascetic life or a frivolous life is a violation of social duty, and a failure to discharge the obligations of social service."[11] As he brought his eight lectures to a close, he summed up the objectives of the World Christian Brotherhood. "The aim of Labour is Christian and it is our aim." Brotherhood means:

We have also to get rid of the Drink Traffic by local option leading on to Prohibition; to make an end of war through the League of Nations; to lift the hand of greed out of the tills of the backward races, and train them in self-management; to educate the child for useful citizenship; to remove the remaining disabilities of women; to succour the aged and feeble and the handicapped; to transform the social and political life of the world so that there shall be nothing left to hurt or destroy any of God's children on His holy mountain.[12]

His ardor for social gospel never dimmed until death claimed him on 20 November 1923.

---

[10] Clifford, *Gospel of World Brotherhood*, 131–32.
[11] Ibid., 132.
[12] Ibid., 156.

Walter Rauschenbusch

Although Walter Rauschenbusch was fortunate to escape the industrial revolution's dehumanizing effects early in life, he felt its full blast when he assumed the role of pastor in New York City's Hell's Kitchen. Walter was the son of Carl August Heinrich and Frida Rauschenbusch, who had migrated to the United States from Westphalia in Germany in 1846. August, who had studied at the University of Berlin, descended from a long line of Lutheran pastors and became a Lutheran pastor himself, but shortly after coming to America, he became a Baptist. Walter was born in Rochester, New York, on 4 October 1861. In sharp contrast to Clifford's ghetto upbringing, by his father's design Walter received his first education in Germany between 1865 and 1869. Back in Rochester, he attended Pfafflin's Private School (1869–1878) and later the Free Academy (1878–1879). During the summers between 1870 and 1879 he worked on a farm in Lycoming County, Pennsylvania. The long hours he labored there for twenty-five cents a day and meager meals undoubtedly "influenced his social thinking in later years."[13] After graduation from the Free Academy, he returned to Germany to enroll in the *Evangelische Gymnasium* at Gütersloh in Westphalia. At the end of four years he was honored with the *Primus Omnium*, recognition as the best student. On returning to Rochester in 1883 Rochester Theological Seminary accepted his study in Germany as equivalent to a college degree but required him to do some remedial work, which he completed at the University of Rochester during his first year in the seminary. He graduated from the seminary in 1886.

Rauschenbusch's early experience was deeply tinged by Pietism. At age sixteen he experienced a conversion which he described in 1913:

> And then, physically, came the time of awakening for me, when young manhood was coming on and I began to feel the stirring of human ambition within me; and what I said to myself was: "I want to become a man; I want to be respected; and if I go on like this, I cannot have the respect of men." This was my way of saying: "I am out in the far country, and I want to get home to my country, and I don't want to tend the hogs any longer." And so I came to my Father, and I

---

[13] Dores R. Sharpe, *Walter Rauschenbusch* (New York: Macmillan Co., 1942) 40.

began to pray for help and got it. And I got my own religious experience.[14]

He recognized the limitations of his perceptions, but he also knew its lasting reality: "Now, that religious experience was a very true one, although I have no doubt there was a great deal in it that was foolish, that I had to get away from, and that was untrue. And yet, such as it was, it was of everlasting value to me. It turned me permanently, and I thank God with all my heart for it. It was a tender, mysterious experience. It influenced my soul down to its depths."[15] The experience carried with it a consideration, typical among Baptists in that day, that he should either be a preacher or a missionary.

Service as an interim pastor of a small German-speaking congregation in Louisville, Kentucky, in the summers of 1884 and 1885 seems to have confirmed a pastoral direction in his vocation. He explained to his friend Munson Ford that it gave him "a chance to do something for others," a selfless action fundamental to Christianity. In this context he began to see more clearly what following Jesus Christ demanded: "I tell you I am just beginning to believe in the gospel of the Lord Jesus Christ, not exactly in the shape in which the average parson proclaims it as the infallible truth of the Most High, but in a shape that suits my needs, that I have gradually constructed for myself in studying the person and teachings of Christ, and which is still in rapid process of construction." One who follows Christ "will find that tho' there is no cross for him to be nailed to, he will die piecemeal by self-sacrifice just as Christ did even before his crucifixion and then he is at one with Christ and placed by God into the same category."[16]

One can see in these thoughts some stakes driven in to mark the outlines of the foundation on which Rauschenbusch would construct his understanding of the social gospel. Pouring the foundation and building on it, however, occurred during the eleven years, 1886–1897, he served as pastor of the Second German Baptist Church in New York City. Hell's Kitchen in this city must have look very much like Paddington in London where John Clifford sought to meet the overwhelming needs of people. As the name clearly implies, this section had a reputation for gangs, prostitution, crime, and all the miseries

---

[14] Ibid., 43. Also cited by Paul M. Minus, *Walter Rauschenbusch: American Reformer* (New York: Macmillan Publishing Co., 1988) 17.

[15] Cited by Sharpe, ibid.

[16] Walter Rauschenbusch to Munson Ford, 30 May 1885; cited by ibid., 46–47.

connected with huge urban ghettoes. At the time New York City was home to thousands of immigrants, about 400,000 from Germany, with a total population of 1.5 million. Second Baptist was no plum. It had gone through years of turmoil with incompetent pastors. It had an antiquated building in a shabby state and only 125 members, mostly factory workers with little income. They were able to pay the young seminary graduate only $600 a year plus an allowance of $300 for rent. One member wrote that Rauschenbusch's acceptance of their call was a "miracle before our eyes."[17] His inaugural sermon was on Jesus' prayer "Thy Kingdom come." The kingdom became the axle around which the social gospel turned. He was ordained 21 October 1886.

As Paul M. Minus has pointed out, Rauschenbusch launched his ministry preaching "a Calvinist version of the gospel, modified by a Pietist-Evangelical heritage in the direction of Arminianism, with only a touch of his nascent theological liberalism apparent."[18] This theology underwent strong testing and expansion, however, as he ministered to his flock and developed a warm friendship with two fellow pastors—Leighton Williams of Amity Baptist Church and Nathaniel Schmidt of First Swedish Baptist Church. At first he did not know how to cope with the unforgiving poverty of many over against the obscene wealth of the privileged few who lived a mile away. He confessed later that he "had no idea of social questions." He did not flounder long, however.

In October 1886 Rauschenbusch discovered Henry George, a journalist seeking election as mayor of New York as a reform candidate of a coalition of labor unions and socialists. George lost, but he won Rauschenbusch: "I owe my own first awakening to the world of social problems to the agitation of Henry George in 1886 and wish here to record my lifelong debt to this single-minded apostle of a great truth."[19] To make up for some elements of George's thought that he found wanting, Rauschenbusch turned to Richard Ely, a professor of political economy at Johns Hopkins University. Ely, an Episcopal layman, argued in *Social Aspects of Christianity* that, in recent centuries, Christians had taught a "one-sided half-gospel" of individual salvation and neglected biblical passion for social righteousness. Sounding themes Rauschenbusch would later espouse, he insisted that "the Gospel of Christ is both individual and social. It

[17] Cited by Minus, *Walter Rauschenbusch*, 50.
[18] Ibid., 55.
[19] Cited by ibid., 62.

proclaims individual and social regeneration, individual and social salvation."[20] Eighteen months after arriving in New York City, the new pastor began to sound his call for a new society that heeded "wails of the mangled and the crushed." In a study program on religion and social issues to which he set himself, he soon sided with workers and with socialism. In November 1889 he joined hands with Leighton Williams and others in publishing a paper intended for workers in New York titled *For the Right*, which endorsed a number of worker objectives—an eight-hour workday, single tax, municipal ownership of utilities, etc. The paper lasted only until March 1891, but Rauschenbusch was already formulating a theological basis for a social mission which would get more Christians involved in reform. He met resistance among Baptist peers, but he persisted. At the Baptist Congress in Toronto in 1889 he affirmed Baptist determination to change the lives of individuals but insisted that there was another equally important object—to bring in the kingdom of God and its righteousness.

Rauschenbusch would probably have remained a pastor had rapid diminishment of his hearing, which he first noticed in 1885, not created such a serious problem. He resigned in 1891 to spend a year studying in Germany, but his people persuaded him to take instead a paid sabbatical. When he returned, they hired someone to assist him in pastoral duties, but in a short time he found this arrangement unsatisfactory. When a second invitation came to teach in the German Department of Rochester Seminary in 1897, he accepted it. In 1902 the number of German-speaking students declining, he moved to the English Department as professor of church history. It helps us to understand his teachings to keep in mind that he was among those who espoused the Anabaptist Spiritual Kinship theory of Baptist history. As Donovan E. Smucker has observed in his study of *The Origins of Walter Rauschenbusch's Social Ethics*, Rauschenbusch drew elements not only from German Pietism and evangelicalism of the Awakenings but also from Anabaptist sectarianism, Protestant liberalism, and Christian social transformationism. From Anabaptist sectarianism he derived his understanding of the church as a voluntary society and the kingdom as gradually evolving.[21] He invoked the names of Francis of

---

[20] Richard Ely, *Social Aspects of Christianity*, new and enl. ed. (New York: 1889) 148–49.

[21] Donovan E. Smucker, *The Origins of Walter Rauschenbusch's Social Ethics* (Montreal and Kingston, London, Buffalo: McGill-Queens University Press, 1994) 65–73.

Assisi, Peter Waldo, John Wycliffe, John Wesley, and William Booth in support of the view that following Jesus rules out selfish acquisition.[22]

From his European sabbatical in 1891 on, Walter Rauschenbusch was in process of framing the ideas which he published as *Christianity and the Social Crisis* in 1907. He had made two attempts to revise a manuscript he had written in 1891 titled *Revolutionary Christianity*. During a two-month vacation in summer 1905, he started over. He worked on it again the next summer. With some trepidation that it might be too radical, he submitted it to a publisher. It appeared in April 1907 just as the Rauschenbusch family departed for a sabbatical in Germany. In the opening pages he made clear that he had produced the book "to discharge a debt" to working people of New York whom he had served as pastor. He wrote, "In recent years my work has been turned into other channels, but I have never ceased to feel that I owe help to the plain people who were my friends. If this book in some far-off way helps to ease the pressure that bears them down and increases the forces that bears them up, I shall meet the Master of my life with better confidence."[23]

Christianity and the Social Crisis is a plea for Christians to take up the challenge of creating a new social order. He used three arguments. On the basis of a study of the prophets, Jesus, and primitive Christianity, he contended, firstly, that "the essential purpose of Christianity was to transform human society into the kingdom of God by regenerating all human relations and reconstituting them in accordance with the will of God."[24] Why did it fail? Because of alien influences on Jesus' followers that caused them to retreat from their original mission. Yet recent developments gave promise of a healthful change as Christians were beginning to realize that to serve Christ they must try to construct a social order in which kingdom ways will prevail.

He maintained, secondly, that both the world and the church would benefit significantly from the recovery of Christianity's social mission. It might prevent the collapse of western civilization such as befell the Roman Empire. An economic system that victimizes everyone whose life it touches is the key problem of industrialized society. Workers do not have a fair return for their labor and suffer loss of health and dignity. Owners take more than they deserve and yet suffer loss of qualities that make life most human. Capitalism,

---

[22] Ibid., 45.

[23] Walter Rauschenbusch, *Christianity and the Social Crisis*, ed. Robert D. Cross (New York, Evanston, and London: Harper Torchbooks, 1964) xxv.

[24] Ibid., xxiii.

moreover, has created a chasm between rich and poor and, as it continues to widen, may result in class warfare. Western civilization's best chance of staving off collapse depends on moral vision that enables people to perceive the immensity of the crisis and thus make a determined effort to build a just and humane society. A church awakened to its social mission provides the only source of such a vision. A revival of that sort is also in the church's interest, for the social crisis has damaged the church by alienating the poor as they perceive it as captive to the rich and affluent.

He sought, thirdly, to persuade aroused Christians that hope lay at hand for corrective action, especially in the growing number of professional and business people who made up a large segment of Protestant churches. The most important corrective is the spiritual regeneration that awakens individuals to their complicity in the sins of society and leads them to commit themselves to social reform. A regenerated preacher will proclaim Jesus' gospel of the kingdom in the knowledge that "if he really follows the mind of Christ, he will be likely to take the side of the poor in most issues."[25] Regenerated lay persons will steadily seek to extend the ways of the kingdom in daily work, modeling more just and humane patterns of thinking and behaving. Both clergy and laity must realize that the movement toward a new society rests chiefly in the hands of the working class and that, for them, socialism holds the messianic promise once enjoyed by religion. Rauschenbusch expected a class struggle: "All that we as [Christians] can do is to ease the struggle and hasten the victory of the right by giving faith and hope to those who are down, that they will not harden their hearts and hold Israel in bondage, but will 'let the people go.'"[26] He was confident that God would give the victory.

Christianity and the Social Crisis elicited much praise and earned Rauschenbusch a permanent prominence in American religious thought. A. H. Strong, president of Rochester Seminary, expected it to be "as epoch-making as Henry George's *Progress and Poverty*.[27] It topped the list of religious best sellers and had to be reprinted. It was translated into numerous languages. Nevertheless, it did not please all. Sadly, the harshest criticisms came from Baptists. Although deeply hurt by such attacks, Rauschenbusch persisted in efforts to respond to pleas of those hungry to hear this prophetic call. In 1909

[25] Ibid., 361.
[26] Ibid., 411.
[27] Augustus Hopkins Strong to Walter Rauschenbusch, 27 June 1907; cited by Minus, *Walter Rauschenbusch*, 161.

he answered a request of *The American Magazine* to write something for them with what was published a year later as *For God and People: Prayers of the Social Awakening*. He wrote two small books on the religious depth and social outworking of love—*Unto Me* (1912) and *Dare We Be Christian?* (1914). He also published a more substantial book titled *Christianizing the Social Order* in 1912, proposing a variety of ways supporters of social transformation could attempt reform. He spent 1915–1916 putting together another popular book on *The Social Principles of Jesus*. In 1917 he gave the Nathaniel Taylor Lectures at the Yale School of Religion published as *A Theology for the Social Gospel*.

World War I, however, put Rauschenbusch in the delicate position of a dissenter. A pacifist, he strongly opposed American entry into the war on the side of England. He told a daughter that if Baptists ever forced him out, he would become a Quaker. He succumbed to cancer on 25 July 1918. Yet his returning to the source, Jesus Christ, like Clifford's, lived on.[28]

Suggested Reading

Bateman, Charles T. *John Clifford: Free Church Leader and Preacher*. London: National Council of Evangelical Free Churches, 1904.

Byrt, G. W. *John Clifford, Fighting Free Churchman*. London: Kingsgate Press, 1947.

Clifford, John. *The Gospel of World Brotherhood According to Jesus*. London: Hodder & Stoughton Ltd., 1920.

Marchant, Sir James. *Dr. John Clifford, C. H.: Life, Letters and Reminiscences*. London et al.: Cassell & Co., Ltd., 1924.

Minus, Paul M. *Walter Rauschenbusch: American Reformer*. New York: Macmillan Publishing Co., 1988.

Rauschenbusch, Walter. *Christianity and the Social Crisis*. Edited by Robert D. Cross. New York et al.: Harper Torchbooks, 1964.

Sharpe, Dores Robinson. *Walter Rauschenbusch*. New York: Macmillan Co., 1947.

Smucker, Donovan E. *The Origins of Walter Rauschenbusch's Social Ethics*. Montreal et al.: McGill-Queens University Press, 1990.

---

[28] For brief discussions of Clifford and Rauschenbusch, see H. Leon McBeth, *The Baptist Heritage: Four Centuries of Baptist Witness* (Nashville: Broadman, 1987) 295, 302, 305–306, 523, 561, 569, 585, 598–99, 731, 734.

CHAPTER 20

Baptists and the Bible and the Turn toward Theological Controversy: The Downgrade Controversy, 1887

Jerry Faught

Introduction

From their beginnings in England in the early seventeenth century, Baptists have struggled with internal tensions. Baptist polity, with its emphasis on local church autonomy, serves to nurture controversy. Since Baptists have no official hierarchy to make decisions for individual Baptist churches, often prominent personalities step forward with an aim toward directing Baptist life. Such was the case in the most significant conflict among nineteenth-century English Baptists. The Downgrade Controversy essentially lasted from 1887 to 1888, although roots of the controversy can be seen in the 1870s, and it would have enduring consequences. The conflict centered on the notion that the Baptist denomination in England had succumbed to widespread doctrinal decay along with rampant moral and spiritual lethargy. The controversy likely would not have grown severe if not for the efforts of England's most popular pulpiteer, Charles Haddon Spurgeon, who advanced the battle consistently and tenaciously. In the end, other Baptist leaders such as the eminent John Clifford refused to allow Spurgeon to control Baptist life in England. This chapter will sketch the course of the controversy, highlighting the roles played by Spurgeon and Clifford, and offer interpretations of the conflict.

Shindler's List and Spurgeon's Scoop: The Occasion of the Controversy

Particular Baptists in England made a major move when they formed a union of churches and ministers in 1813 that eventually became known as the Baptist Union. For the first time Baptists in England had a national organization that could correlate multiple ministries.[1] In 1873 the union modified its constitution in order to facilitate cooperation with General Baptists. Although the official merger of the two groups did not occur until 1891, the groundwork for the alliance was laid nearly twenty years earlier when the union softened its strict Calvinist doctrines and formally recognized the freedom of every local church to "interpret and administer the laws of Christ, and that the immersion of believers is the only Christian baptism."[2] As Leon McBeth notes, these actions launched the Baptist Union on a path toward more of a functional basis of cooperation than a confessional one and set the stage for the Downgrade Controversy as well as later doctrinal debates.[3]

Although conservatives had complained about doctrinal deviation in the Baptist Union in the early 1870s, the Downgrade Controversy did not surface until 1887 with the publication of a series of anonymous articles that appeared in Spurgeon's popular periodical *The Sword and the Trowel*. The first article, published in March 1887, bore the title "The Down Grade," giving controversy its name.[4] The articles, later discovered to be from the pen of Robert Shindler, one of Charles Spurgeon's close associates, charged nearly every Protestant denomination in England with having followed a clear pattern of decline from Calvinist orthodoxy to Arminianism, then to Arianism, and finally to Socinianism.[5] According to Shindler, not all Arminians became Arians and Socinians but Arminian theology made them susceptible to error. Nonetheless, Shindler contended that many English Protestants had abandoned Calvinistic soundness with its high view of scripture and emphasis on divine sovereignty, for cold, dull, speculative viewpoints.[6] Shindler went so far as to contend that Darwinism could be blamed on the Socinianism that was taught at the High Street Church at Shrewsbury where Charles Darwin and his relatives had

---

[1] Ernest A. Payne, *The Baptist Union: A Short History* (London: The Carey Kingsgate Press, 1959) 21–22.

[2] W. T. Whitley, *A History of British Baptists* (London: Charles Griffin & Company, 1923) 109.

[3] H. Leon McBeth, *The Baptist Heritage: Four Centuries of Baptist Witness* (Nashville: Broadman Press, 1987) 294.

[4] Robert Shindler, "The Down Grade," *The Sword and the Trowel* 23/3 (March 1887), http://www.spurgeon.org/s_and_t/dg01.htm (accessed 24 September 2002).

[5] Ibid. Arius (fourth century) believed Jesus to be a created divine being subordinate to God the Father, while Faustus Socinus (sixteenth century) believed Jesus to be merely a human being.

[6] Ibid.

received their religious training.[7] This downgrade had resulted in a decline of spirituality among Protestants evidenced by a lack of evangelical zeal and purity of life. Although Shindler painted a slightly less dismal picture of doctrinal and spiritual decline among Baptists, he argued that the denomination was headed down the path toward doctrinal decay and spiritual lethargy unless some actions were taken.[8]

In August 1887, three months after Shindler's final article, Spurgeon took up the pen and wrote with more militancy and urgency than Shindler. Perhaps Spurgeon found inspiration in Shindler's boldness but knew it would take a popular voice to garner significant attention. Without Spurgeon's powerful voice, the controversy may have been a footnote in English Baptist life. Spurgeon pastored the famous Metropolitan Tabernacle in London constructed to seat 6,000 persons. He first gained notoriety as an eloquent and forceful revival preacher who significantly advanced a spiritual awakening in England beginning in the late 1850s. The immensely popular Spurgeon had to turn away 1,000 persons every Sunday from the 10,000-seat Surrey Gardens Music Hall where he preached before the construction of the tabernacle.[9] When Spurgeon preached or wrote, many people listened.

Spurgeon's first article, "Another Word Concerning the Down-Grade," set forth the key issues upon which he would expand in later writings and sermons. Spurgeon warned of a rapid downward trend in Baptist life characterized primarily by doctrinal falsehood such as a denial of the substitutionary theory atonement, hell as a place for the wicked, the resurrection of Christ, and the infallibility of scripture. Spurgeon stated bluntly, "A new religion has been initiated, which is no more Christianity than chalk is cheese."[10] Spurgeon claimed the new religionists were destroyers of churches and destitute of moral honesty, usurping pulpits designed solely for gospel preaching. Wherever doctrinal error had taken hold, Spurgeon argued that a decline of spiritual life quickly followed, and this was evidenced by prayerless churches, ministers who attended the theater and used theatrical presentations

---

[7] Robert Shindler, "The Down Grade, Part Two," *The Sword and the Trowel* 23/4 (April 1887), http://www.spurgeon.org/s_and_t/dg02.htm (accessed September 2002).

[8] Ibid.

[9] Lewis Drummond, "Charles Haddon Spurgeon," in *Baptist Theologians*, ed. Timothy George and David S. Dockery (Nashville: Broadman Press, 1990) 271, 278–79.

[10] Charles Haddon Spurgeon, "Another Word Concerning the Down-Grade," *The Sword and the Trowel* 23/8 (August 1887), in H. Leon McBeth, *A Sourcebook for Baptist Heritage* (Nashville: Broadman Press, 1990) 198–200.

in worship, and a decline in attendance at worship services. "Many would like to unite church and stage, cards and prayer, dancing and sacraments," declared Spurgeon.[11]

As the controversy developed, doctrinal problems in the Baptist Union became the primary focus. Without naming specific individuals, Spurgeon alleged that more than a few Baptist pastors held to Socinianism, Universalism, and rejected the inspiration and authority of the Bible.[12] Evidently, Samuel Harris Booth, secretary of the Baptist Union, had provided Spurgeon with names of persons he considered heterodox but had asked Spurgeon to keep the information confidential.[13] Booth later indicated that he had supplied Spurgeon with information but that he never expected him to use it to bring charges against others.[14] In any event, Spurgeon's blanket charges seemed to place many Baptist ministers under suspicion of heresy and questioned the integrity of the Baptist Union itself. Add to this the vitriolic nature of his writings and it is not surprising that Spurgeon received minimal support and widespread criticism.

The Lion Goes out Like a Lamb: The Development and Decline of the Controversy

The extensive opposition he encountered no doubt influenced Spurgeon to intensify the conflict by becoming even more trenchant in his articles. He declared that Baptist churches were even worse than he thought. He contended that many ministers had departed the faith and were thieves who hated watch dogs and loved darkness. Even so, he rejoiced that a few men had not "bowed the knee to Baal."[15] Spurgeon repeatedly asserted that he had incontrovertible evidence to support his claims and that no one could or had sought to disprove him. To his critics in the Baptist Union who asked him to name specific individuals who embraced the new theology instead of making general accusations, Spurgeon responded that he did not want to introduce personalities

---

[11] Ibid.

[12] Charles Haddon Spurgeon, "A Fragment upon the Down-Grade Controversy," *The Sword and the Trowel* 23/11 (November 1887), in H. Leon McBeth, *Sourcebook for Baptist Heritage*, 200–202.

[13] McBeth, *Baptist Heritage*, 304.

[14] Lewis Drummond, *Spurgeon: Prince of Preachers* (Grand Rapids: Kregel, 1992) 671, 697.

[15] Charles Haddon Spurgeon, "Our Reply to Sundry Critics and Enquirers," *The Sword and the Trowel* 23/9 (September 1887), http://www.spurgeon.org/s_and_t/dg-04.htm (accessed 25 May 2006).

into the debate.[16] He also believed that since the union had no doctrinal statement that served as a prerequisite for membership, it had no power to discipline specific individuals.[17] Further, Spurgeon may have feared legal action if he named specific persons.[18]

Although he refused to cite specific individuals, many ministers in the Baptist Union knew that Spurgeon strongly objected to the views of Nottingham pastor Samuel Cox who in 1877 penned *Salvator Mundi*, in which he indicated his unwavering support for the universalist view of salvation. Cox wrote that the primary purpose of his book was to draw extensively from the New Testament to convince those who had a faint belief in the "larger hope" to embrace it completely and fearlessly.[19] Since Spurgeon could not tolerate working in the same denomination with individuals who held such beliefs, he proposed that the Baptist Union adopt a conservative confession of faith and utilize it as an instrument of doctrinal accountability. According to Spurgeon's plan, a clear doctrinal statement could provide the Baptist Union with grounds to discipline pastors such as Cox who held unconventional beliefs. "How can we unite except upon some great common truths?" he asked.[20]

That the union ultimately refused to declare its faith in the form of a creed seems incomprehensible to McBeth given the English Baptists' penchant for confessions.[21] Yet, leaders in the union were convinced that Spurgeon sought conformity to his brand of orthodoxy that they deemed too narrow. Even though Spurgeon did not desire to impose upon the union every article in his own personal creed with its emphasis on the doctrines of grace, it is unlikely that the union could have produced a statement of faith pleasing to Spurgeon. For example, Spurgeon held to the verbal plenary theory of inspiration as the only way of understanding biblical inspiration. He insisted that either

---

[16] Charles Haddon Spurgeon, "The Case Proved," *The Sword and the Trowel* 23/10 (October 1887), http://www.spurgeon.org/s_and_t/dg05.htm (accessed 25 May 2006).

[17] Charles Haddon Spurgeon, *C. H. Spurgeon's Autobiography* (Nashville: Publishing House of M.E. Church South, [1900?]) 263.

[18] McBeth, *The Baptist Heritage*, 304.

[19] Samuel Cox, *Salvator Mundi: Or, Is Christ the Savior of All Men?* (London: Henry S. King Company, 1877) in H. Leon McBeth, *A Sourcebook for Baptist Heritage* (Nashville: Broadman Press, 1990) 194–97.

[20] Charles Haddon Spurgeon, "The Baptist Union Censure," *The Sword and the Trowel* (February 1888), in H. Leon McBeth, *Sourcebook for Baptist Heritage*, 202–203.

[21] McBeth, *The Baptist Heritage*, 305.

everything in scripture is inspired, or none of it is inspired.[22] John Clifford, esteemed pastor of the Westbourne Park Baptist Church in London for fifty-seven years (1858–1915) who in 1888 became the president of the Baptist Union and served as the first president of the Baptist World Alliance, rejected this view as the *sina qua non* of inspirational theory. Clifford, who held a high view of scripture, recognized both divine and human elements at work in its writing. He believed that inerrancy did not safeguard the faith but actually undermined it because it failed to stand up under careful scrutiny.[23]

In the end the Union decided not to swim in creedal waters and rejected Spurgeon's agenda. Spurgeon responded quickly and announced in fall 1887, "We retire at once and distinctly from the Baptist Union."[24] He then published articles bemoaning the fact that the union had no disciplinary power because of its functional rather than doctrinal basis. Spurgeon saw no reason why "every form of belief and misbelief" should not be found among union churches as long as they acknowledged baptism by immersion.[25] He could not in good conscience fellowship with "enemies of the cross of Christ."[26] To do so was tantamount to committing treason against the Lord Jesus. Spurgeon could not subordinate the truth for the sake of denominational unity.

Early on Spurgeon had begun to question whether faithful and true Baptists should fraternize with fellow Baptists who had departed from the truth. Rather than forming a new denomination, he suggested the formation of an informal alliance of true evangelicals no matter the denomination.[27] He spent the remainder of his life seeking likeminded individuals with whom to fellowship and being frequently disappointed in this endeavor.[28] Nevertheless,

---

[22] Charles Haddon Spurgeon, *The Greatest Fight in the World* (London: Passmore and Alabaster, 1896) 27, 33.

[23] John Clifford, *The Inspiration and Authority of the Bible*, 3rd ed. (London: James Clark & Co., 1899) 59–78.

[24] Charles Haddon Spurgeon, "The Baptist Union Censure," in McBeth, *A Sourcebook for Baptist Heritage*, 202–203.

[25] Charles Haddon Spurgeon, "A Fragment upon the Down-Grade Controversy," in McBeth, *Sourcebook for Baptist Heritage*, 200–202.

[26] Ibid.

[27] Ibid.

[28] Patricia Stallings Kruppa, *Charles Haddon Spurgeon: A Preacher's Progress* (New York: Garland Publishing, Inc., 1982) 445–51. Kruppa notes that Spurgeon had great difficulty forming alliances with other high profile conservatives because he frequently criticized them.

his desire to create a transdenominational conservative coalition foreshadowed many such fellowships that emerged during the twentieth century.

Given Spurgeon's status, it is surprising that few others followed him out of the union. Even his brother, James, an associate pastor at Metropolitan Tabernacle, remained in the union.[29] In fact, Spurgeon did not publicly urge conservative churches to withdraw from the union either, although he trumpeted his own fearless stand for the truth, likely influencing a few churches to depart.[30] Most conservatives likely stayed in the union because, unlike Spurgeon, they ministered in small churches and could not survive on their own. Further, Samuel Booth, secretary of the union, sought to mollify conservatives by urging it to respond publicly to the controversy.

In January 1888 a delegation of union leaders, which included Samuel Booth and John Clifford, met with Spurgeon at the Metropolitan Tabernacle to persuade Spurgeon to rejoin. Before the meeting, Spurgeon wrote to his wife, "If it means they will surrender it is well, but if it is meant to fix on me the odium of being implacable, it is another matter."[31] Spurgeon would not rejoin the union unless it adopted a clearly evangelical doctrinal statement.[32] Spurgeon and the delegation could not reach a compromise. Days later the delegation presented a report of the meeting to the Council of the Baptist Union who voted overwhelmingly to accept Spurgeon's resignation. The council also passed what Spurgeon referred to as a censure against him. The council stated that Spurgeon had made serious charges publicly and generally that reflected negatively upon the entire body and exposed to suspicion "brethren who love the truth as dearly as he does."[33] They added that since he refused to name specific individuals and provide supporting evidence for his charges, such charges "ought not to have been made."[34] The censure wounded Spurgeon deeply. He replied that he had only desired the union to be formed on the basis

---

[29] W. Y. Fullerton, *Charles H. Spurgeon: London's Most Popular Preacher* (Chicago: Moody Press, 1966) 256.
[30] Charles Haddon Spurgeon, "The Baptist Union Censure," in McBeth, *A Sourcebook for Baptist Heritage*, 202–203.
[31] Spurgeon, *C. H. Spurgeon's Autobiography*, 4, 257.
[32] Ibid., 263.
[33] "Brief Notes," *The Baptist Magazine* 30 (February 1888) 85.
[34] Ibid.

of scripture. He found the objection to a creed "a very pleasant way of concealing objection to discipline, and a desire for latitudinarianism."[35]

On 21 February 1888, the Council of the Baptist Union met and adopted a declaration of evangelical principles commonly held by Baptists. The preamble, however, denied that the declaration held any power to control an individual or enforce legislation. Primarily because of the language of the preamble, Spurgeon refused to accept the declaration as a substitute for a creed.[36]

Another public response to the controversy came with John Clifford's presidential address to the union in April 1888. Clifford, a recognized "soul-winner" and champion of religious liberty and social justice, stood as a giant among English Baptists, although he is not as well-known today as Spurgeon. Clifford's powerful and scholarly address may have prevented a major split in the Baptist Union. Clifford's address surveyed the first forty years of Christianity in order to reveal its real substance and to offer a view on how best to defend the primitive faith. First, he observed that the first Christians did not have perfect agreement as to its "whole contents."[37] He went on to express his rejection of the view that the Baptist Union had abandoned the gospel of the first forty years of Christianity.[38] The way to take care of and defend the faith is to love as Christ loved. Clifford declared, "Better lose all than lose love. He wins who keeps that supreme. He loses who says one bitter word, writes one selfish line, or moves one inch out of the love of God and his brother.... We hurt the faith more by hardness and self-will and unbrotherly behavior than by confused opinions or false definitions."[39] Clifford recognized the presence of "progressive theologies" among Baptists but insisted that "retrogressive" ones abounded as well. He appealed to ministers to study the Bible utilizing the tools of modern biblical criticism and to consider all modern research without simply repudiating what they had not studied. To ban thinking and denounce inquiry would make Christianity irrelevant except for the "aged and apathetic."[40] Clifford doubted that thoughtful persons could be saved by the "clashing of our

---

[35] Charles Haddon Spurgeon, "The Baptist Union Censure," in McBeth, *A Sourcebook for Baptist Heritage*, 202–203.

[36] Payne, *Baptist Union*, 137–38.

[37] John Clifford, "The Great Forty Years; or, the Primitive Christian Faith: its Real Substance and Best Defence," in *A Baptist Treasury*, by Sydnor L. Stealey (New York: Thomas Y. Crowell Company, 1958) 100.

[38] Ibid., 125.

[39] Ibid., 127.

[40] Ibid., 129–31.

creeds" that only produced bewildering noise.[41] In fact, Clifford denied that creeds could produce the type of Christian who would become a personal and social force in society. He proclaimed that if a creed were the best way to defend the Christian faith, then "we could get patent machines by the score" to produce them.[42]

After the censure and Clifford's sermon, Spurgeon no longer considered Clifford a warm, personal friend. Instead, he openly criticized him believing that, with Clifford at the helm, the Baptist Union it would be severely damaged. When Clifford addressed a meeting at a Unitarian chapel in 1889, Spurgeon chided him in print for presenting an address in a room with plaques bearing the words of Voltaire, Jesus, Thomas Paine, and Zoroaster.[43]

By 1888 the Downgrade Controversy had run its course for everyone except Spurgeon and a few of his friends who continued to fan the flames of conflict. Spurgeon became obsessed with the controversy, writing nearly an article a month on downgrade issues until his death in 1892. During his last years Spurgeon suffered terribly from Bright's disease, a terminal illness, that took his life prematurely. According to Spurgeon and his supporters, however, the controversy led to his decline in health.[44] His wife wrote that her husband had died a faithful martyr and witness for Christ.[45] On the other hand, his opponents did not view him as a martyr and some believed his worsening condition accounted for his volatile conduct during the controversy. Spurgeon consistently rejected this assertion believing it to be a red herring.

Interpretations of the Controversy

As McBeth observes, presenting a summary of the controversy is much easier than interpreting it. Although the controversy swirled around Spurgeon and Clifford, it was more than simply a conflict between two influential men. Until the censure, Spurgeon admitted that he differed with Clifford's Arminian views but recognized that the two held essential evangelical truths in common. Only after the censure did Spurgeon's bitterness toward Clifford surface.[46] Only

---

[41] Ibid., 131.
[42] Ibid., 128.
[43] Charles Haddon Spurgeon, "Notes," *The Sword and the Trowel* 25/5 (May 1889), http://www.spurgeon.org/s_and_t/0589nts.htm (accessed 25 May 2006).
[44] Kruppa, 458, 461.
[45] Spurgeon, *C. H. Spurgeon's Autobiography*, 2, 259.
[46] Kruppa, *Charles Haddon Spurgeon*, 452–53.

after the censure did Clifford make a public statement against Spurgeon. In February 1888 Clifford, writing in *The Freeman*, an evangelical paper, referred to Spurgeon's downgrade articles specifically. Clifford proclaimed that he would rather spend a year in jail than present terrible accusations without citing names or evidence.[47]

Neither can the controversy be adequately understood as a renewal of tensions between Particular and General Baptists. Although Spurgeon stood in the Particular tradition and Clifford in the General camp, the primary issues that arose during the Downgrade Controversy transcended the emphases of both groups.[48] Certainly, some Particular Baptists touted their position on divine sovereignty as more biblical than the Arminian stance, but the issues that arose during the Downgrade Controversy were of concern to both Particular and General Baptists, who officially merged in 1891 a year before Spurgeon's death.

The most popular understanding of the controversy comes from modern conservatives who have viewed the conflict as the first major battle in a series of wars between Baptist conservatives and liberals. Some conservatives contend something along the following lines: Conservatives in the Downgrade Controversy represented the true faith and crafty liberals introduced a counterfeit Christianity. Spurgeon stood alone as Christ's true witness against many ministers in the denomination who had abandoned the faith and embraced unorthodox doctrines. The Baptist Union refused to adopt a creed in order to discipline those in error. As a result, the union turned in the wrong direction during the Downgrade Controversy and embraced liberalism. Over the years the Baptist denomination in England has declined significantly. By rejecting Spurgeon's agenda, the union embraced an unacceptable program of doctrinal ambiguity that has led to the decline of Baptist life in England. These conservatives today argue that we face the same struggle in our denomination today. History can repeat itself if we do not stem the tide of liberalism in the denomination by forcing conformity to our creed. The main lesson to be

---

[47] Bill Leonard, *Baptist Ways* (Valley Forge: Judson Press, 2003) 154, citing Nicholas D. Stepp, "The Downgrade Controversy: Following Jesus and Frequenting Theatres" (unpublished paper, Regent's Park College, Oxford, 2000) 20–21, citing John Clifford "Spurgeon's Appeal," *The Freeman* (8 February 1888): 11.

[48] Charles Haddon Spurgeon, "Notes," *The Sword and the Trowel* 23/4 (April 1887), http://www.spurgeon.org/s_and_t/0487nts.htm (accessed 24 September 2002). Spurgeon denied that the issues of the debate concerned Arminianism and Calvinism and viewed the struggle as the truth of God versus the inventions of men.

learned from the Downgrade Controversy is to fight ardently against liberalism or our denomination will decline and perhaps disappear.[49]

Less conservative persons tend to say that there was more complexity in the controversy and argue along the following lines: Several world views competed for ascendancy in the Baptist denomination. Spurgeon represented the conservative position and Clifford the less conservative position. Many Baptists either stood theologically with Spurgeon or Clifford or somewhere in between. A few stood to the left of Clifford. When the disparate voices arose during the Downgrade Controversy, the Baptist Union, still in its adolescence, sought to find an identity but struggled in the process and never really found its way as it aged because conservatives and progressives never learned how to cooperate effectively together.

Liberal ministers certainly existed in the union, but Spurgeon exaggerated their number, casting aspersions upon many ministers in the denomination who were not liberal but less conservative than he. "Spurgeon's Solution" or creedalism must be rejected as the primary method of dealing with doctrinal diversity in a denomination. While this approach might bring a doctrinal uniformity that exists on the surface, the creed ultimately becomes a weapon that destroys Christian fellowship and invites suspicion. If creedalism is the best way to defend a Christian denomination, then that denomination is in trouble.

Spurgeon deserves admiration for many reasons but not for his unwillingness to wrestle with higher criticism and other modern ideas. He dumped all modern thought into one category and labeled it a "deadly cobra."[50] He did not appeal to the educated and informed but to the unsophisticated person. Clifford, on the other hand, sought to utilize historical-critical methodology and engage modern thought in general even if he ran the risk of arriving at untenable conclusions. Spurgeon believed he already had the corner on truth. The decline of the Baptist Union over the years can be explained by a number of factors including secularization and incessant, unproductive debates between conservatives and liberals concerning the authority of scripture and other doctrinal issues.

It is important to note that the questions that arose during the Downgrade Controversy did not disappear from Baptist life. Baptists in America also

---

[49] For an example of this position see John F. MacArthur Jr. *Ashamed of the Gospel: When the Church Becomes Like the World* (Wheaton: Crossway, 1993).

[50] Charles Haddon Spurgeon, "The Case Proved," *The Sword and the Trowel* 23/10 (October 1887), http://www.spurgeon.org/s_and_t/dg05.htm.

struggled with theological issues in the 1920s, and both Northern Baptists and Southern Baptists responded in different fashion.[51]

In the final analysis, the Downgrade Controversy should raise some sobering questions for Baptists today. What are the grounds for Baptist cooperation? Can conservatives and progressives peacefully coexist in a denomination over the long haul? Is the essence of the Christian faith primarily about orthodoxy or orthopraxy, or both?

Suggested Reading

Clifford John. "The Great Forty Years; or, the Primitive Christian Faith: Its Real Substance and Best Defence." In *A Baptist Treasury.* Edited by Sydnor L. Stealey. New York: Thomas Y. Crowell Company, 1958.

Johnson, Philip R. Documents from the Downgrade Controversy. The Spurgeon Archive. http://www.spurgeon.org.

Kruppa, Patricia Stallings. *Charles Haddon Spurgeon: A Preacher's Progress.* New York: Garland Publishing, Inc., 1982.

MacArthur, John F. Jr. *Ashamed of the Gospel: When the Church Becomes Like the World.* Wheaton: Crossway, 1993.

McBeth, H. Leon. *The Baptist Heritage: Four Centuries of Baptist Witness.* Nashville: Broadman Press, 1987.

---

[51] McBeth, *The Baptist Heritage,* 568–78, 679–80.

CHAPTER 21

Baptists and the Turn toward Racial Inclusion: 1955

William M. Tillman Jr.

Baptists arose among western Europeans with theological differences but not with ethnic-racial differences. As Baptists engaged in the missionary movement and blacks came into the Baptist fold, however, race became a huge issue for Baptists. English Baptists of the early nineteenth century vigorously entered the debate regarding abolition of slavery in the English colonies. They energetically supported the need for breaking up the slavery system on which the British Empire had built itself.

In America a long pattern of slavery received strong Baptist encouragement with the formation of the Southern Baptist Convention in 1845. Even with the Emancipation Proclamation, white Baptist churches in the South paternalistically held black members to secondary positions and relationships in most of their settings.[1]

Although white Baptists made positive and overt statements about ministry and mission with Blacks, they still maintained an essentially segregated society as the norm. This segregation was perpetuated as the tacit and legal framework of the United States until the Supreme Court issued its historic decision in 1954 of *Brown v. Board of Education*.

Brown v. Board of Education

This 1954 Supreme Court decision abolished the legal barriers supporting segregation in public schools and public places. The 1896 *Plessy v. Ferguson* Supreme Court decision previously had established separate but equal facilities for black citizens. However, after hearing cases from Kansas, South Carolina,

---

[1] Rufus Spain, *At Ease In Zion: A Social History of Southern Baptists, 1865–1900* (Nashville TN: Vanderbilt University Press, 1961) 44–126.

Virginia, and Delaware, the Supreme Court asserted in *Brown v. Board of Education* that separate facilities were inherently unequal. The circumstances and contexts differed in each state, but a common legal question concerning segregation dominated these various cases.[2] Deeper ramifications of the decision moved the desegregation dynamic throughout American society, challenging deep-seated prejudices, discrimination, and stereotyping.

The Supreme Court of the United States issued *Brown* in May, 1954, and the Christian Life Commission (CLC) of the Southern Baptist Convention (SBC) responded quickly and positively to both the decision and the turmoil that the decision created across the country. The CLC strongly supported *Brown* with a resolution at the June 1954 convention meeting in St. Louis.[3]

Significantly, the SBC executives of both the Foreign and Home Mission Boards supported the resolution. Active SBC missionaries also supported it. They had, through their work beyond the United States, implemented the call of the gospel for racial equality.[4] Though the SBC constituency would largely resist the desegregation decision, the resolution passed overwhelmingly at the 1954 SBC meeting. However, leading pastors such as W. A. Criswell, pastor of First Baptist Church in Dallas, Texas, criticized the SBC action. Some Southern Baptists even issued calls for abolishing the Christian Life Commission of the SBC. SBC executives, however, supported both the court decision and the 1954 SBC resolution, and they published a statement calling for Southern Baptists to obey the federal decision.[5] Those mixed dynamics within the SBC of both resisting and affirming desegregation reflected the outlook of the SBC for another two decades or more. John Lee Eighmy noted the timidity and tardiness of the SBC in supporting desegregation when he said,

---

[2] *Brown v. Board of Education* , 327 US 483 (1954), National Center for Public Policy Research, http://www.nationalcenter.org/brown.html (accessed 30 September 2006).

[3] A. C. Miller was the director of the CLC by this point. He had been a pastor in Texas, director of the BGCT Department of Interracial Cooperation, had been a major part of the formation of the Christian Life Commission for the BGCT, and served as its first director. Substantial academic and vocational preparation coupled with his pastoral style marked by courage lay as background for Miller's entrees to bring Southern Baptists to an understanding and actions toward race relations more reflective of the Gospel. See Robert Parham, "A. C. Miller: The Bible Speaks on Race," *Baptist History and Heritage* 27/1 (27 January 1992): 32–43.

[4] See Alan Scott Willis, *All According to God's Plan: Southern Baptist Missions and Race, 1945–1970* (Lexington: The University Press of Kentucky, 2005).

[5] John Lee Eighmy, *Churches in Cultural Captivity: A History of the Social Attitudes of Southern Baptists* (Knoxville: The University of Tennessee Press, 1987) 190–91.

"It must be admitted, of course, that the largest religious body in the South could claim no credit for initiating or even offering much direct assistance to the Negro revolt. No convention executive publicly associated himself with the movement, and the desegregation of the denomination's schools was most notable in that in nearly every instance it was delayed until after the integration of secular institutions."[6] In short, though certain segments of the SBC leadership made plain their desegregation sympathies, the SBC continued, for the most part, to work within a de facto segregated society, even working against any processes promoting desegregation.

Montgomery Bus Boycott

The real shift in race relations and expressions for clearer civil rights for all Americans came from African Americans, and black Baptists played a big part in this effort. Blacks tested the substance of *Brown* by challenging segregation in an arena that few expected.

Of course, the story of Rosa Parks refusing on 1 December 1955 to sit in the back of a public bus in Montgomery, Alabama, has become legendary as the beginning of the civil rights movement. However, previous experiences doubtless led to her decision. As far back as 1943, a bus driver left her standing outside as she tried to enter the back door of the bus after paying at the front. As well, Jo Anne Robinson, a black professor, was forced to leave the bus as she absentmindedly sat in the front on a day in 1949. These events, and other accounts like them, fueled the intent of the National Association for the Advancement of Colored People (NAACP) to test the practice of bus segregation in Montgomery.

Even though Parks worked as a seamstress, the only job she could find, she was an educated woman. She also had undergone training with the NAACP toward improving civil rights. While her refusal to sit in the back of the bus was a relatively simple act of resistance, it caused her to be arrested by the Montgomery police.

The segregation laws stipulated that blacks could sit no closer than the fifth row of seats on a public bus. As the bus covered its route that day, the situation developed that the first four rows were full with white riders. A white man was left standing. The bus driver asked the blacks sitting on the fifth row to move, for blacks and whites could not sit together. Parks refused to move.

---

[6] Ibid., 194–95.

Her arrest gave impetus to the boycotting of the buses by blacks in Montgomery.

Though other bus boycotts had been tried in Baton Rouge and other Southern cities, they usually did not last more than a day. Parks's actions led to a boycott that was implemented in stages and lasted for more than a year. Responses from the white community typified responses across the Southern United States. Opponents of the boycott used intimidation, threats, and even bombs. As the black community established a transportation system to get people to their workplaces, liability insurance was cancelled on their cars. Trumped charges led to the arrests of blacks. Since blacks did not shop downtown without bus transportation, downtown Montgomery businesses felt the boycott in their pocketbooks. The trauma lasted for a year. A case was presented before the US District Court in Alabama that declared the bus laws in Montgomery to be unconstitutional, based on the rationale in *Brown v. Board of Education*. The district court declared the Montgomery bus laws illegal, and the US Supreme Court supported the opinion as well.[7]

The newly called pastor to Dexter Avenue Baptist Church in Birmingham, Alabama, Martin Luther King Jr., had been involved in planning the bus boycott. As the boycott continued he was elected president of the Montgomery Improvement Association. His leadership in the Montgomery boycott catapulted him in the leadership position of the burgeoning civil rights movement.[8]

Through his wide travel, fundraising, writing, and encouragement, King, a Baptist preacher, influenced the civil rights movement, and one of the most important American movements in the last half of the twentieth century found its leader. King's unusual combination of intellect, articulation, and courage marked him as a person born for the time.[9]

---

[7] See Martin Luther King, Jr., *Stride toward Freedom: The Montgomery Story* (New York: Harper & Row, 1958) for a personal documentary regarding the Montgomery bus boycott.

[8] Cozzens, Lisa. "The Civil Rights Movement 1955–1965." African American History, http://fledge.watson.org/~lisa/ blackhistory/civilrights–55–65 (accessed 6 October 2006).

[9] King left the legacy of five books: *Stride toward Freedom* (New York: Harper & Row, 1958); *The Measure of a Man* (1959; repr., Minneapolis: Fortress Press, 1988); *Strength to Love* (New York: Harper & Row, 1963); *Why We Can't Wait* (New York: Harper & Row, 1963); *Where Do We Go From Here: Chaos or Community?* (New York: Harper & Row, 1967). He was *Time* magazine's man of the year in 1963 and received the

As the dynamism of the civil rights movement's energies spread beyond Montgomery, it claimed more and more of King's time and energy. Soon he was propelled to the leadership of the Southern Christian Leadership Conference that formed a platform for his national, even international, prominence regarding race relations.[10]

One particular event in Birmingham, Alabama, added momentum to the civil rights movement. King had participated in a public, non-violent demonstration against segregation and the police arrested him in Birmingham. Officials placed him in isolation with the hope that his sequestering would put a damper on the demonstrations.

While in jail, King responded to a letter he had received earlier from eight white clergyman calling on him to allow the courts to settle the integration issue and for King to desist from his non-violent demonstrations. The white clergy believed that the demonstrations only incited more problems. King's lengthy and historic response to the white clergy became known as "The Letter from Birmingham City Jail." A black Baptist clergyman was responding white clergy, some of whom were also Baptists. King described his presence in Birmingham and his participation in the demonstrations as rooted in his call for justice:

> Just as the eighth century prophets left their little villages and carried their 'thus said the Lord' far beyond the boundaries of their hometowns; and just as the Apostle Paul left his little village of Tarsus and carried the gospel of Jesus Christ to practically every hamlet and city of the Graeco-Roman world, I too am compelled to carry the gospel of freedom beyond my particular hometown. Like Paul, I must constantly respond to the Macedonian call for aid.[11]

Martin Luther King Jr. understood his ministry in civil rights as tantamount to the proclamation of the gospel. Believing the gospel to be

---

Nobel Peace Prize in 1964. He presented moral leadership which would have marked several lives in that he lived to be only thirty-nine.

[10] See Adam Fairclough, *To Redeem the Soul of America: The Southern Christian Leadership Conference and Martin Luther King, Jr.* (Athens: University of Georgia Press, 1987).

[11] Martin Luther King Jr., "Letter from Birmingham City Jail," in *A Testament of Hope: The Essential Writings of Martin Luther King, Jr.*, ed. James M. Washington (San Francisco: Harper & Row, 1986) 289–302.

inclusive of all people, he saw his efforts as calls to true Christian discipleship.[12] He passionately worked against the long-held oral tradition of biblical interpretation that subordinated blacks and other minorities in American society. King believed that much of the resistance to his efforts stemmed from white Southerners who failed to realize that they were actually practicing a distorted Christianity. George Kelsey identified this distortion in the following words: "Racism is a faith. It is a form of idolatry. It is an abortive search for meaning.... By and large Christians have failed to recognize racism as an idolatrous faith, even though it poses the problem of idolatry among Christians in a way that no other tendency does."[13]

A strange irony appeared in King's confrontation with many of the white Baptists of the South. While he articulated the gospel in extraordinarily powerful ways, King encountered white Baptists in the South who believed that they too possessed a serious commitment to the gospel. Whites generally could not find resonance with King's message. Perhaps there was a certain subconscious jealousy at work. King, with his non-violent strategies, drew astoundingly large crowds and committed followers. He undoubtedly spawned envy among professing Christians in the South.

Coming from a black preacher, King's strategies of non-violent demonstrations combined with a prophetic style of preaching were new to white Christians in the South, even though they have to be characterized as a subculture that thrived on conflict. Many whites desired the way of life that had been shattered by the Civil War. Charles Reagan Wilson developed the thesis that whites constantly tried to recoup from the Lost Cause of the South. Wilson described what may be called a Southern civil religion. Not only the political systems but also religious structures had been incorporated into the segregated antebellum worldview. This worldview became a kind of public theology in the South. This commingling of politics and religion formed an extraordinarily powerful base for rejecting King and his movement. Most white Southerners perceived him as a destroyer of their idyllic way of life.[14]

---

[12] Marty Bell, "Fire in My Bones: The Prophetic Preaching of Martin Luther King, Jr," *Baptist History and Heritage* 34/1(Winter 1999): 7–20. See also Richard Deats, *Martin Luther King, Jr.: Spirit-Led Prophet* (New York: New City Press, 2000).

[13] George D. Kelsey, *Racism and the Christian Understanding of Man* (New York: Charles Scribner's Sons, 1965) 9.

[14] Charles Reagan Wilson, *Baptized in Blood: The Religion of the Lost Cause, 1865–1920* (Athens: University of Georgia Press, 1980). See also Andrew M. Manis, *Southern Civil*

The Next Decade and a Half and Beyond

One should not think that all whites or all white Christians of the South resisted King's work. Indeed, some of the white Southern Baptist pastors supported the civil rights movement. Their churches, however, often terminated the white ministers for taking this very unpopular stand for racial integration. Will Campbell related in a microcosmic way the entrenched paradigm in the Deep South among Baptists as he told the story of Mercer University and its early movements toward integration.

In *The Stem of Jesse: The Costs of Community at a 1960s Southern School*, Campbell demonstrated the irony of white Christianity in the South. Sam Oni, an African young man who had been converted to Christianity through the efforts of Southern Baptist missionaries in Africa, came to the United States for higher education. Although Mercer University accepted Oni as a student in 1963, he was barred from attending the Tatnall Square Baptist Church, located on the campus of Mercer University. To compound the tragedy of excluding Oni, the church also terminated three of the ministers on the church staff for promoting integration in the church.[15] That pattern of the termination of white ministers who supported racial equality was not unusual in the South, and it is largely an untold story.

Though few and far between, spokespersons for building healthier relationships among the races found some hearings. Professors of Christian Ethics in Southern Baptist seminaries, and later their students who came into positions of denominational influence, became major voices for racial equality. Ethics professors such as T. B. Maston of Southwestern Baptist Theological Seminary in Fort Worth, Texas, and Henlee Barnette of the Southern Baptist Theological Seminary in Louisville, Kentucky, promoted racial integration.[16]

Religions in Conflict: Civil Rights and the Culture Wars (Macon GA: Mercer University Press, 2002).

[15] See Will D. Campbell, *The Stem of Jesse: The Costs of Community at a 1960s Southern School* (Macon GA: Mercer University Press, 1995).

[16] Maston had been in the racial debate for decades. His coursework at Southwestern Baptist Theological Seminary reflected such. As well, books published before and after the 1954 decision and Montgomery Boycott demonstrated themes of the Gospel that should be employed: *Of One: A Study of Christian Principles and Race Relations* (Atlanta: Home Mission Board of the Southern Baptist Convention, 1946); *The Bible and Race* (Nashville: Broadman Press, 1959); *Segregation and Desegregation* (New York: The Macmillan Company, 1959). Henlee Barnette characteristically addressed the context as was his style by inviting MLK Jr. to participate in ethics classes at Southern Seminary. As

The Christian Life Commission of the SBC also became a constant voice for racial harmony, sponsoring seminars addressing the racial crisis in the United States.

In 1964 and 1965 the national government adopted two major civil rights bills. The white SBC responded with resolutions addressing the need for better race relations. In 1968 the SBC adopted "A Statement concerning the Crisis in Our Nation." This convention action occurred in the aftermath of the assassination of Martin Luther King Jr. in April. King's assassination motivated Victor Glass, the Home Mission Board's secretary of Department of Work with National Baptists to draft what came to be known as the "Crisis Statement." Glass gained the support of SBC and certain state convention officials and the statement was presented to the convention who gathered in Houston, Texas, in June. The intent was that the statement would represent "the concern, confession, commitment, and appeal" of the majority of messengers present. Up to that point in SBC history, this statement represented the apex of SBC action for racial equality.[17]

Emmanuel McCall, the secretary of the Department of Cooperative Ministries with National Baptists at the Home Mission Board, to whom the responsibility for implementation of the statement was given, said, "The 'Statement Concerning the Crisis in our Nation,' passed by the 1968 Southern Baptist Convention, represented a decisive change in attitudes. This statement reflected our involvement in the making of history, our regret for not having always exercised our influences wisely and our commitment to be God's instruments of reconciliation."[18]

---

well, Barnette marched with King addressing housing in Louisville, Kentucky. A detailed description of Barnette with King is in Henlee Barnett, "The Southern Baptist Theological Seminary and the Civil Rights Movement," *Review and Expositor* 90 (Fall 1990): 77–126. Until his retirement from the Nashville Christian Life Commission, A. C. Miller was a consistent spokesman regarding work toward better black-white relations. His successor, Foy Valentine, who had succeeded Miller in the BGCT Christian Life Commission post and also a graduate student of Maston's, made race a prominent speaking point throughout his years at the CLC helm. Positions on race by the CLC contributed, in fact, drew negative responses through the years and were likely the source of much of the ire from fundamentalists as they began changing the SBC agencies. The CLC was one of the first to suffer from the takeover.

[17] *Annual of the Southern Baptist Convention, 1968*, 67.

[18] Emmanuel L. McCall, "Ministering with Black Americans," in *Missions in the Mosaic*, comp. M. Wendell Belew (Atlanta: Home Mission Board of the Southern Baptist Convention, 1974) 36.

After 1968 there were sporadic resolutions decrying racism or making pleas for racial reconciliation. A conflict erupted in 1972 surrounding a decision of the Sunday School Board in Nashville that may demonstrate the momentum apparently caught in 1968.

The controversy centered upon a Bible study quarterly for teenagers. The material explained New Testament values and attitudes regarding racial understanding. It employed those ideas in explaining the appropriate response if blacks applied for church membership in a white congregation. It included a photograph of an African-American male teenager talking with two white teenage girls. The Sunday School Board elected to recall this quarterly material. The board used the rationale that the material might be construed as promotion of integration. It stated that it considered the issue a matter of individual church polity.

The recall action prompted an avalanche of response, perhaps the most ever in the shortest period of time to any Sunday School Board literature. In fact, "Just 28 days after the decision was first made public through a Religious News Service report, more than 20 Baptist groups had passed resolutions concerning the decision, 15 Baptist state paper editors had written editorials or columns about the matter, and about 400 persons had written letters to the Sunday School Board concerning the decision."[19]

When consideration is given to how many names and people one letter might have represented, it appears that Southern Baptists responded in a significant fashion. One might conclude that a majority of Baptists opposed the Sunday School Board's recall. Such opposition at the least demonstrated some change in thinking among Baptists in the South.

In the decades that followed the SBC's programmatic statements and its agencies' efforts gradually reflected a more balanced and wholesome perspective. Home mission efforts steadily became more overt toward other-than-white ethnic groups. In 1995 the Southern Baptist Convention passed a statement intended to be a public apology to blacks regarding the SBC's historic position on slavery. In reality, most of the SBC's numeric growth in the previous decade and in the years immediately following came from additions of African Americans and other ethnic minorities.[20] The resolution should be

---

[19] Jim Newton, "Revision of Becoming Prompts Record Response toward BSSB," *Baptist Press*, 24 November 1971, 1.

[20] "SBC renounces racist past," *Christian Century* 112, no. 21 (5 July 1995): 671–72. Of the 15.6 million members in the SBC, about 500,000 were African-Americans and

viewed as something extraordinarily positive, although most would agree that it was long overdue. Key statements from it outline a genuine sense of apology and repentance:

> Be it RESOLVED, That we, the messengers to the Sesquicentennial meeting of The Southern Baptist Convention, unwaveringly denounce racism, in all its forms, as deplorable sin....
>
> Be it further RESOLVED, That we affirm the Bible's teaching that every human life is sacred, and is of equal and immeasurable worth....
>
> Be it further RESOLVED, That we lament and repudiate historic acts of evil such as slavery from which we continue to reap a bitter harvest....
>
> Be it further RESOLVED, That we apologize to all African-Americans for condoning and/or perpetuating individual and systemic racism in our lifetime....
>
> Be it further RESOLVED, That we hereby commit ourselves to eradicate racism in all its forms from Southern Baptist life and ministry....
>
> Be it further RESOLVED, That we commit ourselves to be doers of the Word (James 1:22) by pursuing racial reconciliation in all our relationships....
>
> Be it finally RESOLVED, That we pledge our commitment to the Great Commission task of making disciples of all people....[21]

Other major Baptist denominational entities reflected a somewhat similar pattern though a degree of differences can be ascertained.

American Baptist Churches, USA

The American Baptist Convention, with churches mostly in the northern United States, came into the *Brown v. Board of Education* and Montgomery

---

300,000 were other ethnic minorities. By 2005, for comparison, the SBC had 3,000 African-American churches among the 16.2 million members of the SBC. See "Black Southern Pastors Move Past Slavery," *Baptists Today*, 19 June 2005, http://www.baptiststoday.org/ (accessed 26 October 2006).

[21] *SBCNet*, http://www.sbc.net/resolutions/amResolution.asp?ID=899 (accessed 13 October 2006).

Boycott era with a more open attitude toward blacks than Baptists in the South. They declared resolutions on race virtually every year from mid-twentieth century onward. The ABC directed an aggressive membership enrollment drive at gathering blacks. This effort resulted in significant growth in membership numbers and black churches. By 1977 American Baptist Churches, USA, recorded more black members than any other predominantly white denomination.[22]

The American Baptists diligently informed their churches about discriminatory practices and commended King for his efforts. In 1969, the ABC elected Thomas Kilgore Jr. pastor of the Second Baptist Church of Los Angeles and an African American, as president.[23]

The Cooperative Baptist Fellowship (CBF)

As the Southern Baptist Convention increasingly excluded moderates from its processes and agencies after 1979, groups of moderate Baptists began meeting in 1986. Recognizing the SBC's resistance to their input in convention's matters, from the beginning this group expressed an intentional theology of inclusion. In 1991 they organized and took the name Cooperative Baptist Fellowship. The following year the fellowship meeting in Birmingham offered what has been called "the Birmingham Confession." The statement essentially expressed an apology for Baptist complicity in the racism of the past and for the failures to speak against the bombing of the Sixteenth Street Baptist Church, Birmingham, in 1963, and committed to "diligent patience, to sustaining the struggle against racism for all the days of our lives."[24]

Despite this resolve the CBF took until 2005 to choose Emmanuel McCall as the moderator-elect and therefore the moderator the following year. The public acclamation of electing an African American to one of the most visible positions associated with the CBF spoke volumes, however.[25] In a tangible way,

---

[22] Leroy Fitts, *A History of Black Baptists* (Nashville: Broadman Press, 1985) 301 ff.

[23] Dana Martin, "The American Baptist Convention and the Civil Rights Movement: Rhetoric and Response," *Baptist History and Heritage* 34/1 (Winter 1999): 21–32.

[24]Andrew M. Manis, "'Dying From the Neck Up': Southern Baptist Resistance to the Civil Rights Movement," *Baptist History and Heritage* 34/1 (Winter 1999): 42.

[25] Carl Wynn, "Texas laywoman to be nominated CBF moderator-elect," Baptist General Convention of Texas, http://www.bgct.org/texasbaptists/Page.aspx?&pid=2895&srcid=734 (accessed 11 January 2008).

the CBF fulfilled the attempt to become not only multicultural but also intercultural in image.[26]

Baptist General Convention of Texas (BGCT)

Not unlike other states that had been part of the old Confederacy, Texas Baptist churches and leaders have reflected racial exclusivism. At least four factors worked toward opposition to racism. The editors of the *Baptist Standard*, especially in the time frame of this study, regularly addressed racism. Pastors across the state addressed the matters of racism and where the application of the gospel should be in its regard. The presence of Southwestern Baptist Theological Seminary, with T. B. Maston leading the Christian ethics department, moved across the state and beyond extending to anyone the essential message of mission and evangelism. The Christian Life Commission of the BGCT focused upon the ills of racism and offered protocols toward better ways of living out one's faith.

A resolution in 1970 stated the essence of a strong message moving across the BGCT as the messengers requested "the appropriate committees to do everything possible to include all groups in Texas Baptist life, including qualified women, blacks, Mexican-Americans, youth, and leadership of less populous churches on Baptist General Convention of Texas boards, commissions, and committees as quickly as possible."[27]

One might have expected Texas Baptists to have moved toward an expression of multiculturalism, even inter-culturalism, sooner. However, not until 2004 did convention messengers elect Albert Reyes, president of the Baptist University of the Americas, a Hispanic school in San Antonio, as the first non-Anglo president of the BGCT. Michael Bell, the pastor of Greater St. Stephen First Baptist Church—an African-American church in Fort Worth, was elected first vice-president. In 2005 the convention elected Bell as the BGCT's first African-American president.[28]

---

[26] Marv Knox, "Groundbreaking CBF Moderator Yee Urges Intercultural Commitment," 24 June 2006, http://www.abpnews.com/1116.article (accessed 6 October 2006).

[27] *Annual of the Baptist General Convention of Texas, 1970*, 23.

[28] Greg Warner, "Texas Baptists OK restructuring, elect first Hispanic president," Associated Baptist Press, November 2004, http://www.abpnews.com/101.article.print (accessed 11 January 2008) and Ken Camp, "Texas Baptist's elections, speakers reflect diversity," Associated Baptist Press, 16 November 2005, http://www.abpnews.com/679.article.print (accessed 16 October 2006). An interesting compare and contrast

Conclusion

Thus, with perhaps their best efforts and intentions at heart and at least getting expressed, none of the predominantly white Baptist denominational traditions truly reflects a paragon of virtue with regard to positive race relations. Even today, few Baptist churches are truly integrated. Though they may have made statements of inclusion of other-than-white members, their lack of aggressive mission effort toward others shows up in the complexions of those sitting in the pews on Sunday mornings.

We must learn from history. The history of racial inclusion demonstrates that any shift or turn had to be the result of a push. One could make the case that we are, at the least, settling into another cultural context of comfort with things as they are.

What is needed for the turn to be a continuing, perennial expression? Perhaps these possibilities are food for thought. Another civil rights movement? The stirring, again, from the black Baptists or other ethnic groups as they apparently are the best able to get the movement of integration into a cultural change? The rising up of Baptist prophetic types who will courageously sound the challenge of the whole gospel to the culture and to the churches? Likely all of these things and more are needed. For, certainly, history demonstrates the possibility of a movement that can gain considerable momentum only to peak and then go into decline. The further tragedy would be that future historians would record that the movement or turn toward racial inclusion disappeared and its mirror opposite began to be expressed again.

Suggested Reading

"Baptists and the Civil Rights Movement." *Baptist History and Heritage* 34/1 (Winter 1999).

Eighmy, John Lee. *Churches in Cultural Captivity: A History of the Social Attitudes of Southern Baptists.* Knoxville: The University of Tennessee Press, 1987.

King Jr., Martin Luther. *Stride toward Freedom: The Montgomery Story.* New York: Harper & Row, 1958.

Manis, Andrew M.. *Southern Civil Religions in Conflict: Civil Rights and the Culture Wars* (Macon GA: Mercer University Press, 2002).

---

consideration to the BGCT comes with Mark Newman, "The Baptist State Convention of South Carolina and Desegregation, 1954–1971," *Baptist History and Heritage* 34/1(Winter 1999): 56–72.

Wilson, Charles Reagan. *Baptized in Blood: The Religion of the Lost Cause, 1865–1920.* (Athens: University of Georgia Press, 1980).

CHAPTER 22

Baptists and the Turn toward Baptist Women in Ministry

Pamela R. Durso

For nearly 400 years, Baptist women have served as ministers. Yet, during much of Baptist history, women generally have not held formal leadership positions in churches, nor have they been given official titles. Until recently Baptist churches rarely ordained women and even more rarely called women as pastors. Baptist seminaries have been slow to embrace women as serious theological students and to train them for ministry. Many Baptist associations and conventions have refused to recognize women as legitimate ministers of the gospel. Yet, despite their lack of formal training and official recognition, women throughout Baptist history have served as church planters, exhorters, preachers, worship leaders, children and youth workers, and spiritual counselors and advisors.

For nearly 370 years following the founding of the first Baptist church in Amsterdam, Holland, in 1608/1609, the work of Baptist women ministers was rarely recorded. Baptist historians did not preserve the stories of women ministers, and few Baptist women wrote about their experiences. In the past thirty years, however, historians and researchers have intentionally sought to uncover and to tell the stories of these women.

The Earliest Baptist Women Ministers

Possibly among the earliest of the Baptist women ministers were Anne Hempstall, Mary Bilbrow, Joane Bauford, Susan May, Elizabeth Bancroft, and Arabella Thomas, who preached throughout England in the 1630s and 1640s.[1]

---

[1] *A Discoverie of Six Women Preachers in Middlesex, Kent, Cambridgeshire and Salisbury* (n.p., 1641). Although the six women are not specifically identified as Baptists, Baptist scholars such as Edward Caryl Starr and William Thomas Whitley included this

A 1641 document noted that these English women apparently took up preaching because "there was a deficiency of good men, wherefore it was but fit that virtuous women should supply their places."[2] Mrs. Attaway, a lace-maker and member of a General Baptist church in London, was another of these early English Baptist woman preachers. In the mid-1640s, Thomas Edwards, a Presbyterian minister and a vehement opponent of Baptists, labeled Mrs. Attaway as the "mistress of all the she-preachers on Coleman Street."[3] This Baptist "she-preacher" at first confined her preaching to female audiences but later opened her meetings to anyone who wanted to come, and apparently many wanted to come. Edwards reported that "there came a world of people, to the number of a thousand."[4]

During the years in which "she-preachers" proclaimed the gospel in England, the Baptist faith began to spread to other areas of the world. In 1639 Roger Williams founded the first Baptist church in America at Providence, Rhode Island. Within fifty years, some Baptist women were busy instigating the formation of Baptist congregations in their communities, and just over one hundred years after the founding of the Providence church, other Baptist women were preaching and serving as exhorters in worship services. Many of these Baptist women preachers belonged to Separate Baptist churches, and the most prominent of these women was Martha Stearns Marshall, who, beginning around 1754, often prayed and preached during worship services. Although her leadership in worship scandalized many Baptists, Martha's husband and pastor, Daniel, considered her preaching to be a perfectly acceptable way for her to

---

document in their bibliographies of Baptist writings, indicating that the women were Baptists. See Edward Caryl Starr, *A Baptist Bibliography: Being a Register of Printed Material By and about Baptists, Including Works Written against the Baptists*, 25 vols. (Philadelphia: Judson Press, 1947–1976), and William Thomas Whitley, *A Baptist Bibliography: Being a Register of the Chief Materials for Baptist History, Whether in Manuscript or in Print, Preserved in England, Wales, and Ireland*, 2 vols. (London: Kingsgate Press, 1916–1922). Carolyn Blevins also believed these women to be Baptist. See Carolyn D. Blevins, *Women's Place in Baptist Life, Baptist History and Heritage* (2003): 26.

[2] *A Discoverie of Six Women Preachers*, 1.

[3] Quoted in Dorothy P. Ludlow, "Shaking Patriarchy's Foundations: Sectarian Women in England, 1641–1700," in *Triumph over Silence: Women in Protestant History*, Contributions to the Study of Religion 15, ed. Richard L. Greaves (Westport: Greenwood Press, 1985) 96.

[4] Thomas Edwards, *Gangraena: Or a Catalogue and Discovery of Many of the Errours, Heresies, Blasphemies, and Pernicious Practices of the Sectaries of This Time*, 2 vols. (London: Printed for Ralph Smith, 1645) 1:86.

exercise her spiritual gifts. The early Virginia Baptist historian Robert Semple claimed that Daniel's successful ministry in Virginia, North Carolina, and Georgia was largely due to Martha's "unwearied, and zealous co-operation." Semple described her as a woman "of good sense, singular piety, and surprising elocution," who on "countless instances melted a whole congregation into tears by her prayers and exhortations!"[5]

Freewill Baptist women also served as preachers and evangelists during the late eighteenth century. In his 1862 *History of the Freewill Baptists*, I. D. Stewart noted that Mary Savage in 1791 became "the first name on the records as a female laborer in the gospel." Savage traveled to New Durham, New Hampshire, that year and spent nearly twelve months in the town "doing what she could. The melting power of her exhortations was often irresistible, and so great was the effect with which she sometimes spoke at the Quarterly or Yearly Meeting, that a note of the fact was entered upon the book of records."[6]

All of the Baptist women named above plus numerous others ministered to congregations. Some provided strong leadership in their churches, others supplied pastoral care for church members, and still others preached publicly. These Baptist women were effective in their ministries and compassionate in their service, yet they served only informally. None held official church positions or titles, and none were ordained. Formal recognition—that is licensing or ordination—was slow in coming, but perhaps it came earlier than most Baptists think.

"First" Baptist Women Licensed to Preach

Freewill Baptists were most likely the first Baptists to formally recognize women ministers. While some Freewill Baptist writings indicate that Mary Savage and other ministering women such as Sally Parson and Clarissa Danforth may have been licensed to preach in the late eighteenth century, no documentation of those licenses has yet been found. What has been discovered, however, is that Freewill Baptists did license a woman to preach in 1846. In June of that year the Freewill Baptist Home Mission Board commissioned Ruby Bixby and sent her and her husband to minister in Iowa. The couple traveled from their home in Vermont to New York, then to Wisconsin, and finally

---

[5] Robert Semple, *History of the Rise and Progress of the Baptists in Virginia* (Richmond: privately printed, 1810) 374.

[6] I. D. Stewart, *The History of the Freewill Baptists for Half a Century*, 2 vols. (Dover: Freewill Baptist Printing Establishment, 1862) 1:191.

arrived in Iowa in June 1847. While in Wisconsin, the Honey Creek Quarterly Meeting of the Freewill Baptists licensed Bixby to preach and that license was renewed later in Iowa. After arriving in Iowa the Bixbys organized a church at Lodomillo in Clayton County, and that church's reports listed Ruby Bixby as its minister from 1849 until her death in 1877. Her obituary noted that she was "an independent, self-reliant preacher. Her discourses were characteristically persuasive, and she was more than ordinarily successful. She preached much with churches as pastor, and much as an evangelist."[7]

"First" Ordinations of Baptist Women in the Nineteenth Century

In 1876, nearly thirty years after Bixby received her license to preach, the earliest documented ordination of a Baptist woman took place. Since 1876, numerous Baptist denominations throughout the world have ordained women to the ministry. Following is a chronological presentation of known ordinations of women by six Baptist denominational bodies in the United States and by Baptist denominations in Australia, Brazil, Cuba, England, Mexico, and the Philippines. The ordinations cited are the earliest documented. Other earlier ordinations may have taken place, and as more research is done in this field, other ordinations surely will be discovered and documented.

The earliest known ordination of a Baptist woman was that of M. A. Brennan, who in 1876 was recognized as a minister by the Bellevernon Freewill Baptist Church, which was part of the Westmoreland Freewill Quarterly Meeting in Pennsylvania. Brennan served in ministry from 1876 to 1885. While specific information about her ordination has not been found, the fact that Brennan was listed on the quarterly meeting's annual ministerial list of newly ordained and recently deceased ministers indicates that she indeed had been ordained. The ordination of a second Freewill Baptist woman, Lura Maines, most likely occurred in 1877, the year two Michigan churches listed her as a minister, although not the pastor, in their annual reports. In 1880 Maines was called as a pastor, and she served two Freewill Baptist churches. The third ordination may have been that of Louisa M. Fenner, who from 1879 to 1909 served as a minister in Freewill Baptist churches in Rhode Island and Connecticut, pastoring at least two churches and serving in at least two others.[8]

---

[7] Quoted in James R. Lynch, "Baptist Women in Ministry Through 1920," *American Baptist Quarterly* 13/4 (December 1994): 311.

[8] Ibid., 307, 309.

The first ordination of a Northern Baptist (the Northern Baptist Convention is now known as the American Baptist Churches, USA, or ABC-USA) woman occurred six years after the first Free Will Baptist ordination. On 9 July 1882 May C. Jones was ordained at a meeting of the Baptist Association of Puget Sound in Washington. Apparently, her ordination caused quite a controversy. Opponents charged that Jones's church, First Baptist Church of Seattle, had not properly presented a request for ordination to the association or scheduled an ordination council. Instead church delegates, while their pastor was in Europe, had proposed to the association meeting on 9 July 1882 that Jones be ordained that very day after the close of the official meeting. Participants at the meeting who were offended by the proposal walked out, leaving only those supporting Jones's ordination to vote on the recommendation. Following her ordination, Jones served briefly as interim pastor of First Baptist Church, Seattle, and beginning in 1883, she pastored six Baptist churches, sometimes serving two or three churches simultaneously.[9]

A second Northern Baptist woman, Frances E. Townsley, was ordained in 1885. In 1875 Townsley had begun preaching in churches throughout New England and holding evangelistic services. A few years later, a church in her hometown of Shelburne Falls, Massachusetts, licensed her to preach. In 1883 she moved to Fairfield, Nebraska, and settled "among a few unchurched Baptists." Together they constructed a building, and although she continued to travel and preach, Townsley soon began serving as the pastor of the Fairfield Baptist Church. In January 1885 the church's deacons, tired of sending for ordained ministers to preside over the Lord's Supper, asked to ordain her. After initially protesting, Townsley relented, and on 2 April 1885, following a three-hour examination of her experience, call to ministry, and doctrinal views, the ordination council voted to ordain her. Following her ordination, Townsley endured much criticism, but she remained faithful to her calling. She pastored in Fairfield, traveled frequently to preach in towns throughout Nebraska, and served as a temperance leader.[10]

The first Seventh Day Baptist woman to be ordained was Experience Fitz Randolph Burdick. Burdick grew up in West Virginia, and even as a child she felt God's call to preach, but not until 1882, when she was thirty-two years old, did she publicly acknowledge her call and begin to preach. Three years later, in

---

[9] Ibid., 309–10.
[10] Frances E. Townsley, *The Self-Told Story of Frances E. Townsley* (Butler: L. H. Higley Publisher, 1908) 276–81.

1885, she was ordained by the Seventh Day Baptist Church in Hornellsville, New York. From 1885 to 1890 she served several churches in New York, and at the time of her death in 1906, she was pastor of a Seventh Day Baptist Church in New Auburn, Wisconsin. Despite the loneliness and isolation she often experienced in ministry, Burdick conducted fifty weddings, ninety funerals, and preached 890 sermons. Since Burdick's ordination in 1885, fourteen other Seventh Day Baptist women have been formally recognized by the denomination as pastors, chaplains, preachers, and evangelists.[11]

"First" Ordinations of Baptist Women in the Twentieth Century

Edith Gates was the first English woman to serve as a Baptist pastor, serving Little Tew and Cleveley Church in Oxfordshire from 1918 to 1950. Gates did not enter ministry through the traditional English Baptist method, which was to graduate from a Baptist college and then be ordained and added to the list of accredited ministers. Instead, Gates qualified for the pastorate by passing the Baptist Union Examination. Most likely she was ordained in 1922, after having already served in ministry for several years.

A second English Baptist woman, Maria Living-Taylor, also served as pastor during the early years of the twentieth century. Living-Taylor trained for the ministry at universities in London and Dijon and co-pastored four Baptist churches with her husband from 1922 to 1937. Violet Hedger also trained for the ministry, studying at Regent's Park College. She was added to the ministerial list in 1924 and pastored four Baptist churches.[12]

For a period of forty years, from early 1920s to the early 1960s, no other "first" ordinations of Baptist women have been discovered and documented. In 1962 and the years that followed, however, numerous "first" ordinations began to occur. Arlene Churn, an African-American Baptist minister, began preaching at the age of five, and in 1962, at the age of eighteen, was ordained by a church affiliated with the National Baptist Convention, USA, possibly making her among the earliest women to have been ordained within that denominational tradition. In a 1999 interview Churn noted that her experience in ministry had not been "as negative as those of women that have entered into it in the past

---

[11] Patricia A. Bancroft, "Chosen by God: Women Pastors on the Frontiers of the Seventh Day Baptist Denomination," *Baptist History and Heritage* 40/3 (Summer/Fall 2005): 21–22, 24–25.

[12] John H. Briggs, "She-Preachers, Widows and Other Women: The Feminine Dimension in Baptist Life Since 1600," *Baptist Quarterly* 31/7 (July 1986): 346–47.

fifteen or twenty years. Because when I entered it, I was not a woman. I was a girl. I believe the novelty of my being a child sort of neutralized the opinion of men about women preachers."[13] The NBCUSA, Inc., with its 7.5 million members, is the largest African-American Baptist denomination in the United States, and in 1999, the denomination had about one hundred women serving as senior pastors in its churches.[14]

Within Southern Baptist circles, the first woman to be ordained was Addie Davis. On 9 August 1964 Watts Street Baptist Church in Durham, North Carolina, ordained Davis. Not finding a Southern Baptist church that would call her as pastor, she contacted the American Baptist Convention and soon was called by the First Baptist Church of Readsboro, Vermont. Davis served that church for eight years until the fall of 1972, when she accepted a call from Second Baptist Church of East Providence, Rhode Island.[15] She returned to her hometown of Covington, Virginia, in 1982 and co-pastored an ecumenical church until her death in 2005.

In 1972 Druecillar Fordham, an ordained American Baptist minister, became the first woman to pastor a Southern Baptist church and also became the first ordained African-American woman to serve among Southern Baptists. In the early 1970s Fordham was pastoring Christ Temple Baptist Church, an American Baptist congregation in New York City. On 5 October 1972 her church was recognized as a full member of the Metro New York Baptist Association, a Southern Baptist affiliated association, thus making Fordham the first woman to pastor a SBC-affiliated church.[16]

In Australia, Marita Munro became the first woman to be ordained by a Baptist church. Munro felt called to ministry while completing a degree at Queensland University and subsequently enrolled in 1975 at Whitley College to study for the ministry. While a student, Munro pastored several churches, and on 1 October 1978 she was ordained by the Collins Street Baptist Church,

---

[13] Waveney Ann Moore and Twila Decker, "Women's Role in Male-Led Church," *St. Petersburg Times*, 9 September 1999, http://www.sptimes.com/News/90999/news_pf/ TampaBay/Women_s_role_in_male_.shtml (accessed 2 July 2006).

[14] See the National Baptist Convention USA, Inc., website, http://www.national-baptist.com/Index.cfm?FuseAction=Page&PageID=1000014 (accessed 22 March 2007).

[15] Pamela R. Durso and Keith E. Durso, *Courage and Hope: The Stories of Ten Baptist Women Ministers* (Macon GA: Mercer University Press, 2005; Brentwood: Baptist History and Heritage Society, 2005) 18–30.

[16] DeLane M. Ryals, "Southern Baptist Women Ministering in Metro New York, 1970–1995," *Baptist History and Heritage* 39/2 (Spring 2004): 94.

which was affiliated with the Baptist Union of Victoria. From 1979 to 1981 she studied for her master's degree at the Baptist seminary in Ruschlikon, Switzerland, and from 1981 to 1985 she again served as a pastor in Melbourne, Australia. Munro returned to school in 1986 to pursue a degree in education, and for five years after completing that degree she taught school. In the 1990s she served as interim pastor in several churches and taught church history and New Testament Greek courses at Whitley College. A second Australian Baptist woman, Marian Welford, was ordained in 1979, after having pastored for six years in Newmarket. In the 1980s only one Australian Baptist woman was ordained, but seven more women were ordained between 1991 and 1997 by churches affiliating with the Baptist Union of Victoria.[17]

The Convention of Philippine Baptist Churches ordained Angelina Belluga Buensuceso in 1980, making her first ordained Filipino Baptist woman. From 1938 to 1965 Buensuceso had served five Baptist churches, holding the positions of associate pastor, choir director, and pastor. She then began a teaching ministry, serving on the faculty of Central Philippine University from 1967 to 1974. From 1974 until her retirement in 1983 Buensuceso was the director of the Convention Baptist Bible College. Following forty-two years of ministry, Buensuceso, at the age of sixty-three, was ordained on 22 March 1980, at the Rosario Remitio Memorial Hall in Bakyas, Bacolod City, with Filipino pastors and church leaders, American missionaries, and her children participating in the historic event.[18]

In 1992 three Baptist women in Cuba, Ena González Garcia, Clara Rodés, and Xiomara Gutiérrez Diaz, were ordained by the Fraternidad de Iglesias Bautistas (Fraternity of Baptist Churches).[19] Organized in 1989, the fraternity is the newest Baptist body in Cuba. In its brief history this body has "helped ordain or recognized the previous ordinations" of at least sixteen women, and in the early years of the twenty-first century the fraternity had twenty ordained male pastors and thirteen ordained female pastors. Perhaps no other Baptist

---

[17] Darren Cronshaw, "A History of Women's Ordination in the Baptist Union of Victoria," *John Mark Ministries*, http://jmm.aaa.net.au/articles/9020.htm (accessed 14 June 2006).

[18]Carla Gay A. Romarate-Knipel, "Angelina B. Buensuceso: Harbinger of Baptist Ordination of Women in the Philippines," *Baptist History and Heritage*, 41/1 (Winter 2006): 8–15.

[19] "Recent Events Signal New Hope for Women in Ministry in Cuba," *Worldwide Faith News Archive*, 25 February 1998, http://www.wfn.org/1998/02/msg00131.html (accessed 24 June 2006).

body "anywhere in the world can approach this proportion of ordained women."[20]

Sílvia da Silva Nogueira, on 10 July 1999, became the first Baptist woman to be ordained in Brazil. Prior to her ordination service at Primeira Igreja Batista (First Baptist Church) in Campo Limpo, São Paulo, an examining council composed of twenty-seven pastors questioned Nogueira. The church was later "put out of the state convention."[21]

On 25 March 2000 Rebeca Montemayor López became the first woman to be ordained to the ministry by a Baptist church in Mexico. The ordination council and service were held at Shalom Baptist Church in Mexico City, with a six-member delegation of Baptist women from the United States in attendance.[22]

Statistics Relating to Baptist Women Serving as Pastors

Estimating the number of Baptist women worldwide who have been ordained or who are currently serving as pastor is a difficult task. Even offering an accurate estimate of the number of Baptist women ordained within the United States is challenging. Yet, some statistics relating to Baptist women pastors are available. In 2005, 403 women were serving as pastors or co-pastors in churches affiliating with the ABC-USA; 102 women served as pastor, co-pastor, or church planter in churches affiliating with the Alliance of Baptists, the Baptist General Association of Virginia (BGAV), the Baptist General Convention of Texas (BGCT), and the Cooperative Baptist Fellowship (CBF); and three women served as Seventh Day Baptist pastors.[23] Thus, at least 508 Baptist women in the United States held pastoral positions in 2005. Given the number of Baptist churches in the nation, however, the number 508 most likely means that less than 5 percent of all Baptist churches in the United States had a woman serving as pastor.

---

[20] Stan Hastey, e-mail to author, 19 June 2006.

[21] Carolyn Goodman Plampin, e-mail to author, 20 June 2006.

[22] "Baptist Briefs," *Baptist Standard*, 17 April 2000, http:www.baptist-standard.com/2000/4_17/pages/brief.html (accessed 14 June 2006).

[23] Eileen Campbell-Reed and Pamela R. Durso, "The State of Women in Baptist Life—2005" (Atlanta: Baptist Women in Ministry, 2006) 3.

The Ordination of "Non-Preaching" Baptist Ministers

While the percentage of Baptist churches that are willing to call a woman as pastor remains low, the ordination of Baptist women has increased dramatically since the early 1960s. By 1997 Sarah Frances Anders, who was then professor of sociology at Louisiana College and the keeper of statistics about Baptist women, had documented 1,225 ordinations of Southern Baptist women.[24] A recent study undertaken by Baptist Women in Ministry (BWIM) revealed that sixty ordinations occurred in 2005 in churches affiliating with the Alliance of Baptists, the BGAV, the BGCT, and CBF.[25] An educated estimate of the total number of women ordained since 1964 in churches affiliated with Baptist bodies located mostly in the South would be upwards of 1,600. Including women ordained by churches affiliating with American Baptists, Free Will Baptists, National Baptists, Progressive National Baptists, and Seventh Day Baptists would most likely double that number.

The great majority of ordained Baptist women, according to the research of Anders and the recent BWIM study, worked as chaplains or served on church staff, working with children or youth or serving as associate pastor. This late-twentieth-century trend of ordaining ministers who serve in positions other than the pastorate reflected a change in the Baptist understanding of ministry.

For most of their history, when Baptists heard the word "minister," they immediately thought of a pastor or preacher. The term minister, however, took on an expanded definition. This beginning of a new understanding of ministry can be traced to the late nineteenth century, when large, urban Baptist churches began hiring associate pastors or other staff members. Some of those churches hired women and assigned them the title "Bible women" or "local missionary." These women visited non-members, reported on the material needs of people, supervised mission Sunday schools, and counseled women.[26] First Baptist Church of Dallas, Texas, for example, had "Bible women" on its church staff from at least 1887 until 1906. While the church paid these women, they were not given the title of minister, nor were they ordained.[27] With few exceptions

---

[24] Sarah Frances Anders, "Historical Record-Keeping Essential for WIM," *Folio: A Newsletter for Baptist Women in Ministry* 15/2 (Fall 1997): 6.

[25] Campbell-Reed and Durso, "The State of Women in Baptist Life—2005," 3.

[26] Leon McBeth, *Women in Baptist Life* (Nashville: Broadman Press, 1979) 103–104.

[27] Leon McBeth, *The First Baptist Church of Dallas: Centennial History, 1868–1968* (Grand Rapids: Zondervan Publishing House, 1968) 66, 131.

Baptist churches continued to use the title minister and to confer ordination solely on male pastors.

Around the middle of the twentieth century, the understanding of the role of church staff members other than the pastor began to be redefined within the larger Christian community and within Baptist congregations as more churches began to hire staff members to lead and plan their music programs; to work with preschoolers, children, teenagers, college students, and senior adults; and to oversee administration, education, and recreational activities. Eventually, some Baptist churches recognized and publicly identified these staff members as ministers. With these new position titles sometimes came ordination. This changing attitude toward ministers and ministry among Baptists resulted in perhaps thousands of women being given the title of minister and led to many of them being ordained. In 1979 the Baptist historian Leon McBeth noted that there had been a "recent proliferation of ordination for the nonpreaching ministry."[28]

Baptist Opposition to the Ordination of Women

In the past thirty years many Baptists denominations in the United States and around the world have begun to recognize women as ministers of the gospel and to ordain them. Yet, many Baptist groups continue to oppose women ministers. The Original Free Will Baptist denomination, which traditionally endorsed women in ministry, began to exclude women from leadership positions in the 1950s. Since then, while the denomination did not take an official position against female pastors and women's ordination, women have rarely been offered leadership opportunities in the churches, nor have they been approved for ordination. According to David Hines, chair of the Religion Department at Mount Olive College, a Free Will Baptist school, only one of this denomination's seven conferences in 2005 had any ordained women serving in its churches.[29]

National Free Will Baptists also have been reluctant to allow women to serve in ordained ministry positions. According to a National Free Will Baptist pastor, J. Matthew Pinson, some associations have ordained women to the gospel ministry, but most associations disagree with this practice.[30] Some

---

[28] McBeth, *Women in Baptist Life*, 164.
[29] David Hines, telephone interview by Pamela R. Durso, 12 January 2005.
[30] J. Matthew Pinson, *A Free Will Baptist Handbook: Heritage, Beliefs, Ministries* (Nashville: Randall House Publications, 1998) 76.

Landmark Baptists have been more adamant in their opposition to female pastor. Wayne Camp asserted: "When it comes to women preachers I think that any church that has women preach in their services are at best irregular and unbiblical. At worst they are plainly heretical. I believe it is even wrong for a woman to say 'Amen' in a public worship service. I am not alone in that position."[31]

In addition to Landmark Baptists, African-American Baptist denominations and the Southern Baptist Convention (SBC) also have traditionally opposed the ordaining of women as pastors. The policy of the National Baptist Convention of America, Inc., the second largest African-American Baptist denomination, in 2006 was to not ordain women as ministers.[32] Southern Baptists in 1984 stated their opposition to the ordination of women in a resolution titled "On Ordination and the Role of Women in Ministry." The resolution stated that, although "women are held in high honor for their unique and significant contribution to the advancement of Christ's kingdom,...because man was first in creation, and woman was first in the Edenic fall,...we encourage the service of women in all aspects of church life and work other than pastor functions and leadership roles entailing ordination."[33] In 2000 the SBC revised its confessional statement of faith, the Baptist Faith and Message, to contain a clear denouncement of women's ordination and service as pastors: "While both men and women are gifted for service in the church, the office of pastor is limited to men as qualified by Scripture."[34]

Conclusion

With so many Baptist groups opposing women ministers and women's ordination, the surprising reality is that in the past thirty years numerous Baptist women have answered God's call to ministry, have sought church ministry positions, and have been ordained. Given the uphill battle Baptist women have faced and continue to face, one wonders why so many of them have remained within the Baptist tradition. In truth, other denominations have

---

[31] Wayne Camp, "The Sandy Creek Baptist Church, Part 1," *The Grace Proclamator and Promulgator*, 1 February 2002, http://www.gpp–5grace.com/graceproclamator/pp0202_complete.htm (accessed 10 January 2005).

[32] Stephen John Thurston, president of the National Baptist Convention of America, telephone interview with author, 29 June 2006.

[33] *Annual*, Southern Baptist Convention, 1984, 65.

[34] *Baptist Faith and Message* (Nashville: LifeWay, 2000) 13.

benefited from the Baptist opposition to women ministers. Scores of Baptist women have fled their childhood denomination and moved into Methodist, Presbyterian, Disciples of Christ, and United Church of Christ circles. Yet, many Baptist women who have been called to and gifted for ministry have remained Baptist, and their steadfastness has brought renewal and change to the churches to which they belong.

Suggested Reading

Blevins, Carolyn D. *Women's Place in Baptist Life*. The Baptist Heritage Library. Brentwood TN: Baptist History and Heritage, 2003.

———. "Diverse Baptist Attitudes toward Women in Ministry." *Baptist History and Heritage* 38/3 (Summer/Fall 2002): 71–76.

Campbell-Reed, Eileen, and Pamela R. Durso. "The State of Women in Baptist Life, 2005." Atlanta GA: Baptist Women in Ministry, 2006. http://www.bwim.info/index.php/html/main/welcome.html

Durso, Pamela R. "American Baptist Polity and the Inclusion/Exclusion of Women, 1630–2004." In *Walking Together: The Struggles of Baptist with Polity in the 21st Century*. Richmond VA: Center for Baptist Heritage & Studies, University of Richmond, 2005.

———. "Baptist Women in America, 1638–1800." In *Distinctively Baptist: Essays on Baptist History: A Festschrift in Honor of Walter B. Shurden*. Edited by Marc A. Jolley with John D. Pierce. Macon GA: Mercer University Press, 2005.

Durso, Pamela R., and Keith E. Durso, editors. *Courage and Hope: The Stories of Ten Baptist Ministers*. Macon GA: Mercer University Press, 2005.

McBeth, Leon. *Women in Baptist Life*. Nashville: Broadman Press, 1979.

CHAPTER 23

Baptists and Denominational Identity and the Turn toward Creedalism: 2000

C. Douglas Weaver

Baptists have confessed their faith throughout their history. Many, though not all, Baptist individuals, local churches, associations, unions, and conventions have developed written confessions of faith. Only in rare occasions was the goal of these confessions creedal: statements of faith that required assent in order to maintain orthodoxy. In his influential survey, *The Baptist Heritage: Four Centuries of Baptist Witness*, H. Leon McBeth described the differences between confessions and creeds.

A confession designates what people *do* believe, a creed what they *must* believe. A confession is *voluntary* and serves to inform, educate, and inspire; a creed is *required* and serves to discipline and exclude. A confession offers *guidelines* under the authority of scripture; a creed tends to become *binding authority*, in subtle ways displacing the Bible.[1]

In 2000 the devolution of confession to creed occurred in the largest body of Baptists in the world: the Southern Baptist Convention. This chapter reveals how most Baptists have thought that creeds violated the supremacy of biblical authority.

Seventeenth-Century English Baptists

Baptist "founders" John Smyth and Thomas Helwys articulated their beliefs in personal confessions of faith. In addition to individual confessions, the earliest English Baptists (both Particular and General Baptists) developed

---

[1] H. Leon McBeth, *The Baptist Heritage: Four Centuries of Baptist Witness* (Nashville: Broadman Press, 1987) 686–87.

interchurch confessions. The first cooperative effort was the statement of seven Particular Baptist churches, the First London Confession of 1644.

English Baptist confessions were rarely creedal, but they served several purposes. For example, the First London Confession was an apology to refute slanderous rumors about Baptists who were dissenters from the official state Church of England. Baptists did not want to be known as Anabaptists who were caricatured as revolutionaries. Another goal of confessions was to present Baptists as an acceptable group within historic Christian (Protestant dissenters) orthodox beliefs. The Second London Confession (1677), for example, revealed much compatibility with the Puritan Westminster Confession. Early Baptist confessions also addressed doctrinal aberrations in Baptist life.[2]

Colonial America

Baptists in Colonial America often made use of confessions of faith to help delineate their identity. As they did in England, confessions provided a basic doctrinal identity that revealed that Baptist dissent was theologically consistent with historic orthodoxy. Churches and individuals utilized confessions. The First Baptist Church of Boston adopted a confession of faith in 1665, making it the first Baptist congregation in the colonies to do so.

As colonial Baptists grew and developed associations, confessions were often a basis for cooperation. Baptists in the influential Philadelphia Baptist Association—the first permanent association in American Baptist life—affirmed the final authority of the Bible in religious matters. Nevertheless, doctrinal agreement was a condition for associational membership. In their struggle to survive, these Baptists desired to define themselves as orthodox as their neighbors. While associational minutes indicate that a confession was "owned" as early as 1724, the association officially waited until 1742 to adopt the Second London Confession of 1689. This confession, produced by the Particular Baptists of England, became known in America as the Philadelphia Confession of Faith. The Philadelphia Baptist tradition opposed associational creedalism. In 1749 Benjamin Griffith penned a tract on behalf of the association that analyzed associational power. He noted that the association should never usurp the authority and independence of the local church.[3]

---

[2] To read these confessions, see William L. Lumpkin, *Baptist Confessions of Faith* (Valley Forge: Judson Press, 1969).

[3] A. D. Gillette, *Minutes of the Philadelphia Association* (Philadelphia: American Baptist Publication Society, 1851) 27, 46, 60–63.

The occasional use of the Philadelphia Confession as a standard of orthodoxy was evident in the case of Elhanan Winchester, who became pastor of First Baptist Church of Philadelphia in 1780. Winchester discarded Calvinism and became a Universalist soon after accepting the Philadelphia pastorate. Controversy erupted. A majority in the church supported the eloquent Winchester, but his opponents appealed to the association. It sided with the opposition party who had affirmed the Philadelphia Confession of Faith and recommended excommunication for the Winchester group.[4]

The Separate Baptist tradition also represented the anti-creedal perspective of colonial Baptists. Separate Baptists, who developed out of the New Light Congregationalists during the First Great Awakening, often felt the wrath of state religion that required approval of preaching licenses and meetinghouses. Separate Baptists claimed to preach based on a divine calling and desired to practice New Testament Christianity. Consequently, they disliked confessions and believed that creedal statements led to formality, spiritual stagnation, and diverted believers from the authority of the scriptures. No colonial Baptist was more anti-creedal than Separate Baptist evangelist John Leland. For Leland, to be Baptist was to have an unfettered conscience before God:

> Confessions of faith often check any further pursuit after truth, confine the mind into a particular way of reasoning, and give rise to frequent separations...It is sometimes said that hereticks are always averse to confessions of faith. I wish I could say as much of tyrants. But after, all, if a confession of faith, upon the whole, may be advantageous, the greatest care should be taken not to sacralize, or make a petty Bible of it.[5]

Using a typical Protestant aversion to all things Catholic, Leland said that a creed was a "Virgin Mary" between the soul and God. Such props were barriers to direct access of the individual conscience to God.

The two largest groups of Baptists in the colonial era, the Regular Baptists, heirs of the Philadelphia Baptist Confession, and the much more modified

---

[4] Ibid., 174–78. Winchester's supporters left the church; he helped form the Society of Universal Baptists.
[5] John Leland, "The Virginia Chronicle," *The Writings of John Leland*, ed. L. F. Greene (1845; repr., New York: Arno Press, 1969) 114

Calvinistic Separate Baptists, eventually united. The quest for religious liberty during the era of the American Revolution was the climactic push toward union. Separates initially rebuffed efforts to unite in the South, but gradually modified their aversion toward using confessions as long as the documents were not creedal; a confession could not be a binding statement of faith on anyone's conscience.[6]

Nineteenth Century

During the first half of the nineteenth century, the democratization of American Christianity brought new emphases to the religious landscape. Calvinism was attacked or softened in favor of an Arminianism that gave credence to each person's free will.[7] The Baptist emphases on the sacredness of the individual conscience and the necessity of individual conversion were very compatible with revivalism and the burgeoning democratic idealism which expressed much confidence in the abilities of a free common people. Baptists, along with the Methodists (theologically Arminians), were the fastest growing religious bodies in the young nation.

In this context of freedom Baptist leaders in the North and South distanced themselves from any coerced creedal definition of Christianity. Interchurch cooperation was needed, but individual freedom and local church independence were paramount. In his assessment of Baptist identity, Brown University president Francis Wayland linked the importance of the individual conscience to the sole authority of scripture. "Soul liberty," the "peculiar glory" of Baptists, meant that each believer had the right of private interpretation. Denominations that require creeds still had schism; in contrast, "the Bible without the hindrance of a creed is allowed to be pure truth." Wayland acknowledged that Baptists had confessions of faith, but "probably not one in ten thousand of our members ever heard of their existence." In triumphal fashion, he declared that Baptists were different from other Christians because only they relied completely on the New Testament in religious matters."[8]

---

[6] David Benedict, *A General History of the Baptist Denomination in America*, 2 vols. (Boston: Manning & Loring, 1813) 1:62.

[7] For the idea of "democratization," see Nathan Hatch, *The Democratization of American Christianity* (New Haven: Yale University Press, 1989).

[8] Francis Wayland, *Notes on Principles and Practices of Baptist Churches* (New York: Sheldon, Blakeman and Co, 1857) 13–16, 132–33.

The most influential Southern Baptist at mid-century had views similar to Wayland. William B. Johnson, the first president of the Southern Baptist Convention, wrote *The Gospel Developed through the Government and Order of the Churches of Jesus Christ* (1846) in which he articulated an anti-creedal stance. Johnson affirmed "the supreme authority of Scripture" and "the right of private interpretation of Scripture" as fundamental principles found in Baptist life. In *"An Address to the Public"* the explanation for the formation of the Southern Baptist Convention, Johnson declared that the schism was over the right of Southerners (i.e., slaveholders) to practice missions. The schism was not over doctrine because Baptists in the North and South "differed in no article of the faith." No creed was created since Baptists had only one creed, the Bible.[9]

In the nineteenth century many local Baptist churches and associations continued to use confessions. In the battle against Alexander Campbell's anti-confession stance, frontier Baptists affirmed their right to have confessions that served as general guides to biblical study.[10] At the same time, Baptists again declared that these confessions were not creeds because the Bible was the sole Baptist creed. In describing Virginia Baptists, for example, J. L. Burrows insisted "personal liberty of interpretation" accompanied any adoption of a confession of faith by an association. During doctrinal or polity discussions, confessions were discarded in favor of the Bible. According to Burrows, "(Baptists) have always irreverently pushed them [confessions] aside with the question, What saith the Lord?... They never would attempt to settle differences by quoting human formulations, but at once passed beyond them to find the import of the inspired Word."[11]

Twentieth Century

Entering the twentieth century, Northern Baptists joined other Protestants in the quest for denominational efficiency. Long known for highlighting the independence of the local church, a dramatic methodological shift toward unity resulted in the formation of the Northern Baptist

---

[9] William B. Johnson, *The Gospel Developed Through the Government and Order of the Churches of Jesus Christ* (Richmond: H. K. Ellyson, 1846) 16. William B. Johnson, *Address to the Public*, in *A Baptist Source Book*, by Robert A. Baker, (Nashville: Broadman Press, 1966) 120.

[10] McBeth, *Baptist Heritage*, 380.

[11] J. L. Burrows, "Centennial Discourse, Dover Baptist Association—1783–1883," *The Chronicle* 3/2 (April 1940): 71–72.

Convention in 1907. In the convention's fourth year, Henry Morehouse, the dominant denominational executive of the day, affirmed that the mission of Northern Baptists was built upon "time honored Baptist principles" such as the right to private judgment in matters of faith, affirmation of the "authority and sufficiency of the scripture, as against imposed creeds," and democratic church government.[12]

Other leading American Baptists articulated a similar vision. Social Gospel advocates Walter Rauschenbusch and Shailer Mathews opposed creeds. Rauschenbusch said that "personal experience was the crux" of the Baptist faith. Genuinely democratic (and apostolic) churches were "based on religious experience, and not intellectual assent to a creed." Prominent Baptist liberal Shailer Mathews affirmed the importance of the Bible but said that doctrinal formulations needed continuous updating in light of the best modern scientific analysis available. He noted that creeds historically had been used as coercive tools of conformity to exclude nonconformists from the church. Mathews concluded, "Confessionalism is the evangelicalism of the dogmatic mind. Modernism is the evangelicalism of the scientific mind."[13]

A push toward creedalism was manifested in the "Fundamentalist-Modernist" conflict of the early twentieth century. Fundamentalists believed that missionary work and academic institutions had become infected with the heresy of Bible-denying liberalism. The fundamentals of the faith had to be rescued. At the 1922 convention of Northern Baptists, a "Fundamentalist Fellowship" attempted to adopt a creed to safeguard orthodoxy. Leaders promoted biblical inerrancy in their rallies. Militant fundamentalist William B. Riley, who liked to call liberals "Unitarian Baptists," offered a resolution to adopt the New Hampshire Confession of 1833 as a doctrinal standard. While most Baptists accepted the conservative theology of fundamentalists, they did not believe that intellectual assent and conformity to a creed was necessary or Baptistic. Consequently, Riley's resolution was defeated by a substitute motion:

---

[12] Henry Morehouse, "The Making and Mission of a Denomination," in *Baptist Life and Thought: 1600–1980, A Source Book*, ed. William Brackney (Valley Forge: Judson Press, 1983) 293.

[13] Walter Rauschenbusch, "Why I Am a Baptist" (1905), *Christian Ethics Today: Journal of Christian Ethics*, www.christianethicstoday.com/issue/001/ (accessed 5 June 2006). Shailer Mathews, *The Faith of Modernism* (New York: AMS Press, 1924) 35–36.

"The Northern Baptist Convention affirms that the New Testament is the all-sufficient ground of our faith and practice, and we need no other statement."[14]

After Northern Baptists refused to adopt a creedal statement, the Baptist Bible Union (BBU), a more militant independent organization, developed outside the convention to press for creedal conformity. The BBU—strongly exhibiting the separatist tendencies in fundamentalism—told churches to refrain from giving financial contributions to any mission group or school that failed to affirm the fundamentals of the faith. In 1933 the BBU disbanded and reorganized as the General Association of Regular Baptist Churches. The New Hampshire Confession, with a required premillennial understanding of Jesus' second coming, became a creedal standard.[15]

The Fundamentalist Fellowship remained in the Northern Baptist Convention, but relations with denominational leaders were tense. Fundamentalists demanded a doctrinal litmus test for missionaries, but the convention continued to affirm the authority of the scriptures and refused to amend its "inclusive" policies (evangelical beliefs were diverse and thus broadly defined). Ultimately, the convention leadership believed the fundamentalists wanted a narrow creed and fundamentalists did not trust the doctrinal orthodoxy of convention leaders.

In December 1943 the Conservative Baptist Foreign Missionary Society was formed, and subsequently on 17 May 1947 the Conservative Baptist Association of America was born. Hundreds of churches left the Northern Baptist Convention, formed a "movement" that opposed the centralization of power, and adopted a creedal statement that affirmed the inerrancy of scripture.[16]

Throughout the twentieth century, American Baptists maintained its anti-creedal perspective. In 1972 Northern Baptists, at the time called the American Baptist Convention, reorganized into the American Baptist Churches, USA. The name "American Baptist Church" was rejected to avoid any implication of being "a connectional system, a creed other than the New Testament...a possible violation of local autonomy."[17] At the outset of the twenty-first century

---

[14] Fundamentalism was also strong in Northern Presbyterianism. Numerous accounts of the fundamentalist conflict among Northern Baptists exist. See William Brackney, *The Baptists* (Westport CT: Greenwood Press, 1988) 28–34. See also Robert Torbet, *A History of the Baptists*, 3rd ed. (Valley Forge: Judson Press, 1963.

[15] The GARBC's current articles of faith are found at http://www.garbc.org/artfaith.php.

[16] The CBA's current declaration of faith can be found at http://www.cbamerica.org/.

[17] McBeth, *Baptist Heritage*, 581.

some American Baptists were demanding a creedal statement to exclude churches that affirm homosexual lifestyles.

In the early twentieth century Southern Baptists continued to emphasize their commitment to the freedom of the individual conscience and the sole authority of the Bible on matters of faith. Numerous Baptist voices declared that creeds must not void a believer's right to personal interpretation of the scriptures. E. J. Forester, pastor and college professor, said that a creed could function as an "expression of beliefs," but it was abused when used as an authority because it usurped the Bible as the standard for orthodoxy.[18] The leading Baptist theologian of his day, President E. Y. Mullins of Southern Seminary, concurred that voluntary confessions were an acceptable method of sharing the truth, but when church bodies imposed creeds on human consciences, they were tyrannical and a "shadow between the soul and God."[19]

A milder Southern version of the fundamentalist conflict in the 1920s resulted in a push for a confession of faith. Few Southern Baptists could be called liberal theologically; nevertheless, a battle to denounce evolution by the boisterous fundamentalist J. Frank Norris and others led denominational leaders to propose a confession in order to maintain unity in the convention. The confession, the Baptist Faith and Message of 1925, was largely written by E. Y. Mullins and was based on the New Hampshire Confession of Faith. The statement's preface indicated that confessions were not creeds, but voluntary formulations of faith. The mildly Calvinistic confession affirmed the sole authority of the Bible for "all religious opinions" but avoided mentioning evolution. No one on the "confession committee" advocated evolution, but they did not believe a theological confession needed a statement on science.[20]

Detractors continued to press for an explicit anti-evolution statement. The convention passed one (McDaniel Statement) the following year, but Southern Baptists mostly ignored the confession until the 1960s. Nevertheless, a few Baptist progressives of the 1920s feared Southern Baptists had taken an

---

[18] E. J. Forester, *The Baptist Position as to the Bible, the Church, and the Ordinances* (Baltimore: Woodward and Co., 1893) 30–33.

[19] E. Y. Mullins, "The Baptist Conception of Religious Liberty," in *The Life of Baptists in the Life of the World*, ed. Walter B. Shurden (Nashville: Broadman Press, 1985) 59.

[20] *SBC Annual*, 1925, 75. *Religious Herald* (Virginia), 25 June 1925, vol. 98, pp. 11, 22–23.

unfortunate step toward creedalism, or to use Leon McBeth's descriptive phrase, "The camel's nose was in the tent."[21]

Southern Baptists galloped toward creedalism when a second wave of fundamentalism erupted. The religious earthquake called the "Fundamentalist-Moderate" conflict had early tremors in the 1960s. Seminary professor Ralph Elliott suggested in his book, *The Message of Genesis*, that Genesis 1–11 was theological rather than literal history. Published by Broadman Press, the official press of the Sunday School Board of the Southern Baptist Convention (SBC), the book caused a backlash of protest.

The convention's official response to the "Elliott controversy" was the adoption of a revised version of the 1925 confession, this time named the 1963 Baptist Faith and Message. As with the 1925 statement, denominational loyalists sought to unify the convention with this voluntary confession. Influential denominationalist Herschel Hobbs, the chief commentator of the confession, emphasized its voluntary and non-creedal nature that was fully described in a preamble. As with the 1925 confession, most local churches ignored the 1963 statement for a couple of decades.

Theological tension seemed relatively quiet or at least isolated for almost two decades. Actually, a network of persons developed that believed that seminaries and convention agencies needed to be purged of liberalism. With the election of Adrian Rogers as convention president in 1979, a ten-year plan devised by Paige Patterson and Paul Pressler was successfully implemented to takeover the SBC. The plan involved electing convention presidents committed to the creedal litmus test of biblical inerrancy. The presidents then used their appointive powers to select committees that remade trustee boards of SBC institutions into guardians of inerrancy. Moderates unsuccessfully warned that the controversy was not a "conservative versus liberal" conflict, but while there were some theological differences, it was a political power play that demanded creedal control, squelched dissent, and was shaped by the Religious Right. The moderate appeal to "unity amidst diversity," belief in the Bible without the red herring of inerrancy, and freedom of conscience fell on deaf ears. While

---

[21] H. Leon McBeth, *Texas Baptists: A Sesquicentennial History* (Dallas: Baptistway Press, 1998) 187.

presidential elections were fiercely contested, the fundamentalist agenda had won by 1990.[22]

The crowning achievement of the "conservative resurgence" in the SBC came with the adoption of a revision of the 1963 confession, called the 2000 Baptist Faith and Message.[23] New items included a statement that excluded women from the pastorate, a statement on the submission of the wife to the husband in family life, and the importance of doctrinal accountability. The preamble that had emphasized that the confession was a voluntary statement and not a creed was discarded. Denominational employees and theological seminary faculty are required to subscribe to the confession. Critics said the fundamentalist adoption of a creed was complete.

Baptists Abroad

Confessions have been widely used in European Baptist life. Similar to their roles in early English or American contexts, confessions expressed Baptist identity to assert commonalities with other Protestant bodies. In addition, European Baptists who struggled to survive in countries with state supported churches had to write confessions in order to receive government toleration. A few countries (Spain, Portugal, and Greece) have adopted the 1963 Baptist Faith and Message of the Southern Baptist Convention. At the same time, European Baptists have strongly resisted creeds, especially since state supported churches had used their creeds to inflict persecution upon minority religious groups. The German Baptists' confession, for example, insists that it is a voluntary statement of faith that has no compulsory powers. Baptists in some regions (for example, Britain, Sweden, Norway) only use brief general

---

[22] Numerous accounts of the SBC controversy exist from both sides. For the moderate perspective, see Walter Shurden, *Not a Silent People* (Macon GA: Smyth and Helwys, 1995) 69–112.

[23] For the Baptist Faith and Message 2000, see http://www.sbc.net/bfm/. For an extensive theological analysis of the rise of creedalism in the SBC, see the study of a 1994 statement, "The Report of the Presidential Theological Study Committee." Like McBeth, Jeff Pool says that Southern Baptists erased the historic Baptist distinction between confession and creed. He elaborates that this is due to an extreme Calvinistic revision of traditional Baptist perspectives on several basic doctrines of the faith. See Jeff B. Pool, *Against Returning to Egypt: Exposing and Resisting Creedalism in the Southern Baptist Convention* (Macon GA: Mercer University Press, 1998).

statements of principles.[24] Commenting upon British Baptists' detachment from creeds, English biblical scholar H. Wheeler Robinson commented in 1927, in a vein similar to E. Y. Mullins, that they held to the contents of the historic Christian confessions as loyally as other Christian bodies, but they "feel the peril of stereotyping that which must be living to be real, and the peril of substituting a formal assent for what is of value only as a personal conviction."[25]

Throughout the history of the Baptist World Alliance (BWA), international Baptist leaders have affirmed the use of confessions but opposed creedalism. At the opening Baptist World Congress in 1905, British leader Alexander MacLaren invited the delegates to stand and repeat the ancient Apostles' Creed to demonstrate to the world that Baptists were doctrinally orthodox within the larger Christian community. He said:

> So I have suggested that, given your consent, it would be an impressive and a right thing, and would clear away a good many misunderstandings and stop the mouth of a good deal of slander—if we here and now, in the face of the world, not as a piece of coercion or discipline, but as a simple acknowledgement of where we stand and what we believe, would rise to our feet and, following the lead of your President, would repeat the Apostles' Creed. Will you?[26]

The editor of the proceedings added, "The whole gathering then instantly rose and repeated, slowly and deliberately, after Dr. MacLaren the whole of the Apostles' Creed."

MacLaren's action was spontaneous, not choreographed. It was not a crusade for creedal adoption. As he emphasized, recitation of the creed was "not a piece of coercion or discipline," and the editor's note makes it sound like the crowd did not know the creed, so they had to repeat it after MacLaren. His use of the Apostles' Creed, moreover, also revealed that Baptists had never had a consensus statement of faith beyond the Bible.

---

[24] G. Keith Parker, *Baptists in Europe: History & Confessions of Faith* (Nashville: Broadman Press, 1982) 18–26, 57, 243.

[25] H. Wheeler Robinson, *The Life and Faith of the Baptists* (London: Kingsgate Press, 1927) 80.

[26] Alexander MacLaren, "In the Name of Christ...By the Power of the Spirit," in *The Life of Baptists in the Life of the World*, ed. Walter B. Shurden (Nashville: Broadman Press, 1985) 17.

Future world Baptist congresses clearly opposed creedalism. At the second BWA gathering in 1911, English minister J. Moffatt Logan said that the world would not be Christianized through the use of creeds. Ancient creeds had been used as "instruments of cruelty," Logan declared, and Christ's message should be trusted to an environment of freedom.[27] To a BWA audience of European Baptists in 1913, the most influential British Baptist of the era, John Clifford, preached that "no confession is final. No church order is infallible or beyond improvement." Clifford implored his colleagues to be open to fresh understandings of the Scriptures as they were enlightened by the Holy Spirit.[28]

As the BWA matured and gained greater representation beyond its early American/British dominance, international voices also denounced creedalism. At the tenth Baptist World Congress in 1960 in Rio de Janeiro, Alfonso Olmedo, a pastor and missionary from Argentina, emphasized that Baptist unity across the world could not be based on a type of organization or adherence to a creed, but a common commitment to "deeds" and "subjection" to God. Denton Lotz, the most recent General Secretary of the BWA (1988–) has continued the BWA's commitment to a non-creedal Baptist witness. He declared that Baptists have "core doctrines that must be confessed" but reaffirmed "the Bible rather than imposed creeds as our sole source of authority in matters of faith."[29] Southern Baptists, with their recent insistence on creedalism, withdrew from the BWA in 2004. Whether some international Baptist groups, perhaps a few indebted to Southern Baptist mission efforts, follow the Southern Baptist Convention into a joint creedal arrangement is yet to be determined.

Twenty-first Century

Baptist groups in America have responded differently to confessions/creeds at the threshold of the twenty-first century. A small group of Baptist scholars in the South issued the Baptist Manifesto in 1997 seeking to "re-envision" Baptist identity. The manifesto did not call for a creed, but it criticized individualism in favor of a communal identity of faithful discipleship: "Scripture wisely forbids and we reject every form of private interpretation that makes Bible reading a practice which can be carried out according to the dictates of individual conscience (2 Peter 1:20–21)." Non-supporters criticized the attack on the role

---

[27] Richard Pierard, ed., *Baptists Together in Christ, 1905–2005: A Hundred-Year History of the Baptist World Alliance* (Falls Church: BWA, 2005) 37.
[28] Ibid., 42.
[29] Ibid. 306.

of the individual, prominent throughout Baptist history. They also said that the document underappreciated the role of congregational governance by suggesting it reflected a willingness to rely on "spiritual masters" to interpret the scriptures for church laity.[30] The long-term influence of the Baptist Manifesto remains to be seen. A parallel interest in the reaffirmation of historic Christian creeds like the Apostles' Creed, the Nicene Creed, and the Catholic tradition is also a trend to be watched.

Other Baptists have continued to highlight the individual's ability to read the scriptures under the guidance of God's Spirit as an integral Baptist distinctive. American Baptists have an "Identity Statement" (2005) that echoes their response to the fundamentalist conflict of the 1920s. They continue to affirm the Bible as "final authority" and "accept no humanly devised confession or creed as binding."[31] The Cooperative Baptist Fellowship, formed in 1990 by "moderates" who had been disenfranchised from the Southern Baptist Convention, has adopted a set of "Core Values." The authority of scripture is affirmed as is "the freedom and responsibility of every person to relate directly to God without the imposition of creed or the control of clergy or government."[32]

In addition to the Southern Baptist Convention's adoption of the creedal 2000 Baptist Faith and Message, the road to creedalism was also traveled by other Baptists who responded negatively to the challenges of modern theology in the twentieth century (for example, the General Association of Regular Baptist Churches, Conservative Baptist Association of America). The real or

---

[30] Mikael Broadway, Curtis Freeman, Barry Harvey, James W. McClendon, Jr., Elizabeth Newman, and Philip Thompson, "Re-Envisioning Baptist Identity: A Manifesto for Baptist Communities in North America," Perspectives in Religious Studies 24/3 (Fall 1997): 303–10. Walter Shurden notes the strong influence of Duke ethicist Stanley Hauerwas on the manifesto. Hauerwas has written that the Bible should be taken out of the hand of the laity; "spiritual masters" should then teach the scriptures to the Church. See Walter B. Shurden, "The Baptist Identity and the Baptist Manifesto," Perspectives in Religious Studies 25/4 (Winter 1998) 321–40. Manifesto supporters have responded that their views have been distorted. See Greg Warner, "'Manifesto'supporters say role of community misinterpreted," Associated Baptist Press, 1 Februrary 2006, http://www.abpnews.com/810.article (accessed 11 January 2008).

[31] An Expression of Christian Faith Representative of American Baptists adoped by the General Board, American Baptist Churches in the U.S.A., November 2005. "American Baptist Identity Statement, 2005," American Baptist Churches, U.S.A., http://www.abc-usa.org/identity/idstate.html.

[32] Cooperative Baptist Fellowship, "Our Core Values," Cooperative Baptist Fellowship, http://www.thefellowship.info/ (accessed 11 January 2008).

perceived threat of liberalism was usually the stated factor. The need for certainty amidst the swirling, rapid changes of twentieth-century modernity is another. These Baptists believe theological creedalism is necessary to defend moral absolutes in an age considered decadent and morally relativistic.

Suggested Reading

"American Baptist Identity Statement, 2005." An Expression of Christian Faith Representative of American Baptists adopted by the General Board, American Baptist Churches in the U.S.A., November 2005. American Baptist Churches, USA. http://www.abcusa.org/identity/idstate.html (accessed 10 June 2006).

"Comparison of 1925, 1963 and 2000 Baptist Faith and Message." Baptist General Convention of Texas, Baptist Heritage. http://www.baptiststandard.com/postnuke/themes/PostNukeBlue/comparison.html (accessed 12 June 2006).

Cooperative Baptist Fellowship, "Our Core Values," Cooperative Baptist Fellowship. http://www.thefellowship.info/ (accessed 15 June 2006).

Lumpkin, William L. *Baptist Confessions of Faith.* Valley Forge: Judson Press, 1969.

Parker, G. Keith. *Baptists in Europe: History & Confessions of Faith.* Nashville: Broadman Press, 1982.

Pierard, Richard, editor. *Baptists Together in Christ, 1905–2005: A Hundred-Year History of the Baptist World Alliance.* Falls Church VA: BWA, 2005.

Rauschenbusch, Walter. "Why I Am a Baptist" (1905). *Christian Ethics Today: Journal of Christian Ethics.* http://www.christianethicstoday.com/issue/001/ (accessed 5 June 2006).

CHAPTER 24

Baptists at the Twenty-First Century: Assessments and Challenges

Walter B. Shurden

If you have read all the chapters in this book, you have an introduction to the Baptist story for the last 400 years. Each of the chapters has a date or dates associated with it. When you study history of any kind, you will discover that dates are mere "nails" on which historians hang significant events. The nails in this book mark pivotal turning points in Baptist history.

Some of the nails in this book help you assess the distinctive traits of the Baptist people. These traits can be listed as the following.

(1) Baptists affirm the importance of a believers' church in which people testify to their personal experience with God. This individual and personal encounter of the individual with God in Christ is critical to understanding the Baptist people. Moreover, baptism is reserved for those people who voluntarily make that commitment. Many people think that the most important thing about Baptist baptism is the *mode* of baptism, the practice of immersion. It is true that Baptists today universally practice immersion. However, you have learned that for the first three decades of Baptist life the most important aspect of baptism for Baptists was the *subject* of baptism, the person being baptized. Baptists practice believers' baptism, rather than infant baptism, because they think it is the best way to insure what they call a "regenerate" church.

(2) Baptists passionately advocate freedom of conscience. Religious liberty and its political corollary, the separation of church and state, constitute Baptists' single most significant contribution to the broader culture, especially in America. One should note, however, that Baptists have pled for religious freedom in all geographical contexts. Freedom has been a recurring word in every phase of Baptist life. Freedom, not fear, is the atmosphere in which

religion flourishes best. Baptists argue that the individual conscience must be free.

(3). Baptists stress congregational rule in their churches. They believe that the best way to discern the mind of Christ is through all the members of a local church, not through bishops, clergy, or extra-local church councils imposing their wills on the fellowship of believers. Each local Baptist church, under the Lordship of Christ, is free to determine their membership and leadership, order their worship and work, and ordain whom they perceive as gifted for ministry. Baptists think that congregational church government is the best means to guarantee the equality of all believers. It is also the best method of evoking and utilizing all the gifts of all the members of the churches for the mission of Christ. The diversity in Baptist life is largely due to the independent polity of Baptist churches. While Baptist churches voluntarily cooperate together in associations, conventions, and unions, these churches remain free from the coercion of these organizations. Take away congregational church polity from Baptists and you have made them something other than Baptists.

(4). Most Baptists are known today for their missionary zeal. From their beginning, Baptists fervently proclaimed their understanding of the gospel. However, it was not until the time of William Carey in the latter part of the nineteenth century that Baptists embraced the responsibility for carrying the Christian message throughout the world. With the birth of the missionary spirit among Baptists in 1792 (a very important nail for Baptists), they led the rest of Christendom in this important enterprise.

(5). In terms of religious authority, Baptists stress that the Bible is their sole authority for faith and practice. In this, however, they do not differ from most other Christian denominations. Where they do differ is in the ongoing interpretation of the Bible. With the canonization of the Bible in the fourth century, the problem of religious authority did not disappear. We still have the task of the continuing interpretation of scripture and sensing God's will for our lives. The Bible is not an almanac with answers to all contemporary questions such as the role of women in ministry, stem cell research, and homosexuality. So, how do Christian groups discern the Lordship of Christ in their lives today? Some have used a single person such as the Pope, others have used a council of bishops, and others rely on theological creeds, while still others use a combination of clergy and laity at a general assembly. Baptists have no bishop but the local congregation. Each individual in Baptist life is encouraged to read, study, and interpret the Bible for oneself, and to bring that interpretation to the local body of believers. It is the local congregation that is the final interpreter of God's will in Baptist life.

The peculiar distinctives of Baptists outlined above may be described and categorized in many different ways. Whatever terms are utilized, however, one will certainly end up with a belief in a believers' church protected by believers' baptism, freedom of individual conscience, congregational church polity, biblical authority, and the Great Commission.

When one reads and studies the Baptist story, one discovers far more than the so-called "Baptist distinctives." You have read in this volume about the Baptist effort to confess faith without creedalizing it. Also, the Baptist struggle to form a denominational structure that brings local churches together while protecting congregational polity has been an effort that continues to this very day. Baptist participation in and opposition to revivalism has also been a powerful shaping force in Baptist life. The concern for social justice has never been absent from Baptist life. People such as Isaac Backus, John Leland, John Clifford, Walter Rauschenbusch, and Martin Luther King Jr. played a prominent role in sensitizing Baptists to justice issues. Baptists have had somewhat of a love/hate relationship with education, yet they have established some major institutions of higher learning. Race and gender have been huge issues in Baptist life, as in the life of most other denominations.

In light of the Baptist saga, what are the challenges that Baptists face in the twenty-first century? Many challenges could be enumerated, but I will list six that I think are important.

First, despite Baptists' peculiar distinctives and unique history, they are very much a part of the larger Church of Jesus Christ. Baptists desperately need to march into this new century affirming their surname as well as their given name. We are "Baptist Christians." Baptists at various points in their 400 year history have been obsessed with an exceedingly narrow sectarianism. Landmarkism is exhibit A of this tendency, but it is by no means the only example. The challenge is to overcome this limiting and limited sectarianism that sees itself as the whole of the Christian Church or, at least, as better than all the rest.

Sadly, some Baptists have used baptism as a barrier rather than a bridge. Baptists in this new century would do well, as John R. Tyler urges, to revisit our view of baptism when it separates rather than unites.[1] For too long now,

---

[1] See his argument in John R. Tyler, *Baptism: We've Got it Right...and Wrong* (Macon GA: Smyth & Helwys Publishing, 2003).

Baptists have used baptism the same way that those earliest Jewish Christians used circumcision, as a litmus test to exclude. When other faithful followers of Christ wish to identify with us, should Baptists make their practice of believer's baptism by immersion a barrier to church membership? One of the challenges for Baptists in this new century is to learn how to accept and relate to other Christians.[2]

If any one idea has been missing from the Baptist vision over the years, it is a close, binding relationship with the continuous, historic, and universal tradition of the Christian community. That is precisely why at the first meeting of the Baptist World Alliance in 1905 sagacious old Alexander MacLaren, the Baptist saint from Manchester, England, and the presiding officer of the meeting, asked Baptists from around the world to stand and repeat the Apostles' Creed. Of course, being anti-creedal,[3] as was their heritage, those Baptists could not repeat the creed because most of them did not know it. So they had to repeat it *after* MacLaren. This wise old Baptist saint wanted Baptists from around the world to show their identification with Christians throughout the world. Three cheers for wise ole MacLaren!

A second challenge for Baptists in this new century is to maintain a believers' church. With the temptation to gain more members and to evaluate "successful" church ministry solely on the basis of increasing numbers, Baptists run the risk of compromising their concept of a believers' church.[4] Even efforts to make sure that our children and grandchildren "join the church" make us vulnerable to sacrificing the ideal of a regenerate church. In some Baptist churches pre-school age children are now accepted into full church membership. Early Baptists would doubtless be horrified at such practices that fall only a few years short of infant baptism. One must seriously ask, "What is the difference in child baptism and infant baptism?"

Baptists simply must make clear in this new century that becoming a Christian is more than intellectual assent to doctrine. Becoming a Baptist Christian is about far more than learning the right answers to religious questions; it is commitment to a new way of life, a life incarnated in Jesus of

---

[2] To see how one Baptist pastor confronts this challenge see G. Todd Wilson, "Why Baptists Should Not Rebaptize Christians from Other Denominations" in *Proclaiming the Baptist Vision: Baptism and the Lord's Supper*, Walter B. Shurden, ed. (Macon GA: Smyth & Helwys Publication, 1999) 41–47.

[3] See chap. 23 in this book.

[4] For a more extensive discussion of this issue, see Alan Neely, "Church Membership: What Does It Mean? What Can It Mean?" in *Proclaiming the Baptist Vision*, 39–48.

Nazareth. Whatever else it means to be a Christian, it means to take seriously what Jesus took seriously. If you want to know what Jesus took seriously read the four Gospels of Matthew, Mark, Luke, and John. "Credo," or "I Believe" means "I give my heart to," "I pledge my love to," "I turn my life over to," "I give my undivided allegiance to." That is very different from a nodding head that says "I agree with these ideas."

Third, Baptists face a challenge of living up to believer equality. Baptists have said they believe that the local church is built on flat ground. Each believer has equality with other believers. The clergy cannot pull rank on the laity. The old cannot pull rank on the young. Whites cannot pull rank on blacks. Men cannot pull rank on women.

One of the challenges of Baptists in the twenty-first century is to maintain that equality, especially as it relates to race and gender. Baptists have not always lived up to their ideal of the priesthood of *all* believers. A few times Baptists have slipped into the priesthood of *clergy* believers and falsely trumpeted pastoral authoritarianism. Throughout much of Baptist history in America, Baptists have affirmed the priesthood of *white* believers and created churches along racial lines. For a long, long time, Baptists, as so many other Christian denominations, practiced the priesthood of *male* believers.

Charles E. Poole, Baptist pastor, preached a sermon titled "We Ordain Women Because We Baptize Girls."[5] His text was Galatians 3:27–28 where Paul said, "For as many of you as were baptized into Christ have put on Christ. There is neither Jew nor Greek, there is neither slave nor free, there is neither male nor female; for you are all one in Christ Jesus." The water of baptism may symbolically wash away sin, but it also washes away class and race and gender. When we "put on Christ," we also "take off" class and race and gender. Baptists still struggle to understand that.

Fourth, Baptists face a vexing and recurring challenge in the twenty-first century in terms of their congregational polity. On the one hand, they face, in some cases, a centralizing denominationalism that tends to overwhelm local congregational church life. Local church freedom in this instance is sacrificed for the sake of denominational unity. Local churches, because of a deadening passivity, yield up their lives to a centralized authority. On the other hand,

[5] Charles E. Poole, *Between the Gates: Helpful Words from Where Scripture Meets Life* (Macon GA: Smyth & Helwys Publishing, 2006) 97–99. See William E. Hull's *Beyond the Barriers* (Nashville: Broadman Press, 1981) for another Baptist approach to the issue of inclusion in the life and ministry of the church.

congregationalism can easily become an exaggerated localism that fails to participate in the larger Body of Christ. Finding a balance between these two extremes has always been a difficult assignment for Baptists. It will be no less so in the twenty-first century.

Fifth, Baptists' passion for the issues of religious liberty and separation of church and state is needed as much in the twenty-first century as in previous years. One of the major threats to religious freedom today is that Baptists will "assume that there is no danger" or that "the danger is too slight to bother."[6] Baptists today are not a minority people whipped on the street as was Obadiah Holmes in seventeenth-century Boston. Nor are they jailed as were those eighteenth-century Baptist preachers in Colonial Virginia. Threats to religious liberty and separation of religion and government continue, however.

William E. Hull has noted that "in recent years, geopolitical developments have redefined the church-state agenda in ways that may make it a dominant issue for years to come."[7] He wisely observed that the same dynamics exist today in some countries that gave rise to the Baptist movement in England and America. Religious clergy who make absolute claims enjoy the full protection of theocratic states that limit the freedom of others. A quick reading of the day's newspaper headlines indicates that religious incivility continues unabated. The Baptist cry for freedom still needs to be heard.

Another danger, especially in America, is the existence of a shallow patriotism where citizenship is confused with discipleship. Baptists, now numbered among the majority rather than the minority, will have to work even harder to distinguish between pietism and patriotism. To assess critically where one begins and the other ends is not always child's play. But we can be sure that when the cross of Christ is wrapped in the flag of any nation, danger, if not downright heresy, lurks close by. Prayer in public schools, channeling public tax dollars into the support of private religious programs, and defending America as a "Christian nation" simply are not in keeping with the Baptist tradition of dissent and their plea for equality for all people.

---

[6] E. Glenn Hinson, *Soul Liberty: The Doctrine of Religious Liberty* (Nashville: Convention Press, 1975) 122.

[7] William E. Hull, *The Meaning of the Baptist Experience* (Brentwood: Baptist History and Heritage Society, 2007) 20. This little twenty-four-page booklet is the best statement on the Baptist identity that I have ever read. It deserves wide reading by the Baptist people and by all others who want to understand Baptist Christians.

Sixth, Baptists will be challenged in this new century to continue to be a Great Commission people. Few Baptists can witness a baptismal experience without calling to mind the Great Commission of Jesus when he said, "All authority in heaven and earth has been given to me. Go therefore and make disciples of all nations, baptizing them in the name of the Father and of the Son and of the Holy Spirit, teaching them to observe all that I have commanded you."[8] Since the time of William Carey in the late eighteenth century, Baptists have been a missionary people. Why have Baptists in the modern period engaged in such a lively missionary spirit? William E. Hull nails one of the reasons when he said that "the faith most freely chosen is the faith most freely shared." Further, Hull superbly characterized the missionary spirit of Baptists at their best when he said, "Because of the crucial importance of an uncoerced conscience, this [Baptist] witness is offered, not to proselyte, nor to judge one's inherited religion, not to claim superiority, but to give all persons a choice regarding Jesus Christ as Lord of their lives."[9]

Without a doubt, Baptists face a major challenge in keeping alive that enthusiasm for the Great Commission in this new century. Additionally, one of the premier challenges for Baptists in this new century is to understand that the Great Commission includes word and deed, speaking/preaching and living/doing, evangelism and social justice. Baptists, as you have learned in this book, certainly have not been void of acts of social justice, but without a doubt we have made our mark more in missions and in the preaching of the gospel than in caring for the poor and speaking up for the oppressed. This has been especially true for the last 200 years of Baptist history. Baptists will be challenged to carry a whole gospel into the needs of the twenty-first century, a gospel that addresses both the spiritual needs and the physical and emotional hurts of humanity. Baptists would be smart in the coming decades if we heeded the counsel of St. Francis of Assisi, a Catholic, who said, "Preach the gospel at all times; if necessary use words."

---

[8] Matt 28:18–20.
[9] Ibid., 17–18.

List of Contributors

Wm. Lloyd Allen, Sylvan Hill Baptist Church, professor of Baptist heritage, James and Carolyn McAfee School of Theology, Mercer University

Rosalie Beck, associate professor of religion, Baylor University

William H. Brackney, Millard R. Cherry Distinguished Professor of Christian Thought and Ethics, Acadia University

Karen O'Dell Bullock, fellow of the Institute, professor of Christian Heritage, director for the Ph.D. program, B. H. Carroll Theological Institute

Terry G. Carter, Associate Dean of the School of Christian Stuides, W.O., Department Christian Ministries, Vaught Professor of Christian Ministries, Ouachita Baptist University

J. Bradley Creed, provost, executive vice president and professor of religion, Samford University

Charles W. Deweese, executive director-treasurer, Baptist History and Heritage Society

Pamela R. Durso, associate executive director, Baptist History and Heritage Society

Jerry L. Faught II, Dickinson associate professor of religion, Oklahoma Baptist University

E. Glenn Hinson, senior professor of church history and spirituality, Baptist Seminary of Kentucky

Carol Crawford Holcomb, associate professor of religion, University of Mary Hardin-Baylor

Fisher Humphreys, professor of divinity, Beeson Divinity School, Samford University

W. Glenn Jonas, Howard Professor of Religion and Chairman of Religion and Philosophy, Campbell University

Alan J. Lefever, director, Texas Baptist Historical Collection and adjunct professor, George W. Truett Theological Seminary

Bill J. Leonard, dean of the divinity school and professor of church history, Wake Forest University

Sandy Dwayne Martin, professor and head of the department of religion, University of Georgia

Walter B. Shurden, Callaway Professor of Christianity and executive director, the Center for Baptist Studies, Mercer University

Stephen Stookey, professor of Christian history and leadership studies, Gary Cook School of Leadership and Christian Education

William M. Tillman Jr., T. B. Maston Professor of Christian Ethics, Logsdon School of Theology, Hardin-Simmons University

Doug Weaver, assistant professor of religion, director of undergraduate studies, department of religion, Baylor University

Michael E. (Mike) Williams Sr., dean of humanities and social sciences, professor of history, Dallas Baptist University

Highlights from the Life and Ministry of Harry Leon McBeth

Alan Lefever

1931 Born in Rotan, Texas, 5 August

1950 Enrolls Wayland Baptist College
     Marries Ada Lucille Miller, 9 June

1954 Receives Bachelor of Arts from Wayland Baptist College
     Enrolls at Southwestern Baptist Theological Seminary

1956 Begins pastoring First Baptist Church, Rio Vista, TX

1957 Receives Bachelor of Divinity from Southwestern Seminary

1958 Daughter Ruth Ann born, 8 January

1959 Son Mark Wayne born, 31 December

1960 Appointed adjunct professor of church history at Southwestern Seminary
     Resigns as pastor of FBC, Rio Vista

1961 Receives Doctor of Theology in Church History from Southwestern Seminary

1962 Elected to Southwestern Seminary Faculty

1963 Son David Lee born, 18 June

1966 *The History of Southern Baptist Higher Education* is published
     Victory through Prayer: A History of Rosen Heights Baptist Church 1906–1966 is published

1968 *The First Baptist Church of Dallas: Centennial History 1868–1968* is published

1976 Begins service as a member of the Historical Commission of the Southern Baptist Convention

1977 *Strange New Religions* is published

1978 Receives Norman W. Cox Award for Best Article published in *Baptist History and Heritage*

Begins term as president, Southern Baptist Historical Society (Baptist History and Heritage Society)

1979 *Women in Baptist Life* is published

Ends term as president, Southern Baptist Historical Society (Baptist History and Heritage Society)

1983 Ends service as a member of the Historical Commission of the Southern Baptist Convention

1985 *The Baptist Heritage: Four Centuries of Baptist Witness* is published

1989 Receives W. O. Carver Distinguished Service Award from Southern Baptist Historical Society

1990 *Sourcebook for Our Baptist Heritage* is published

1991 *Celebrating Heritage and Hope: The Centennial History of the Baptist Sunday School Board, 1891–1991* is produced

1998 *Texas Baptist: A Sesquicentennial History* is published

2001 Death of Ada Lucille McBeth, 27 October

2002 Marries Thelma Grace Smith, 17 November

2003 Retires as Distinguished Professor of Church History, Southwestern Seminary

2004 Baptist History and Heritage Society creates the H. Leon McBeth Fund

A Selected Bibliography of the
Works of Harry Leon McBeth

Alan Lefever

Books

The Baptist Heritage. Nashville TN: Broadman Press, 1987.
Celebrating Heritage and Hope. N.p., 1990.
English Baptist Literature on Religious Liberty to 1689. New York : Arno Press, 1980.
The First Baptist Church of Dallas: Centennial History, 1868–1968. Grand Rapids: Zondervan, 1968.
The History of Southern Baptist Higher Education. Nashville TN: Education Commission of the Southern Baptist Convention, 1966.
Men Who Made Missions. Nashville TN: Broadman Press, 1968.
A Sourcebook for Baptist Heritage. Nashville TN: Broadman Press, 1990.
Strange New Religions. Nashville TN: Broadman Press, 1977.
Texas Baptists: A Sesquicentennial History. Austin TX: Eakin Press, 1999.
Victory through Prayer: A History of Rosen Heights Baptist Church, 1906–1966. Fort Worth TX: Rosen Heights Baptist Church, 1966.
Women in Baptist Life. Nashville TN: Broadman Press, 1979.

Articles

"America's Southern Baptists: Who They Are." *Christianity Today* 32/4 (November 1988): 17–21.
Autonomy and Cooperation. Foundations of Baptist Heritage series. Nashville TN: Historical Commission of the Southern Baptist Convention, 1989.
Baptist Beginnings. Baptist Heritage series. Nashville TN: Historical Commission of the Southern Baptist Convention, 1979.
"Baptist Beginnings." *Baptist History and Heritage* 15/4 (October 1980): 36–41, 65.

"Baptist Church Covenants." *Baptist History and Heritage* 27/1 (January 1992): 9–60.

"Baptist Fundamentalism : A Cultural Interpretation." *Baptist History and Heritage* 13/3 (July 1978): 12–19, 32.

"Baptist or Evangelical: One Southern Baptist's Perspective." In *Southern Baptists and American Evangelicals* (Nashville TN: Broadman & Holman, 1993) 68–76.

"Baptists See Black." *Southwestern Journal of Theology* 12/2 (Spring 1970): 135.

"The Broken Unity of 1845: A Reassessment." *Baptist History and Heritage* 24/3 (July 1989): 24–31, 48.

"Challenges to Religious Liberty." *Southwestern Journal of Theology* 36/3 (Summer 1994): 45–51.

"The Changing Role of Women in Baptist History." *Southwestern Journal of Theology* 22/4 (Fall 1979): 84–96.

"Cooperation and Crisis as Shapers of Southern Baptist Identity." Baptist History and Heritage *30/3 (July 1995): 35–44.*

"Expansion of the Southern Baptist Convention to 1951." *Baptist History and Heritage* 17/3 (July 1982): 32–43.

"Fundamentalism in the Southern Baptist Convention in Recent Years." *Review & Expositor* 79/1 (Winter 1982): 85–103.

"George W. Truett: Baptist Statesman." *Baptist History and Heritage* 32/2 (April 997): 9–22.

"God's Last and Only Hope: The Fragmentation of the Southern Baptist Convention." *Review & Expositor* 88/4 (Fall 1991): 449–50.

"Has it Been Worth the Cost: Some Theological Reflections." *Faith and Mission* 5/4 (Fall 1987): 27–30.

"Images of the Black Church in America." *Baptist History and Heritage* 16/3 (July 1981): 19–28, 42.

"J Frank Norris and Southwestern Seminary." *Southwestern Journal of Theology* 30/3 (Summer 1988): 14–19.

"John Franklyn Norris: Texas Tornado." *Baptist History and Heritage* 32/2 (April 1997): 23–38.

"The Legacy of the Baptist Missionary Society." *Baptist History and Heritage* 27/3 (July 1992): 3–13.

"The New Shape of Religion in America." *Southwestern Journal of Theology* 38/3 (Summer 1996): 19–27.

"The Ordination of Women." *Review & Expositor* 78/3 (Fall 1981): 515–30.

"Origin of the Christian Life Commission." *Baptist History and Heritage* 1/4 (October 1966): 29–36.

"Patterns of SBC Presidential Authority." *Baptist History and Heritage* 31/3 (April 1996): 12–22.

"Perspectives on Women in Baptist Life." *Baptist History and Heritage* 22/3 (July 1987): 4–11.

"Piety and Politics: Evangelicals and Fundamentalists Confront the World." *Southwestern Journal of Theology* 31/4 (Fall 1988): 58.

"Preaching Values in Baptist History." *Southwestern Journal of Theology* 6/2 (April 1964): 111–22.

"Role of Women in Southern Baptist history." *Baptist History and Heritage* 12/1 (January 1977): 3–25.

"Social Gospel in America, 1870–1920." *Southwestern Journal of Theology* 9/4 (Fall 1966): 100–101.

"Southern Baptists and Race Since 1947." *Baptist History and Heritage* 7/3 (July 1972): 155–69.

"Texas Baptists and Ordination." *Perspectives in Religious Studies* 29/4 (Fall 2002): 245–58.

"The Texas Tradition: a Study in Baptist Regionalism." *Baptist History and Heritage* 26/1 (January 1991): 37–57.

"Tongues as of Fire: Pentecostalism in Contemporary Christianity." *Southwestern Journal of Theology* 12/2 (Spring 1970): 134–35.

"Two Ways to be Baptist: An Introduction." *Baptist History and Heritage* 32/2 (April 1997): 7–8.

Addresses

"J. Frank Norris and Southwestern Seminary." Chapel address, Southwestern Baptist Theological Seminary, Fort Worth TX, 12 March 1987.

"The Primacy of Christ." Chapel address, Southern Baptist Theological Seminary, Louisville KY, 28 July 1981.

"A Study in Baptist Regionalism: Parts 1–2." Chapel address, Southwestern Baptist Theological Seminary, Fort Worth TX, 19–20April, 1988.

Acknowledgments

Any editor of a collection of essays is indebted to many who helped the work come to fruition. In addition to the nineteen other contributors to this volume, I want to say a special word of thanks to my co-editor, Walter Shurden. Dr. Shurden is, like Leon McBeth, one of the premier Baptist historians in the world. His belief in this project from its inception has been essential. Without his many contributions in editing, writing, and rewriting, and his great encouragement, this work would not have been possible. I wish to thank Pat Manuel in the Computer and Technology Department, Dallas Baptist University, for her assistance in editing and merging documents from different computer programs and from more than twenty sources. Likewise, I am grateful once again for the support of my provost, Dr. Gail Linam, and of the faculty and staff of the College of Humanities and Social Sciences, Dallas Baptist University, especially the departmental secretary, Jillian Pryor, and my administrative assistant, Wanda Allen. Finally, as always I appreciate the love and support of my wife, Robbie, and sons, Michael, Josh, and Carey.

Index

Graves, James R., 80, 81, 179-93
Great Awakenings (First and Second), 115, 121, 129, 144, 155, 165, 212, 235, 290
Great Reform Bill of 1832, 143
Greater St. Stephens Baptist Church, 272
Green, Molly Marshall, 87
Grenz, Stanley, 87
Grievance Committee of Warren Baptist Association, 154
Griffin, Benjamin, 289
Gutenberg, Johannes, 5

Habermas, Gary, 88
Hall, Robert, Jr., 77
Hall, Robert, Sr., 77, 116, 117
Hamilton, William, 87
Handy, Robert T., 164
Hard Times, 236
Hardcastle, Thomas, 20
Hardin-Simmons University, 138
Hardshell Baptists (see also Primitive Baptists), 148
Harper, William Rainey, 82, 134
Harrington, Caroline, 215
Harrison, Wes, 34-35
Harvard Divinity School, 88, 132
Harvard College/University, 82, 93, 130
Harvey, Hezekiah, 77
Hasseltine or Hazeltine, John, 122
Hatch, Nathan, 163
Hauerwas, Stanley, 88
Hayden, S. A.; Haydenism, 188, 191
Haystack Prayer Meeting, 122
Hedger, Violet, 280
Help to Zion's Travelers, 116, 117
Helwys, Thomas, 3, 11, 14, 16, 17, 23-25, 28-32, 36, 75, 288
Hemphill, Kenneth, 137
Hempstall, Anne, 275
Henry, Carl F. H., 77, 84, 87
Henry, Patrick, 156
Henry VIII of England, 9-10
Henrician Reformation, 207

High Flying Churchman, 159
Hines, David, 285
Hinson, E. Glenn, 87
Hinton, John Howard, 77
History of Foreign Baptists, 185
History of the Freewill Baptists, 277
History of New England with Particular Reference to the Denomination of Christians Called Baptists, 164
Hitler, Adolph, 227-29
Hobbs, Herschel, 296
Holliman, (or Holyman) Ezekiel, 17, 41
Holmes, Obadiah, 27, 43, 307
Home Mission Board, (also Domestic Mission Board) SBC, 262, 268
Honey Creek Quarterly Meeting of the Freewill Baptists, 278
Honeycutt, Roy, 136
Howell, R. B. C., 151, 186
Hull, William E., 307, 308
Hurlbert, Eri, 134
Huss, John, 6
Hutchinson, Anne, 17, 40-42

Ill Newes from New England, 23, 26, 28
Independents (England), 51, 52, 54, 55, 61
Independent Baptists, 74
Industrial Revolution, 143
Ivimey, Joseph, 44

Jackson, Andrew, 80, 141, 142
Jacob, Henry, 12, 16, 37
James I of England, 16, 24, 25, 29, 31
Japanese Baptist Convention, 218
Jefferson, Thomas, 157, 160, 162
Jenckes, Daniel, 129
Jerusalem Council, 67
Jessey, Henry, 16, 37, 38, 45
Jessey Memoranda/Records, 37
Jeter, Jeremiah B., 175, 176, 183
Jews, 143
Jim Crow Laws, 175
JLJ Church, 12, 16, 37, 38
Johns Hopkins University, 82, 134, 244